FLUENCY IN READING

Synchronization of Processes

FLUENCY IN READING

Synchronization of Processes

Zvia Breznitz
University of Haifa, Israel

LEA LAWRENCE ERLBAUM ASSOCIATES, PUBLISHERS
2006   Mahwah, New Jersey   London

KH

Lawrence Erlbaum Associates, Inc., Publishers
10 Industrial Avenue
Mahwah, New Jersey 07430
www.erlbaum.com

Cover design by Kathryn Houghtaling Lacey

Library of Congress Cataloging-in-Publication Data

Breznitz, Zvia.
   Fluency in reading : synchronization of processes / Zvia Breznitz.
      p.   cm.
   Includes bibliographical references and index.
   ISBN 0-8058-4144-X (cloth : alk. paper)
   1. Dyslexia.   2. Reading—Physiological aspects.   3. Synchronization.   I. Title.

LB1050.5.B74   2005
371.91′44—dc22   2005045499
                                                                          CIP

Books published by Lawrence Erlbaum Associates are printed on acid-free paper,
and their bindings are chosen for strength and durability.

Printed in the United States of America
10 9 8 7 6 5 4 3 2 1

10/19/06

*To Shlomo, who taught me the meaning of science,
my kids at home and my students in the laboratory,
and Pieter, who helped me to gather my thoughts.*

*My mother and father, Hannah and Vevik,
first showed me the light of books.
This book is dedicated to their memory.*

Contents

Preface   xi
     The Structure of the Book   *xv*

1   Fluency in Reading: Approaches and Definitions   1
     The Use of Fluency in the Literature: A Review   *2*
     Current Definition of Fluency   *4*

2   Reading Rate   9
     Reading Rate as a Dependent Variable   *9*
     Reading Rate as an Independent Factor   *17*
     Project 1: Verification of the Reading Rate Manipulation on
         Reading Performance   *20*
     Project 2: Cognitive Mediation of the Acceleration Phenomenon   *28*
     Conclusions   *34*

3   Automaticity in Fluent Reading   36
     Characteristics of Automaticity   *37*
     Theories of Automaticity   *38*
     Automaticity and Reading   *42*
     The Importance of Automatic Decoding   *43*
     Dyslexia and Automaticity   *45*
     Conclusions   *48*

4   Prosody as an Indication of Fluency   50
    What Is Prosody?   51
    Acquisition of Prosody   52
    Prosody and Structure in the Speech Comprehension Process   55
    Prosody in Reading   58
    The Role of Prosodic Representation in the Reading Process   61
    Conclusions   64

5   Naming Speed: A Review   66
    Discrete Versus Sequential Naming   67
    Developmental Differences in Naming Speed   71
    Naming Speed Deficits Among Dyslexics   74
    Possible Explanations for Naming Speed Deficits   75
    Possible Connections Between Naming Speed
        and Reading Disability   83

6   Speed of Processing   90
    What Influences Speed of Processing?   91
    Age-Related Changes in Speed of Processing   91
    Speed of Processing: A Domain-General
        or Domain-Specific Component?   92
    Speed of Information Processing Among Dyslexics   99

7   Visual Processing: Regular and Dyslexic   105
    The Physiology of the Visual System   105
    Low-Level Visual Processes and Dyslexia   112
    Visual-Orthographic Processing and Dyslexia   124
    Conclusions   126

8   Auditory-Phonological Processing: Regular and Dyslexic   127
    The Structure of the Auditory Modality   128
    Lower Level Auditory Deficits   133
    Linguistic Level Phonological Processes   145
    Higher Level Auditory-Phonological Deficits in Dyslexia   147
    Conclusions   149

9   Speed of Processing of Visual and Auditory
    Modalities: Research Evidence   150
    The Study   150
    Behavioral Measures Project—Introduction   156
    The Tasks   157
    Orthographic-Phonological Transformation   165
    Discussion and Integration of Findings   167

10 Event-Related Potentials (ERPs) in the Study of Dyslexia 170
ERP Evidence on Dyslexic Readers *172*
Our Studies *183*
Conclusions *192*

11 Cross-Modal Integration 195
The Connection Between Reading Ability
and Cross-Modal Integration *195*
Our Cross-Modal Studies *200*
Cross-Modality Tasks Behavioral Experiments *201*

12 The Synchronization Phenomenon 211
Research on the Asynchrony Hypothesis *212*

13 Reading Fluency, Training, and Dyslexia 218
Training and Brain Plasticity *218*
Language and Brain Plasticity *220*
Can Word Reading Fluency Be Improved Through Training? *225*
Description of the Study *226*
Conclusions *232*

**14 Conclusion: The Key Role of SOP Within the
Orchestration of Reading** 235
Conclusion *240*

References 241

Author Index 287

Subject Index 303

Preface

The human brain has existed for approximately 60,000 years, but the alphabetic code has been around for only 5,000 years. The ability to read is not part of our evolutionary heritage, because no brain system has been developed specifically for the reading process. Reading is a highly composite cognitive task, which relies on brain systems that were originally devoted to other functions. In most cases, the reading process is successful, but in some cases it does fail. Reading is an action of decoding and comprehension of the printed materials. Word decoding implies the activation of different brain entities such as the visual and auditory modalities and the orthographic, phonological, and semantic systems. These entities activate separately and simultaneously during reading (PDP Model; Breznitz, 2000; Seidenberg & McClelland, 1989). Moreover, because it is a cognitive process, reading requires activation of the information-processing system at different stages, including perception, memory, processing, and output. Each entity has a different function in the reading process, and each has a different biological structure. Each activates in different brain areas, and each processes information in a different manner and at a different speed. This complexity poses a major challenge for the human brain, which proves too much for some readers. Failures in reading are usually expressed through inaccurate and slow/nonfluent word reading. These failures are commonly termed *developmental dyslexia*.

In most known languages, developmental dyslexia has a high incidence, at around 5% to 10% of the population. In literate societies, reading deficits that persist into adulthood can lead to considerable disabilities. The study of dyslexia has historically focused on word reading accuracy and has shown that dyslexic readers experience profound difficulties in grapheme-to-phoneme decoding. A long line of research into phonological deficits indicates that the primary source of the difficulties experienced by dyslexics lies in word reading accuracy (see Badian, 1997; I. Y. Liberman & Shankweiler, 1991, for a review). Some studies have found a fundamental orthographic deficit that had been accumulating among disabled readers (Barker, Torgesen, & Wagner, 1992; Cunningham & Stanovich, 1990; Stanovich & West, 1989; Zecker, 1991). Other studies have also found that dyslexic readers exhibit higher level linguistic difficulties in such areas as semantics (Nation & Snowling, 1998; Roth & Spekman, 1989), syntax (Bentin, Deutsch, & Liberman, 1990; Morice & Slaghuis, 1985; Roth & Spekman, 1989; Scarborough, 1991; Webster, 1994), morphology (Ben-Dror, Bentin, & Frost, 1995; Vogel, 1983; Wiig, Semel, & Crouse, 1973), and metalinguistics (Tunmer, 1989; Tunmer, Pratt, & Herriman, 1984). Consistent evidence has also pointed to dysfluent-slow word reading rate as a characteristic of dyslexia (Breznitz, 2003b; Carver, 1990; Wolf, 1999, for a review). In 1997, the Committee of the Health Council in the Netherlands (Gersons-Wolfensberger & Ruijssenaars, 1997) put forward an additional factor to explain the dyslexia phenomenon, suggesting that dyslexic readers may suffer from a lack of automaticity in word reading as expressed by inaccurate and slow word reading performance (Nicolson & Fawcett, 1990; Yap & Van der Leij, 1993b). However, it has been argued that the lack of automaticity might be confusing, because it might constitute a causal explanation for inaccurate word reading, rather than a description of reading failures (see Snowling, 2000, for more details). For this reason, the British Psychological Society (BPS) replaced the term *automatization* with *fluency and accuracy* in 1999 (Snowling, 2000). The following working definition was suggested for developmental dyslexia: "Dyslexia is evident when accurate and fluent word reading and/or spelling develops very incompletely or with great difficulty" (BPS, 1999, p. 18).

In recent years, a growing body of evidence has indicated that dyslexics exhibit dysfluency in word reading, which affects reading comprehension (see Meyer & Felton, 1999, for a review). Comparisons of young dyslexics to age-matched regular readers have pointed to the fact that dyslexic readers not only make a higher number of decoding errors, but also exhibit longer performance times when decoding words (Bjaalid, Hoien, & Lundberg, 1993; Manis, Szezulski, Holt, & Graves, 1988; Young & Bowers, 1995; Zecker, 1991), pseudowords (Ben-Dror, Polatsek, & Scarpeti, 1991; Bruck, 1990; Gallagher,

Laxon, Amstrong, & Frith, 1996; Rack, Snowling, & Olson, 1992), and connected text (Meyer & Felton, 1999). These findings have led researchers to mention that rapid word decoding skills are an additional factor discriminating between regular and irregular reading performance (Chabot, Zehr, Prinzo, & Petros, 1984) and that poor readers are characterized not only by difficulties in accuracy, but also by dysfluent word reading (Kame'enui, Simmons, Good, & Harn, 2001; Torgesen, 2000; Wolf, Bowers, & Biddle, 2000).

Recent changes in our understanding of dyslexia have led to a growing emphasis on the fact that accuracy and fluency are two different processes. The high demand for rapid and accurate decoding in our technology- and knowledge-based societies gives an extra impetus to the necessity of focusing on the factors that influence fluency in reading. However, the relations between accuracy and fluency in normal and impaired word reading are not yet fully understood. For instance, it is important to distinguish between causal explanations and symptom descriptions of the reading failures. At the level of description, inaccuracy in word reading is mainly expressed through decoding errors (e.g., Torgesen, 2000). Regarding fluency, there is an agreement in the field that fluency in reading is expressed by performance time. The terms *reading time*, *speed*, *rate*, *duration*, and *latency* of reading performance are being used in parallel in an attempt to portray the time-related aspects of fluency in reading. This book argues that at the level of description fluency in reading is mainly expressed through reading rate and dysfluent reading is mainly evidenced by a slow word decoding rate (see also Breznitz, 2000). At the level of causal explanation, inaccurate word decoding can be viewed as an outcome of poor word recognition skills (e.g., Adams, 1990). A large amount of data pointed to the impairment in phonological processing as the source of word reading accuracy (e.g., Share, 1999). The lack of orthographic, semantic, syntactic, and morphological skills was also suggested as affecting word decoding accuracy (e.g., see Adams, 1990, for a review). However, the causes of dysfluency are not yet clear. Moreover, there is ambiguity in the literature concerning whether dysfluent reading is an effect or a cause of word decoding inaccuracy (e.g., Torgesen, 2000). These questions are a central focus of this book.

Given the belief that the primary source of dyslexia is located mainly within phonological processes, the traditional view has been that reading fluency is a result of the effectiveness of phonological processing (for reviews, see Ackerman, Dykman, & Oglesby, 1994; I. Y. Liberman & Shankweiler, 1991; Lyon & Moats, 1997). However, in recent years, a number of converging lines of evidence have brought about a shift in this perspective. First, reading intervention studies demonstrate that whereas direct, intensive training in phonemic awareness improves decoding and word identification in poor readers (accuracy), it yields only minimal gains in reading fluency (for a recent comprehensive review, see Meyer & Felton, 1999; Torgesen, Rashotte, & Wagner, 1997; Wolf & Katzir-Cohen, 2001; Young & Bowers, 1995). Second, evidence increasingly points to the presence of a second core deficit in dyslexia, indexed by naming-speed deficits (Wolf, 1997, 1999; Wolf & Bowers, 1999, 2000) and manifested in fluency and comprehension problems. Recent research has consistently singled out discrete groups of reading impaired children who exhibit a naming speed or phonological deficit, or both (Badian, 1996; Breznitz, 2001a, 2003b; Compton, Chayna, DeFries, Gayan, & Olson, 2001; Levy, 2001; Lovett, 1987; Lovett, Steinbach, & Frijters, 2000; Manis, Doi, & Bhada, 2000; Wolf & Bowers, 2000). This conception is known as the double-deficit hypothesis (Wolf & Bowers, 1999, 2000). A third line of emerging evidence is based on cross-linguistic data. Purely phonological deficits are manifested to a lesser extent in languages characterized by regular orthographies (Wimmer, 1993, 1996; Wimmer, Mayringer, & Landerl, 1998). In marked contrast to this, deficits in slow reading and naming speed are consistently found across languages that utilize regular orthographies. Languages examined in such studies include German (Wimmer et al., 1998), Dutch (Van Daal & Van der Leij, 1999; Van den Bos, 1998; Yap & Van der Leij, 1993b, 1994), Finnish (Korhonen, 1995), Spanish (Novoa, 1988; Novoa & Wolf, 1984), and Hebrew (Breznitz, 2001a). A fourth factor originates mainly from studies carried out by Tallal (1993). These support the thesis that there is a basic (low-level) multisensory processing deficit in the linguistic domain. This deficit may originate in impairment of perceptual and motor areas and may cause slow processing rate in dyslexics (see reviews in Farmer & R. Klein, 1995; Nicolson & Fawcett, 1994a; Stein, 2001; Waber, 2001; Wolf, Bowers, & Biddle, 2000; Wolff, 2000a).

Fifth, compensated dyslexic adults (see Bruck, 1998) who had been exposed to printed materials for years and had received years of remedial programs were found to read words accurately (Breznitz & Leiken, 2002a; Bruck, 1998; Brunswick, McCrory, Price, C. D. Frith, & U. Frith, 1999; Gallagher et al., 1996; Lefly & Pennington, 1991). However, these readers still continued to read text at a slower rate, which caused them to have difficulties in comprehending the text (see Breznitz & Berman, 2003, for a review). Why did these dyslexics, despite overcoming some of their decoding accuracy difficulties, continue to read slowly? Furthermore, there is evidence that performance accuracy of dyslexics in phonological and orthographic tests was similar to that of regular readers. Yet, task performance time for these dyslexics again continued to be significantly longer than for regular readers (Ben-Dror et al., 1991; Breznitz, 2003b;

Shaul, in press). Moreover, performance time in lexical decision tasks has been found to be the best predictor of adult dyslexia (Shaul, in press; Shaul & Breznitz, in press). If nonslow (fluent) reading is an outcome of the effectiveness of decoding accuracy (e.g., Torgesen, 2000), then why is it that adult dyslexics were able to overcome some of their decoding accuracy limitation, yet continued to be slow (dysfluent) readers?

The basic claim of this book is that fluency is separate from accuracy of word reading. Moreover, fluency lies at the core of dyslexia and its manifestations. Stated differently, the argument is that the various symptoms of dyslexic readers can all be traced to a central causal factor, namely, slow information processing. Because the focal interest of this volume is in the systematic exploration of the causal factors underlying slow reading, the emphasis will, by necessity, be on low-level processes such as perception and pre-meaning decoding of symbols. Thus, the role of semantic involvement is necessarily minimal, and so is the reliance on connected text. It follows that rather than focusing on fluency of reading connected texts, the emphasis clearly shifts to speed of decoding single words.

The main argument of this book is that speed of processing of the modalities and the systems that are activated in word reading are the initial underlying factors—determining the rate of word decoding. The speed of processing (SOP) of each participating system is the outcome of its biological structure and of its function in processing the information. The crucial systems that are activated in word reading are the visual and the auditory brain modalities, as well as the orthographic, the phonological, and to a lesser degree, the semantic brain systems. The visual-orthographic systems process the information in a holistic manner and the auditory-phonological systems in a sequential one. These differential processing styles imply that each entity processes the information at a different speed and contributes differently to the word decoding rate. Moreover, constraints imposed by the stages of activation of the information-processing mechanism require the timely arrival and subsequent integration of the relevant information from these different brain sources. In other words, it is not just the individual SOP within each entity, but also the need for synchronization of the information between the entities that are causal factors for successful word decoding rate to occur.

THE STRUCTURE OF THE BOOK

The book distinguishes between the description of fluency, on the one hand, and the causes of fluency, on the other. It is divided into three main parts.

Description of Word Reading Fluency

For many years, research in fluency has mainly focused on accuracy. Recently, a number of additional skills have been put forward as a basis for fluent reading, including reading rate (speed and time), automaticity, prosody, and rapid automatized naming tasks (RAN). The latter skills are often used as a diagnostic measure for the quality of reading. Chapter 1 looks at several recent reviews on fluency in reading. Chapters 2 through 5 focus on descriptive aspects of fluency: Chapter 2 discusses studies arguing that reading rate is the central factor in fluent and dysfluent reading. Studies that treat reading rate as a dependent variable are contrasted with those that view it as an independent variable. Chapters 3 and 4 focus on automaticity and prosody, respectively, as additional fluency measures. Chapter 5, in turn, critically reviews studies that treat slow naming speed as a core measure of dysfluency.

The Determinants of Word Reading Fluency

The second part of the book comments on the causes or the underlying factors that determine reading fluency. Chapter 6 reviews the literature on speed of processing. Chapters 7 and 8 discuss the manner and speed of activation of the visual and auditory modalities as factors in word reading. Evidence from our various research projects that were conducted over the years on the determinants of fluent word reading are presented in the following chapters. Chapter 9 presents behavioral evidence (reaction time and accuracy) and chapter 10 presents data on electrophysiological measures using evoked potential methodology (ERP) on the speed at which the visual and auditory modalities and the phonological and orthographic systems are activated among regular and dyslexic readers. Chapter 11 focuses on the speed of cross-modal integration where behavioral and electrophysiological evidence are presented.

The "Synchronization Hypothesis"

Based on our approach, which presented speed of processing of information in the modalities and the linguistic brain systems as a crucial factor in fluent reading, the third part focuses on the "synchronization hypothesis" as an underlying factor in fluent reading. This section puts forth the idea that it is not only the speed of processing in each modality and system but also the synchronization between the various components that are activated in reading and both contribute to the fluency and accuracy of the reading process. Chapter 12 introduces the synchronization hypothesis as an explanation for fluent reading and, conversely, relates the "asynchrony phenomenon" to dysfluent reading. Chapter 13 presents evidence from our intervention studies that attempt to overcome dysfluency by using the "reading rate acceleration" paradigm, which manipulates speed of processing by training. Chapter 14 concludes the book by presenting a theoretical model concerning the determinants of reading fluency.

—Zvia Breznitz

1

Fluency in Reading: Approaches and Definitions

A child that encounters the printed materials at the initial stages of reading acquisition deciphers the text in a slow and nonautomatic manner, while ignoring punctuation marks and exhibiting a monotonous (nonprosodic) expression. This is commonly described as dysfluent reading. As reading skills develop, most children pass this stage and their reading becomes more fluent. However, for some children, especially poor or dyslexic readers, reading fluency is harder to achieve—even after years of print exposure and remedial teaching (Bruck, 1998; Lefly & Pennington, 1991; Shaul & Breznitz, in press; Young & Bowers, 1995). In recent years, the issue of fluency has evoked interest among researchers dealing with reading and dyslexia. This has resulted in the inclusion of the term *fluency* in the current definitions of the dyslexia phenomenon as a separate factor from accuracy (BPS, 1999).

Over the years, the terms *fluency* and *dysfluency* have gone through different stages in the study of reading. Research during the 1980s mainly dealt with the phonological decoding theory at the level of single-word recognition. When phonological decoding was normal and performed automatically, reading was regarded as being fluent. In the 1990s, following the in-depth observation of cognitive processes by new technologies, additional explanations of reading difficulties were offered. Theories such as automaticity, the double deficit hypothesis, the systems analysis approach, and speed of information processing were suggested as explanations for fluency and dysfluency in reading. These theories are based on the notion that the cerebral processes in reading are multi- rather than unidimensional and are based on interactive processes of the various components that are activated in reading.

CHAPTER 1

THE USE OF FLUENCY IN THE LITERATURE: A REVIEW

The focus on fluency in reading is not new in reading research. Although not directly named "fluency," some of the components that make up this term today were mentioned as early as the end of the 19th and the beginning of the 20th century. Terms and ideas suggested as important for effective reading include practice and repetition (James, 1886, in National Institute of Child Health and Human Development, 2000), automatic-like rates of recognition of the reading components (Cattell, 1886), and reducing the processing time in reading in order to free the mind from attention to details (Huey, 1905). A further landmark in reading research was the appearance of "the model of automaticity" by LaBerge and Samuels (1974), which argued that reading becomes increasingly efficient as a result of the development of automaticity in decoding skills. This allows limited attentional resources to be reallocated to higher level comprehension skills. Automaticity has become a central factor in the contemporary study of fluency (see chaps. 3 and 6).

Doehring (1976) provided the first systematic direct studies, using kindergarten to end-of-high-school readers, on the developmental rate of the various reading subskills, such as symbols (colors and objects), letters, letter combinations, words, random word sequences, and sentences (see also chap. 2). It was suggested that a skilled reader is one who masters the latter skills beyond the level of simple accuracy. That is, a reader could be classified as fluent only when his accurate processing became rapid enough. Reading rate of the various components that are activated in the reading process has become a central characteristic of the current conception of fluent reading. Fluency as a developmental outcome of the reading skills was also presented in Chall's (1983) model, which suggested that fluency develops around the second and third grades, when decoding skills are consolidated and word recognition automaticity develops. A similar developmental perspective was suggested by Ehri and Wilce (1983), who claimed that word recognition is the basic skill on which other dimensions of reading skills depend. Accordingly, word recognition can be divided into three stages. In the first stage, accuracy is important and, via accuracy, words can be identified independently. In the second stage, the new words acquired by practice become automatically recognizable, without direct attention to pronunciation. In the third stage, word recognition speed increases to the maximum development level at which the processing components become assimilated into memory. In other words, two central components of fluency, automaticity and speed, were suggested as underlying factors in the development of word recognition.

Many studies have examined the validity of reading fluency measured with curriculum-based measurement (CBM). CBM is a compilation of strategic tests that measure oral reading fluency in order to make a decision regarding reading skill. The findings provide wide support for oral reading fluency as a valid and reliable measure for reading skill in general, and for comprehension in particular (Deno, Mirkin, & Chiang, 1982; L. S. Fuchs, D. Fuchs, & Maxwell, 1988). Examining the characteristics of fluent and nonfluent readers in the fourth grade, White (1995) defined 55% of fourth-grade readers as fluent. Their reading is characterized by accuracy (96% accuracy among fluent readers as opposed to 94% accuracy among nonfluent) and rapid speed (an average of 140 words per minute as opposed to 80 words per minute). In addition, a significant correlation was found between higher levels of fluency and higher levels of comprehension. L. S. Fuchs et al. (1988) hypothesized that fluency is more than "encoding speed" and they compared reading fluency to common comprehension measures. Reading fluency measured using CBM showed a significantly high correlation with SAT scores, and even more with other tests that examine comprehension. In addition, the correlation between this test and comprehension was significantly higher than the correlation with reading single words. In a factor analysis on the components of reading and linguistic processing skills, J. L. De Soto and C. B. De Soto (1983) found that fluency in encoding meaningful and meaningless words was a separate factor in addition to comprehension. Examining the contribution of experienced readers' oral reading fluency to investigate the connection between encoding, comprehension, and fluency, Collins (1989) found that fluency is a more discriminating factor than other components. However, the connection between fluency and comprehension is not clear yet. Some studies (R. C. Anderson, Wilkinson, & Mason, 1991; Hoffman & Isaacs, 1991) suggested that fluency stems from high comprehension levels. In other studies (Breznitz & Leiken, 2000b; Reutzel & Hollingsworth, 1993), fluency was found to affect the level of comprehension. Although the causal link from accuracy to comprehension is thus well established, this book concentrates on a prior link in the chain of reading: that from fluency to accuracy (chap. 2, and chaps. 6–12).

The verbal efficiency theory by Perfetti (1977, 1985) represents a landmark in the study of reading. Perfetti's model stresses the importance of accurate and rapid word recognition, working memory processes, general symbol activation and retrieval, lexical access and retrieval, and learning and practice as crucial factors in enhancing reading effectiveness. Within the overall account of reading ability, the notion of fluency was presented in terms of "effective reading speed," which was itself seen as an outcome of comprehension, decoding accuracy, and rate of reading (measured by words per minute). Moreover, the "bottleneck theory" (Perfetti, 1985; Perfetti & Hogaboam, 1975) addresses the relation between word recognition, reading speed, and meaning production (see chaps. 2 and 6). Perfetti's theories served as the basis for the speed of processing theory of fluent reading (Breznitz, 2003b).

CURRENT DEFINITION OF FLUENCY

There is presently no consensus concerning the definition of fluency as related to reading (Reutzel & Hollingsworth, 1993). Neither is there an agreement as to whether fluency is a dependent variable and as such represents a diagnostic measure for the quality of reading (L. S. Fuchs, D. Fuchs, Hosp, & Jenkins, 2001), or whether it is an independent variable that affects the quality of reading (Breznitz, 2001a). Lastly, it is not clear how reading fluency can be trained and remedied (Meyer & Felton, 1999).

Existing definitions can be divided into three separate positions. The first views reading fluency as an outcome of the quality of the oral reading of words and connected text. As such, it has been measured by accuracy, prosody, and in some cases by rate of oral reading. The second viewpoint breaks reading into linguistic components, which are acquired and developed in a series of stages. Fluency is perceived as an outcome of the development of accuracy and automaticity in each component. A third view, the system analysis approach, presents reading fluency as an outcome of the effectiveness of various biological and cognitive systems. Based on this view, the speed of processing perspective of fluency is presented.

Fluency as an Outcome of the Quality of Oral Reading Skills

Different definitions posit the view of fluency as an outcome of the quality of oral reading (L. S. Fuchs et al., 2001). In general, the quality of oral reading is measured by accuracy, rate and prosody of words, and connected text. Accordingly, Schreiber (1980) defined fluency as "that level of reading competence at which textual material can be effortlessly, smoothly, and automatically understood" (p. 177). Similarly, Meyer and Felton (1999) proposed that fluency can be perceived as "the ability to read connected text rapidly, smoothly, effortlessly, and automatically with little conscious attention to the mechanics of reading such as decoding" (p. 284). Hudson, Mercer, and Lane (2000) viewed fluency as "accurate reading at a minimal rate with appropriate prosodic features (expression) and deep understanding" (p. 16). In addition, the National Institute of Child Health and Human Development (2000) defined fluency as "the immediate result of word recognition proficiency" (pp. 3–5), and listed the components of fluency as word phrasing as expressed by intonation, stress, and pauses observed in the reader; syntactic comprehension; and expression in oral reading, which transmits elements of emotion, expectation, and description (see White, 1995).

Torgesen, Rashotte, and Alexander (2001, p. 4) suggested a minimalist definition of fluency, according to which reading fluency is a result of rate and accuracy in oral reading of curriculum-based materials (see also Shinn, Good, Knutson, Tilly, & Collins, 1992).

Clearly, the definitions presenting fluency as a consequence of the quality of oral reading skills put forward the idea that fluency may be achieved only after reading skills such as word and connected text decoding are acquired and established. In accordance with this view, fluency can be measured by looking at the number of oral reading errors, reading time, and vocal expression levels of written material.

A Linguistic and Developmental Perspective

In a comprehensive review, Meyer and Felton (1999) summarized the source for dysfluent reading and claimed that it relates to three linguistic levels: the *word level*, the *syntactic level*, and the *meaning level*. Each level incorporates some aspects of fluency.

Word Decoding.   At this level, dysfluent reading is an outcome of difficulties in word recognition systems (phonology and orthography). The deficits may arise from phonological, visuospatial, and/or working memory processes that may be manifested in the slowed mapping of verbal labels to visual stimuli (grapheme to phoneme correspondence; see also Snyder & Downey, 1995; Wolf & Bowers, 1999). Thus, poor readers take more time than regular readers to identify single words. Moreover, the more complex a word, the longer it takes them to learn it (Manis, Custodio, & Szeszulski, 1993). In order to learn a word pattern, poor readers need to be exposed for a longer time than regular readers to the pattern of the words (Ehri & Wilce, 1983). The slow manner of word decoding for poor readers results from their attempt to match letters to sounds within an unfamiliar word pattern (Meyer & Felton, 1999). Recognition of single words depends on storage and the speed of word retrieval. Inaccurate word decoding leads to the storage of incorrect patterns in the mental lexicon. At the same time, dyslexics recorded word retrieval processes that were slow and impaired (Meyer, Wood, Hart, & Felton, 1998). Thus, many poor readers suffer from word recognition problems that make fluency problematic. The source of the difficulty may vary among different readers. Slow and inaccurate word reading is exhibited in the rate (speed or time) at which the reader decodes words (see chap. 2).

Syntactic Processing. At this level, dysfluency is exhibited in a lack of prosody and rhythm in oral reading, which are caused by the lack of sensitivity to syntactic cues (Leiken, 2002; Schreiber, 1980; see also the following section). Schreiber (1980) suggested that the lack of fluency among poor readers occurs because they are unable to perceive the prosodic and rhythmic characteristics of the language in written text. According to Schreiber, the reader's ability to perceive the syntactic structure of the language leads to automaticity (see also the next section). Schreiber mentioned that young children often rely on prosodic and rhythmic characteristics in order to extract meaning before they acquire real linguistic skill. However, prosodic clues are not accessible to beginning readers with poor word recognition skills, who do not understand how the sounds of spoken language are represented in written text.

Failure to Make Higher Order Connections Between Word Recognition Skills and Semantic Information, or Between Words, Meanings, and Ideas. Researchers agree that there is a connection between dysfluent reading and deficient comprehension. Two models have been suggested to explain the effect of slow word recognition on comprehension. The first is the information-processing model (LaBerge & Samuels, 1974) derived from information-processing theory (e.g., Norman, 1968; Posner, Lewis, & Conrad, 1972). According to this model, reading becomes increasingly more fluent as the result of automaticity development within subskills: "When one describes a skill at the macrolevel as being automatic, it follows that the subskills at the microlevel and their interrelations must also be automatic" (LaBerge & Samuels, 1974, p. 295). The first stage of this process involves the visual code and the unitization of visual stimuli. These may include letters, spelling patterns, words, and highly frequent word groups (e.g., "high school"). With exposure and practice, the visual features in stimuli like letters become unitized and are then perceived as a single unit. As these units accumulate and letter perception becomes increasingly automatic, attention to early visual coding processes decreases. This allows attentional resources to be reallocated to other areas, such as the semantic (or meaning) code. As noted in this model, word recognition and comprehension cannot be carried out simultaneously if the reader has to focus disproportionately on word recognition.

The second model is the verbal proficiency model (Perfetti, 1977, 1985), which also assumes that readers become more proficient due to learning and practice, which releases cognitive resources for the higher requirements of reading. Perfetti's model claims that slow word recognition interferes with the reader's ability to retain large units of text in the working memory, which prevents reading from being efficient. The model has also been described as the serial processing, or bottleneck, theory.

A Developmental Perspective.   Over the last few years, a number of researchers have presented evidence indicating that reading fluency may be comprised of components that are built up alongside the development of other reading components at various stages during the acquisition of reading skills. Kame'enui et al. (2001) put forward this perspective. In their view, at lower levels of processing during the initial stages of reading acquisition, fluency is affected by the quality of letter recognition and phoneme awareness, whereas at more advanced stages of reading, at the higher levels of processing, fluency is a result of mastering reading skills such as word recognition and text comprehension. Within this developmental perspective, the onset of fluency should appear at the early stages of reading acquisition.

Wolf and Katzir-Cohen (2001) developed their own working definition of fluency, which incorporates a wide range of components relevant at different levels of activity. They suggested that

> in its beginning, reading fluency is the product of the initial development of accuracy and the subsequent development of automaticity in underlying sublexical processes, lexical processes and their integration in single word reading and connected text. These include perceptual, phonological, orthographic, and morphological processes at the letter, letter pattern, and word levels, as well as semantic and syntactic processes at the word level and connected text level. After it is fully developed, reading fluency refers to a level of reading accuracy and rate where decoding is relatively effortless; where oral reading is smooth and accurate with correct prosody; and where attention can be allocated to comprehension. (p. 219)

Wolf and Katzir-Cohen (2001) were the first to break down the activity of reading fluency into subskills and components. They suggested that there are three connected levels of reading subskills: letter, word, and connected text. Each level, in turn, is based on underlying components such as perceptual, cognitive, linguistic, and motor systems that include visual and auditory perception, memory, lexical access and retrieval, and motor output. Finally, reading fluency involves integration of information from phonological, orthographic,

semantic, and morphological processes. This comprehensive working definition enables systematic tracking of the underlying factors of fluency and
dysfluency in reading.

The Theoretical Systems Analysis Approach

It is clear from the previous discussion that fluency and dysfluent reading have
been mainly used in order to describe behavior or style of reading. But investigations of the causes of fluency have been limited in the literature on reading. A
new perspective on fluency in reading was developed in Berninger's (2001) systems analysis approach. Berninger conceptualized fluency as being based on
several basic biological and cognitive components including: the rate and persistence of visual and speech signals in reading materials; the efficiency and
automaticity of the development of phonological, orthographic, and morphological systems; and the coordination of responses by the executive functions
system.

Berninger's definition points to rate, automaticity and coordination as basic
components activated to achieve fluency and it adds the concept of the existence of underlying systemic conditions that affect fluency.

Speed of Processing Approach.   Breznitz (2003b) elaborated on Berninger's (2001) systems analysis position by suggesting that fluency in reading is primarily based on the rate of decoding single words. Rate of decoding words is in
turn an outcome of *speed of processing* (SOP) of the systems that are activated in
word reading. The main argument of this approach is that each of these brain
systems processes information at a different speed. Consequently, synchronization of the information arriving from the different systems is an essential prerequisite for decoding words. Thus, the symptoms of dyslexic readers are manifested by slow decoding rate and can be traced to a central causal factor,
namely, that of slow SOP. This slowness can derive from one or more of the systems that are activated in word decoding. That also often leads to speed
asynchrony between these components.

This book attempts to provide theoretical foundations and empirical evidence for the speed of processing approach as an explanation for fluent reading.

2

Reading Rate

A consensus exists among researchers that reading rate is a crucial factor in determining reading fluency at all levels. Interest in this factor has increased in recent reading research. Reading rate is perceived in two ways in the literature. The consensus holds that reading rate is an outcome of effective reading skills. As such, it is most often presented as a dependent variable or as a diagnostic measure. An alternative research paradigm has put forward another view presenting reading rate as an independent factor influencing the quality of the reading skills (see Breznitz, 2003b, and Breznitz & Berman, 2003, for a review). This position is presented herein.

READING RATE AS A DEPENDENT VARIABLE

It is commonly understood that effective reading rate results from the efficiency of decoding skills and comprehension (Greene, Kincade, & Hays, 1994). Several hypotheses have been suggested to explain decreased reading rate based on the assumption that word reading rate is a dependent variable. For example, it has been suggested that the level of word reading accuracy, the reader's age, the acquaintance with reading skills, and development of word reading automaticity are all accountable for decreased reading rate (see Biemiller, 1978; Carver, 1990; Gough & Tunmer, 1986; Greene et al., 1994, for reviews). Slow word recognition interferes with the reader's ability to retain large units of text in the working memory (bottleneck theory), which prevents reading from being efficient (see the Verbal Efficiency Theory—Perfetti, 1977, 1985; Shankweiler & Crain, 1986).

However, the basic view among researchers positing reading rate as a dependent factor is based on the claim that reading is a linguistic process. As such, its effectiveness is based on the level of acquisition, mastering and performance of its sublexical components that are letters, graphemes and phonemes, multiletter units, words, pseudowords, and connected text. Greene and Royer (1994) summarized studies in the English language that measured identification and decoding rate of these sublexical components. In the following sections, reading rate is presented accordingly.

Reading researchers agree that fluent reading is based primarily on the quality and rate of identification and recognition of the symbols and sounds of single and multiletter units. In the regular development of reading fluency, research has clearly indicated a developmental trend in the speed at which letters and/or letter units are identified. The average time it takes to identify single letters in the English language is 3 s for kindergarten children, 800 ms at the beginning of the first grade, 600 ms at the end of the first grade, and about 100–200 ms less by the sixth grade (Compton & Carlisle, 1994; Doehring, 1976; J. F. Mackworth & N. H. Mackworth, 1974; G. M. Sinatra & Royer, 1993; Stanovich, Nathan, & Vala-Rossi, 1986). College students are able to identify letters within 50 ms, which is about 500 ms faster than children (Biemiller, 1978; Jackson & McClelland, 1979; Mason, 1982; Sloboda, 1976, 1977).

Studies designed to verify differences in the speed of letter identification between good and poor readers indicate that poor readers are about 300 ms slower than good readers in the first grade, 200 ms slower in grades three and four, 400 ms slower in grades five and six, and about 100 ms slower at college level (J. F. Mackworth & N. H. Mackworth, 1974). Similar results were obtained in studies measuring multiletter speed of processing (Biemiller, 1978; Doehring, 1976; Frederiksen, Warren, & Rosebery, 1985; Greene et al., 1994). Large increases in the speed at which one or more letters are identified seem to occur at the end of first grade. An asymptote in letter identification rate appears between the fifth and sixth grades. Differences between good and poor readers continue at least until college level (for reviews see Table 1, pp. 146–147, Table 2, pp. 150–151 in Greene et al., 1994).

Word and Pseudoword Processing

The first comprehensive study to measure the rate of word reading at different age groups was carried out by Doehring (1976). The researcher requested that subjects match a word they heard to one they read. Students in the first grade took over 2.5 s to match the words, but by the first half of the second grade the average reaction time (RT) to the task decreased by approximately 300 ms. Another 200 ms difference was observed between grades six and seven. An asymptote in word reading identification rate was observed from the seventh grade on. Chabot, Petsos, and McCord (1983) looked at the RT for word matching among students in grades two, four, and six. A 535 ms decrease was found by the fourth grade and another 255 ms decrease was observed in the sixth grade (see also Bowey, 1985; Hogaboam & Perfetti, 1978; J. F. Mackworth & N. H. Mackworth, 1974; Stanovich et al., 1986a).

Young and college-level poor readers were found to be slower than age-matched good readers in the speed at which words were identified (see Compton & Carlisle, 1994; Greene et al., 1994; Jackson & McClelland, 1979; J. F. Mackworth & N. H. Mackworth, 1974, for reviews). Stanovich (1981) and Stanovich et al. (1986) found that poor readers in the first grade identified words about 350 ms slower than age-matched good readers. Hogaboam and Perfetti (1978) and Booth, Perfetti, and MacWhinney (1999) found large response time differences and a priming effect for word identification among good and poor readers in grades two through six. The differences between good and poor readers decreased in magnitude with increasing grade level. With regard to decoding time, Stanovich et al. (1986) looked at oral reading of words as a function of grade level, reading ability, and the relatedness of preceding context. The good readers were consistently faster than the poor readers, and the fifth-grade students were faster than the third-grade students. The pattern of decreased word reading rate (decoding) among poor readers tends to be different and less steady compared to that of good readers (see Greene et al., 1994, for review).

Compton and Carlisle (1994) summarized studies investigating words and pseudowords during oral reading rate among reading disabled (RD) as compared to subjects matched for chronological age (CA) and reading level (RL). The RD group was consistently slower than the CA and RL groups (see Baddeley, Ellis, Miles, & Lewis, 1982; Ben-Dror et al., 1991; Lundberg & Hoien, 1990). The group differences in reading rate were more pronounced when the task involved pseudowords (see Compton & Carlisle, 1994; Reicher, 1969, for reviews). However, reading time for pseudowords also appears to decrease over the years in the normal course of reading skill development (Bowey, 1985; Doehring, 1976; Greene et al., 1994; Stanovich, 1981; Stanovich et al., 1986).

Stanovich et al. (1986) also looked at differences between good and poor readers in different age groups on pseudoword oral reading time and rhyme production time. The good readers in the third grade were only 28 ms faster at reading pseudowords than poor readers, but by the fifth grade the good readers were

174 ms faster than the poor readers. For the rhyme production tasks, the largest difference between good and poor readers was found in the third grade. Wiegel-Crump and Dennis (1986) looked at word reading times when subjects were provided with different types of cues: pictures, rhyming information, and semantic information. Across the three tasks, the youngest subjects were slowest, and reaction times decreased with increasing grade level. Doehring (1976) found decreases of 300 ms in reading single words from fourth to fifth grade and from eighth to ninth grade. Schwantes (1981) compared third and sixth graders on word reading and found that the sixth-grade students were 245 ms faster. Bowey (1985) compared good and poor readers in the fourth and fifth grades and found that the poor readers in each grade were slower than the good readers. Hogaboam and Perfetti (1978) looked at good and poor readers in the third and fourth grades and also compared latencies for words with one and two syllables. The observed difference for one-syllable words was 160 ms in both the third and fourth grades. For two-syllable words, the third-grade poor readers were 870 ms slower than the good readers, and the fourth-grade poor readers were 640 ms slower than the good readers.

Hess (1982) compared good and poor readers in grades four and six, and found that the larger differences in latency were due to ability differences rather than to grade level differences. G. M. Sinatra and Royer (1993) examined vocalization latency differences between students in grades two, three, and four. They found a large grade level difference between students in grades two and three. Frederiksen et al. (1985) examined the gains poor high school readers made as a function of instructional interventions that targeted speeded practice of component processes in reading. They consistently found decreases in latency when their subjects were tested following the intervention. Perfetti (1985) found that for each grade level and task, the discrepancy in reaction time between words and pseudowords was considerably greater for poor readers than for good readers. R. Sinatra (1989) provided further evidence that efficient processing of pseudowords develops in the third grade. Decreases in reaction time were observed from second to fourth grade, but the larger decrease was found from third to fourth grade. However, with real word data, the larger decrease was found to occur from second to third grade. R. Sinatra's (1989) data provides the clearest evidence for developmental trends in processing pseudowords. Frederiksen et al. (1985) examined latency performance on pseudoword vocalization tasks across two test administrations separated by instructions involving speeded practice. Their high school subjects were consistently slower at vocalizing pseudowords than words. The gains poor readers made tended to be less than those made on the word vocalization task, but consistent decreases in reaction time were nonetheless observed across test administrations.

A review of empirical data points to a developmental trend of decreased reading rate over time. Among younger readers, reading words in a list takes longer than reading letters. However, among older children, the rates at which these two tasks are decoded is similar (Biemiller, 1978). Biemiller's (1978) study also raised the possibility that poor readers do not experience difficulties at the single feature identification level but rather need more processing time when more features are involved at the word level. It is conceivable that poor readers have difficulty extracting and/or remembering orthographic structure, relating letters within words that permit able readers to reduce the number of features that must be processed in order to identify a word (Smith & Holmes, 1970–1971). Good readers may extract the holistic pattern of words, whereas poor readers rely on the individual features that compose words (Meyler & Breznitz, submitted), a manner of decoding that takes longer (Biemiller, 1978). It has also been suggested that poor reading may be an outcome of reduced opportunity to extract orthographic structure, resulting from insufficient reading due to a general speed of processing problem. As such, reading speed may be a central factor in identifying reading disability (see Wolf, 2001).

The Rate of Reading Words in Connected Text

Various studies have examined word reading fluency by investigating oral reading rate of curriculum-based materials (CBM) (Deno et al., 1982; L. S. Fuchs et al., 1988; White, 1995). For example, White (1995) distinguished between fluent and nonfluent fourth-grade readers by the average number of words correctly read in a minute. The words were taken from fourth-grade reading materials. Data indicated that fluent readers read an average of 140 words per minute and nonfluent readers read only 80 words per minute. White's study also indicates a positive correlation between fluency level and comprehension.

Nathan and Stanovich (1991) also found a high correlation between the speed and effort with which reader's process text and text comprehension. When a reader battles with reading rate, it can negatively affect comprehension and motivation to read (Stanovich, 1991). In other words, decreased reading rate in word recognition leads to dysfluency in reading and to an unrewarding reading experience, which reduces involvement in text-related activities. Hence a vicious cycle is created whereby dysfluent reading leads to less reading. Lack of practice and exposure causes a failure to develop automatic word recognition. As a result, poor readers continue avoiding practice or perform it with no real cognitive involvement, thereby continuing the cycle. Vocabulary and other cognitive skills accelerated by reading may be delayed to the extent that the failure to develop reading fluency results in an extended impairment (Nathan & Stanovich, 1991).

The bottleneck theory presented by Perfetti (1985) and Perfetti and Hogaboam (1975) attempts to explain the relation between word recognition, reading speed, and production of meaning. According to this theory, slow word recognition creates an obstacle for maintaining large units of text in working memory, causing reading to be less efficient. According to Tan and Nicholson (1997), the relation between rapid decoding of words and sentence comprehension does not mean that the faster readers read, the better they understand. By using word fluency rather than reading rate, L. S. Fuchs et al. (1988) hypothesized that fluency is more than "decoding speed" and compared reading fluency to common comprehension measures. These researchers showed that reading fluency measured using CBM has a high and significant correlation with SAT scores, and even more with other tests that examine comprehension. In addition, the correlation between fluency of connected text and comprehension was significantly higher than the correlation of comprehension with single word reading.

In their study, J. L. De Soto and C. B. De Soto (1983) carried out a factor analysis on the components of reading and linguistic processing skills. They found that fluency measured by rate in decoding meaningful and meaningless words was a distinct factor, which was highly important for comprehension. In a simple experiment examining the importance of decoding as an independent skill, pupils were trained to recognize words faster and were checked to see whether this led to improved comprehension. Fleischer, Jenkins, and Pany (1979) trained fourth- and fifth-grade pupils in rapid decoding using single words for practice purposes. After practicing, the pupils read a section containing the key words. The practice did improve recognition speed and accuracy for the training words. However, this improvement was not transferred to comprehension. A wide range of researchers examined these findings and concluded that poor comprehension is not a result of poor decoding skills.

Cromer (1970) claimed that in addition to fast and accurate single word reading, the reader needs the ability to collate meaningful words into patterns (e.g., sentences or phrases). In this manner, readers are made aware that words exist in larger linguistic units and cannot be learned solely within lists containing unrelated words. Tan and Nicholson (1997) trained children to encode words rapidly and accurately using flash cards and examined the effects of training on comprehension. The training involved either single words or words in sentences. The results showed that practicing words within sentences was more efficient than practicing single words. In addition, there was more variance under the sentence condition than the single word condition, suggesting a wider range of individual differences for this practice condition.

Thus, reading is a complex ability in which the reader is required to use a number of different cognitive processes including word recognition, access to word meaning, syntactic division, semantic analysis of sentences, and interpretation of the overall text—all of which need to occur rapidly (Young & Bowers, 1995).

Doehring (1976) examined oral reading rates for various levels of connected text. His subjects were students in grades 1 through 11. The most important decrease in reading rate occurred during the second grade. Cirilo and Foss (1980) examined how the time needed to read a sentence depends on the importance of the sentence and its position in the passage. Their college-level subjects took longer to read more important sentences and sentences that appeared earlier in the passage. Schwaneflugel and Shoben (1983) looked at how the sentence reading times of college students were affected by whether or not the sentence was concrete or abstract, and whether or not the sentence was embedded within a larger context. They found that the concrete versus abstract manipulation did not have an effect in the presence of context, but subjects took longer to read abstract sentences in the absence of context.

Freedman and Forster (1985) looked at the time it takes to match sentences that are either identical or varied by one word, and either grammatically correct or incorrect, and found that college students took longer to match the latter set of sentences. L. Katz and Wicklund (1971) examined differences between good and poor readers in the fifth grade when scanning sentences of either two or three words for target words. Although the poor readers were consistently slower than the good readers, both groups took longer to scan the two-word sentences and to give negative responses.

Lesgold and Curtis (1981) measured words per minute (WPM) among first and second graders as they advanced through an instructional reading program. Time was measured across six or seven occasions of reading passages that varied in familiarity and difficulty. The young readers remained faster at reading familiar text as they progressed through their reading instruction, but steady increases were noted with both types of text. Stanovich, Cunningham, and Feeman (1984) examined the reading times of good and poor first-grade readers in the fall and spring. They found that good readers were consistently faster at reading paragraphs than poor readers. With coherent text, both the good and poor readers made significant gains in reading speed from the fall to the spring test administrations. With a random text, both groups were slower than with a coherent text, and both groups made much smaller gains in reading speed from fall to spring. Hess (1982) looked at passage reading time for fourth- and sixth-grade good and poor readers. The poor readers at both grade levels were considerably slower than their good reader peers, and the sixth-grade students were faster than the fourth graders in both groups. Kintsch and Monk (1972) measured college students' inference and reading times based on simple or complex paragraphs. They found that whereas subjects took longer to read more complex texts, the time it took to make inferences was slightly shortened when based on complex texts.

Carver's Reading Rate Theory

One of the leading theories attempting to explain reading rate was put forward by Carver (1991, 1997) in his "rauding theory." This theory includes a model that depicts four levels (referred to as "echelons") of factors that affect the achievement of optimal reading rate and accuracy. Proceeding from the last level inward, the fourth level includes three teaching factors: individual differences in cognitive power, age, and individual differences in cognitive speed; and three "aptitude" factors (cognitive power, thoughts rauded, and cognitive speed). These factors, in turn, influence the third level, which includes verbal knowledge, as well as a decoding speed and naming speed.

Carver (1991, 1997) explicitly focused on the links between fluency and comprehension. He introduced a different perspective to fluency-related research by emphasizing the different purposes of reading and the different rates that these purposes elicit in readers. These include the scanning, skimming, rauding, learning, and memorizing processes. According to Carver, most reading is done in the rauding mode, that is, the mode used by an individual to comprehend each consecutively encountered, complete thought in a passage. Operating in the rauding mode, for Carver, represents the fastest rate at which an individual can successfully understand complete thoughts in each sentence: "The rauding rate is the individual's highest rate of comprehension whereby comprehension is relatively accurate" (p. 144). Such a rate involves the underlying components of lexical access, semantic encoding, and sentential integration.

In sum, when reading rate is being presented as a dependent variable it is clear that it is an outcome of the quality of decoding and comprehension in reading. As such, the better the decoding and comprehension skills are, the faster the reading rate. Viewing the reading rate as a dependent factor suggests that fluency in reading is also perceived as a dependent factor based on the qualities of reading skills. However, consistent findings suggest that reading rate should also be viewed as an independent factor affecting the quality of the reading skills.

Moreover, the current definition of dyslexia views fluency in word reading as independent of accuracy. As such, when expressed by reading rate, fluency by definition can also be perceived as an independent factor. The next section develops this argument further.

READING RATE AS AN INDEPENDENT FACTOR

As a first step toward a more thorough understanding of the role of reading rate, the causal relations between reading rate, decoding accuracy, and reading comprehension were measured. Breznitz (1987a) performed a study in which 450 subjects in the last quarter of first grade participated. All subjects had already completed the stage of acquiring the Hebrew alphabetic code and were focused on stabilization of decoding skills. It was hypothesized that reading skills were not yet fully established among this population and that the causal relations between reading skills during their development could therefore be observed. All subjects read 24 items orally (Reading Comprehension Test; Ortar & Segev, 1970). Reading time, decoding errors, and comprehension were measured for each item. Most subjects, regardless of decoding accuracy and comprehension levels, exhibited a wide range of reading rates across the items. It was suggested that reading rate has a wide range of variants, at least at the initial stage of reading acquisition when reading skills have not yet developed fully. Based on these results, the notion that a discrepancy may exist between ability and performance in reading emerged for the first time, stimulating extended research (Breznitz, 1991).

In an attempt to verify the causal relations between reading time, decoding errors, and reading comprehension, several path analyses were performed. The causal relations between decoding errors and comprehension are well documented in the literature (Adams, 1990; Perfetti, 1985). The study focused only on the causal relations between reading rate, decoding, and comprehension. Path analyses were performed on four different hypothesized models. The first measured the extent of the influence of decoding accuracy on reading rate. The second measured the effect of reading rate on decoding accuracy. The third measured the extent of the effect of comprehension on reading rate and the fourth measured the extent of the effect of reading rate on comprehension. Reading rate was revealed to affect decoding accuracy ($r = .49$) to a greater extent than decoding accuracy affected reading rate ($r = .33$). Reading rate affected comprehension ($r = .-44$) to a greater extent than comprehension affected reading rate ($r = .-30$).

These surprising results necessitated an in-depth investigation of the role of reading rate in the reading process. Specifically, we aimed to check whether or not reading rate also influences the quality of reading. Three consecutive comprehensive research projects were designed. Project 1 put forward the hypothesis that reading rate may also be perceived as an independent variable influencing the quality of decoding and comprehension reading skills (see Breznitz, 2001a, for a review). This assumption was verified among various groups of readers at all levels reading both the Hebrew and English languages. In these studies, the "acceleration phenomenon" was discovered. Project 2 was designed to examine the cognitive mediators of the acceleration phenomenon, and Project 3 was designed to examine its underlying factors.

The Basic Reading Rate Manipulation

As the Breznitz (1987a) study indicated, novice readers exhibit a wide range of reading rates even when the reading materials are matched on length and level of decoding and comprehension. This rate range was used as a basis for the basic reading rate manipulation, which was used in the experiments comprising the three projects. In the experimental setup, the reading rate of each subject was controlled and manipulated individually. As such, it became an independent variable in the studies (see Breznitz, 2003b, for a review).

Materials. Reading materials were chosen based on the type and design of the experiment (behavioral or electrophysiological), the age of the subjects, and the language (Hebrew/English). There were always two to four parallel forms of the reading tests, matched for length and level of decoding and comprehension difficulties. Each form contained 12–24 reading items of increasing difficulty and length. Items consisted of one to three declarative sentences followed by a short, inferential, multiple-choice question (see Breznitz, 2001a, 2003b; Breznitz, DeMarco, Shammi, & Hakerem, 1994; Leiken & Breznitz, 1999, for reviews).

Test Procedure. In each experiment, subjects were asked to read aloud the appropriate level-matched test in one of the reading rate conditions: self-paced or fast-paced. In several experiments, a slow-paced reading rate condition was also incorporated. All test items were presented, one at a time, on an IBM personal computer screen. The experimenter or the subject controlled the appearance and disappearance of each reading item on the screen. Prior to testing in each of the experimental rate conditions, two training trials were administered.

As standard procedure in each experiment in the first condition, subjects read the test items at their own natural routine pace (self-paced 1). They were instructed to start immediately upon appearance of the text. To eliminate the possible confounding effects of regressive eye movements, items were erased as soon as reading was completed. The computer, which recorded the reading time for each item, was activated by the experimenter or by the subject when reading began and deactivated once the last letter was pronounced. Per-letter reading rates were calculated for each item by the computer program, yielding a range of per-letter rates depending on the number of items. These rate ranges served as base input for the reading rate manipulations in the following experimental conditions. A multiple-choice question appeared on the screen following the erasure of each reading item and was erased as soon as the subject had responded by pressing the appropriate number on the keyboard (1 to 4).

In the second condition (fast-paced), each subject was prompted to read at the fastest per-letter rate they had achieved in the self-paced condition. Only those items that the subject had correctly comprehended were eligible. Thus, the test material was presented at the highest rate of demonstrated ability for each subject. To minimize the disruption of natural eye movements, as soon as the start button was activated, the text was automatically erased letter by letter at the highest rate attained in stage 1 (from right to left in Hebrew and from left to right in English). When the entire item had disappeared from the screen, the multiple-choice question appeared automatically and was displayed until the subject had indicated an answer. The early experiments also measured any possible warm-up effects by introducing a third condition that was given to the subjects following the fast-paced condition, in which subjects again read at a self-paced rate (self-paced 2).

In some experiments, an additional condition (slow-paced) was performed. In the slow-paced condition, subjects were forced to read at the slowest per-letter rate they had achieved in the self-paced 1 condition. Only those items that the subject had correctly comprehended were eligible. When the entire item had disappeared from the screen, the multiple-choice question appeared automatically and was displayed until the subject had indicated an answer.

In most of the studies, reading errors were monitored in all of the conditions by requesting subjects to read all of the items aloud as accurately as possible. The measures assessed for each form in all conditions were: total number of oral reading errors, total comprehension score, per-letter reading time (in seconds) for each of the test items, and total reading time for each item, form, or test.

PROJECT 1: VERIFICATION OF THE READING RATE MANIPULATION ON READING PERFORMANCE

Project 1 was designed to examine the hypothesis that different reading rates may effectively enhance the reader's quality of decoding and degree of comprehension. This hypothesis was tested in a series of studies in which individual oral reading rates were controlled and manipulated according to each subject's routine reading rate, as exhibited in the self-paced reading condition. Accuracy and comprehension were measured under each condition.

Detection of the Acceleration Phenomenon

Study 1

The first study (Breznitz, 1987a) included four different experiments. Three of them examined the effect of reading rate manipulation on decoding accuracy and comprehension among novice first graders in Israel, reading Hebrew. The fourth experiment studied the rate manipulation among novice first graders in the United States, reading English (Breznitz, 1987a). All subjects participating in the four experiments were in the last term of the first grade, at the stage of stabilizing decoding skills after having acquired the alphabetic code. Subjects read three parallel forms of the reading test (discussed earlier). The first form was read at each subject's routine self-paced rate (self-paced 1), whereas the second one was read at each subject's own fastest rate achieved in self-paced 1. Readers read a third form, once again at a self-paced reading rate (self-paced 2). Reading time (per-letter), decoding accuracy, and comprehension were measured for each item.

Experiments 1 (Hebrew) and 4 (English).   Results indicated that for most of the subjects in both experiments, reading at the fast pace decreased decoding errors and increased reading comprehension significantly (see Breznitz, 1987a, 2003b). Once again, both experiments revealed a wide range of per-letter reading rates in the self-paced 1 condition for most subjects. However, when they were forced to read at the highest rate they had achieved in self-paced 1, almost all subjects were able to maintain the high speed across all items presented. Upon returning to their self-paced rates in self-paced 2, subjects also returned to the decoding accuracy and comprehension scores they achieved in self-paced 1.

Experiment 2.   This experiment was designed to determine the effects of reading at the slowest reading rate achieved in the self-paced 1 condition. The experiment followed the basic reading rate manipulation procedure, incorporating the slow-paced reading rate condition. Results indicated that the extra time allotted by the manipulation in the slow-paced condition enabled subjects to perform the decoding process more accurately despite the reduced contextual cues. Moreover, slowing the subjects' reading rate significantly decreased their comprehension despite the increase in reading accuracy (see Breznitz, 2003b).

Experiment 3. This experiment attempted to determine the effects of deliberately inserted spelling errors in the reading material on the subjects' accuracy and comprehension in self- and fast-paced reading rate conditions. Results showed significant improvement in the fast-paced condition, which led to enhanced comprehension and automatic correction of the words containing the spelling mistakes (see Breznitz, 2003b).

In sum, the four experiments show that the reading rate of novice readers is varied. When prompted to accelerate their reading rate according to the highest rate achieved by each individual reader in the self-paced condition (self-paced 1), young readers at the initial stage of stabilizing reading skills could read about 20% faster than they were able to at their own self-paced reading rate. This faster reading rate was maintained across all reading items in the fast-paced condition (6–12 items). Furthermore, accelerating reading rate on the basis of individual self-paced ability significantly reduced decoding errors and enhanced comprehension while individually decelerating reading rate below individual self-paced reading rate (slow-paced), improved decoding accuracy but reduced comprehension (Breznitz, 1987a). The stronger effect of accelerating reading rate on decoding accuracy and comprehension was mainly discernible among the poor readers of the sample. The results of the first study raised the idea that reading rate can be perceived as an independent variable that affects the quality of reading skills. Accelerated reading rate decreased decoding errors and increased comprehension. This phenomenon was named the *acceleration phenomenon.*

At this point in time, the acceleration phenomenon had only been found among novice readers. Additional verification and replication among a larger variety of readers at different reading levels were necessary.

The Study of the Acceleration Phenomenon Among Young Regular and Impaired Readers

Study 2. The next study (Breznitz, 1987b) addressed the question of a possible gap between the reading performance of garden variety (Stanovich, 1986b) lower and middle-class first graders and their potential reading ability.

Disadvantaged children are more easily distracted, depend more on familiarity of written text with spoken language, and have poorer vocabulary. It was therefore hypothesized that they would benefit from the acceleration manipulation, which allows children to achieve their potential reading ability as measured by rate, comprehension, and decoding errors. Reading comprehension and decoding skills were measured under accelerated reading rate conditions. The reading rate manipulation applied in this experiment succeeded in overcoming reading skill differences between advantaged and disadvantaged first graders. Under the fast-paced condition, the performance of the disadvantaged subjects approached that of the advantaged group. Although significant differences remained with respect to comprehension, oral reading errors disappeared. This is consistent with the fact that competence in decoding skills precedes competence in comprehension.

Study 3. The third study (Breznitz, 1997d) examined the acceleration phenomenon from a developmental perspective. Eighty-one subjects from elementary schools located in a middle-class, urban neighborhood in northern Israel participated in a 5-year longitudinal study that examined the relation between reading rate, decoding, and comprehension during consecutive stages of reading acquisition. The hypothesis was that progressive improvement in reading skills would be reflected in a progressive decrease in the effect of acceleration. To check this theory, subjects at the end of each grade level in school (one through five) were requested to read aloud from appropriate level-matched tests in three reading rate conditions: self-paced 1, fast-paced, and self-paced 2. Following the basic acceleration manipulation, results indicated that as compared to the self-paced 1 condition, the fast-paced reading condition revealed the following: (a) significant gains of at least one item in comprehension at each grade level, and (b) an upward linear trend in decoding accuracy was evident until the third grade, indicating a reduction of almost 30% in reading errors. By the fourth grade, the number of decoding errors was dramatically reduced and appeared to have become stable. Between grades four and five, the reduction in reading errors was less dramatic, although it remained significant. Thus, subjects in the first grade exhibited a striking improvement in their decoding scores during reading acceleration. However, this improvement gradually decreased with each subsequent grade, indicating that reading acceleration is most advantageous when decoding skills are unstable.

Consistent with the results of previous studies (see Breznitz, 2001a, for a review), these data demonstrate that readers attain increasingly proficient reading skills in each successive year of elementary school. The benefits of reading acceleration are maintained at least up to the fifth grade, during which readers are able to accelerate their reading pace about 25% to 35% above their normal, self-paced rate. The self-paced reading rate followed a downward linear trend through grade three and appeared to stabilize thereafter. An asymptote appeared around the fourth grade. Differences between self- and fast-paced reading rates followed a similar pattern. Hence, the "leveling-off" of the fast-paced reading rate parallels the pattern found in the self-paced condition. As readers reach an asymptote in their normal pace of reading, they likewise reach an asymptote in their ability to accelerate. Thus, the discrepancy between self- and fast-paced reading rates is greatest in the lower grades, significantly decreases in grade three, and then stabilizes in grade four. With respect to poor and good readers, both groups profited from reading acceleration in general. However, in all five grades, the gains in comprehension were significantly greater for poor readers. In the fourth and fifth grades, oral reading errors were almost nonexistent among good readers, but poor readers improved significantly on decoding accuracy during reading acceleration.

These findings delineate developmental aspects of reading rate in relation to decoding accuracy and comprehension. The relations of the three component skills during self-paced (routine) reading developed in two distinct patterns. Progressive improvement in each subskill was observed until third grade, and the best predictor of performance in each subskill was earlier performance in the same subskill. From fourth grade on, comprehension continued to improve while decoding ability and reading rate appeared to stabilize, and the best predictor of reading performance at this point was reading rate in the second grade. These two patterns can be interpreted as reflecting two stages of reading acquisition: acquisition and practice of subskills and acquisition of proficient coding with fluctuating comprehension. In addition, these results indicate that there may be a transition point at which reading rate becomes more independent. In the early stages of reading acquisition (between first and third grade), reading rate both influences and is influenced by word recognition ability, making it both a dependent and an independent variable. By the fourth grade, reading subskills are firmly established and the reader enters a second stage of reading development, in which reading rate acquires increasing independence.

Study 4. Study 4 investigated the acceleration phenomenon in the reading of impulsive hyperactive children as compared to dyslexic readers and regular subjects (Harpaz & Breznitz, 1997). We tested the assumption that dyslexic readers' speed of processing is slower as compared to regular readers, whereas impulsive-hyperactive readers' processing speed is faster. In addition, regardless of processing speed, both groups are less accurate when performing decoding tasks, reading comprehension, and cognitive tasks. Eighty children participated in this study (equal numbers of boys and girls), and were divided into two test groups each containing 20 subjects. The first test group included dyslexic readers and the second impulsive-hyperactive children. The remaining 40 subjects were regular readers divided into two control groups, one matched to test groups in chronological age and the other in reading age. Again, three reading conditions were used in order to determine the speed of processing in each subject: self-paced, fast-paced, and slow-paced. The fast- and slow-paced reading conditions were calculated for subjects separately in accordance with the reading time obtained in their self-paced condition. According to the research hypotheses, fast-paced manipulation of the subjects' reading rates will improve accuracy among dyslexics, whereas slow-paced manipulation will improve accuracy among impulsive-hyperactive readers.

Our findings supported the assumption that dyslexics are slower and less accurate during most reading and cognitive processing tasks than regular readers. Moreover, impulsive-hyperactive readers are slower and less accurate than regular readers on most tasks. The results also showed a difference in the speed of processing of dyslexic as compared to impulsive-hyperactive subjects. The dyslexics were faster and more accurate than the hyperactive readers. Most significantly, dyslexic readers were slower than all other subjects (regular and hyperactive) on naming and phonological processing tasks. This indicates that dyslexics suffer from a specific decoding disability (phonology), as well as word vocabulary and naming deficits, whereas the impulsive-hyperactive children possess general disabilities both in reading and cognitive processing. These results support the claims of Stanovich (1988), who indicated that dyslexics have a core phonological deficit, and of Fodor (1983), who purported that hyperactive children have general cognitive problems.

Thus, the assumption that accelerating the reading rate of dyslexic subjects will improve their comprehension was sustained, whereas the assumption that slowing down the reading rate of impulsive-hyperactive subjects will lead to improved comprehension was not. In fact, accelerating reading rates improves the comprehension of all subjects, especially among the hyperactive subjects, who exhibit better comprehension than the other groups during the fast-paced condition. This emphasizes the beneficial effects of reading acceleration for subjects with lower cognitive abilities (i.e., attention span capacity, sustained attention, low verbal ability, low visuomotor ability, and slow speed of processing). It may be that the hyperactive subjects improved their comprehension due to the fact that when reading at their usual pace, the attention system interferes with the processing system, and a balance is created between the attention on

PDP processing systems when they accelerate their reading (Mozer, 1988). This balance may enable processing of larger language chunks and may create opportunities for allocation of attention to comprehension (McClelland, 1985, 1986).

In sum, fast-paced reading was found to improve attention with regard to capacity, working memory, distractibility, and available cognitive resources. The fast pace also helped the dyslexic and hyperactive readers to partially overcome the limitations connected to reading—such as decoding skills (Gough & Tunmer, 1986; Snowling, 1980), verbal working memory, and the ability to concentrate and avoid distractions (Siegel, 1988).

The Effect of the Acceleration Phenomenon on the Reading Performance of Adult Readers

Studies 5 to 8.   The fifth and sixth studies were designed to examine the effects of the acceleration phenomenon on university-level adult regular and dyslexic readers in Israel, reading Hebrew (Breznitz & Leiken, 2000b; Leiken & Breznitz, 2001). Studies 7 and 8 looked at the acceleration phenomenon among university-level adult regular readers in the United States, reading English (Breznitz et al., 1994; Breznitz, DeMarco, & Hakerem, 1993). The experiments explored if mature readers can derive the same benefits from the acceleration phenomenon as elementary schoolchildren do. Following the basic acceleration manipulation, decoding errors, reading comprehension, and reading time were tested during the self-paced 1, fast-paced, and self-paced 2 reading rate conditions. Results indicated that in both languages, adult-college level regular readers could read about 10% faster (Breznitz et al., 1993; Breznitz & Leiken, 2000b) than their routine self-paced reading rate. As the subjects were regular mature readers, no decoding errors were detected in any of the experimental reading rate conditions. However, comprehension significantly increased on one item or more in all of the experiments during the fast-paced reading condition as compared to both of the self-paced reading rate conditions. Once again, the dyslexics in this experiment gained the most from the acceleration manipulation. They significantly reduced their decoding errors, increased comprehension, and could read about 15% faster.

Studies 9, 10, 11, and 12.   Breznitz and Leiken (2000a, 2000b) and Leiken and Breznitz (1999, 2001) conducted a series of studies regarding the effects of the acceleration phenomenon on syntactic functioning among Hebrew-speaking adult dyslexics, as compared to age-matched controls. The results from these experiments indicate that the various grammatical functions of words contribute differently to sentence processing in the fast- and slow-paced conditions. The effect was expressed in varying degrees for different sentence elements, indicating that processing of the predicate was hardly affected by accelerated reading rate, whereas other sentence elements (i.e., subjects, direct objects, and prepositions) were significantly affected. Thus, reading rate acceleration affected the process of identifying the grammatical functions of words. This suggests that reading rate can influence some aspects of sentence processing, which confirms the view of reading rate as an independent variable (Leiken & Breznitz, 2001). Regarding dyslexic readers, results provided evidence of a syntactic processing "weakness" in dyslexia. However, the acceleration manipulation increased the processing speed of syntactic parsing (interpretation of word strings), which in turn improved comprehension. These effects were observed among regular and dyslexic readers but were more prominent among dyslexics, perhaps because regular readers used their processing resources in the self-paced condition more effectively (Breznitz & Leiken, 2000a).

Furthermore, word order in Hebrew does not significantly influence the process of identifying syntactic functions of words. Rather, readers of this language rely on other means to determine relations among language elements. It is therefore possible that in the self-paced condition, a predicate-centered (morphologically based) strategy is used whereas in the fast-paced condition a word-order strategy is used (Leiken & Breznitz, 2001). However, with regard to dyslexic readers, the modification of processing manner in the fast-paced condition led to changes in the processing strategies used. In the self-paced condition, the predicate-oriented strategy was found to be most efficient for sentence processing in Hebrew. However, the dyslexic readers demonstrated a more primitive mode of identifying the grammatical roles of words, namely, the word-order strategy (Breznitz & Leiken, 2000b). This strategy is simpler, in that it seems to reflect the fundamental cognitive strategy of information processing. Although it is not the most effective for linguistic processing in Hebrew, it is typically used during the early stages of language development among Hebrew-speaking children (Berman, 1985; Sokolov, 1988). The predicate appeared to be significantly affected by reading rate, which is an important finding, because the verb occupies the central position in Hebrew sentences and is singled out from other words by its morphological characteristics. Dyslexic readers paid significantly less attention to the predicate in the self-paced condition than normal readers did. This tendency changed in the fast-paced condition, but the predicate did not shift to first place in the activation pattern as it did with the verb-oriented strategy (Breznitz & Leiken, 2000b).

Study 13. In this final experiment (Birnboim, Breznitz, Pratt, & Aharon, 2002), the acceleration phenomenon was investigated among adult frontal lobe head injury patients, as compared to dyslexics and regular readers. Data were collected under self-, fast- and slow-paced reading rates. The subjects were 60 male participants, divided into three groups. Two groups consisted of university students: 20 normal readers and 20 dyslexic readers. The third group included 20 frontal lobe, closed head injury patients. In-depth analysis reveals that this manipulation differentially affects head injured, dyslexic, and normal readers in terms of the strength of the acceleration effect on different reading skills. In contrast with previous studies (Breznitz, 2001a, for a review), reading comprehension in this study was determined on the basis of the ability to distinguish between semantically appropriate and semantically inappropriate sentence endings and not on the basis of comprehension questions.

Comparisons of reading speed in each of the three conditions indicated that, overall, the subjects with frontal head injuries read slowest, normal readers read fastest, and dyslexic readers read at an intermediate pace. Comparisons between average-paced and fast-paced reading within each reading group revealed that in terms of increased reading speed, acceleration was most advantageous to dyslexic readers. Head injured subjects performed worse than the other two groups not only on the measures of reading but also on most of the other baseline measures. This population was slower and less accurate on word retrieval from semantic memory, had a shorter attention span, was more susceptible to distraction, and achieved lower scores on the baseline reading comprehension test. Only decoding accuracy during oral reading was unimpaired. Although dyslexic readers achieved lower scores on this measure, head injured subjects performed as well as normal subjects.

The study revealed that head injured patients, who were characterized by the poorest reading skills, benefited from reading acceleration more than the normal readers but less than the dyslexics. One explanation for this finding may be that the effects of acceleration may be limited under circumstances of acute brain damage. Hence, whereas both dyslexic and frontally brain injured subjects exhibited similar patterns of impaired cognitive processing in terms of poor attention and memory skills, the slow and inefficient cognitive processing of the head injured subjects was due to confirmed, localized damage in the frontal lobe. This was not the case for dyslexic readers, who displayed no "hard" neurological signs.

Conclusions

The experiments described consistently indicated that various groups of readers at different ages can read faster than their routine self-paced reading rate. And, importantly, reading at faster rates enhanced decoding accuracy and comprehension. These findings were exhibited across two languages and were more pronounced among poor readers. These results have raised the possibility that among readers at all levels, good and poor, young and adult, there is a discrepancy between ability and performance in reading. That discrepancy appears foremost in reading rate. In our experiments, the routine reading rates of readers at all levels were found to be from 10% to 35% slower, on average, than the reading rates they were capable of exhibiting under the acceleration manipulation. The larger discrepancy appeared mainly among novice and dyslexic readers, whose reading skills are not yet stabilized. Our data showed that the larger the discrepancy, the larger the effect of the acceleration phenomenon on enhancement of the reading skills. Moreover, the fact that the acceleration phenomenon also affected the reading performance of more advanced young readers, as well as adult regular readers, strengthens the belief that readers at all levels and ages do not routinely read at their highest possible level. The accelerated reading rate may help to reduce some of the discrepancy between ability and performance, thereby enhancing reading effectiveness. At the slower rate, decoding accuracies were highest. The slow-paced condition may have allowed subjects (mainly novice and dyslexic) more time for rehearsal and self-correction of decoding mistakes. However, under this condition, comprehension was lowest. Lastly, the slow reading pace also reduced the amount of contextual information available in short-term memory and impaired reading comprehension. These strong and consistent findings raised a central question concerning the basic cognitive mediating factors involved in the acceleration phenomenon. Answering this question was the aim of the second project.

PROJECT 2: COGNITIVE MEDIATION
OF THE ACCELERATION PHENOMENON

As reading is a cognitive process that functions according to constraints on information processing, we proposed that several mediating cognitive factors contribute to the positive effect of the acceleration phenomenon on reading performance. These factors were studied systematically among young regular and dyslexic readers (see also Breznitz, 2003b, for a review). The initial research dealt with attention span and reduction of distractibility during reading (Breznitz, 1988). This was followed by two studies focusing on overcoming some of the limitations imposed by short-term/working memory on reading (Breznitz, 1997a; Breznitz & Share, 1992). A fourth study focused on the ability to surmount, to some extent, the effects of impaired word recognition skills (Breznitz, 1997a), and the final study focused on the idea of overcoming some of the prosodic difficulties in reading (Breznitz, 1990).

Study 1: Attention and Distractibility

This study (Breznitz, 1988) was designed to examine the hypothesis that the acceleration phenomenon reduces distractibility and increases attention capacity for reading material. It was hypothesized that prompting children to read at their maximal normal reading rate would improve their comprehension and reading accuracy, even in the presence of proximal distracters. Participants included 30 regular and 30 dyslexic readers in the fourth grade. In the first condition, subjects were tested with the basic acceleration manipulation. In the second condition, the acceleration manipulation was run again while visual pictorial distracters were inserted into the reading materials. In both conditions, subjects read the materials orally, and reading time, decoding errors, comprehension, and recall recognition tests of the distracters were measured.

As in previous studies, this study supported the effect of the acceleration phenomenon under both reading conditions. No significant differences in decoding accuracy and comprehension were found among the regular readers when comparing the two self-paced reading rates (with and without distracters). However, comprehension decreased significantly in the dyslexic group when they read at the self-paced reading rate with distracters as compared to the self-paced rate without them. Both groups were able to remember the distracters in the self-paced reading rate condition, but only the regular readers remembered the distracters in the fast-paced condition.

The regular readers were already at the advanced stage of mastering decoding skills. For them, decoding words was already an automatic skill and they could direct their attention to reading comprehension and simultaneously allocate spare attention capacity to the visual distracters without interfering with either their comprehension or decoding accuracy. The visual distracters captured the attention span of the dyslexics in the self-paced reading rate condition and interfered with their reading skills. However, reading at an accelerated rate helped the dyslexics to focus their attention on the reading materials, eliminat-

ing distractibility and improving reading. Still, due to limited attentional resources, they could not remember the distracters.

Studies 2 and 3: Short-Term Memory

Four experiments were conducted in each of two studies, one on regular readers
and one on dyslexics, to investigate the hypothesis that comprehension gains in
fast-paced reading can be attributed primarily to changes in short-term memory
(STM) functioning (Breznitz, 1997a; Breznitz & Share, 1992). Based on the
claim that the fast-paced manipulation increased the units (either number or
size) available in STM and thus enlarged the context in which the reading process occurs, it was suggested that subjects engaged in fast-paced reading would
show significant performance gains on tasks sensitive to STM function. Two
groups of second graders participated in the studies, 23 regular readers and 23
dyslexics.

Experiment 1.   The first experiment in each study assessed the influence of
the acceleration manipulation on measures more closely associated with STM
function, such as recognition and recall for semantic (propositional) content
and for exact wording. The texts were read in self-paced and fast-paced reading
rate conditions. For both groups of subjects, significant differences between the
self-paced and fast-paced conditions were obtained on all measures. Among the
regular readers, reading speed increased by 28%, reading accuracy by 48%, inferential comprehension by 21%, and propositional recall by 29%. The two
measures closely related to STM functioning also showed significant improvement. Recall of exact wording improved 24% and recognition 59%. For the dyslexics group, reading rate increased by 19%, reading accuracy by 28%, inferential comprehension by 26%, and factual content recall by 6%. No significant
gain for recall and recognition of exact wording was found. For the regular readers, data suggested that the effects of the fast-paced manipulation occur primarily through STM. In contrast, dyslexic children did not improve their memory
for exact wording in the fast-paced condition.

Experiment 2.   This experiment examined memory for wording and word
order in sentences read in a fast-paced, as opposed to a self-paced, condition in
order to provide more explicit evidence for the STM hypothesis. Primacy and
recency effects were also examined based on the hypothesis that if the fast-
paced manipulation operates primarily through STM, then recall of the last
(most recent) item should show a greater fast-paced advantage than recall of

the first (primacy) item, because recency effects are more dependent on STM. For both groups of subjects, significant gains for speed, accuracy, and comprehension (as measured by propositional recall) were revealed in the fast-paced condition. Among the control groups, equal gains were shown for measures of item and order recall. These powerful effects on STM-sensitive measures support the view that improvements in reading comprehension obtained through fast reading result from an increase in the number of elements being held in STM. With respect to recency and primacy, improvement in recall of the primacy items was negligible, whereas recall of recency items doubled in the fast-paced condition.

The dyslexic readers showed significant gains only in forward recall order on the measures of item and order recall. These results support the view that, among dyslexic children, improvements in comprehension obtained with fast-paced reading can result from an increase in the number of elements being held in STM. In addition, the increased forward recall performance among dyslexics may indicate a reliance on contextual information. Regarding primacy and recency, the data indicated that dyslexic children recalled more primacy than recency elements during both fast- and self-paced conditions. To the extent that recall of recent items is relatively more dependent on STM processes than recall of primacy items, these results fail to support the view that the fast-paced manipulation operates among dyslexics directly through STM processing.

Experiment 3. This experiment was designed to directly compare memory for wording with memory for semantic information. If the fast-paced manipulation works primarily through STM, then an interaction would be expected between memory condition (semantic vs. wording) and pace condition, with fast-paced reading producing relatively more accurate detection (i.e., fewer false alarms) or wording than semantic changes. The results suggested that among the regular readers in the self-paced condition, correct identification of the unaltered version was superior in the semantic condition. Thus, subjects were more often fooled by a substitute word that preserved meaning than by meaning-altering changes. This replicates the well-established finding that semantic memory for text is superior to memory for surface features. The fast-paced condition produced significant gains in memory for wording but not in memory for semantic information. Among the dyslexic readers in both the self- and fast-paced conditions, correct identification of the unaltered version of the passage was superior in the wording conditions than in the semantic wording conditions. Thus, the dyslexic children were more often fooled by meaning-altering changes than by words that preserved meaning. These results are the reverse of those found among normal novice readers

Experiment 4.   In the fourth experiment, subjects were given a target item from the text they had just read aloud and asked to recall the items immediately preceding and following the probe. We hypothesized that the fast-paced manipulation would produce significant improvements in recall relative to self-paced reading in both groups of subjects. As predicted, the regular readers recalled more items in the fast-paced condition. The dyslexic children recalled more prior words than subsequent words during self- and fast-paced reading, which indicates that the recall of items among dyslexic readers is related to context.

In sum, results from the regular readers in all experiments provided strong evidence for the hypothesis that the fast-paced manipulation operates primarily through STM functioning. The magnitude of the gains suggests that the fast-paced manipulation was operating specifically on the STM component of the reading process. With regard to individual differences, there is a tendency for subjects with smaller STM spans to benefit more from the experimental manipulation. The fast-paced phenomenon can be regarded as strong support for the causal role of STM functioning in reading. However, results suggested that STM functioning among dyslexic children was only facilitated when reliance on context was feasible, as opposed to normal novice readers, who showed sizable gains on STM tasks that were free of context effects. In addition, the findings also suggested that STM resources might be used in a different manner among dyslexic readers, who depend more on sentence content to deduce meaning. Although this strategy is not cognitively economic in terms of engagement of limited resources, it may offer a means of lexical access that is inefficiently achieved through phonological or orthographic codes.

It is conceivable that for context dependent dyslexic readers, acceleration induces postlexical text integration processes (improvement in WM [working memory] responsible for short-term processing functions), whereas for novice readers a fast pace may enhance prelexical word identification processes (increased efficiency in STM responsible for passive storage functions). Thus, the effects of reading acceleration may enhance processing operation among dyslexics and it may increase capacity for normal readers. A fast reading pace might improve the reading effectiveness of dyslexic readers by facilitating the interaction between short- and long-term memory storage functions through increased WM activity. An additional possibility is that WM may act as a coordinating mechanism for information arriving from each of the subsystems involved in the reading process (phonological, orthographic, and semantic). Fast-paced reading may improve this coordination by forcing information to arrive in WM more quickly, thereby creating a situation in which corresponding information from the three subsystems is present simultaneously.

Study 4: Overcoming Phonological Impairment

In the fourth study (Breznitz, 1997b), an attempt was made to reduce the effect of a basic phonological deficit at the core of dyslexics' word recognition problems using two independent and mutually supporting methods: reading acceleration and auditory masking.

Auditory Masking.   Interference in the auditory channel might obstruct the use of phonological codes during reading and encourage dyslexic readers to use alternative, less impaired information. As the phonological system is presumably intact in control readers, its masking might actually reduce their reading effectiveness. As indicated by previous results, the dyslexics benefited from acceleration, particularly in terms of improved comprehension, although to a lesser degree than normal controls. The rationale behind the auditory masking manipulation was based on the notion that one method of reducing the reliance of dyslexic children on their impaired phonological skills is to overload it with task-irrelevant information. As expected, auditory masking was somewhat detrimental for normal readers, who were deprived of an effective information-processing route. In the case of dyslexic readers, however, even in the self-paced condition, auditory masking significantly decreased all types of oral reading errors, increased their reading speed and, indirectly, the beneficial effects of acceleration.

Auditory masking during fast-paced reading interferes with the performance of normal novice readers who depend primarily on their effective phonological processing during word recognition. It appears that although they have sufficient spare capacity in the self-paced condition to overcome the extra load on the auditory channel, the combination of masking and reading acceleration impedes their capabilities. It is possible that both acceleration and auditory masking effectively altered the distribution of processing resources among phonological, orthographic, and semantic processing systems. This may have led to some changes in processing within and between the systems and between the two groups. The analysis of decoding errors lends further support to the notion that both auditory masking and acceleration, separately and in combination, reduced the dyslexic children's reliance on the phonological route.

Study 5: Vocalization

This study (Breznitz, 1990) examined the relative sensitivity of various temporal features of reading to increased reading rate. The main objective was to determine whether or not increased input rate would lead to increased output rate (vocalization–utterances). Would the subject speak faster, or would the output rate remain stable when the pauses between utterances became fewer or shorter? Seventy-six first-grade subjects participated, all of whom were tested with the acceleration manipulation. Oral reading time, decoding accuracy, and comprehension were measured. In addition, oral reading times were recorded and analyzed by an analog-to-digital conversation analyzer (automatic vocal transaction analyzer, AVTA). Two temporal parameters were derived from the AVTA: a vocalization unit (a segment of sound uninterrupted by any discernible silence) and a pause (a silent segment bounded by vocalizations). Vocalization time and pause time were examined to determine the changes in each when subjects were prompted to read faster than their own natural pace. Results indicated that during self-paced reading, 45% of the total reading time was taken up by vocalization and 55% was consumed by pauses. During accelerated reading, both vocalization and pause time decreased significantly. However, pause time decreased to a greater extent. During fast-paced reading, subjects made fewer and shorter pauses, spoke faster, and tended to speak in longer units. It is plausible that the "good pauses" (i.e., those conducive to adequate information processing and comprehension) were retained during fast oral reading, and the less necessary pauses were eliminated.

CONCLUSIONS

According to our argument, reading rate is the central factor in fluent word reading. When it is perceived as a dependent variable, the focus ought to be on the underlying processes that bring about a fast and fluent reading rate, namely, accuracy and comprehension. However, when reading rate is viewed as an independent variable that itself influences the quality of reading, the central focus should shift to the way in which it affects accuracy and comprehension. This suggests a further in-depth investigation of the underlying causes that determine reading rate as an independent factor enhancing word decoding effectiveness. The second and the third sections of this book present this notion.

Viewing the data of our research projects, several results emerge that require specific attention. First, our data have consistently revealed a discrepancy between reading rate ability and the actual self-paced reading rate in most readers. When pushed to read faster under the acceleration manipulation, our subjects not only operated at a faster reading rate but they also improved their decoding accuracy and comprehension. Two questions thus arise. Why is there such a discrepancy even among good readers? And why was a faster reading rate not automatically maintained without manipulation, given that its benefits are clear and substantial?

Perfetti's (1985, 1997) verbal efficiency theory suggested that the quality of the various components that are activated in reading is crucial for reading effectiveness. Many researchers (e.g., Adams, 1990; Perfetti, 1997, for a review) agree that decoding accuracy is crucial for good reading. In order to achieve good word decoding among students, teachers commonly tend to slow down students' reading rate (Breznitz, 1981). Over the years, the brain acquires these kinds of reading habits. With maturation, there is a natural increase in reading rate. But, due to bad habits, few readers reach their optimal rate. Moreover, because reading requires the processing of information in particular brain modalities and systems that were originally developed for other tasks, it has to adopt the operational mode of these brain entities. Generally speaking, a more accurate or cautious process typically implies a slowing down of any brain activity. However, in the case of reading, a better performance requires, first, the timely arrival of inputs from each of the various sources and, second, the synchronization of inputs between these sources. In other words, reading is an inherently time-constrained activity. Paradoxically, therefore, a faster—not slower—SOP in the brain entities activated in reading is likely to be crucial for effective reading performance in general and for fluent word reading rate in particular. This hypothesis is explored in the following chapters.

3

Automaticity in
Fluent Reading

Researchers agree that effective decoding of print is a prerequisite for reading comprehension (Adams, 1990). Effective word decoding is determined by accuracy and flow. These are believed to be achieved only when word recognition skills become automatic—that is, without much conscious effort (LaBerge & Samuels, 1974). The contribution of automaticity to fluent reading is widely seen to be crucial. The Committee of the Health Council in the Netherlands (Gersons-Wolfensberger & Ruijssenaars, 1997; Snowling, 2000) recommended a new working definition of dyslexia, which includes the following conditions:

1. It should be descriptive, with no causal explanations.
2. It should be specific enough to recognize dyslexia among a variety of reading and spelling problems.
3. It should be general enough to allow for a variety of causal explanation models.
4. It should be applicable to research objectives and suitable for intervention.

This led to the following working definition: "Dyslexia is present when the automatization of word identification (reading) and/or word spelling does not develop, or does so very incompletely or with great difficulty" (Health Council of the Netherlands). In this definition, the term *automatization* refers to reading and writing styles characterized by a high level of speed and accuracy that require a small amount of deliberately allocated attention resources. The following sections focus on the contribution of attention and automaticity to fluent reading.

CHARACTERISTICS OF AUTOMATICITY

People perform many actions automatically, with little effort or conscious thought. The automaticity evident in perceptual-motor skills extends to cognitive skills such as reading. Researchers have composed various lists of characteristics that define automaticity (Posner & Snyder, 1975; Schneider, Dumais, & Shiffrin, 1984). Logan (1997) presented four characteristics that are common to most of these lists, as well as significant in definitions of automaticity: speed, effortlessness, autonomy, and lack of conscious awareness.

The development of automaticity is characterized by an increase in speed. Learning curves for tasks that become automatized show that performance becomes faster and more accurate with practice, with most gains being made at the beginning and the magnitude of the gains diminishing with further practice. Thus, performance follows a power law stating that reaction time will decrease as a function of practice until a certain irreducible limit is reached (Logan, 1997). Accordingly, although the first few trials exhibit a dramatic improvement, with more practice, a much larger number of trials will be required to create a significant change in speed (Logan, 1988b, 1992). This illustrates the relativity of the speed characteristic of automaticity.

Dual task interference has been used in studies attempting to demonstrate that automaticity also involves effortlessness. The underlying assumption is that if two processes can be accomplished simultaneously, without leading to any interference, then at least one of the processes is automatic (Logan, 1978, 1979; Schneider & Fisk, 1982, 1984). Studies have shown that effortlessness is a criterion of automaticity in reading. For example, using a dual task paradigm, Posner and Boies (1971) found that skilled readers automatically decode letters. Automatic processing is also considered to be autonomous in that it can begin and end without intention (Zbrodoff & Logan, 1986). The Stroop effect is commonly used to demonstrate this. This effect occurs when subjects are asked to name the color of the ink in which names of colors are written. Subjects take longer to name the color of the ink if the written word spells the name of a different color (e.g., RED written in blue ink) than if the word name and the ink are of the same color (e.g., RED written in red ink). This phenomenon is interpreted as evidence for autonomous reading of the color word, even in situations where such reading is unnecessary and makes the task more difficult. It has been shown that interference in the Stroop task increases as children learn to automatize words. For example, Schiller (1966) found that first graders showed less interference on the Stroop task than second graders, who had more developed reading skills. Automatic processes are not always characterized by all the properties described earlier, and for each process, one property may be more developed than the rest. This view of automaticity maintains that different properties may change at different rates, leaving the less practiced or impaired reader with a process that may continue to be effortful and dysfluent (Logan, 1997).

THEORIES OF AUTOMATICITY

Limited Capacity

The connection between automaticity and decoding was noted in the influential LaBerge and Samuel model of reading. LaBerge and Samuels (1974) presented a general theory of automatic processing in reading. They outlined a basic limited-capacity argument, which holds that reading is a complex skill in which simultaneous word recognition and comprehension are possible only when they present a combined cognitive demand that does not exceed the reader's available resources. Furthermore, LaBerge and Samuels held that automaticity in word recognition develops through practice, because practice decreases the attention requirements for word recognition, freeing up limited cognitive resources to process meaning. In nonfluent readers, a single process alone might require the full extent of cognitive resources. In such cases, when word recognition uses up all of the reader's cognitive resources, other component processes of reading, such as comprehension, cannot be processed simultaneously. LaBerge and Samuels argued that when faced with the task of both recognizing and comprehending words, unskilled readers switch attention back and forth between these two processes. Such attention switching is slow and burdensome for memory, and it interferes with comprehension. They proposed that repeated practice could lead unskilled readers to increased efficiency and automaticity.

Perfetti and Hogaboam (1975) showed that poor comprehenders differ from good comprehenders in the speed at which they decode single words, with good comprehenders reading words faster, especially words that are unfamiliar and low in frequency. They concluded that poor comprehenders lack automatic word identification skills and they proposed a "shared limited capacity hypothesis," according to which the available memory capacity is limited for performance of two tasks simultaneously: word recognition and comprehension. The automaticity of word identification allows the mind to deal with higher order linguistic skills important for comprehension. The term *bottleneck* was used to describe the problem that arises as a result of sharing a limited resource.

Posner and Snyder (1975) similarly employed the idea of limited capacity. Their two-process model of cognitive expectancies formats the time course and facilitative/inhibitory patterns of two expectancy methods. One is a capacity-demanding conscious mechanism, whereas the other is a resource-free automatic priming mechanism. The conscious attention mechanism is thought to cause both inhibition and facilitation of unexpected signals. In contrast, the automatic process is thought to facilitate the processing of related signals, but not to inhibit the processing of unrelated signals. Mackay (1982) argued that practice under consistent conditions leads to an increase in firing between the nodes in an existing neuronal framework, which in turn causes gains in speed and accuracy. This strength theory concludes that automaticity is the result of connections made stronger and easier to follow due to repetition.

Shiffrin and Schneider (1977) provided further support for the idea that automatic processing develops as a result of practice with consistent stimulus–response relations. They believed that without consistency, automaticity could not develop, and the degree of automaticity depends on the extent of consistency (Schneider & Fisk, 1982). Shiffrin and Schneider's theory of automaticity includes two modes of information processing. One is controlled processing and refers to a set of operations that are under conscious control, require active attention, and are limited by capacity. Such processes are thought to operate in new situations where stimulus–response relations are prone to variability. The second mode is automatic processing, which is fast, often insensitive to capacity limits, and very difficult to modify once initiated. Shiffrin and Schneider saw the Stroop effect as reflecting a difference in processing speed, with word reading being the faster and more automatic process and color naming being the slower, controlled process. Such differences in processing speed suggested by Stroop interference are consistent with their distinction between controlled and automatic cognitive processes.

J. D. Cohen, Dunbar, and McClelland (1990) preferred to view automaticity as a continuum rather than a dichotomous activity. In their view, different tasks exist along a processing continuum depending on the degree of automaticity of each task. They claimed that as a continuous process, automaticity in performing a task is subject to attention control. They designed a parallel-distributed processing (PDP) model of the Stroop task that incorporated the concepts of relative speed of word and color processing and automaticity. According to J. D.

Cohen et al. (1990), the Stroop effect can be captured in a relatively simple connectionist network that assumes that the weights of the connections among color and word pathways vary on the basis of differing levels of experience with these two processing dimensions. With experience, the connections gain more weight, and processing becomes more automatic. In addition, the J. D. Cohen et al. model nicely captures many Stroop phenomena, including the asymmetry between facilitation and interference, stimulus onset asynchrony effects, practice effects, and response set effects. This theory is consistent with the ideas of LaBerge and Samuels (1974), Shiffrin and Schneider (1977), and Mackay (1982), implying stronger connections as the cause of faster processing speed.

Strengthened connections are also part of the explanation for automaticity in J. R. Anderson's (1992) ACT theory, which argues that production rules that specify the steps of cognition control all cognitive behavior. Three learning processes are incorporated in the ACT theory. The first is decoding of knowledge derived from experience. Such knowledge is saved as facts in memory and is called *declarative knowledge*, which is not specific for any particular use or goal. In contrast, *production rule knowledge* is committed to a certain use. The second stage of learning involves the gradual proceduralization of declarative knowledge into automatic production rules, which capture the procedural knowledge on how to achieve specific goals. The third learning process involves strengthening the production rules and the declarative facts. Anderson noted that a production is automatic to the degree that it is strengthened each time it is used, and it receives the same increment of strength each time it is practiced. Furthermore, he showed that his theory is applicable not only to motor tasks, but to a range of cognitive skills, including geometrical reasoning and development of language and letter recognition. Anderson's mechanism can also be perceived as a chunking theory, because it collapses several tasks onto a single step. Newell and Rosenbloom (1981) also offered a chunking theory, wherein stimulus and response elements are chunked. This enables complex stimuli to be perceived and responded to as single, rather than complex, units. Thus, due to the reduced number of steps involved in processing, the cognitive load is reduced. This makes the task less effortful, and the response faster and more automatic.

Modularity

The notion of limited attention processes and capacity, as initially presented by LaBerge and Samuels (1974), has been incorporated into many theories of automaticity. However, Stanovich (1990) offered another view of the mechanisms driving automaticity. Stanovich pointed out the merits of viewing automaticity of reading from a modular perspective, in which independent, autonomous expert processing systems control the identification of words. These systems are designed to perceive and retrieve the appropriate information and to direct information processing. Whereas the limited capacity models emphasize the amount of processing resources used by a certain task, the modular approach emphasizes the quality and efficiency of actual processing. In the modular approach, each perceptual cue is directed to the appropriate processing system. This allows the independent processing centers to equip themselves only with the information relevant to their function. Such increased efficiency in processing, Stanovich claimed, leads to the construction of a high quality representation in memory. This encapsulation process essentially explains automaticity as a memory phenomenon. Due to the accuracy and precision of the stimuli, access to representations in memory is seemingly effortless and immediate (Stanovich, 1990). Studies of context dependency support the modularity theory. Such studies show that unskilled readers are more dependent on context than skilled readers (Nicholson, 1991; Stanovich, 1986b). Presumably, this is because the word recognition skills of skilled readers are so good that they need not rely on context, whereas unskilled readers must rely more on context due to underdeveloped word identification skills (Nicolson & Tan, 1999). Thus, good readers have high-quality word representations, which, as modularity theory predicts, operate independently of higher level processes so that they are not subject to the influences of context. Similarly, this theory is also supported by research showing that reliance on higher level processes, such as prediction and guessing, is more typical of poor than of skilled readers (Nicholson, 1991).

Logan (1988a, 1997) also emphasized the notion of automaticity as dependent on memory processes and advanced the concept of increased specificity of function in automaticity. He suggested episodic memory as the primary learning mechanism responsible for automaticity. Logan proposed that a separate memory trace is laid down with each experience of a task. This trace can be retrieved if the task is repeated. A task-relevant knowledge database is built with increasing practice, which comprises more and more instances in memory. Logan claimed that automaticity is achieved when performance is based on the retrieval of memory traces of past solutions to relevant problems and not on algorithmic computations based on thinking or reasoning. He posited that with each exposure to a stimulus, the algorithm competes with each memory instance, in parallel and independently. The response given depends on the winner of this race. When the knowledge base becomes large enough, performance can come to be based entirely on memory retrieval. With more memory episodes, the probability that one will win the race increases until the algorithm can be abandoned entirely. Speed and effortlessness of automaticity result because memory retrieval is faster than algorithmic retrieval and involves fewer steps.

AUTOMATICITY AND READING

Before proceeding to our discussion of the role that automaticity plays in reading, it is useful to differentiate between higher order and lower order processing (Spear & Sternberg, 1987). Lower order, or bottom-up, processing is data driven. Reading processes that rely heavily on lower order processing include letter identification and word recognition. On the other hand, higher order, or top-down, processing is concept driven. When one begins to read, reading comprehension is dependent on the success of lower order processing and word identification, but as competence is gained, reading comprehension comes to be explained more by higher language competence than by word identification skills (Perfetti, 1985). This progression from lower level to higher level processes was outlined by LaBerge and Samuels (1974) in their model of the stages of perceptual learning. In the first stage, time and effort are spent mostly on the detection of relevant features. In reading, this stage involves turning the majority of effort and attention to the recognition of letters and their association with phonemes. At this stage, performance is accurate but very slow. In the next phase, mastery is reached through practice. This is the utilization stage, wherein familiar words are recognized as single units and performance is very close to perfectly accurate, although still slow. During the last phase, the skill is practiced to the point where it can be performed without conscious concern. It is at this third stage that full automaticity is reached. In terms of accuracy and speed, the model suggests that full accuracy will be mastered during the second stage, whereas speed will increase throughout the phases, ending at an asymptote. Consequently, upon completion of the phases, performance is characterized by both rapidity and accuracy. According to the LaBerge and Samuel's model, automaticity occurs first at the letter coding level, and only then at the spelling and word levels.

Other models of reading acquisition and automaticity recognize that word reading involves an interaction between orthographic, phonological, and semantic systems (Bowers & Wolf, 1993). It has been posited that the effortless and automatic recognition of letters, letter patterns, and whole words is a critical factor in the development of fluent reading (Adams, 1990). A child must learn that each letter represents a sound, in a process aided by knowledge of letter names. When the child knows the letter names and is able to retrieve them quickly, then more attention can be devoted to letter sequences. This enables the child to build up an orthographic pattern. When this pattern is further associated with a sound, then a phonological-orthographic connection is constructed, enabling the child to further recognize and remember words. Thus, rapid processing at each level is what enables the child to progress to the level of rapid word recognition. Readers following a normal progression are able to develop letter cluster codes automatically while they attend to the specific letter sequence that corresponds to a specific subword sound unit. This helps to increase the speed with which they recognize familiar words. Thus, readers are dependent on orthography for phonological processes and on phonology for properly recognizing orthographic clusters. Consequently, a disability in word reading may result from a failure of the orthographic or the phonological code to develop, as well as from a failure of the codes to connect or to do so in a temporally appropriate manner (Berninger, 1990). Studies have shown that first graders who achieved more automaticity in letter naming also learned more words and recognized those words more quickly than did poor readers, who achieved a lesser degree of automaticity (Blachman, 1984).

Speed of word recognition is also acknowledged as an important indicator of automatic reading (Perfetti, 1985). Bowers and Wolf (1993) found that many subjects with slow word reading speed exhibit naming speed deficits and they hypothesized that slow naming speed can be seen as an indication of disruption in one or more of the processing domains that are activated in word reading or in the precise timing mechanisms that operate within particular domains or across them. They posited that such disruption might affect the automatic induction of high quality orthographic codes, as well as their rapid connection to phonological representations.

THE IMPORTANCE OF AUTOMATIC DECODING

LaBerge and Samuels (1974) cited two criteria for measuring reading skill development: accuracy and automaticity. They claimed that the development of decoding skill to the point of automaticity is essential. According to their theory, fluent reading is only attained when all decoding levels, from visual to semantic, work automatically, so that attention is free to produce meaning. One of the reasons for the mounting interest in the word recognition process is the consistent finding that word recognition development is involved in improving comprehension (Calfee & Piontkowski, 1981; Stanovich, 1985; Young, Bowers, & MacKinnon, 1996). To understand how word recognition skill influences other reading processes, comprehension included, the components of word recognition, accuracy, and automaticity must be explored.

Although achieving accuracy in word recognition is an important milestone in reading (Wolf, Miller, & Donnelly, 2000), it is not the only skill that determines reading ability and it is not sufficient to attain reading fluency. Without fluency, it is possible that comprehension will not be achieved. Thus, to become proficient readers, children not only need good phonological representations of words, but they must also be able to process these words quickly and with minimal resources. Once words can be processed with a high level of accuracy, fast speed of processing is the next stage of reading development on the way toward automatic reading, which is the final stage of effective word processing (Ehri & Wilce, 1983; LaBerge & Samuels, 1974).

Automatic processing of words enables allotment of attention to higher processes and acts as a basis for better comprehension (Yap & Van der Leij, 1993b). According to Samuels and Flor (1997), the reading process requires fast and accurate decoding (see also Stanovich, 1993) and simultaneous comprehension. Thus, readers who have attained automaticity in decoding processes can allot attention resources to comprehension and expression. A fluent reader is one who can perform a number of tasks, such as word recognition and comprehension, simultaneously. Typically, readers arrive at this stage of skill acquisition after a long period of practice, including repetitive exercising of reading skills. As such in the normal course of reading, speed and accuracy can be considered to be tightly connected constructs, both of which are crucial for effective automaticity in word reading.

On the one hand, automaticity is presented as resulting from the efficiency of reading skills that are tested using processing speed and accuracy. On the other hand, it can be claimed that automaticity is a general cognitive trait, which therefore relies on the processing efficiency of the basic systems involved in the reading process. The main argument in this book is that accurate word recognition relies, among others, on the speed of processing of the modalities and systems activated during reading and their synchronization. This also contributes to the development of automatic processes in information processing. Thus, it can be maintained that automaticity tested by the processing speed of the aforementioned skills also stems from the speed of processing of the modalities and systems involved in this activity. As word recognition relies on processing in the visual and auditory modalities, the speed of processing of these systems and their synchronization constitutes a crucial factor for the development of automatic word recognition. Consequently, automaticity can not only be presented as a dependent variable relying on the quality of the systems activated in reading, but also as a variable influencing the quality of word retrieval from the lexicon as well as comprehension.

DYSLEXIA AND AUTOMATICITY

Studies have demonstrated that dyslexic children process words slowly (Lovett, 1987), and this speed deficit extends beyond printed words to a more general deficit in retrieving names of visual objects, colors, digits, and letters (Bowers & Swanson, 1991; Denckla & Rudel, 1974; Wolf, Bally, & Morris, 1986). Such studies indicate a problem in dyslexics that is not only related to decoding, but may also arise from poor automaticity of lower order reading skills, such as name retrieval ability. Dyslexics also tend to have poorly automatized motor balancing skills, leading to the claim that dyslexia is caused by an automatic processing deficit that hinders skill acquisition in general (Nicolson & Fawcett, 1990). This, along with the fact that automatic skills and phonological awareness constitute two separate skills (Bowers & Swanson, 1991), led Yap and Van der Leij (1993b) to investigate whether dyslexics have a deficit in automatic phonological decoding skills. They compared the performance of dyslexics to that of normal readers and poor readers on tests of varying phonological requirements and of automatic processing. On the explicit phonological task, dyslexics showed a deficit in automatic phonological decoding, whereas poor readers' responses resembled normal readers. When phonological processing requirements were simpler, dyslexics showed a deficit in automatic word processing. The more demanding the task became with respect to phonological processing, the poorer dyslexics performed on the speeded condition, which was a measure of automaticity. Thus, Yap and Van der Leij (1993b) concluded that dyslexics not only have qualitatively poor phonological representations, they also have severe problems with rapid, automatic processing of phonological information. In light of the theory presented here, the source of the slowness of dyslexic readers in automatic processing of phonological information can be explained as an outcome of slow speed of processing of the phonological system itself.

Van der Leij and Van Daal (1999) further tested their automatic decoding deficit hypothesis in a study in which students with dyslexia were expected to show slower response latencies than chronological age controls, even for accurately read words of high frequency. They explored whether the slowness of processing is also apparent at the level of sublexical units and when reading nonwords. Students with dyslexia were found to process highly familiar words more slowly than nondisabled students their own age. This speed limitation extended to many other orthographic stimuli, resulting in response latencies that were comparable to or worse than those of younger readers. This was taken to indicate that the reading of dyslexics, even when carried out accurately, does not reach the level of the relatively attention-free automaticity seen in normal readers. Thus, the automatization of dyslexics' reading skills is deficient, as expressed in slowness even when reading words that are familiar and accurately read. The explanation of Van Daal and Van der Leij relies on a theory of dyslexia as an automatization deficit specific to phonological decoding skills. However, the fact that dyslexics are slow even when accurately reading familiar words suggests additional causes for their lack of automaticity in word reading. Along this line, Nicolson and Fawcett (1990, 1993a) proposed that children with dyslexia have a general deficit in automatizing skills. Their dyslexic automatization deficit (DAD) hypothesis claims that dyslexics have trouble acquiring fluency both in reading and in other areas, such as cognitive and motor skills. They posited that dyslexia is not necessarily unique to one modality, but can be expressed across several different modalities. Nicolson and Fawcett further proposed that dyslexics can mask or hide their impairments in basic skills through "conscious compensation" and they contended that dyslexic children can achieve normal performance on a wide range of tasks by simply committing a large part of their attention resources to the task at hand. Because they work so hard, the hypothesis predicts that dyslexic children will get tired more easily and will be more susceptible to stress, and their performance will break down during resource-intensive tasks.

To demonstrate the scope of the automatization deficit, Nicolson and Fawcett compared dyslexic and normal readers across a series of motor balance tasks, which should be automatized and have little connection to reading skills (Fawcett, Nicolson, & Dean, 1996; Nicolson & Fawcett, 1999). Dyslexic subjects performed at the level of age-matched controls on baseline tasks, such as simple balancing. However, they showed impaired performance as the tasks became more complex. On a selective choice reaction time task, there were differences in speed between the dyslexic and control groups, whereas on simple reaction time tasks no such difference was detected. In addition, when the subjects were asked to perform a dual task that included balancing as the primary task and a task that required attention (counting backward, auditory tasks) as the secondary task, the performance of dyslexic subjects deteriorated. The control subjects showed no balance deficit, indicating automatization of balance. The DAD theory has been challenged based on several unsuccessful attempts to replicate Nicolson and Fawcett's findings. Yap and Van der Leij (1994) found support for the automatization deficit in only one of two dual task conditions. Wimmer et al. (1998) and Stringer and Stanovich (1998), however, reportedly did not find any supporting evidence for the DAD hypothesis.

The longer processing time among the dyslexics in more complicated tasks requiring the processing of information from more than one source points to an additional factor underlying automaticity in word reading. When a task requires information from more than one source, the speed at which the information is processed at each source and the speed of synchronization between the various sources are both likely to be crucial in order to achieve automaticity. Automatic retrieval of words requires a stable representation of word patterns in the mental lexicon. A potential explanation for the lack of stable word patterns in the mental lexicon among dyslexic readers is that information from the various entities activated during reading does not arrive on time for a proper integration to occur. This is the asynchrony hypothesis, which is dealt with in chapters 8, 9, and 10.

Cerebral Involvement

Fawcett et al. (1996) suggested that phonological impairments may be a product of cerebral impairment. Specifically, they raise the possibility that mild cerebral impairment may lead to limited articulatory control, which causes difficulty in building up phonological representations as well as problems with more complex motor tasks. Nicolson and Fawcett (1999) further developed this cerebral deficit hypothesis. They pointed to the deficits in motor skills and automatization seen in dyslexics as a strong indication of cerebral involvement, based on recognition of the cerebellum as an area responsible for motor functioning. The cerebellum has also been claimed to be involved in the automatization of motor skills, as well as in adaptive learning control (Ito, 1984, 1990). Nicolson and Fawcett cited a PET study in which cerebral activation was associated most extensively with new learning and with the process that makes motor tasks automatic (Jenkins, Brooks, Nixon, Frackowiak, & Passingham, 1994). They claimed that the cerebellum is linked not only with the frontal motor area, but also with areas further in the frontal cortex, such as Broca's area. They also presented evidence that the cerebellum is involved in language as well as motor functions, citing a study by H. C. Leiner, A. L. Leiner, and Dow (1989, 1993) that implicates the cerebellum in language dexterity, advancing the proposition that the cerebellum is involved in the automatization of skills, be they motoric or cognitive. Studies using various brain imaging techniques (Aksoomoff & Courchesne, 1992; Decety, Sjoholm, Ryding, Stenberg, & Ingvar, 1990; Paulesu, Frith, & Frackowiak, 1993; Roland, Eriksson, Widen, & Stone-

Elander, 1989) also support the notion that the cerebellum is involved in cognitive activities.

Nicolson and Fawcett claimed that the cerebellum has a role in the execution and automatization of motor skills, as well as a possible role in the proceduralization of cognitive skills. H. C. Leiner et al. (1989) pointed out that the cerebellum improves the performance of those areas to which it is linked by two-way neural connections. They noted that as the cerebellum has bidirectional ties to Broca's area, it is likely to be involved in improving language dexterity, which has both mental and motor components. The cerebellum may have the ability to support the development of a cognitive skill by using its timing and error analysis mechanism (Ito, 1990). A cerebral deficit could also account for the difficulties in spelling and handwriting experienced by dyslexics.

In explaining the validity of their hypothesis, Nicolson and Fawcett (1999) purported that the link between cerebral impairment and dyslexia is to be expected, as reading is a complex task requiring automatization and combination of its component skills. Although their performance may appear normal, closer examination of readers with cerebral impairment can reveal subtle deficits in fluency. Nicholson and Fawcett further offered a causal chain that explains the manner in which cerebral impairment may cause deficits in reading processes. They indicated it will first present itself in childhood as a mild motor difficulty and then as slowness in speaking and babbling, as well as decreased dexterity. If readers with cerebral impairments are less fluent in articulation, then they have fewer resources for processing sensory feedback, placing them at a disadvantage in the processing of auditory and phonemic structures of spoken words.

CONCLUSIONS

Several researchers have suggested that a lack of automaticity in word reading may lead to dysfluency in reading. The National Institute of Child Health and Human Development (2000) viewed fluency as "the freedom from word recognition problems that may prevent comprehension," and automaticity as "fluent processing of information requiring little effort or attention" (p. 7; see also Harris & Hodges, 1995). The terms *automaticity* and *fluency* overlap in the literature, as both are based on accurate repetition and practice. Researchers typically use the term *fluency* to denote a variety of specific linguistic processes including reading. With respect to reading, fluency refers specifically to the performance of word reading. However, the term *automaticity* can be presented as a broader concept, including a wide variety of behaviors ranging from motoric skills to cognitive skills. Seen in this way, automaticity incorporates a larger number of underlying factors that contribute to the development of linguistic skills such as fluent word reading rate. However, according to the view of this book, a primary factor for enhancement of automaticity in word reading is the speed at which the modalities and systems process information when decoding words. Without a certain level of SOP in these components, no word forms can be created and no substance for the automaticity process can be available. At this level of analysis, automaticity and word decoding rate share common factors. This idea is elaborated in later chapters of this book.

4

Prosody as an Indication
of Fluency

Different studies have pointed to the importance of spoken language in the acquisition of reading. Much of the research has focused on the importance of phonology and its contribution to correct reading. Within the bounds of the relation between spoken and written language, there exists an additional channel that focuses on prosody in language. Prosody refers to the aspects related to the chronometrics of oral expression, in other words, the clues connected to language expression. The reference is to intonation, sound, and silence during oral flow and speech fluency. All of these constitute evidence for discourse comprehension.

Different researchers claim that appropriate prosody (phrasing, intonation, and stress) during oral reading characterizes fluent reading (Chomsky, 1978; Rasinski, 1990; Samuels, Schermer, & Reinking, 1992). According to these researchers, proper prosody during the reading process is a result of efficient word recognition and comprehension, and its expressions are characterized by correctly stressed reading fluency and text comprehension.

This chapter surveys the relevant literature related to prosody in spoken and written language. The central question discussed is the extent to which prosody, as a basic trait, can be seen as influencing the quality of reading and the extent to which prosody develops as a result of the efficiency of the reader's reading skills.

WHAT IS PROSODY?

Prosody, the rhythm or intonation accompanying language, is not a linguistic byproduct but rather an aspect of language that is significant in its own right. We are most often aware of the importance of prosody when it is lacking, for example, when we have difficulty understanding synthetic, "robotic" speech (when interacting with a computerized answering service, etc.). The prosodic pattern is actually another dimension of speech that reflects and transfers different types of information. It is often said about babies and speakers of a foreign language that they "understand the tone." That is, they extract some information from the prosody of an utterance even if they do not understand the language in which it is said. According to Carroll and Slowiaczek (1987), prosody is comprised of meter, intonation, and inflection, and constitutes an abundantly organized pattern that provides additional information regarding the sentence. Prosody thus carries additional linguistic information to that of the verbal and syntactic information transferred in speech. In addition, Dowhower (1991) claimed that expressive and fluent reading is characterized by the appearance of prosodic features such as pitch (intonation), stress (loudness), and duration (timing). Finally, speakers and listeners use prosody to facilitate a wide variety of information processing, including marking and decoding lexical meaning, noting and disambiguating emotional intent, and marking and comprehending new information (Kimelman, 1999).

H. Cohen, Josee, and Mayada (2001) suggested two alternative conceptions of prosody. The first maintains that prosody is part of linguistic structure and affects the processing of language by providing clues for resolving other levels of linguistic structure, be they lexical (distinguishing lexical combinations, e.g., red coat vs. redcoat), syntactic, or semantic (resolution of ambiguities). In the second view, prosody is seen as a physical characteristic of the speech signal (marking the state of the speaker, e.g., anger, happiness, surprise), an integral part of the final representation of an utterance in memory, and a contributing factor in decoding and reconstruction in memory.

Hierarchically structured language incorporates phonological, morphological, syntactic, and semantic information. Additional nonlinguistic information, such as physical characteristics of the message and metalinguistic knowledge, also contribute to the communicative act. Prosody is one of the contributors to this process. It is the perceptual pattern of intonation, stress, and pause, the physical correlates of which are frequency, amplitude, and duration. The contribution of prosody is manifested in the provision of necessary cues, which influence language at multiple levels:

1. *Psycholinguistic processing*: Prosody can directly facilitate the resolution of semantic and syntactic structure necessary to extract meaning from a spoken message.

2. *Short-term memory processing*: Prosody can provide an initial structure in memory, in which incoming input is situated.

3. *Long-term memory processing*: Prosody can facilitate the activation of meaningful associations.

ACQUISITION OF PROSODY

Kehoe (2000) contrasted two different approaches to prosodic acquisition, the prosodic structure approach, which proposes that during development children's outputs are constrained by prosodic shape constraints and the correspondence approach, which proposes that alignment and faithfulness effects between input and output play the greatest role in explaining children's prosodic patterns. These findings provide support for both prosodic accounts by explaining that shape constraints play the dominant role at the earliest stages of development, and correspondence plays the dominant role at later stages. In fact, the correspondence account can be viewed as an extension of the prosodic structure account. Constraints that yield shape restrictions in early acquisition are demoted and outranked by constraints that yield outputs of varying size and shape. Children's preservation patterns are subject to developmental effects. First, children attend to stressed syllables on the right side of the word, regardless of primary or secondary stress. Second, they attend to the distinction between primary and secondary stress, and this leads them to focus on stressed syllables leftward in the word. Third, children attend to all stressed syllables in the target form, regardless of word position or stress prominence. It is also important to note that components of prosodic and segmental acquisition develop independently and at different rates (Goffman, 1999). Prosodic acquisition is still in progress in children age 4 to 6 years, and the capacity to produce rhythmic and modulated articulatory movements contributes to this developmental process. The capacity to produce rhythmic structure plays a role in the type of prosodic distinction that appears in a child's output.

This chapter presents theoretical models and empirical findings related to the production and comprehension of speech and attempts to understand the place of prosody in these processes. It seems that the important contribution of prosody to linguistic processing stems from its connection to language structure, and a number of theorists have referred to this connection. For example, Neisser (1967) noted a "close relationship between phrase structure and pronunciation" (p. 262). Around the same time, Chomsky and Halle (1968) formulated a rule system that connects a sentence's phonological representation and surface structure. These rules describe the connection between the stress and segmentation patterns of elements in a sentence and the syntactic structure of that sentence. Lieberman (1975) and Lieberman and Prince (1977) described the phonological representation behind the prosodic pattern as a structure whose branches and hierarchy are identical to those of a syntactic representation. Selkirk (1980) suggested that prosodic structure is not isomorphic to syntactic structure. Nevertheless, mapping these two structures can and should be defined because prosodic structure reflects syntactic structure in certain ways.

Although the nature and extent of the connection between prosodic and syntactic structure are not completely clear, many researchers seem to believe in the existence of such a connection. Due to recent technological developments that enable exact multidimensional sound analysis, evidence has accumulated regarding the manner in which structural information is reflected in prosody. For example, in a series of studies by Grosjean et al. (Gee & F. Grosjean, 1983; F. H. Grosjean, L. Grosjean, & Lane, 1979), syntactic structure (surface structure) was found to be the best predictor of pause patterns in a sentence, namely, their length and location. Schafer provided additional support for the connection between prosody and syntactic structure (Schafer, Carlson, Clifton, & Frazier, 2000; Schafer, Speer, Warren, & White, 2000). Schafer, Speer et al. (2000) mentioned that a wide range of sentence comprehension studies have shown that prosody can disambiguate syntactic structure, and explained that speakers are more likely to use prosody to disambiguate syntax when explicitly instructed to do so, or when the sentence is not disambiguated by context (Straub, 1997). They argued that production resulting from reading tasks may not accurately reflect the prosody of natural conversation and may misrepresent the degree of prosodic disambiguation in everyday speech. Their finding that adult speakers use disambiguating prosody for a structure already disambiguated by context suggests that prosodic disambiguation might be quite common in natural speech. This supports the claim that prosodic effects on comprehension must be incorporated into any satisfactory model of sentence processing. Schafer, Speer et al. (2000) also found that variability in the prosody used to disambiguate helps to constrain how it might fit into processing models. This supports the argument that the relation between prosody and syntactic disambiguation is complex and involves more than just the ability to be sensitive to the presence or absence of prosodic boundaries in an utterance.

The results from this study regarding comprehension confirm that naïve listeners can use the prosodic differences found in phonological and phonetic analyses to disambiguate syntactic structure. They also indicate that other types of prosodic information, such as choice of pitch accents and edge tones or the use of varying pitch ranges, seem to aid in disambiguation. These findings also provide further evidence that prosody is an important source of information for sentence comprehension in a wide range of discourse situations, and that prosodic structure is not fully predictable from syntactic structure, even in a highly constrained discourse situation. It has been shown that a disambiguated syntactic structure can be associated with multiple prosodic structures, which vary in such features as high versus low pitch, accents, and edge tones.

In a separate study, Schafer, Carlson et al. (2000) investigated whether or not adult listeners use pitch accents to disambiguate syntactic strings. The results of their study indicate that the presence of a pitch accent conveying focus can disambiguate the structure of ambiguous sentences, as placing a pitch accent on a function word (who or when) affects the syntactic analysis of the clause that it contains. The experiments used in this study attempted to identify ways in which the effects of a pitch accent were influenced by phrasal length and by intonational phrasing. Contrary to expectation, they found a simple effect of pitch accent, unmodulated by other prosodic factors. Schafer and colleagues believed that the effects of prosody on language comprehension will best be understood by viewing the listener as constructing and using a full prosodic description of a heard utterance.

Fox Tree and Meijer (2000) maintained that although syntactic ambiguity has often been the focus of research, ambiguous sentences are rarely noticed in everyday speech. One plausible explanation is that prosody can be counted on to disambiguate the sentences, another is that context is used. It was therefore of interest to discover which type of clues—context or prosody—plays the more important role in determining the listener's final interpretation. Fox Tree and Meijer focused on two questions: Do native speakers automatically insert disambiguating prosody into their ambiguous utterances? And, do listeners use this information? They found that native adult speakers do not produce useful prosody for syntactic disambiguation, and their ambiguous sentences do not contain enough prosodic cues to steer listeners toward the intended interpretations. Both prosody and context can influence the interpretation that listeners assign to a syntactically ambiguous utterance. The contextual influence, however, is particularly strong, and masks the effect of prosody. Thus, when prosody is the only disambiguating cue, accuracy at interpreting meaning is far from perfect.

PROSODY AND STRUCTURE IN THE SPEECH COMPREHENSION PROCESS

Much evidence points to a connection between the structural aspects of language and the prosodic patterns that characterize it. Collier and Hart (1975) described this connection as an interaction in which prosodic clues directly assist syntactic structure decoding. The functional importance of the connection between prosody and structure is found more clearly in relation to speech comprehension processes. Although the speech production process begins with a concept and ends with auditory output, the speech comprehension process can be described as doing the opposite (H. Clark & E. Clark, 1977). It begins with the auditory stimulus and aspires to reach decoding and comprehension of ideas. Various researchers (e.g., Forster & Ryder, 1971) believe that as listeners are exposed to a rapidly fading continuous stimulus, they must act according to hypotheses to deal efficiently with the flow of incoming information. The first hypotheses raised by the listener are based on a rapid scanning of the auditory input, which focuses mainly on the syntactic structure of the sentence. The semantic processing of the message begins only after the structural representation is created (Forster & Ryder, 1971). According to the structural approach to speech comprehension, the listener scans the input while searching for structural clues to use for segmentation and reconstruction of the relations between the different elements in the sentence (Fodor & Garrett, 1967; Kimball, 1973). This is where the functional importance of prosody comes in.

It seems that prosody provides the listener with important structural clues during continuous auditory input processing. Carroll and Slowiaczek (1987) found that when the prosodic pattern suits the syntactic structure, listeners understand the message more easily than in a situation where the prosodic messages are incompatible with the sentence structure or are missing completely. Their explanation is that rhythm functions as an organization principle, and the prosodic timing hierarchy (see Carroll & Slowiaczek, 1987) helps the listener to organize the hierarchical structure of sentence components. Different types of prosodic information assist the listener in reconstructing different aspects of the structure. For example, based on the stress pattern, subjects can distinguish between content words and function words and between nouns and adjectives. Thus, the stress pattern of a given word provides the listener with reliable information regarding its grammatical category (Kelly, 1992).

Prosodic information helps the listener divide syllables and separate words presented in sequence (Cutler & Butterfield, 1987). Prosodic information is also relevant to larger units, such as phrases and sentences, and contributes to the reconstruction of syntactic structure (Butterworth, 1980; Goldman-Eisler, 1972). Indeed, its contribution is important to processing even larger units of expression, such as the ability to recognize topical structure (Swerts & Geluykens, 1994), the finishing points of an utterance, dialogue turn change, and the like (Geluykens & Swerts, 1994). This indicates that prosody has an important function in the communication between speaker and listener, as it provides the listener, swamped by an auditory stimulus that must be processed rapidly, with initial information regarding the message's structure. This information is important to the process of constructing and examining hypotheses, because it constitutes the basis for constructing hypotheses to guide content processing. Based on this information, the listener will build the structural framework into which he will later insert the content (Forster & Ryder, 1971).

Kimelman (1999) similarly provided evidence that prosody facilitates auditory comprehension in adults. His purpose was to determine whether or not there is a critical relation between the ability to benefit from prosody, which has a positive influence on auditory comprehension, and the severity of aphasia. An additional aim was to examine the role of linguistic complexity in determining how much comprehension benefit aphasic listeners can derive from prosody. Results indicated a significant positive effect of prosody on auditory comprehension for mild, moderate, and severe aphasics. This confirms the role of prosody as an auditory comprehension facilitator. In addition, for severe aphasics, there was a resource limitation resulting in a performance trade-off. As linguistic processing demands increase, the available resources for prosodic processing decrease among severe aphasics, causing them to benefit less from prosody when performing linguistically complex tasks.

In sum, it can be said that the strong connection between prosody and structure is common to both speech perception and speech production processes, and in both cases this connection is of functional value. According to Selkirk (1980), the units of prosodic structure, defined by processes such as "prepausal-lengthening," "boundary-tones," and pauses mediate the creation of syntactic segmentation during speech production or the accessibility to this segmentation during speech perception. Ferreira (1993) expanded this idea and explained that the importance of prosody to linguistic processing stems from its role as mediator between thought and speech. She claimed that speech-related processes (comprehension and production) have a common purpose, namely, mapping the disordered information in ideas and thoughts into ordered information transferred through the speech channel. This mapping is not done in one step, but rather during a process of producing increasingly linear intermediate representations. The ideas and thoughts, which are multidimensional and hierarchical, are translated into a syntactic structure that is hierarchical and bidimensional only. This, in turn, is translated into a prosodic representation that is hierarchical, but linear. This representation constitutes the basis for producing a linear phonetic representation. Thus, in both speech comprehension and production, prosody constitutes one of the transfer stages between the linear representation of speech to a multidimensional representation of thought, or vice versa.

Speer, Crowder, and Thomas (1993) offered empirical support for the existence of a prosodic representation. They believed that due to the rapid transfer and fading of spoken language, the listener cannot utilize prosodic information in real time to the utmost efficiency, and must therefore retain the prosodic representation of the utterance. Their study is based on a sentence recognition test, which was intended to examine if the listener has a prosodic representation of an auditorily presented sentence. They presented subjects with a series of sentences spoken in natural prosody. Subjects were then presented with test sentences, and were requested to determine if each sentence was new (did not appear in the first series) or old (did appear). In some cases, the old test sentences were presented with the same prosody as in the original series and, in other cases, they were presented with a different prosody. The subjects exhibited difficulty in recognizing sentences that appeared with a different prosody, leading the researchers to conclude that during the process of sentence perception and processing the listener also creates a prosodic representation that constitutes an inseparable part of the sentence's grammatical representation.

Wingfield, Lindfield, and Goodglass (2000) focused on the extent to which the stress patterns of words affect word identification and whether or not this ability declines with age or remains stable. The purpose was to determine the extent to which younger and older adults can make use of prosodic information in word recognition. The findings were consistent with prior studies showing that older adults can make good use of sentence prosody in comprehension and recall of connected speech. They suggested that listeners can detect and utilize word stress in making perceptual judgments. This study indicated that older and younger adults correctly recognize spoken words in significantly shorter gate sizes when the prosodic pattern of the full word is made available to the listener along with the segmental information in the onset gate (plus whatever cues to full word prosody may have been present within the onset gate). In addition, once hearing sensitivity is taken into account, a comparison of the ability of the younger and older adults to use word prosody in word recognition shows little change with age, implying that prosodic stress information, as well as phonemic information, is accessible to listeners and that neither the quality of the information, nor the ability to use this information in conducting a perceptual match, changes appreciably in normal aging.

J. G. Martin (1972) emphasized the structural nature of prosody, claiming that listeners use the prosodic pattern as a temporal structure, organizing information according to the dimension of time. This type of organization facilitates perceptual processes and enables buildup or expectations regarding the rest of the utterance based on structural regularity (J. G. Martin, 1972). However, it seems that prosody as an organizational principle also assists information retention (Cutler, Dahan, & van Donselaar, 1997). A number of studies providing empirical support for this claim examined how prosody influences Epstein's (1961) findings that it is easier to remember pseudosyllables when they are presented with a morphosyntactic structure (e.g., meeving gups keebed gompily). These studies showed that Epstein's (1961) findings could be reproduced in an auditory presentation only if the syllable sequence was presented with sentence prosody (Leonard, 1974; O'Connell, Turner, & Onuska, 1968). Beyond its contribution to online speech perception processes, prosody thus functions as a representation, which due to its structural nature can be used as an organizing principle that also improves information retention.

PROSODY IN READING

Oral reading, like speech, is based on the processing of linguistic information. Reading and speech are similar in some aspects and different in others. Similar to reading, speech comprehension is based on the reception and processing of linear information into a multidimensional semantic representation. However, the functions differ from each other in a number of ways:

1. Manner of information representation: Speech is based on a rich auditory code that contains a surplus due to the representation of information in three dimensions: time, intensity, and frequency, which create prosody and provide the listener with information in addition to linguistic information. Reading is based on a relatively meager orthographic code, presented monodimensionally (linear—the only dimension is the order of symbols in a row), and it contains fuzziness (unclear message).

2. Manner of transfer: Listeners receive information passively, as it is transferred relatively quickly and fades rapidly. Readers, however, can control the pace of information reception. As all the information is always available and does not fade, they can preview and even go back if necessary. (However, it is important to note that the more proficient the readers, the less they do so.)

3. Modality: Whereas speech is based on auditory representations, reading is based on visual representations. Carroll and Slowiaczek (1987) attributed great importance to this difference. They claimed that the fact that reading is acquired later than speech and is not acquired naturally but requires directed teaching reflects the difficulty of receiving linguistic information via the visual modality. They argued that the auditory modality is directly incorporated into the language processing mechanisms that perform structural processing; therefore, the initial input representation contains both structural and prosodic information. It seems that this representation has an advantage with respect to its accessibility to language processing and its resilience for information retention. The visual information reception system is not directly connected to language processing systems, and thus the initial representations it produces are not accessible to linguistic processing systems. Phonological representations are produced during processing of the text, and their importance stems from their accessibility to linguistic processing mechanisms and their resilience for information retention in working memory. Questions arise, then, regarding whether these representations also contain prosodic information.

Few studies have dealt directly with prosody in reading, and most of these have only dealt with oral reading. It is often assumed that oral reading is based at least in part on speech production processes, and therefore prosody in reading, like prosody in speech production, is produced on the basis of a structural representation that precedes full lexical and semantic processing.

Dowhower (1991) identified six markers of prosodic reading: the presence or absence of pausal intrusions, the length of phrases between pauses, the number of appropriate and inappropriate phrases, the duration of final words of syntactic phrases, the change of pitch at final punctuation marks, and stress or accent. Readers capable of using these markers appropriately are able to transfer their knowledge of syntax from speech to text by effectively applying these features to their reading. As a result, these readers maintain the features of expressive oral language in addition to their accuracy and rate (Kuhn & Stahl, 2003).

Goldman-Eisler (1972; in Koriat, Greenberg, & Kreiner, 2002) claimed that "the reader's prosody is even closer to the ideal of grammatical structure than the speaker's prosody" (p. 271). Subsequent findings indicate that although during spontaneous speech less than one third of the pauses occur in the boundaries between commas, during vocal reading all the pauses occur between these boundaries (Goldman-Eisler, 1968, 1972). Therefore, appropriate prosody in reading, measured by the amount of pauses and vocalization in oral reading, enhances comprehension (Breznitz, 1990). In the Breznitz (1990) study, the vocal prosody patterns of oral reading and reading comprehension of 76 first graders were examined twice, first during the last week of the first quarter of the academic year, at the stage of acquiring reading skills, and once again during the last quarter of the year, at the stage of establishing reading skills. Voice analysis was accomplished using automatic vocal transaction analysis (AVTA; Jaffe & Feldsten, 1970). The parameters included the length of vocalization and pause time in segments of oral reading and their relations to reading comprehension. In the first quarter of the year, 38% of the total reading time was taken up by vocalization and 62% was filled by pauses. This pattern was reversed during the last quarter of the year, where the length of pauses was 41% and vocalization was 59%. Relative to total reading time, the average vocalization increased significantly and pause time decreased to an even greater extent.

As compared to the initial stages of reading acquisition, during the establishment of reading skills in the last quarter of the first grade, readers made shorter and fewer pauses, and tended to read with more and longer vocalization units. To further clarify the nature of these changes, Breznitz (1990) calculated the vocalization time per word and the number of words per vocalization unit in the two reading periods. The total length of vocalization for the entire duration of reading was divided by the number or words (161) in each reading period. The vocalization time per word during the first quarter was .85 s and during the last quarter was .59 s. To obtain the number of words per vocalization unit, the average length was divided by .85 and .59 for the first and last quarters, yielding 3.2 and 4.9, respectively. Thus, during the last quarter of the year, the readers spoke 53% more words per vocalization unit.

In an attempt to investigate the relations between prosody (defined here by the speech pattern) and reading comprehension, a Pearson correlation was computed between the parameters. During the first quarter of the year, the correlation between reading comprehension and frequency of pauses was $r = -.54$ $(p < .001)$, and the correlation between reading comprehension and average vocalization length was $r = .45$ $(p < .01)$. During the last quarter of the first grade, the correlation between reading comprehension and pauses was $r = .-51$ $(p < .001)$, and between vocalization and reading comprehension, $r = .66$ $(p < .001)$. In both cases, fewer pauses and more vocalizations were associated with higher comprehension. It is conceivable that better reading skills are associated with more vocalizations and less pauses. In this case, pauses might be an expression of hesitation in reading. The larger the hesitation, the less prosody can be achieved, leading to dysfluency in reading. The strong connection found between prosody and structure in oral reading implies that prosody may be an indication of a successful transformation of visual input into phonological code, bringing an accurate pattern into working memory for further processing. This representation is more accessible to linguistic processing mechanisms, and is apparently also efficient in retaining information during processing.

H. Cohen et al. (2001) investigated the influence of prosody and its visual analogue, punctuation, in text comprehension in two experiments. The first was related to the processing of oral discourse and was aimed at assessing the role of prosody in the comprehension of gist and recognition of lexical units in aurally presented text under three conditions: normal, monotone, and altered. The results indicated better comprehension under the normal condition than the monotonous or altered conditions. In addition, recognition of words was better when prosody was normal than when it was altered or monotonous. The second experiment involved the processing of written text. The purpose was to assess the role of punctuation in text comprehension and recognition of lexical units in visually presented text under three conditions: normal, absent, and altered. The results indicated better comprehension when punctuation was normal than when it was absent or altered, although absence or alteration did not prevent comprehension entirely. In addition, the absence of prosodic structure provided by punctuation impaired word recognition.

Overall, the results reveal that altered prosody and punctuation affect performance in a similar fashion and seriously impair text comprehension and word recognition in adult subjects. Prosody and punctuation differ in their effects to the extent that different processes are involved in listening and reading tasks. The absence of punctuation did not impair comprehension of visually presented text whereas the equivalent condition in the aural mode did impair comprehension. In addition, punctuation is important to the reading process and altering it in a way that is incongruent with the underlying syntax makes the reading task more time consuming and more difficult in terms of the number of words read per second.

THE ROLE OF PROSODIC REPRESENTATION IN THE READING PROCESS

As noted earlier, J. G. Martin (1972, p. 506) described prosody as consisting of "auditory temporal patterns." Each of the three characteristic included in this description attributes a certain advantage to prosody as an information retaining representation:

1. Pattern—J. G. Martin (1972) emphasized the fact that the prosodic pattern has internal organization, created by certain perceptions based on rhythm,

intonation, and stress. Epstein's (1961) findings illustrate the advantages of a morphosyntactic pattern as an organizing principle that improves memory, and the findings of O'Connell et al. (1968), as well as Leonard (1974), emphasize that during auditory presentation the prosodic patterns function as an organizing principle (see pp. 26–27).

2. Temporality—J. G. Martin (1972) claimed that a representation based on temporal patterns has an advantage, as the reception and processing of information is serial. He emphasized the importance of temporal patterns in guiding serial behavior (see Lashley, 1951) using top-down information and suggested that these patterns can guide serial processes of information reception and processing in working memory. There are two advantages to this. First, the temporal pattern can contribute to the timing compatibility between the input and processing processes. Second, as the prosodic pattern is also related to syntactic structure, it can contribute to the coordination between processing cycles and syntactic units. Support for this claim can be found in findings indicating that incompatibility between the prosodic pattern and the syntactic structure makes comprehension difficult for listeners.

3. Auditory—J. G. Martin (1972) noted the importance of the auditory nature of the representation. He claimed that spoken language processing is coordinated with and based on auditory information, and it is therefore important that the representations used by both modalities be compatible.

These advantages seem clear with respect to representations developed in the spoken language processing system. These spoken inputs must enter the auditory system rapidly in order to prevent them from fading out before they are recognized. The central question in this study is if these representations are also used in the reading process. A number of claims support this idea. From an evolutionary point of view, reading is a function that developed relatively late (Baddeley, Vallar, & Wilson, 1987). It can be assumed that when humans developed this system, processing mechanisms unique to comprehension and production of language were already developed and entrenched. It would be inefficient for developing reading skills not to make use of the developed and sophisticated mechanisms already available in the linguistic processing system (Patterson & Coltheart, 1987).

As stated, the visual channel for information reception is not a part of the linguistic processing system, as opposed to the auditory channel, which is directly integrated into this system (Carroll & Slowiaczek, 1987). Thus, it can be assumed that at a certain stage in text processing, representations accessible to the auditory system are produced. If these claims are accepted, then it follows that the advantages of a prosodic representation to the speech comprehension process also apply to the reading process. It can be assumed that the organizational pattern is also efficient in retaining information during the reading process. In fact, Epstein's (1961) findings indicate this to be the case. It can be assumed that an advantage based on temporal patterns also exists in reading as information reception and processing in reading is also serial, and the coordination between processing cycles in working memory and syntactic units is important. Finally, the findings indicating the importance of the phonological channel in reading and the importance of phonological representations for retaining information during text processing imply that perhaps the most important contribution of prosodic representations to reading stems from their being auditory representations. In other words, they may serve as a means of auditorily presenting abstract information, such as syntactic structure. In this manner, information is more readily available to the linguistic processing systems and more resilient for working memory storage.

There is no doubt that, during speech comprehension processes, the listener uses prosodic information, leading to the hypothesis that readers also use prosodic representations. However, it must be remembered that the listener receives the prosodic information as an inseparable part of the linguistic input, whereas the reader does not. In order to use prosodic representations, the reader must first produce them, and the question arises as to whether and how this can be done. Various findings imply that the reader does produce a prosodic representation during reading. In previous chapters, evidence was discussed to show that there is a strong connection between the prosodic and structural representations of a sentence. Models of speech production (Garrett, 1988; Levelt, 1989) describe prosody production as part of the syntactic structure production stage, independent of lexical item placement. Findings in the field of text processing indicate that in reading, as in speech comprehension and production, structural processing precedes content processing.

Prosody of language is connected to a temporal chronometric pattern of pauses and vocalization in the stream of spontaneous speech (e.g., Dechert & Raupach, 1980; Goldman-Eisler, 1968) or reading (Breznitz, 1990). Pauses during reading tend to be related to cognitive and physiological needs (e.g., Goldman-Eisler, 1968; Grosjean, 1980; Siegman, 1978). As such, pauses in a stream of spoken or written language are for the purpose of processing information or breathing. Both of these components determine the length and the frequency of pauses. Prosody in reading is also expressed in the amount and the length of vocalizations and pauses in oral reading. The complements of pauses are vocalization units (utterances), with each vocalization bounded by two pauses. A vocalization can be regarded as the verbal output of the thought processing that preceded it (e.g., W. Klein, 1980; Siegman, 1978). The length of utterance is variable and its determinants have been debated in the literature. O'Connell (1980) and Chafe (1980) concluded that the length of a vocalization unit is probably characteristic of a given speaker, context, and content. Few studies have investigated the role of pauses in oral reading situations or in nonspontaneous speech (Goldman-Eisler, 1968; Grosjean & Collins, 1979; Lieberman, 1969), and those that do exist deal with mature and fluent readers. These studies indicate that in reading situations, the temporal patterning of vocalizations and pauses (see also Goldman-Eisler, 1968) is organized according to the syntax and semantic organization of the text. It is claimed that even necessary breathing pauses occur at grammatical junctions. Moreover, fluent readers make breathing pauses primarily according to content organization. Reading faster leads fluent readers to produce shorter and fewer pauses (Grosjean & Collins, 1979).

CONCLUSIONS

The term *prosody in reading* is taken from the prosody of spoken language. Prosody in spoken language relies on the proper development of language, its rules, and dictates. Thus, prosody can be presented as a measure relying on the oral expressions of language and as such its measures are related to patterns of silent speech and intonation. These measures combine to create a characterization that requires fluency in speech. The ability to use these language clues is acquired during a lifetime as a result of interpersonal verbal interaction and becomes an integral part of the spoken language expression necessary for communication. In this manner, prosody functions as a dependent variable and a diagnostic measure for the quality of spoken language and characterization of interpersonal verbal communication.

An examination of prosody in spoken language indicates characteristics related to speakers, as well as the existence of interpersonal differences in their manner of language expression. For example, rate of speech, which is an interpersonal variable, does not only stem from the content of speech but also from traits characterizing the speaker. In this way, prosody can be presented as an independent variable that influences the manner of speech.

The aforementioned details regarding spoken language and prosody also pertain to prosody in reading. Prosody in reading is also used as a diagnostic measure for the quality of the reading activity and is a measure that requires oral expression. Thus, the pattern of utterances and pauses in oral reading contributes a measure of reading fluency. As such, prosody itself cannot be one of the determinants of word decoding fluency, but rather can be seen as a diagnostic measure for the quality of word decoding and reading comprehension.

5

Naming Speed:
A Review

In recent years, the rapid automatized naming (RAN) of visually presented symbols has come to assume pride of place as a measure for fluency in reading. Consistent results indicate that dyslexic subjects perform these tasks at a slower rate than regular readers. These findings have led to an abundance of literature examining the connection of RAN to reading fluency, which is critically reviewed in this chapter. Many dyslexic children encounter daily naming difficulties in their attempts to speedily name familiar visual stimuli such as letters, digits, colors, and simple objects. Research in this area, originally based on work in the field of brain science, stemmed from a hypothesis raised regarding naming colors. Geschwind (1972) hypothesized that the ability to name colors may predict a child's reading ability. He surmised that the cognitive components involved in naming colors constitute a good representation of the cognitive components needed for the reading process. As in reading, naming requires the attachment of verbal labels to abstract, visual stimuli. This hypothesis was examined and developed in a series of studies carried out by Denckla and Rudel (1974, 1976a, 1976b). In these studies, the researchers used a sequential naming task to examine children's abilities in naming familiar visual stimuli (e.g., letters, digits, colors, and simple objects.) These researchers concluded that the speed, not the accuracy, at which children named these stimuli was strongly related to their reading ability.

These interesting findings initiated a long series of studies on the connection between naming speed and reading ability. Naming speed for visual objects presented sequentially discriminated between dyslexic and normal readers (Berninger, Abbott, & Alsdorf, 1997; Bowers, Steffy, & Tate, 1988; Denckla & Rudel, 1976a, 1976b; Snyder & Downey, 1995; Spring & Davis, 1988; Wolf, 1982; Wolf et al., 1986; Wolff, Michel, & Ovrut, 1990), between dyslexics and underprivileged poor readers (garden variety) (Ackerman & Dykman, 1993; Badian, 1994, 1995; Wolf & Obregon, 1992), between dyslexics and other learning disabled readers (Ackerman & Dykman, 1993; Denckla & Rudel, 1976b; Felton & Brown, 1990; Wood & Felton, 1994), and between dyslexics and young normal readers at the same reading level (Ackerman & Dykman, 1993; Biddle, 1996; Segal & Wolf, 1993; Wolf, 1991). Moreover, these differences were not connected to intelligence (Bowers et al., 1988; Spring & Davis, 1988).

What are the common aspects shared by effective naming speed and effective reading activity, and how do they differ? Both reading and naming speed are expressed in processing time measures, so it may be hypothesized that these processes share a common cognitive factor, which involves the speed at which information is processed. Processing speed will be critical in understanding the naming and reading deficits that utilize the same brain functions.

DISCRETE VERSUS SEQUENTIAL NAMING

Although there is a significant body of evidence linking naming speed and reading ability, there are some inconsistencies regarding the types of stimuli and naming tasks for which a relation was found. One important distinction lies between discrete and sequential naming tasks.

Discrete naming tests are exemplified by the Boston naming test (Kaplan, Goodglass, & Weintraub, 1983), in which pictures of objects are presented according to a decreasing frequency of names in the English language. The pictures, on cards, are presented one by one, and the subject is asked to name them as quickly and accurately as possible. The time required by the subject to name each stimulus is measured, and the reaction time is averaged for all stimuli.

In sequential naming tasks, the subject is required to name a set of visual stimuli presented sequentially, as quickly as possible. One example is the rapid automatized naming (RAN) task created by Denckla and Rudel (1974), in which participants are required to name an array of familiar digits, pictures, letters, or color patches in sequential order, as rapidly as possible. Each set consists of 5 letters (or digits, or colors, or objects) that frequently appear in the language, and these stimuli are repeated 10 times in 5 rows, for a total of 50 stimuli. The final score is the overall time required to name all the stimuli in the set. A similar task is the rapid alternating stimulus (RAS) test, which was created by

Wolf (1986). This task consists of an array that includes 5 letters and 5 numbers, presented in 5 rows for a total of 50 items. The specific stimulus that appears is determined randomly, but the set pattern remains permanent (letter-number-letter-number, etc.) to encourage use of contextual information.

Whereas a significant connection between naming speed and reading ability has been found on both RAS and RAN tasks, this connection has not been confirmed in studies employing discrete naming tasks. Perfetti, Finger, and Hogaboam (1978) found that no difference in naming speed between good and poor readers exists when naming was examined using a discrete naming test. Similarly, Walsh, Price, and Gillingham (1988) found that naming speed for letters in a second-grade discrete naming test was not significantly related to the reading level of children at the beginning of the third grade. Stanovich (1981) also found that the naming speed of poor readers does not differ from that of regular readers in the first grade. He claimed, in support of the discrete test, that this test is methodologically cleaner, and constitutes a more accurate measure of item recognition speed, because it removes nonrelevant variance related to scanning, tracking, and motor strategies. Thus, sequential and discrete tasks have been considered different in their connection to reading ability, and several explanations have been proposed to account for this difference.

Still, other studies have not consistently found that sequential naming tasks, as opposed to discrete tasks, differentiate between good and poor readers. Several of these studies, placing more emphasis on the task stimuli employed and the specific reading ability aspects tested, are detailed next.

Swanson (1989) claimed that the cognitive requirements of sequential naming are more compatible with those of the reading process. Both processes require lexical access and retrieval, within the context of scanning and tracking material, which is presented sequentially. According to Swanson, discrete naming tasks remove the variant sources that naming shares with reading. Additionally, she claimed that methodological problems in these studies have failed to find a connection between discrete naming and reading ability. In a controlled study, she compared well-defined groups of good and poor readers from the first, third, and sixth grades using discrete and sequential naming tasks, with an alternating interval between discrete stimuli. She found differences between the good and poor readers on every task and at every age level, with the sequential naming task distinguishing better between the groups of older readers. Thus, she concluded, good readers differ from poor readers even on retrieval of discrete symbols.

Bowers and Swanson (1991) found that both discrete naming speed and sequential naming speed are significantly related to length of word recognition and to comprehension among children in the second grade. However, only sequential naming speed is significantly related to accuracy of word and pseudoword recognition among these children. These findings support the claim that poor readers already possess a lexical retrieval deficiency at the discrete stimulus stage, and this lack of proficiency affects reading speed and comprehension measures more than the accuracy measures, as claimed by LaBerge and Samuels (1974) in their theory on reading automation.

Wolf et al. (1986; discussed later as well) presented the claim that these two types of naming tests are complementary, because they provide information on two different levels of lexical access and retrieval. Discrete naming, which does not require scanning, tracking, or integration of subprocesses, does not distinguish between good and poor readers, whereas sequential naming, which is comprised of more subprocesses and requires temporal integration, clearly distinguishes between the two reading groups. Thus, an integration difficulty may be at the base of the differences between readers.

Wolff et al. (1990) found that adolescent dyslexics differ from regular readers in both discrete and sequential naming. It seems that the difference between these studies and earlier ones, which found a difference only in discrete naming, is the level of reading disability. Stanovich (1981) used a group that included poor readers, with a reading gap of only a few months, and Perfetti et al. (1978) used poor readers whose reading level was only a year below their age level, and apparently not deficient enough to exhibit a difficulty in discrete naming. It is possible that a name retrieval problem exists among readers with a severe disability, even at the most basic level of name recognition.

In their study, Meyer et al. (1998) considered the differential predictive value of rapid naming tests for various aspects of reading among nondisabled and poor readers. The researchers found that rapid naming was predictive only for poor readers, and not for average readers, thus suggesting that poor rapid naming is not sufficient to cause poor reading. In this study, phonological skill was the best predictor of early poor readers, whereas rapid naming skill was the best predictor of which poor reader would improve.

Conversely, rapid naming tasks generally failed to predict later reading comprehension, which suggests that comprehension depends on more than single-word reading, and improvement in single-word reading is not a sufficient condition for improvement in reading comprehension. It also seems it is the automaticity of retrieval, not the knowledge of the names themselves, that gives naming its predictive power.

In a study investigating rapid automatized naming skills among normal and language-impaired adults and children, Wiig, Zureich, and Chan (2000) found that measures of accuracy for continuous naming of single or multidimensional stimuli do not seem to consistently and reliably differentiate between clinical (language disorder vs. no language disorder) or educational groups (dyslexia vs. no dyslexia). Naming speed of latency measures for letters, numbers, and alternating letters and numbers, however, consistently differentiated students with dyslexia from their academically achieving peers. In addition, color–shape naming speed measures in this study differentiated students with primary language disorders from their typical age peers for the majority of the age levels compared. These researchers also observed that continuous naming speed measures decrease significantly with age among students without dyslexia or language disorders.

Wiig et al. (2000) found important differences between regular language disorders and dyslexic subjects when performing color and alphanumeric naming tasks. As compared to regular readers, the language disorder subjects performed significantly slower on both tasks whereas dyslexics were slower only on the alphanumeric tasks. Moreover, the Fawcett and Nicolson (1994), Felton, Naylor, and Wood (1990), and Wolff et al. (1990) studies found that color–shape naming times did not differentiate between learning-disabled and nonlearning disabled students aged 15–16, which may have resulted from color–shape combination stimuli losing diagnostic sensitivity in adolescence. This result contradicts findings that rapid automatized naming time measures for letters and numbers maintain diagnostic sensitivity for dyslexics throughout adolescence and young adulthood (Felton et al., 1990; Korhonen, 1995). However, based on this data, it can be suggested that only alphanumeric tasks continue to represent deficits among adult dyslexics.

A second difference found is that naming times for single dimension stimuli (colors or shapes) did not differentiate between the learning disabled and regular groups. In contrast, studies of students with dyslexia show that rapid naming times for colors differentiate students with and without dyslexia, if those compared had similar intellectual abilities (Fawcett & Nicolson, 1994; Felton et al., 1990; Wolff et al., 1990).

Two different models have been proposed to account for naming time deficits on continuous, alternating stimuli tasks in clinical groups of students with dyslexia (Kinsbourne, Rufo, Gamzu, & Palmer, 1991; Satz, Fletcher, Clark, & Morris, 1981). The first model, the *developmental lag model*, maintains that observed differences in naming time or accuracy measures reflect a lag in the rate of development and presumes that students with dyslexia will eventually catch up with their peers. However, the second model, the *deficit model*, claims that observed performance differences reflect deficits in underlying neuropsychological processes, which are important for the development of the skills examined. Therefore, according to this model, students with dyslexia will not be able to close the gap with their peers by age 16. Acceptance of the developmental lag model over the deficit model is dependent on whether or not, in middle school, individual students who show rapid color–shape naming deficits catch up with peers, who did not exhibit naming deficits.

DEVELOPMENTAL DIFFERENCES IN NAMING SPEED

From the findings obtained in the aforementioned studies, it appears that linguistic and cognitive components, shared by both reading and naming, largely depend on the nature of the task, as well as on the age and achievement level of the reader. It is important to follow the development of naming speed, on the one hand, and the development of reading, on the other hand, in order to understand the difference in the connection between them.

One interpretation of the developmental changes occurring in naming speed and reading relates to these variables' link to processing speed. Kail (1988b) claimed that age differences in processing speed can be explained as part of a general developmental change. An increase in processing resources, along with an age increase, may result in increased processing speed. In studies carried out by Kail (1991a, 1991b), motoric-perceptual tasks and cognitive tasks were used in order to show how performance speed improves with age, with degree of improvement higher in early and middle childhood than in later childhood and adolescence.

Kail and Hall (1994) claimed that the development of a general speed factor among regular readers explains the changes in naming speed. They examined 144 children, from age 8 to 13, using general processing time measures, naming measures, and various reading measures, thereby examining the overall changes in these measures. It was found that along with the increase in age, there were systematic increases in speed of processing, naming speed, and reading ability. The nature of the causal connection between these variables was examined using pathway analysis leading to the following model. Changes in speed of processing lead to changes in naming speed, which in turn lead to changes in word recognition, which then explain changes in reading comprehension. According to Kail and Hall, naming speed is influenced by a general processing speed, which develops with age, and is not the direct result of an increase in age or experience (Kail & Hall, 1994).

In a study carried out by Wolf et al. (1986), the connections between naming rate of familiar visual stimuli during a sequential naming task (RAN) and three

reading measures—word recognition, reading aloud, and reading comprehension—were examined. Naming rate was measured for two types of symbols, varied in the extent to which they become automatic. Automaticity is reached
when rapid naming of symbols is accomplished in the presence of a minimum in-
vestment of attentional resources. The first type, alphanumeric symbols, elicits
rapid and automatic naming. This group of symbols is general, and includes
numbers, as opposed to letters that are specific alphabetic symbols. Additionally, there are nonalphanumeric symbols, for which naming does not become automatic. This latter type includes symbols with a wide semantic base,
such as objects, and symbols with a restricted semantic base, such as colors.
Wolf et al. found that naming speed for all stimuli types, tested at kindergarten
age, was significantly related to each of the reading measures, tested in second
grade. However, in second grade, naming speed differentiation for alphanumeric and nonalphanumeric symbols begins. Naming speed of alphanumeric
symbols, solely, remained significantly related to second-grade reading ability,
specifically to word recognition ability. Naming speed's connection to reading
comprehension remains significant after second grade, but weakens. In other
words, lower level requirements, existing in letter and number naming tasks,
maintain a strong and stable connection to lower level requirements in word
recognition tasks, and an unstable and poor connection to higher level requirements present in reading comprehension tasks. Reading comprehension had a
strong and stable connection only with naming speed of objects, seemingly
based on their shared high-level semantic processing requirements. It is important to note that word recognition was significantly related to naming of both
numbers and letters, consequently making the connection to fast retrieval of
automatic symbols rather than to letter recognition ability.

In another study, Wolf and Goodglass (1986) examined the connection between object naming performance, which is semantically more complex, and
various reading measures. The results of this study contradicted those of the
previous study: Object naming in kindergarten predicted all reading measures
in second grade; object naming's connection to reading comprehension was
strong, and remained stable for an extended period, until fourth grade. This
connection could not be explained by variance of vocabulary, because the significant connection between object naming and reading comprehension remained even after the removal of this variance. Thus, according to this study,
high-level retrieval processes, required for object naming tasks, are related to
higher processes involved in reading comprehension.

Spring and Davis (1988) examined the connections between sequential
naming speed for digits, word recognition, and reading comprehension meas-

ures among 4th- to 10th-grade children. Their findings also suggested that digit naming speed had a stronger relation with word recognition than with reading comprehension.

It seems that there are two axes that define the relations between naming and reading: first, a developmental axis and, second, the differentiation of task requirements. The relation between naming speed and reading are dictated by the changing nature of task requirements combined with the changing nature of reading capabilities. In the early stages of development, all naming tasks predict later reading capabilities. In these stages, when children are required to rapidly name visual stimuli, they use subprocesses, which are related to the subprocesses required for reading in second grade.

In higher elementary school grades, the subprocesses used for rapid naming of automatic symbols differ from the subprocesses used for naming of colors or objects. In parallel, the connection between decoding and comprehension changes, so that decoding becomes fluent and more automatic. The result is that at the end of third grade, performance of object naming tasks, which have semantic requirements, has a strong connection only to reading comprehension measures, whereas naming of automatic symbols is directly related to decoding measures. It is important to note that the connection between reading measures and naming, appearing in third grade, remains stable thereafter.

Biddle (1996) carried out a study on the development of naming speed from kindergarten to fourth grade. She reported that the most progress in naming speed occurs for the majority children by first grade, and by second grade at the latest. This finding may explain why the connection between naming speed and word recognition remains strong among regular readers, although there is no meaningful change if differentiation of word recognition occurs after second or third grade. Despite this, children with a naming speed deficit, who do not suffer from phonological processing difficulties, show gradual improvement of their naming rate albeit not significant in any year. Due to the fact that automaticity of word recognition, and probably naming, is not reached among reading disabled children, it is easy to understand the finding (McBride-Chang & Manis, 1996) that naming abilities of disabled readers continue to hold a strong and stable connection with word recognition until at least fourth grade, whereas among regular readers phonological awareness, and not naming speed, sustains a strong and stable connection with word recognition.

The previous findings emphasize the importance of differentiation in the use of naming measures to predict reading, as well as for remedial and educational purposes.

Van den Bos, Zijlstra, and Spelberg (2002) addressed developmental relations between naming and reading speed. Their subjects included children from elementary school, grades two (age 8), four (age 10), six and seven (age 12), students from secondary education classes (age 16), and parent pairs (age 46). The purposes of the study were to determine how continuous naming speeds for four stimulus types (letters, numbers, pictures, and colors) and reading speed for a word list increase across a life span, to investigate changes in the interrelations of naming speed of these four stimulus types across various age levels, and to determine the development of naming and word reading speed associations at various age levels.

Results indicated that word reading speed and naming speeds of colors and pictures continue to increase into mature adulthood, and confirm the hypothesis that naming speed increases as a function of age, with the sharpest increase apparent in early grades. For letter and number naming, asymptote scores are reached at around age 16. An increased common speed factor was observed, as well as a differentiated and increasingly independent pattern of alphanumeric associations. The researchers believed that these findings reflect a gradual strengthening of initial, loosely connected alphabetic and numeric access routes into an integrated alphanumeric lexical network, which is explained by the hypothesis that letter and number naming speed interact with both reading and arithmetic practice.

In addition, regression analyses and correlations between naming factor scores and reading speed showed a developmentally increasing relation between reading and alphanumeric naming speeds, whereas unique contributions of color and object naming speeds to reading speed were erratic. Thus, as children grow older, there is a selective increase in the relation between word reading speed and naming speed, as the increase applies only to alphanumeric naming stimuli and not to the more erratic relation between word reading and color-and-objects naming speeds.

This study supports the theory, which describes reading recognition development as a domain-specific learning process with reciprocal facilitating links to alphanumeric symbol-naming speed development.

NAMING SPEED DEFICITS AMONG DYSLEXICS

Many studies deal with the special relation between naming speed and reading among children with a severe reading disability. In a 5-year longitudinal study, Wolf and Obregon (1989) divided disabled readers into two groups, underprivileged readers and dyslexics. They found that from kindergarten until fourth grade the dyslexics were significantly slower than the underprivileged readers on every sequential naming measure (RAN). Conversely, a significant difference in accuracy on object naming tasks, which are based on semantic ability, was found between dyslexics and normal readers, but was not found between dyslexics and underprivileged readers. When the subjects were given a multiple-choice recognition test of words to name, dyslexics were more successful than underprivileged readers. The explanation offered by the researchers was that underprivileged readers had difficulty naming a word because they did not know it, whereas dyslexics found naming difficult because their hurdle was retrieving the word.

Felton, Wood, Brown, Campbell, and Harter (1987) studied naming speed differences between dyslexic children and children with other learning disabilities, among them children with attention disorders, and revealed naming deficits specific to dyslexic children that do not exist in other disorders (see also Spring & Davis, 1988). Felton et al. (1990) found that these differences remain in adulthood despite remedial teaching and acquisition of phonological skills. In the latter study, the researchers found that tasks requiring sequential retrieval of visual symbols (e.g., RAS and RAN) revealed differences between adult dyslexics and adults without reading disabilities in the most accurate manner.

Wolff et al. (1990) also found that these differences exist among adolescents and young adults. They compared adult dyslexics who received systematic, long-term remedial teaching with those who did not come by such instruction. They found that although both groups differed in their naming speed from normal readers, these groups did not differ from each other, despite their different reading levels. It seems that naming difficulties were consistent, stable, and not overly affected by remedial teaching. Nevertheless, it is important to note that the type of remedial teaching given appears significant, and thus general conclusions should not be drawn yet regarding the improvability of naming speed. The findings of this study support the claim that the connection between naming speed and reading ability grows poorer with time, even though it still exists among adult dyslexics. It is clear that the decoding process becomes more automatic with age, thereby creating the differentiation of the two processes; the reading process requires higher level subprocesses, whereas naming of visual symbols continues to be based on lower level subprocesses or on a general speed of processing factor.

POSSIBLE EXPLANATIONS
FOR NAMING SPEED DEFICITS

Phonological Difficulty

There is virtually no disagreement in the literature regarding the existence of some form of naming speed deficit in dyslexia. It has been proposed that behind deficits in naming speed lie phonological deficits, as naming speed is traditionally seen as a phonological processing ability. Naming is commonly treated as retrieval of phonological codes from long-term memory (Wagner, Torgesen, Laughon, Simmons, & Rashotte, 1993) or as phonological encoding with lexical access (Wagner & Torgesen, 1987).

There is some important evidence, however, both theoretical and empirical, which disputes this phonological explanation for naming deficits. First, as studies have indicated, the naming process requires capabilities such as attention to stimuli, perceptual processes specific to the visual modality, access to lexical information stored in long-term memory (both semantic and phonological), access and retrieval of phonological labels, articulation, and precise integration and timing within and between subprocesses. Second, the correlation between naming speed and various measures of phonological processing is low (Cornwall, 1992) or nonexistent (Felton & Brown, 1990).

Current reading models assume that reading and naming have several common levels of processing, including visual analysis, semantic access, access to the phonological output lexicon (POL), and selection and sequencing of phonemes for production (Breen & Warrington, 1995).

However, a common route to the POL, shared by naming and reading, could not account for disassociations found between semantic errors in naming and oral reading (Southwood & Chatterjee, 1999, 2000). These researchers presented a case of a deep dyslexic, who exhibited semantic errors in naming that exceeded those in oral reading. The researchers proposed a model related to the organization and processing structure of the reading system, the simultaneous activation hypothesis (SAM). They suggested that object naming is primarily constrained by the semantic route, and if damaged, renders the selection of the appropriate phonological code extremely difficult.

The researchers extended the simultaneous activation hypothesis (SAM) by assessing error patterns associated with phonological dyslexia. Based on their study, they proposed a SAM framework to account for dissociations in semantic and phonological errors. In line with this view, semantic errors are absent during oral reading if additional information, available from other reading routes, facilitates activation of the appropriate phonological entry. During naming, degraded semantic information, rather than the correct phonological entry, constrains the activation of a semantic associate in the POL. The presence of phonological errors in oral reading and their near nonexistence in object naming occurs because additional information from other reading routes activates a partial phonological entry in reading, as opposed to naming.

Wagner et al. (1993) identified three phonological skills related to reading ability: phonological awareness, phonological encoding in working memory, and access rate to phonological information. They have reported some surprising results, which state that one source explains performance differences between good and poor readers on tasks involving phonological awareness and phonological encoding in working memory, and another source explains differentiation on sequential naming tasks. This result, according to the researchers, indicates the existence of two separate abilities at the basis of phonological processing. However, it can also be interpreted as supporting a basic difference between cognitive requirements of naming and those of phonological awareness and encoding.

A low correlation between naming speed and phonological awareness measures was also found in the German language. The German orthography is flat in comparison to English, with more grapheme–phoneme regularity. This means that phonological requirements are reduced. It has been shown that in this type of language, dyslexics have less difficulty on phonological tasks. However, they do exhibit clear naming speed difficulties (Wimmer, 1993). This finding also supports the existence of two separate abilities.

Research results also show that naming speed and phonological measures interact differently with various reading measures. In a series of studies carried out by Bowers and her colleagues, performance on phonological tasks strongly predicted recognition of words and pseudowords, but did not predict word and text reading speed. However, it appears that naming speed does not predict recognition of pseudowords at all, but rather predicts accuracy and recognition speed of words of relatively high frequency in the language (Bowers, 1993, 1995; Bowers et al., 1988; Bowers & Swanson, 1991). Cornwall (1992) found that phonological awareness clearly and independently predicted word recognition, as well as reading speed and accuracy. It is important to note in this context that developmental factors have an affect on the various naming and reading measures, as mentioned earlier.

Further evidence that naming speed deficits are not dependent on phonological processing deficits is derived from the fact that reading disabilities can be classified into subgroups based on these deficits. Lovett (1984) was the first to suggest classification of reading disabilities into subgroups—the first containing those with a reading rate deficit and the second made up of those with a reading accuracy deficit. Children with reading rate deficits were characterized by slow naming, slow but accurate word recognition, good phonological processing abilities, and reading comprehension difficulties. Those children with an accuracy deficit exhibited phonological processing difficulties, as well as slow, troublesome word recognition and comprehension. Lovett therefore concluded that naming speed deficits may exist among poor readers who do not have phonological difficulties.

Wolf and Bowers conducted a series of studies that dealt with the "double deficit hypothesis," according to which most readers fall into one of four subgroups: no deficit, phonological processing deficit, naming speed deficit, or a double deficit, both in phonological processing and naming speed (Bowers, 1995; Bowers, Golden, Kennedy, & Young, 1994; Bowers & Wolf, 1993; Wolf & Bowers, 1999; Wolf & Obregon, 1992). The researchers found that phonological processing of readers with a naming speed deficit did not significantly differ from that of regular readers. However, their naming speed was slower compared to both regular readers and readers with phonological processing deficits. In comparison, the naming speed of readers with phonological processing deficits did not differ from that of normal readers, whereas phonological processing was lower than that of both regular readers and readers with naming speed deficits. In addition, children with a double deficit displayed both slower naming speeds and lower phonological processing when compared to regular readers, and did not differ from readers with phonological deficits on phonological processing or from readers with naming speed deficits on naming speed. Readers with phonological processing deficits scored lower on measures of word recognition accuracy than readers with naming speed deficits, whereas those with speed deficits scored lower on measures of reaction time in word recognition. Both groups with single deficits achieved relatively low scores on all reading ability measures when compared to regular readers, with a gap of 1 to 2 years. The readers with a double deficit achieved lower scores than regular readers, with a gap of 2½ to 3 three years. Thus, the group with a double deficit displayed a more severe deficit. It is interesting to note that readers with single phonological deficits or those with a double deficit are those primarily recognized in early stages of reading acquisition, this due to their obvious decoding problems. Those with naming deficits are usually identified later, around fourth grade, when the lack of decoding automaticity disrupts their reading comprehension, at a stage when it is expected to be at a relatively high level. These findings provide important support for the claim that phonological processing ability and naming speed are two independent abilities, and a deficit in each one of these abilities manifests reading difficulties with disparate characteristics.

The important results of the aforementioned studies have been replicated in other studies. Lovett (1995) replicated these results in a large clinical study of children with severe reading disabilities, and found that although most of the children fell into the double deficit group, others had either a single phonological processing deficit or a naming speed deficit, with similar characteristics to those found by Wolf and colleagues. Lovett also examined subject responses in the different subgroups, to intervention, and found that most subjects profited from a phonologically based intervention method. However, subjects with a single phonological deficit showed the greatest improvement in reading ability as a result of this intervention. She concluded that subjects with naming speed deficits, both in the single and the double deficit subgroups, required an intervention method with a different emphasis in order to achieve maximum results.

McPherson, Ackerman, Oglesby, and Dykman (1996) provided primary evidence of neurophysiological differences between the phonological and naming speed subgroups in an evoked potentials study. The subjects were divided into two groups, with and without phonological deficits. Those with phonological deficits exhibited a pronounced lack of phonological priming. These subjects presented a longer and larger priming effect than other subjects, mostly on the lateral sides of the brain. It seems they were less inclined to move from one processing stage to another.

Wimmer, Mayringer, and Landerl (1998) examined whether the characteristic reading speed impairment of German dyslexic children results from a general skill automatization deficit (Nicolson & Fawcett, 1990) or from a more specific deficit in visual naming speed and phonological skills. The hypothesized skill automatization deficit was assessed using balancing of peg movement and visual search. RAN tasks served as a measure of impaired visual naming speed, and the phonological deficit was assessed by speech perception, phonological sensitivity, and phonological memory tasks. The researchers did not find evidence for a skill automatization deficit, as the dyslexic children did not differ at all on the balancing tasks, and to a small extent on the other nonverbal tasks. However, the dyslexic children exhibited impaired visual naming speeds and impaired phonological memory performance.

Manis et al. (2000) explored coexisting relations among measures of naming speed, phonological awareness, orthographic skill, and other reading subskills in a sample of second graders. They used naming speed, as measured by the RAN task, to account for unique variance in reading; vocabulary and phonemic awareness data were controlled. Naming skills had a stronger unique contribution to orthographic skills, whereas phonemic skills had a stronger contribution to nonword decoding.

Marked difficulties on a range of reading tasks, including orthographic processing, were exhibited by the double deficit subgroup (slow naming speed and low phonemic awareness), but not by the groups with only a single deficit. These results were partially consistent with Bowers and Wolf's (1993) double deficit hypothesis of reading ability. The researchers found that the group with both deficits had relatively poor reading, and differed from children with single deficits on the orthographic choice task. The greatest impairments in reading

were associated with the slowest naming times. Manis et al.'s (2000) results differed from those of Bowers and Wolf (1993) in the degree of impairment seen
among children with only a naming speed deficit. This group was the least impaired compared to the subgroups with naming speed or phonemic awareness
deficits, and did not show the deficient orthographic skills noted by Bowers
(Bowers, Sunseth, & Golden, 1999; Sunseth & Bowers, 1997).

Nation, Marshall, and Snowling (2001) investigated the object naming skills
of dyslexic children, children with poor comprehension, and children with normally developing reading skills. The researchers used pictures with names varying in word length and frequency, and found that compared to regular age-
matched readers, dyslexic children were less accurate at naming pictures with
long names. The dyslexic readers also made a disproportionate number of phonological errors. In contrast, children with poor comprehension exhibited normal effects of word length, but were slower and less accurate at naming pictures
than the control group. They were particularly poor at naming pictures with low
frequency names. Unlike the majority of results from the studies already described, these findings led to the conclusion that phonological processing deficits are at the core of object naming difficulties in children with developmental
dyslexia.

It is important to note that individual differences in naming arise from the interaction of strengths and weaknesses in phonological and semantic processing,
as illustrated by the fact that dyslexic children did not experience greater difficulty in dealing with low frequency words than the reading age controls. Thus,
it is possible that the source of the children's difficulties varies in accordance
with the nature of their underlying language strengths and weaknesses.

Vocabulary Acquisition Difficulty

Wolf and Goodglass (1986; discussed earlier) examined the hypothesis that
naming speed and effective reading are connected by the quality of readers' vocabulary. In this study, subjects were given a receptive vocabulary test and the
Boston naming task. Results indicated differences between good and poor readers on the naming speed task, but not on the vocabulary test.

Wolf and Obregon (1992) chose the same discrete naming task to examine
the connection between naming speed and reading measures among dyslexic
readers and older regular readers aged 9–10. They found a significantly strong
connection between performance on the naming task, reading comprehension,
and reading aloud, and a significant but poor connection to word recognition.
This finding corresponds with the developmental direction discussed earlier. In

order to examine the question of vocabulary influence in this context, the naming test included a multiple-choice component presented at the end of the test. Each subject was requested to select the target word from four possibilities. No difference in accuracy was found between dyslexics and regular readers on this task, indicating no vocabulary difficulty. It appears that the differences between normal and dyslexic readers stem from retrieval ability rather than a vocabulary deficiency.

Articulation Difficulty

Ackerman and Dykman (1993) examined the connection between naming deficits among dyslexic readers and slow rates of articulation. According to Baddeley (1986), all deficits related to dyslexia, including lack of phonological sensitivity, slow naming, and poor short-term memory, can be explained by the slow rate at which dyslexics express units of sound. He showed that the memory range of verbal stimuli is significantly related to their articulation rate. For example, the average memory range for one-syllable words is longer than the memory range for five-syllable words. This finding can be explained by the fact that the articulation time of words with one syllable is shorter than the articulation time of words with five syllables. Thus, if the articulation rate of dyslexics is slower than their memory range, then the range is shorter, and thus their phonological sensitivity is lower. The claim is that these children cannot retain phonetic information in short-term memory for the length of time necessary to create phonetic patterns. In order to examine this claim, the articulation rate of dyslexic children from age 7 to 12 was measured. They were asked to count from 1 to 10 as many times as possible in a given time frame, repeat their ABCs in a given time frame, and repeat words with an increasing number of syllables, and their performance rate was measured. The dyslexics' performance was compared with that of children with attention disorders and with underprivileged children, but no significant differences were found.

However, dyslexic readers did differ from the other two groups of readers on three measures: phonological sensitivity, sequential naming, and short-term memory range. Thus, based on this study, these differences cannot be attributed to articulation rate.

Obregon (1994) continued to examine the articulation rate hypothesis using a computer program that analyzed children's speech fluency during the RAN task. He did not find significant differences between normal and dyslexic readers when comparing the time it took to articulate visually presented symbols. However, he did find differences in interval times between stimuli; dyslexics took longer to retain the previous stimulus, perceive and recognize the current stimulus, and activate lexical access and retrieval processes for the following stimulus.

Short-Term Memory Difficulty

Short-term auditory memory errors are a characteristic of dyslexics' perform-ance that repeatedly appears in the literature. There are theories suggesting that dyslexics do not use memory strategies correctly, or that they have rela-tively slow access to the lexicon from the visual and auditory channels (Ellis & T. R. Miles, 1981). Other theories attribute this short-term memory difficulty to a more specific deficit in the use of phonological codes. Evidence supporting this claim includes the finding that dyslexics exhibit less of an advantage in re-membering rhyming words as opposed to nonrhyming words, compared to regu-lar readers (Mann, 1984), and they encode spoken sounds more slowly (Tallal, 1980). According to the proponents of these theories, the difficulty in rapid naming stems from the same phonological deficit.

In a study conducted by Bowers, Steffy, and Swanson (1986), the researchers examined the contribution of short-term auditory memory, naming speed, and speed of visual processing to the reading ability of children from age 7 to 12, whose reading age was 2 years lower than their chronological age-matched peers. As in previous studies, a positive correlation was found between short-term memory levels and reading ability. However, memory contributed signifi-cantly less to this correlation, when the children's intelligence and attention levels were controlled. A strong connection was found between performance on the Wechsler Intelligence Scale for Children–Revised (WISC–R) digit span test, sentence memory test, and measures of attention and intelligence, whereas no connection was found between naming and these measures. In addition, the variance common to memory and reading ability, not explained by attention or intelligence measures, was explained in full by digit naming speed.

Visual Scanning Difficulty

Spring and Davis (1988) suggested that the gap often found between reading and sequential naming measures, as opposed to discrete naming measures (dis-cussed earlier) can be explained by visual scanning difficulties among poor read-ers. According to these researchers, good readers are able to name a stimulus, while simultaneously processing the next stimulus to its right, or in other words, perform parallel processing of a number of stimuli. On the other hand, poor readers are only capable of serial processing. Good readers use parallel processing in sequential naming of word lists, but not in discrete naming, which therefore does not reveal the advantage of good readers.

Swanson (1989) tested this claim in a controlled study in which she manipulated the interval between stimuli. In the first condition, subjects were requested to perform discrete naming as in previous studies, with an adequate interval between stimuli, whereas in the second condition the interval was shorter. In addition, the stimuli surrounding the target stimulus were also manipulated. The target stimulus appeared either alone or in an array of three stimuli as the center stimulus, with no gap between the stimuli. However, in the first condition, the stimulus to the right of the target stimulus became the target stimulus in the next stage, whereas in the second condition this was not the case. The results were that naming speed in the simple condition, in which the stimulus was presented alone and had an adequate interval, explained most of the naming speed variance between good and poor readers in first, third, and sixth grades. Each of the conditions distinguished between the two reading groups, whereas the stimulus to the right of the target had no influence. Swanson concluded that the differences between readers were not related to their ability to perform parallel processing. A later study carried out by Bowers and Swanson (1991) had similar findings for good and poor readers in second grade.

POSSIBLE CONNECTIONS BETWEEN NAMING SPEED AND READING DISABILITY

Naming Speed and Difficulty Creating Orthographic Patterns

Bowers and Wolf (1993) suggested that naming speed is related to the rate at which children create orthographic patterns when exposed to print. According to this hypothesis, slow naming of visual stimuli can contribute to reading difficulties in three ways: First, it prevents the creation of connections between phonemes and orthographic units at the word and subword levels, and their amalgamation into patterns; second, it restricts the quality of orthographic codes that memory is based on; and third, it increases the exposure required to create stable orthographic patterns.

Adams (1981) suggested a model of orthographic surplus, according to which good readers learn to associate between letters in a certain sequence, so that with time they recognize orthographic patterns and not just single letters. If recognition of single letters is slow, then letters in a word are not activated at a time proximity sufficient to allow creation of frequently repeated orthographic patterns. This results in lack of familiar orthographic patterns (sight words) by the reader, who needs these patterns for fluent reading. Thus, the reader requires more practice time and exposure to create quality orthographic patterns.

Based on neurocognitive evidence, Wolf (1991) claimed that there is a connection between slow visual naming and deficient development at the cellular level. As discussed in the visual processing chapter, there is a significant amount of converging evidence supporting deficits in the magnocellular systems of dyslexics, possibly influencing the speed at which they process information. A reduction in processing speed, at the base of the naming speed deficit, may support the explanation offered by Bowers and Wolf (1993). If visual recognition of single words occurs slowly among dyslexics, it does not allow production of connections between letters, which appear with high frequency simultaneously in words, and thus orthographic patterns are not created (Seidenberg & McClelland, 1989).

Naming Speed Representing General Temporal Processing

As discussed in previous chapters, there is extensive behavioral evidence that a temporal processing deficit exists in dyslexics in three areas: visual, auditory, and motor (see Breznitz, 1996; Farmer & R. Klein, 1995; Wolf & Bowers, 1999, for detailed surveys). A number of important points, pertaining to the connection between naming and reading, arise from an examination of this evidence (see chap. 6 as well).

First, it seems that the evidence, although comprehensive, cannot be solely explained by slow reaction time. Timing differences appear only when a choice or integration task, including a number of subprocesses, is involved. With respect to motor functions, problems occur when dyslexics are required to arrange a number of behavioral units into larger patterns by temporal organization (as performing two actions one after the other). It seems that both in motor functioning and in the two sensory modalities differences between dyslexics and regular readers are not present at the basic level of reaction time, but rather occur when temporal selection and coordination, which overload the cognitive system, are required.

Another point clearly arising from this evidence is the critical role that speed and sequence have in distinguishing between dyslexics and regular readers, specifically in visual and auditory areas. For instance, dyslexics perform as well as regular readers when basic judgment, regarding the presence or lack of a stimulus, is required, even when it is presented rapidly (e.g., a short flash of light).

However, when a distinction must be made concerning whether one or two stimuli have been presented in a sequence, dyslexics require a longer interval in order to discern the existence of two stimuli. Additionally, when a distinction must be made between two stimuli, and the presentation of stimuli is either simultaneous, or in sequence with very short intervals, dyslexics do not perform as well as regular readers. When judgment regarding the order of stimuli is required, dyslexics exhibit difficulties only when presentation time is rapid. The difficulty ceases when intervals between stimuli are sufficiently long.

Some neurological evidence may explain these behavioral findings. In addition to Galaburda's findings regarding the irregularity of the magnocellular subsystem in the lateral geniculate nucleus, which is involved in rapid processing of visual information, Galaburda and his associates also found evidence for magnocellular irregularity in the medial geniculate nucleus, which is the area responsible for coordination of auditory information (Galaburda, Menard, & Rosen, 1994). The latter area determines the speed at which auditory information is processed, and thus deficient development of this area may impair a child's ability to discriminate between phonemes and create accurate phoneme representations.

Merzenich, Tallal, and associates (Merzenich et al., 1996; Tallal, 1993) carried out studies on children with language deficits. They claimed that a temporal processing deficit causes problems with perception and discrimination of auditory stimuli presented rapidly, leading to problems in discriminating between language sounds. This difficulty interferes with retrieval of phonological codes and creates deficient phonological awareness, which leads to a reading acquisition deficit.

Farmer and R. Klein (1995) distinguished between auditory temporal processing deficits, which lead to phonological dyslexia characterized by phonological processing difficulties, and visual temporal processing deficits, which lead to surface dyslexia characterized by orthographic processing difficulties (in agreement with the first explanation offered by Bowers & Wolf, 1993).

Wolff and associates (Wolff, 1993; Wolff et al., 1990) offered a different explanation for behavioral findings regarding deficient temporal processing among dyslexics. They found that dyslexics have problems on tasks that require a rapid pace, mostly when output comes from both hemispheres. For example, when required to perform various actions with both hands simultaneously, dyslexics' performance was worse than that of regular readers. They concluded that differences between dyslexics and regular readers stem from differences in interhemispheric information transfer rates. In an MRI study carried out on a small group of dyslexic children, Hynd and associates (1995) found a number of anatomical differences in the front and rear areas of the corpus colossum, which regulate transfer of information between hemispheres. This finding supports the claim of Wolff and his associates.

Ojemann (1983, 1984) suggested an alternate way of looking at the connection between naming speed and reading. He indicated that reading, naming, and miming of sequential facial movements can be disrupted when the front (anterior) areas of the frontal lobe are blocked by electrical stimulation. He claimed that the common mechanism in these linguistic and motor functions may prove to be a precise timing mechanism. According to Ojemann, a deficit in this mechanism may explain the frequent disorders of linguistic and motor functions common to aphasia and apraxia. Tzeng and Wang (1984) also claimed that a timing mechanism exists, and referred to dyslexia as a special case of documented deficits in this mechanism. According to these researchers, rapid use of a sequential strategy is the critical factor at the base of linguistic lateralization in the left hemisphere, where temporal control is located. Readers with a severe reading disability cannot utilize the left hemisphere's timing mechanism, in order to encode the precise letter order in written language, and are consequently unable to use grapheme–phoneme coordination rules to achieve reading fluency.

Llinas (1993) conducted a neurological study in an attempt to explain the connection between perceptual, motor, and linguistic timing deficits among dyslexics. He claimed that a more general temporal deficit, related to the nuclei in the thalamus, is at the base of the disorder. These nuclei function as a general timing mechanism, which regulate neuron stimulation rates in various motor and sensory areas of the brain.

A larger number of researchers proposed that linguistic processes rely on a timing mechanism in the brain, which is responsible for the regulation of the speed of the incoming information (Ojemann 1983, 1984; Tzeng & Wang, 1984; Wolf & Biddle, 1997). A later study suggested that this time mechanism might be in the cerebellum (Nicholson, Fawcett, & Dean, 2001).

Speed of Processing Hypothesis for Effective RAN Processes

Written language processes, including naming, are based on various brain sources and require the timely arrival and integration of the incoming information. Given the limitation of the information-processing system, these processes are strongly time constrained. It is well documented that dyslexic readers are slower than regular readers in performing RAN tasks (see Misra, Katzir, Wolf, & Poldrack, in press, for a review). But what are the sources of this slowness?

The literature to date has mainly measured this slowness using subjects' behavioral reaction time. When behavioral measures are used in RAN studies, information concerning the entire sequence of cognitive activity is provided only at the conclusion of processing, at the output stage. This stage only occurs after the completion of sensory, cognitive, and motor processes (Bentin, 1989). It is therefore difficult to determine, on the basis of behavioral measures alone, the extent to which dysfunction or slowness at any particular stage along the information-processing sequence contributes to slow RAN performance. The use of ERP methodology in cognitive research allows us to track online the timing of cognitive activities involved in the processing of information, such as the perception and discrimination of stimuli, the classification and retrieval of stimuli, and the processing of information in working memory (Bentin, 1989; Breznitz, 2001a; Breznitz & Meyler, 2003; Breznitz & Misra, 2003).

In an attempt to investigate the source of the RAN slowness in dyslexic readers, Breznitz (2005) studied the speed of processing of the cognitive components activated during letter and object-based RAN tasks among regular and dyslexic readers by using electrophysiological measures with ERP methodology. When using the ERP method, the presentation of the RAN stimuli required some modification. Instead of a matrix presentation, the stimuli appeared on the computer screen in blocks of five symbols at a time. In this way, the sequential basis of RAN could be maintained while preventing the intrusion of motoric movements in the ongoing EEG (Breznitz, 2005). In all of the experimental tasks, N100–P200–N200 (related to perceptual processing) and P300 components (related to memory processing) were identified among all subjects (see chap. 10 for more details). The peak latencies of all ERP components appeared significantly later in the dyslexic group. In both RAN tests, the between group differences were observed both with the ERP latencies and with reaction time (RT). The ERP components appeared later and the RT were longer in the dyslexics. In both letter and objects the between group differences in N100–P200 were between 30 ms and 40 ms, and in the P300 between 63 ms and 70 ms. In the letters task, the difference in RT was 192 ms and in the objects it was 276 ms. Breznitz (2005) suggested that during the processing of the RAN tasks, speed of processing at all stages in dyslexic readers is slow. This slowness starts with the perception of the stimuli (N100), continues in the stimuli discrimination process (P200) and the working memory process (P300), and is expressed finally in terms of a slow output (reaction time). Similar results were found in a word recognition ERP study where the stimuli were words and pseudowords (Breznitz, 2002; Breznitz & Meyler, 2003; Breznitz & Misra, 2003; see also chap. 10).

In order to further investigate the underlying processes of the RAN tasks, an additional study was carried out whereby 73 dyslexics and 73 regular adult readers were tested with four RAN tests: letters, numbers, objects, and colors (Breznitz, 2005; see also chaps. 10 and 11). A factor analysis of the four RAN measures yielded a single factor explaining 86.46% of all the factor variance. The following are the specific loadings of the variance: .95 for letters, .95 for numbers, .93 for colors, and .87 for objects. A stepwise multiple regression analysis was performed for each group differently. The dependent variable was the RAN factor and the independent factors were word decoding fluency (1-minute tests for words and pseudowords), phonological (omission, deletions), orthographic (parsing test), digit span (STM), working memory, verbal fluency, speed factor (WAIS–R), and automaticity (Stroop test) (for details, see chap. 9, and Breznitz, 2002).

The analysis revealed different results in the two groups:

The dyslexic group: Two measures entered into the regression equation and explained 49% of the variances in the RAN task among the dyslexics. The first was the latency of P300 in the letter RAN task with $Rsq = .41, \beta = .65$. The second was orthographic time measure (parsing time) with $Rsq = .8, \beta =.25$.

The average readers group: Three measures entered into the regression equation and explained 48% of the variances in decoding among the control group. The first was the P200 of the RAN letter test $Rsq = .32, \beta = .44$. The second was automaticity measure (Stroop time) $Rsq = .11, \beta = .36$. The third was the phonological performance time measure, $Rsq = .5, \beta = .22$.

These results suggested a fundamentally different process between the dyslexics and the regular readers when processing the RAN tasks. The perception stage for the regular readers (as expressed by P200 latency) and working memory for the dyslexics (as expressed by P300 latency) explain most of the variances in processing RAN tasks. In regular readers, the stimuli are stored accurately in the mental lexicon, and little else besides perception is subsequently needed for fast retrieval. As such, the regular readers are able to finish processing the information very early on, at the stage of perception. In contrast, among dyslexic readers, the presentation of stimuli in the mental lexicon is impaired, which leads to incomplete storage. Consequently, perception is insufficient for stimuli identification and the dyslexics must carry the (uncompleted) processing of the initial stimuli on to the working memory stage, and perhaps even further into long-term memory. It appears that RAN is more strongly connected to word decoding fluency score for dyslexics than for normal readers. Among the dyslexic readers, the RAN factor correlates with word decoding fluency score, $r = .59$, $p < .001$, and in the controls, $r = .39$, $p < .01$.

In sum, effective RAN processing relies on fast speed of processing at all stages. The dyslexic subjects were slower than the controls at all stages of processing the RAN tasks. Whereas for regular readers SOP at the perception stage is the crucial factor for fast RAN processing, among the dyslexics it is the SOP in the working memory stage. Similar results were found when the two groups processed linguistic information (see chap. 11 for more details).

6

Speed of Processing

Mental behavior involves cognitive activities, which greatly vary in nature and level of complexity. These activities, viewed as sets of disparate cognitive processes, take time to complete. The precise duration of a mental activity is an outcome of individual processing abilities. The literature terms this concept *speed of processing* (SOP). An operational definition of SOP is "the total speed required for a person to perform a cognitive task at any processing level." In other words, each cognitive activity is composed of a sequence of actions, each requiring a certain execution time. *Response time* is the time it takes to perform each subprocess of the complete task. Therefore, speed of processing is the time passing from external stimulus presentation until the behavioral response to the stimulus (Kail, 1991a).

During this time, the information is perceived and processed via various modalities and systems, activated in different brain locations and through several stages of activation within the information-processing system (Atkinson & Shiffrin, 1971). According to Kail (1991a), the modalities and systems activated in a particular task with their differential processing speed, united with the complexity of stimuli, are contributing factors to speed of processing. Thus, Hale (1990) suggested that any information-processing activity also incorporates a basic speed of information processing. Rapid SOP is crucial for effective task performance, given the rapid decay of stimuli, which imposes time limitations on information processing.

Reading is an example of a cognitive activity that requires information processing under time constraints. Hence, SOP may be a crucial factor in accurate and fluent reading. A slow speed of processing might be a crucial factor in dysfluent reading. This chapter is divided into two parts. The first part reviews the concepts of SOP during cognitive activity, and the second presents evidence for slow SOP in dyslexic readers.

WHAT INFLUENCES SPEED OF PROCESSING?

The research on SOP during cognitive activity is divided into several topics. However, studies in this field generally focus on the age-related and developmental aspects of SOP. Researchers have debated as to whether SOP is a global characteristic (domain general) of the human brain with a genetic component, or a part of a general ability (G factor), and they have focused mainly on the connection between IQ and SOP. Others view SOP as task dependent (domain specific) and related to cognitive processing levels. These issues are addressed next.

AGE-RELATED CHANGES IN SPEED OF PROCESSING

Age-related changes are the most prevalent topic within research on speed of information processing. The most compelling finding on SOP is that it changes with age. Young children have been compared to older children and to young and elderly adults. Developmental changes in SOP have even been examined among 5-month-old infants using a novelty preference task. The latter study incorporated measures of time duration and number of trials needed to reach a conclusion, such as the time infants needed to look at a familiar face before recognizing it (Rose, Feldman, & Jankowski, 2002). The number of trials decreased by 18% between 5 and 7 months of age, and by an additional 34% between 7 and 12 months. Similarly, Hale (1990) reported that 10-year-old children were 1.82 times slower than 15-year-olds and young adults, whereas 12-year-olds were only 1.5 times slower.

Investigations into age-related changes have consistently shown that a nonlinear change in SOP is evident across the life span. Two main findings stand out. First, regardless of the task employed, response time decreases as a function of age until adulthood. Thus, older children are faster than younger children, but they are slower than young adults at performing a wide variety of tasks (Kail, 1979, 1991a; Wickens, 1974). Second, elderly adults process information slower than young adults (Cerella, 1985; Neubauer, Spinath, Riemann, Borkenau, & Angleitner, 2000; Posthuma, Mulder, Boomsma & de Geus, 2002;

Salthouse & Somberg, 1982). One of the important issues raised in these studies is that the processing speed of elderly people is significantly slower than that of young adults, even when their accuracy in processing information is similar. We can thus hypothesize that SOP is separate from accuracy. If so, what are the factors underlying SOP?

SPEED OF PROCESSING: A DOMAIN-GENERAL OR DOMAIN-SPECIFIC COMPONENT?

SOP has been presented in two ways in the literature. On the one hand, SOP is an outcome of a global mechanism (domain-general) that develops with age. On the other, it is presented as a domain-specific component (task dependent) that develops with learning and practice.

SOP as Domain General

Several studies have presented SOP as a domain-general skill (Jensen, 1982; Kail, 2000; Levine, Preddy, & Thorndike, 1987). Kail (2000) provided developmental evidence in support of the thesis of a global mechanism that limits the speed at which children and adolescents process information. The mechanism is not specific to particular tasks or domains, but is rather a fundamental characteristic of the developing information-processing system. It is hypothesized that the underlying biological factor corresponding with SOP is the spread rate from one node to another within the neural network (Kail 1986b, 1988a, 1991a). In other words, age-related changes in SOP may reflect developmental changes in neural communication rates, which are affected by the number of transient connections in the central nervous system and age-related increases in myelinization (Miller, 1994).

In experiments performed by Kail (1986a, 1988a), children, adolescents, and adults aged 8 to 22 were given various tasks, such as mental rotation, analogical thinking, mental additions, memory search, and visual search. Results indicated that SOP developed similarly with age in all tasks. As children become older, their SOP decreases. Kail (1991a) conducted a comprehensive review of studies on SOP at various ages. The probes included a long list of linguistic and nonlinguistic tasks (Hale, 1990; Hale, Myerson, & Wagstaff, 1987; Kail, 1985, 1986a, 1986b, 1988a, 1990, 1991a, for a review). Data analyses indicated a linear connection, with a gradient above one, between SOPs at different ages. This indicates that within age-matched normal readers, SOP is generally uniform. It was suggested that SOP is a global, task-independent feature and it changes rapidly in childhood and much slower in adulthood.

The studies by Kail (1991a) and Hale (1990) support the *global trend hypothesis*, which suggests that all information-processing components develop simultaneously at a similar rate. Hale (1990) lent support to Kail's (1986b) findings that processing times in various tasks change in concert from age 10 through 15, at which point SOP appears fully mature. Moreover, ratios of individual reaction times to average reaction times are relatively constant across tasks (Hale & Jansen, 1994).

Two factors influence the *global trend hypothesis* on SOP. One is the intrinsic efficiency of individual processing steps, or style (see C. Roth, 1983); another is the efficiency with which these steps are communicated (Hale, 1990). The development of these two factors presumably depends on neurobiological changes (Hale & Jansen, 1994). It is conceivable that SOP is affected by the time neural messages require to reach cortical sensory areas, to leave cortical motor areas, and to be perceived as output, for a given reaction time. Similarly, Ridderinkhof and Van der Molen (1997) found that changes in SOP are global, and therefore affect all cognitive functions (see also Travis, 1998).

Kail (1991a) discussed three principal interpretations of the characteristics and operation of the general component in SOP. The first interpretation relates to the positive transfer among speed processes. Kail (1991a) speculated that skills used for performing certain tasks subsequently generalize to other domains. However, as Kail casually pointed out, this interpretation suffers from one major drawback, namely, that time-constrained tasks are domain specific. Kail claimed that performance on these tasks does not usually transfer to tasks lacking highly related processing requirements (Kail & Park, 1990). However, time-constrained tasks such as reading, which are based on the precise integration of information from more than one entity (e.g., a grapheme–phoneme correspondence), are not just based on speed of processing within each entity. Rather, a mutual *dialogue* between the various entities with respect to the content and the speed of transfer of information is crucial for reading effectiveness. This idea of a dialogue is developed in the synchronization theory spelled out in chapter 13.

Kail's second interpretation holds that, as children grow older, their available processing resources grow as well. Thus, an older child can allocate more resources for a given time-constrained task, thereby reducing the time needed to complete it. There are two possible ways in which this resource increase may occur. There may be a purely quantitative increase in processing resources, such that a general maturational change affects SOP in younger and older subjects. Alternatively, SOP may decrease as a result of increasing automatization in task performance, thereby reducing subject response latencies (Kail, 1991a). Kail and Salthouse (1994) agreed that speed of processing decreases with increases in cognitive resources. However, they claimed that SOP decreased because adults could ignore stimuli, information, or processes that interfered with task performance. They stated that an executive mechanism, responsible for inhibitory control, develops over the years and promotes quick and efficient processing, unaffected by hindering factors. However, the existence of a resource capacity has been questioned in recent years. According to Stanovich (1990), encapsulation is a more suitable concept, because it emphasizes the representation of knowledge in memory, rather than the pool of available processing resources. It can be suggested that appropriate resources enhance knowledge in memory. The quality of task-related resources may be affected by the speed at which the information is processed within and between these resources.

Kail's third interpretation is based on an analogy of computer software (Salthouse & Prill, 1983). Two computers may use the same software, provided they have different cycle times. But one computer would require more time to execute single commands. Similarly, a given person may require additional time to scan task instructions into working memory, or to initiate a response. Thus, reduced time cycles are analogous to decreased durations in cognitive operations.

Kail (1991a) claimed that general SOP changes, across tasks, are an outcome of the following factors: improvements in memory (see also Geary, Brown, & Samaranayake, 1991; Whitney, 1986), more resources allocated for a task, a developmental decrease in SOP of cognitive operations, and neurobiological changes in the central nervous system (see also Hale, Fry, & Jessie, 1993; Hale & Jansen, 1994; Vernon, 1987). Effective SOP is also found to be connected to metacognitive processes (Kail, 1988a). It was found that SOP increases the effectiveness of processes such as stimulus encoding, stimulus recognition, sensory storage, memory comparison, and mapping of signals onto the appropriate responses (Kerr, Davidson, Nelson, & Haley, 1982; Maisto & Baumeister, 1975).

Whitney (1986) suggested that speed of memory retrieval may be crucial to SOP of cognitive information, because cognitive information at various levels (e.g., word meanings, concepts, and symbols) is both stored and retrieved from a general database.

Speed of processing was closely observed with respect to rates of semantic memory retrieval, which is fundamental to both simple and complex tasks. Data from multiple studies support the idea that developmental changes in rates of semantic memory retrieval cause changes in global SOP, in much the same manner as other factors, such as the use of strategies or changes in the knowledge base (Ford & Keating, 1981; Keating & Bobbitt, 1978). It is likely that the content and organization of children's semantic categories affect the speed of information retrieval at different ages (Prawat & Cancelli, 1977; Sperber, Davies, Merrill, & MacCauly, 1982).

One of the factors that affects memory retrieval may be the speed at which the information is perceived and stored in the brain. A slow inflow of information into the brain might slow the storage and impair the retrieval processes.

The Relations Between G Factor and SOP

A number of studies have focused on the hypothesis that SOP as a domain-general factor is part of a global G factor (part of the IQ). SOP was tested when processing various kind of intelligence (IQ) measures. Generally, a negative correlation around $r = -.50$ was found between measures of SOP (Reaction Time—RT/Inspection Time—IT) and measures of intelligence (IQ). The faster the SOP, the higher the IQ score (Deary, 1993; Deary & Stough, 1996; Finkel & Pedersen, 2000; Kranzler & Jensen, 1989; Luciano et al., 2001; Neubauer et al., 2000; Posthuma et al., 2002; Vigneau, Blanchet, Lorenger, & Pepin, 2002). Moreover, SOP was found to contribute nearly 50% of the variance in intelligence score (Jensen, 1982; Vernon, Nador, & Kantor, 1985). Several IQ tests therefore incorporated, in addition to the verbal and the performance measures, a speed factor measure. For example, in the WISC–R IQ test (Wechsler, 1974), the speed factor was composed out of two subtests: the Digit Symbols and Symbols Search.

The strong connection between SOP and IQ was interpreted in several ways. Some have suggested that cognitive activities are all performed in working memory, which has a limited capacity. The limitations on the quantities of stored material and processed material complicate even simple tasks. The existence of decreased SOP allows more efficient processing. The quicker the speed, the faster the information is encoded and processed into chunks, allowing the processing of additional information. Moreover, the faster the processing, the quicker the retrieval from long-term memory, and the more likely that information in short-term memory will not fade. Consequently, those who answer correctly on more questions in IQ tests are those with faster SOPs (see also Luciano et al., 2001; Vigneau et al., 2002). However, Sternberg (1966) questioned these interpretations and argued that as the complexity of tasks increases, longer time measures reflect the increasing meta-componential requirements of a task. That is, longer processing time can be also associated with more in-depth and higher level processing, rather than with difficulties in information processing. Thus, Sternberg discussed the importance of measuring time allocations for the separate component processes, rather than emphasizing the central and/or indiscriminate SOP.

Other studies suggested that the correlations between intelligence and SOP are based on increased neural efficiency of the central nervous system. In these studies, methods such as evoke respond potential (ERP) (Blinkhorn & Hendrickson, 1982), regional blood flow in the cortex (Risberg, 1986), metabolic activity of glucose (Parks et al., 1990), and peak alpha wave (Posthuma, Neale, Boomsma, & de Geus, 2001) were used. Higher intelligence was found to be related to increased neural efficiency of the central nervous system (Vernon & Mori, 1992). T. E. Reed (1984) hypothesized that intelligence and neural efficiency are correlated, based on genetic factors related to structure and quantity of neurotransmitters that affect SOP, which in turn affect intelligence. In other words, faster neural conduction enables faster SOP, leading to better results on IQ tests. Reed revealed a connection between SOP and neural conduction velocity. Conduction velocity is the speed at which an electric impulse is transferred along nerve fibers and synapses (T. E. Reed, 1984). This is presumably associated with the quantity of transmitters at the end of a synapse, and the speed at which they are released (M. A. Reed, 1989), or associated with the myelin, which insulates the nerves and leads to faster and better conduction of the electric impulse (Miller, 1994). These researchers examined whether conduction velocity is hereditary and how it connects to IQ. The study used 210 pairs of 16-year-old twins; all were given the RAVEN IQ test, and neural velocity was measured through the arm. Significant high correlations ($r = .52-.76$) between IQ and the various conduction velocity measures (i.e., beginning, peak, and end of conduction) were found only between identical male and identical female twins (monozygotic) and not in dizygotic twins (for similar results, see also Rijsdijk & Boomsma, 1997; Vernon & Mori, 1992). It was suggested that the heredity factor in neural conduction is high. Moreover, these studies indicated that conduction velocity and reaction time significantly contributed to predictions of IQ. Higher IQ and faster SOP were both related to faster and more efficient neural conduction. However, it was maintained that although a strong connection among these three factors exists, it is impossible to assert which of these relations is causal.

Another attempt to present SOP as a domain-general factor can be seen in studies of the genetic aspects of SOP. Most of these focused on the relations between SOP, IQ measures, and genetic factors. Phenotypic correlations between

SOP and measures of IQ were found to be linked to genetic factors. The portion of phenotypic correlation resulting from genetic mediation was substantially high and ranged from $r = .68$ to $r = .72$ (Baker et al., 1991; Boomsma & Somsen, 1991; Eysenck, 1986; Finkel & Pedersen, 2000; Luciano et al., 2001; McGue, Bouchard, Lykken, & Feuer, 1984; Neubauer et al., 2000; Vernon, 1989). In general, these findings support the notion that more intelligent subjects have faster selective response activations (Eysenck, 1986; Vernon, 1987, 1993) The fast selective processing mainly appears at the early perceptual stage (Posthuma et al., 2002).

Another genetic study (Eysenck, 1986), consisting of a large sample of monozygotic and dizygotic adult twins, investigated the relation between reaction times on elementary cognitive tasks and measures of psychometric intelligence. As previously, the portion of phenotypic correlation resulting from genetic mediation was substantially high ($r = .68$). It was suggested that SOP can be presented as an indicator of biological intelligence and can be expected to be genetically determined (Eysenck, 1986). Added to this was the myelination hypothesis, which holds that increases in myeline on the exson tend to increase SOP of the nervous system (Neubauer et al., 2000).

Speed of Processing as Domain Specific

Other theorists (Chi, 1977; Roth, 1983; Siegler, 1987) have questioned the scientific validity of a central mechanism that regulates age changes in SOP. They have presented findings that involve domain-specific components showing that the use of strategies and task-appropriate knowledge either reduce or eliminate time differences between younger and older adults (Rabinowitz, Ornstein, Folds-Bennett, & Schneider, 1994). In a longitudinal study, children between the age of 6 and 9 were tested on an inspection time (IT) task, tested again 5 minutes later, and again after a year. On the one hand, the decrease in IT times was much greater one year after testing than 5 minutes later. On the other hand, young children retested a year after their initial test performed better than older children on initial testing. This indicates that prior experience on a task has greater impact than maturational processes per se (e.g., changes in SOP). Exposure to a particular class of tasks generates changes and reorganization in underlying knowledge, and elicits strategic behavior (M. Anderson, Reid, & Nelson, 2001).

It is conceivable that at least some age-related changes in SOP are due to shifting of strategies. Less efficient strategies of young subjects are replaced by optimal strategies of older subjects (Childs & Polich, 1979; McCauley, Kellas,

Dugas, & De Vellis, 1976; Pick & Frankel, 1974). Chi (1977) and Chi and Gallagher (1982) argued that adults employ control processes, which are more efficient than those used by children, and adults have more available knowledge stored in long-term memory. Moreover, short-term memory capacity is more associated with a person's knowledge than it is a function of a person's age.

In general, Chi (1977) questioned the assumption that a central processing deficit affects the speed of mental operations in children compared to adults. Chi suggested three possible causes for slower reaction times in children. First, children take longer to perform elementary mental operations. Abundant data have been gathered on the Sternberg (1966) short-term memory scanning task, which is an estimate of an elementary mental operation. Most developmental studies probed by the Sternberg paradigm were conducted on children aged 8–14 years, with no significant developmental differences found in memory scanning rates (Dugas & Kellas, 1974; G. J. Harris & Fleer, 1974). Second, children do not have efficient organization of processes to perform a particular task. Finally, in discussing central processing limitations in children, these limits should be differentiated from nonprocessing factors. The latter include increased durations of motor reaction time, difficulty in maintaining the rate of information loss from short-term memory, and a less accessible, or deficient, semantic knowledge base within long-term memory. Developmental differences in reaction time do not necessarily mean slower elementary mental operations, and often reflect different control processes across age groups (Chi, 1977).

Chi and Klahr (1975) conducted a study in which 5-year-olds and adults had to quantify random dot patterns. They concluded that children's central processing speed was not necessarily slower, but rather that adults and children used different processes to quantify the dots. This suggests that there is no need to postulate age differences in speed of central processing. When reaction time differences arise, they can often be accounted for by means of a different aggregate of mental operations by children and adults, or by means of different control processes. Moreover, Chi's (1978) study presumed that if knowledge or strategies determine rates of processing, children who are knowledgeable in a given domain would show superiority over adults that are less knowledgeable in that domain.

More support to domain specificity of SOP can be found in studies that connected noncentral speed of processing limitations with motivation (Elliott, 1970), extended practice (Elliot, 1972; Newell & Rosenbloom, 1981), and knowledge base (Egan & Schwartz, 1979; C. Roth, 1983). Others have indicated that developmental increases in the speed of mental operations are due to attentiveness (Elliot, 1970, 1972), maturation of modules, inhibitory ability, attentional processes (Davis & Anderson, 2001), strategic selection, organization, control (Chi, 1977; Chi & Gallager, 1982), and regulation of speed-accuracy requirements (Brewer & Smith, 1989).

SPEED OF INFORMATION PROCESSING AMONG DYSLEXICS

Dyslexia is a reading impairment phenomenon and is characterized by slow reading rate. The notion that reading rate is a dependent variable affected by the quality of the reading skills (see Carver, 1990, for a review) clearly precludes any attempt to view speed of processing as a causal factor. However, if reading rate is viewed as separate from performance accuracy and presented as an independent factor that itself affects the quality of the reading skills (see chap. 2 for a review), we need to investigate its underlying factors. The main theme of this book is that reading rate represents the duration of the processing time of all its constituents. Because reading is a time-constrained process, SOP of its constituencies is crucial. Slower SOP in one or more of the activated components can be a cause of reading impairment.

Of central interest to reading research is the mapping of the various components that are active in reading. On the one hand, it has been claimed that reading is a linguistic activity and that reading difficulties can be seen only in the verbal domain (see Adams, 1990, for a review). Others have suggested that nonlinguistic processes also play a role in accounting for reading difficulties and that dyslexic readers exhibit impairments in the nonlinguistic domain as well (i.e., Stein & McAnally, 1995). What is the impact of SOP in the regular and deviant reading process? Is it restricted to speed of activation in the language-related areas alone (domain specific) or does it have more generalized (domain general) influence?

Because there has to date been no consistent research design measuring both linguistic and nonlinguistic processes within the same subject group, there is no conclusive evidence to answer any of the aforementioned questions. The available evidence mainly focuses on the linguistic domain alone, testing reaction time rates for the recognition of graphemes and phonemes, words and pseudo-words, and connected text in dyslexic readers as compared to age-matched and reading-level regular readers. Although the record is not clear-cut (see Stringer & Stanovich, 2000), most studies pointed to a slow reaction time in dyslexics as compared to the controls at all levels of reading (i.e., Breznitz, 2003b; Breznitz & Meyler, 2003; Compton & Carlisle, 1994). Moreover, the speed of reaction time to the reading stimuli and the reading rate not only distinguished between good and poor readers, but also affects the level of decoding and comprehension. Fast reaction time and reading speed decreased decoding errors and increased comprehension (Breznitz, 1987a, 2003b; Catts, Gillispie, Leonard, Kail, & Miller, 2002; see also chap. 2 for a review).

Recent studies have provided indirect evidence indicating that a slow rate of information processing in dyslexics is not limited to the reading process. Dyslexics are slower in performing rapid automatized naming (RAN) tasks (Bowers & Wolf, 1993, see also chap. 5). Dyslexics were also slower in tapping tasks (Wolff et al., 1990; Wolff, 2000b), and motor functions combined with counting tasks (Nicolson & Fawcett, 1993a; see also chap. 3). Further evidence on the differences in SOP between dyslexics and regular readers derives from studies that placed a different emphasis on the determinants of speed of information. One current theory explains dyslexia by means of the time serial processing deficit (Tallal, 1980; Tallal, Curtis, & Kaplan, 1988; Tallal, Miller, & Fitch, 1993; Tallal, Stark, Kallman, & Mellits, 1981; and see also chap. 8 for a review). Tallal, Miller, and Fitch (1995) suggested that impaired temporal processing under time constraint is at the root of children's language problems. This impairment impedes the integration of rapid sensory information that is needed for effective reading. Additional evidence concerning the effect of slow SOP on reading skills can be seen in Yap and Van der Leij (1993a; see also chap. 11), who claimed that dyslexics lack the ability to coordinate simultaneously between stimuli coming from different modalities and systems. This book explains this coordination problem as due, ultimately, to the fact that each entity processes information at a different speed. Appropriate coordination requires a limited between entity gap in SOP. However, as chapter 12 indicates, the crucial difference between dyslexics and normal readers is precisely that the former have systematically slower within entity SOP rates and larger between entity SOP gaps. It is these differences that lie at the heart of the coordination problems experienced by dyslexic readers.

Another body of evidence regards the lack of automaticity of dyslexics during dual tasks performance. In all dual tasks, the reaction time performance of dyslexics was slower (Nicolson & Fawcett, 1993a; see also chap. 3). Other studies pointed to the slowness of dyslexics in retrieving stimuli from memory. The resulting "between stimuli time intervals hypothesis" claimed that the slow SOP of information in dyslexics occurs mainly between the stimuli and affects their memory retrieval (Bowers & Wolf, 1993; Wolff, Michel, & Ovrut, 1990; see also chap. 5). Further evidence supporting slow SOP as an explanation of dyslexia derives from the "mistiming hypothesis" (Bowers & Wolf, 1993). This hypothesis is based on the fact that the process of word decoding in reading requires exact integration of the incoming orthographic and phonological information. A successful word reading process is based on the effectiveness of a timing mechanism that regulates the incoming information according to the task needs. Bowers and Wolf (1993) suggested that the timing mechanism in dyslexics is impaired and causes mistiming between the orthographic and the phonological information, which deteriorates the integration needed for successful word reading (see also Breznitz, 2000; Breznitz & Misra, 2003; and chaps. 9 and 10).

In sum, the common element in all interpretations regarding the slow SOP among dyslexic readers regards the activation of more than one stimulus, or more than one sensory modality or process (see Laasonen, Halme, Nuuttila, Service, & Virsu, 2000; Wolf, Bowers, & Biddle, 2000). However, there are also some studies suggesting that the slow SOP rates can be also been seen with a single stimuli, or a single modality (Farmer & R. Klein, 1995, for a review; Breznitz & Meyler, 2001).

Additional explanations of dyslexia have been put forward over the years. One of these is the "transient deficit hypothesis," which posits that dyslexics' reading deficiencies are the result of inefficient, or *mistimed*, interactions between two separate but interactive parallel visual pathways for the processing of temporal and pattern information, namely, the sustained visual system and the transient visual system (Lovegrove, 1993b). This mistiming occurs as a result of impaired operation of the transient system. The transient and sustained processing systems each have different spatiotemporal response characteristics and are specialized for analyzing different aspects of perceptual information. In general, the transient system is held to be a fast operating early warning system that extracts large amounts of global information. The sustained system is thought to react more slowly and subsequent to the transient response. The responses of the transient and sustained systems are mutually suppressive (see Breitmeyer, 1993, for a review, and chap. 7 for more details). The observation of problems among dyslexic readers in rapid, sequential, or temporal processing in the visual system has led to the proposal that the abnormalities may also be found in similar fast responding neurons of the auditory and somatosensory systems (Breitmeyer, 1993; Livingstone, 1993; Livingstone, Rosen, Drislane, & Galaburda, 1991). Stein and McAnally (1995) examined this hypothesis in adult dyslexics. The test was analogous to a visual test, and examined sensitivity to auditory sound waves. Dyslexic subjects completed the task in a longer time frame, and made more mistakes than regular readers. This supported the assumption that the development of synchronized auditory processing is impaired among dyslexics.

The issue of modality-general temporal SOP deficits as a cause of dyslexics' reading problems put forward another hypothesis, according to which the reading of dyslexics may be hampered by some form of asynchrony or mistiming (Breznitz, 2000; Breznitz & Misra, 2003; see also chap. 11). This occurs within and between the modalities and the systems that are activated in reading or at some stage or stages of the information-processing sequence. As dyslexic readers typically show an impaired capacity to organize elements into coordinated ensembles, some researchers have stressed the coordination and integration of events in relation to impaired SOP (Breznitz & Misra, 2003; Llinas, 1993; Wolff, 1993). Wolff (1993) maintained that temporal resolution ability may be decomposed into component variables of timing precision and serial ordering. These variables are seen as responsible for dyslexics' deficits in the ability to coordinate and integrate stimuli, particularly under conditions of increased processing demands. Different neuropsychological models of dyslexia assume that the sources of such difficulty are in the left hemisphere (LH), or in selective dysfunctions of the cerebral hemispheres. Others view dyslexia as a problem relating to time and content coordination impairments between both hemispheres. According to one contemporary theory, the characteristic timing deficits of dyslexic readers are held to stem from a lack of synchronization between the operations of the two hemispheres during the process of reading. Poor synchronization is held to result from impaired and slow interhemispheric transfer via the corpus callosum (Davidson & Saron, 1992; Gladstone & Best, 1985; Goldberg & Costa, 1981).

The cerebral hemispheres differ in their rates of information processing, or time bases. Although perception of temporal order is independent of sensory system, the left, language-dominant hemisphere is a more precise temporal processor (Hammond, 1982). The LH has specialized mechanisms for rapid sensory integration within the tens of milliseconds range. The temporal components of speech must be analyzed within this critical temporal range. It has been speculated that the LH specializes in linguistic processing because of the temporal specialization of the LH (Tallal, 1994).

Although the right hemisphere (RH) is capable of processing verbal information semantically, normal people tend to rely primarily on the LH's superior abilities in this domain. The RH is specialized for the processing of spatially structured information (Davis & Wada, 1977). The LH is superior at utilizing well-routinized codes, but the RH plays a critical role in the initial stages of acquisition of new descriptive systems, or of novel stimuli (Goldberg & Costa, 1981).

Learning to read requires complex interactions between left and right hemisphere processes. Reading acquisition is essentially a process of acquiring a new descriptive system, in that a novel visual code is imposed on an established auditory-linguistic code. Possibly, this would make the RH processes initially crucial for acquiring reading, as identifying printed words is both a novel and a visual task. There is evidence that the RH may play a special role in reading acquisition, but not for maintaining basic reading skills once they have been learned (Zaidel, 1983). Once reading skills are established, the LH may play a larger role in the reading process. It has been suggested that skilled reading may require a controlled modulation of interhemispheric interaction, in that the LH (or some other control mechanism) may regulate reading subprocesses by selectively "inhibiting" or "disinhibiting" RH function (Hutner & Liederman, 1991). Another suggestion is that a cross-callosal inhibitory mechanism prevents conflicting RH processing from interfering with LH processing, but facilitates interhemispheric transfer when RH and LH processes complement each other (Kershner & Graham, 1995; Zaidel & Schweiger, 1985).

According to the interhemispheric transfer deficit hypothesis, dyslexia is an outcome of insufficient interhemispheric collaboration when transferring information about novel visuospatial patterns of letters with the familiar auditory-linguistic properties of spoken language (Gladstone & Best, 1985; Goldberg & Costa, 1981). To be maximally useful, the information arriving from each of the hemispheres must be coordinated within a narrow time window. A failure to do this will interfere with the smooth execution of responses. In short, when visual information about letters is not associated with the appropriate auditory information, the ability to recognize words is impeded (Davidson, Leslie, & Saron, 1990; Davidson & Saron, 1992).

Recent research appears to support the interhemispheric transfer deficit hypothesis. Dyslexics have a faster interhemispheric transfer time (IHTT) from right-to-left and slower IHTT from left-to-right hemisphere compared to controls. In addition, faster left-to-right reading performance is associated with poorer performance on reading and cognitive measures among dyslexics, whereas the opposite is true of faster left-to-right transfer (Davidson & Saron, 1992).

Llinas (1993) advanced additional theory of a general cellular slow SOP dysfunction in dyslexics. He suggested that the normal properties of neural circuits responsible for temporal aspects of cognition are impaired among dyslexic readers, and argued that these abnormalities may cause a type of dyschronia, or mistiming, between different interconnected neural sites, particularly in the high frequency range (35–45 Hz). Llinas suggested that there may be impairment in a central "clock" that controls the rate of neural firing patterns, or oscillations. These oscillations are hypothesized to be an essential component for binding sensory information in cortico-thalamo-cortical networks. He pointed out that a slowing down may have occurred due to some developmental variation in central nervous system organization.

The question of whether or not the slower SOP of dyslexics can be also related to a general G factor was studied in Breznitz (2003b, in press, and chap. 9). Young and adult dyslexics as compared to reading-level and age-matched readers were tested with the WISC–R IQ test (Wechsler, 1974). No significant differences were found between the good and the poor readers in general ability score. However, the dyslexics at all ages achieved significantly lower scores in the IQ speed factor. This score is based on a computed measure driven out of Symbols Search and Digits Symbols subtests performance. This computed score introduced a speed factor in the general ability measure. Data also yielded a correlation of $r = .44$ in the young and $r = .51$, $p < .01$ in the adult dyslexic groups between the speed factor and word decoding score. No significant correlation between these measures was found in the good readers groups.

In sum, the evidence reviewed supports the notion of a more general slow SOP in dyslexic readers that is not merely limited to reading. Yet, it is not clear as to how this slowness relates to the effectiveness of the reading skills in general and to reading rate in particular. The reading activity starts with visual and the auditory-acoustic systems by recognizing the visual and the sounds of the written symbols and incorporates processing in the phonological, orthographic, and semantic systems. All are activated at the level of letters, words, and connected text. Furthermore, as reading is a cognitive process, its activation relies on perceptions, memory, and output processes. As such, the reading process incorporates a wide range of processes that are driven from different modalities and brain systems; each processes information in a different manner and at a different speed. As effective reading requires integration of information from the different sources, we claim that SOP within and between these activation sources is crucial for effective reading. Lack of SOP in one or more of the reading components or insufficiency in speed synchronization between the components is likely to cause reading problems. This hypothesis is developed in the following chapters. The modalities and the systems that are activated in reading are described and the specific biological structure of each modality and its relation to SOP is discussed. Data from our own research projects on this theme are presented.

7

Visual Processing:
Regular and Dyslexic

Examining the contribution of visual deficits to reading impairment requires familiarity with the anatomy and function of the visual system, extending from the eyes to higher association areas in the cortex. Knowledge of specific characteristics of the visual system is fundamental for understanding its role in various aspects of reading, both regular and impaired. The complexity of the visual modality, consisting of many processing stages and subsystems that require integration, provide a likely substrate for rate irregularity and asynchrony problems. The idea that impaired reading is, to some extent, the result of abnormal visual processing speeds is further strengthened by findings of behavioral, evoked response potential (ERP), and imaging studies. This chapter first reviews the stages and subsystems of visual processing, followed by an examination of broad evidence regarding visual deficits in dyslexia.

THE PHYSIOLOGY OF THE VISUAL SYSTEM

Visual information, contained in written language, is perceived by the brain's visual pathways. This perception begins with retinal detection of visual features in printed material. The retina contains millions of ganglion neurons of different classes, which are designated to receive information from the environment via the visual field. The perceived visual information continues from the retina to the optic nerve, to the optic chiasm, through the optic tract, and to the various layers of the lateral geniculate nuclei (LGN), composed of magnocellular

(M), or transient layers, parvocellular (P), or sustained layers, and koniocellular (K) layers in the thalamus, to the optic radiation area, and then to primary visual and visual association areas in the occipital lobe. From there, visual information continues into the visual cortex along two largely parallel streams, the ventral (the "what pathway," or P stream) and the dorsal (the "where pathway," or M stream).

From the Eyes to the Cortex

The optic nerves leave the eyes and jointly form the optic chiasm, where they undergo partial decussation, crossing over of axons from the nasal retina to the contralateral side of the brain. Thus, past the chiasm, the left optic tract contains information on the right hemifield, whereas the right optic tract contains information on the left hemifield.

A small number of optic tract axons continue to the hypothalamus, where they synchronize a variety of biological rhythms. In addition, direct projections run from the retina to the pretectum in the midbrain; the pretectum controls the size of the pupil and certain eye movements. Approximately 10% of the retinal fibers bypass the thalamus and project to the tectum, to the part of the midbrain called the superior colliculus (i.e., retinotectal projections). Neurons in the superior colliculus command eye and head movements via indirect connections with motor neurons in the brain stem. These eye and head movements bring an image to a point in space where a new stimulus appears in the fovea.

However, the majority of optic tract axons innervate the (LGN) of the thalamus. The afferent neurons of the LGN project to the primary visual cortex (i.e., optic radiations). This pathway mediates conscious visual perception.

Visual Cortex

Information about the environment, entering through the eyes, is processed by a visually responsive cortex, which is subdivided into functionally distinct areas. Each area constitutes a single topographic representation of the visual field (Amir, Harel, & Malach, 1993; Knierim & Van Essen, 1992). Definitions of these visual areas are based on several criteria: The retinotopic representation of visual space; functional characteristics, as selective responses to stimuli according to physical properties; histological architecture, as revealed by staining of myelin, Nissl, and cytochrome oxidase; and connectivity (Felleman & Van Essen, 1991).

Intensive study in the past 30 years has revealed over 30 visual areas in the macaque monkey (Van Essen, Fellemen, DeYoe, Olavarria, & Knierim, 1990). Among the areas described, researchers agree on the existence of areas V1, V2, and MT (Kaas & Morel, 1993; Malach, Amir, Harel, & Grinvald, 1993; Malach, Schirman, Harel, Tootell, & Malonek, 1997). Area V1, also called the striate cortex, receives 70% of its neural input directly from the LGN in the thalamus; therefore, it is considered to be the main station of visual processing in the cortex. From the striate cortex, visual information is transferred further along the hierarchy of visual cortex areas, including the V2 and MT. Area V2 has a set of reciprocal connections, on the one hand, with area V1 and, on the other hand, with higher order areas in the cortex, such as MT, DM, and DLc. The human brain is likely to exhibit a similar organization.

The functional organization of the striate cortex, or area V1, is characterized by ocular dominance and orientation columns (Malach et al., 1993). Another set of functional domains shows preference for different colors, for low spatial frequencies, and no preference for orientation. These are the cytochrome oxidase blobs, so called due to the high cytochrome oxidase activity in them (Malach, 1994; Malach et al., 1993; Tootell, Hamilton, & Silverman, 1985).

Area V1 transfers a major part of the ascending information to area V2, the next area in the hierarchy (Salin & Bullier, 1995). Three segregated processing streams have been identified within monkey area V2, each associated with a stripelike formation, seen when stained with cytochrome oxidase:

- Thick stripes—the motion and disparity stream.
- Thin stripes—the color stream.
- Pale stripes—the shape analysis stream.

Each receives distinct sets of connections from area V1, and projects to different targets (Levitt, Yoshioka, & Lund, 1994; Malach, Tootell, & Malonek, 1994). It has been suggested that area V2 contains multiple, interleaved visual maps, one for each color, orientation, and disparity domain (Roe & Ts'o, 1995).

Two Visual Processing Streams

Visual processing continues thereafter, following two large-scale cortical streams. Segregation into these streams begins in the retina itself, and then in magnocellular and parvocellular layers in the LGN. The separation of streams continues within the cortex, as one pathway stretches from the striate cortex toward the parietal lobe, and the other toward the temporal lobe. Area MT, located in the parietal lobe stream, responds to stimulus movement and direction of movement. Beyond area MT, the so-called where stream, are several areas involved in guiding eye movements. Area V4 has been the most studied in the temporal stream; it is sensitive to color and orientation, and significant for both shape and color perception. Beyond V4, the "what pathway," are areas with more complex functions, such as face recognition. These functions are important for both visual perception and visual memory. The anatomical and functional divisions of the two visual processing streams are discussed in detail in the following section.

Anatomical and physiological evidence indicate that the magnocellular (M) and parvocellular (P) pathways are segregated and largely independent throughout the visual system, originating in separate classes of A and B ganglion cells in the retina, projecting onward into either magnocellular or parvocellular layers within the LGN in the thalamus, and continuing to the dorsal and ventral pathways in the cortex.

Magnocellular and Parvocellular Layers in the LGN. The two visual processing systems have apparent differences, distinctively in distribution within the six layers of LGN in the thalamus. Two layers belong to the magnocellular (transient) system (Livingstone & Hubel, 1988), consisting of larger neurons responsible for timing perception and motion direction, and sensitive to contrast. Four layers belong to the parvocellular (sustained) system (Livingstone & Hubel, 1988), consisting of smaller neurons, which are sensitive to color. These cells are responsible for perception of finer pattern, shape, and texture features.

Psychophysical studies on channels of temporal-spatial visual processing point to several important differences between the two visual systems. The magnocellular, or M system, is characterized by rapid processing, high-contrast sensitivity, sensitivity to motion, and relatively low acuity. Research further indicates that the M system is insensitive to color, carries stereoscopic information, and may be responsible for spatial localization, depth perception, figure-ground separation, and hyperacuity. The parvocellular, or P system, with its sustained characteristic, appears primarily responsible for the perception of color, texture, fine stereopsis, and object recognition (see Table 7.1; Kalat, 1992; Livingstone, 1993; Livingstone & Hubel, 1988).

The M and P distinction continues along the visual pathway into the cortex; cortical processing streams play a leading role in current models on visual processing of form, color, motion, and depth information (Breitmeyer, 1993; Cavanagh, 1991; Livingstone, 1993; Livingstone & Hubel, 1987, 1988; Maunsell & Newsome, 1987; Tyler, 1990).

TABLE 7.1
A Comparison of the M System and the P System

Magnocellular (transient) System	Parvocellular (sustained) System
Maximum sensitivity to low-spatial frequencies	Maximum sensitivity to high-spatial frequencies
Maximum sensitivity to high-temporal frequencies (i.e., sensitivity to motion)	Maximum sensitivity to low-temporal frequencies (i.e., sensitivity to permanent stimuli)
Response to appearance or disappearance of stimuli	Response during stimuli presentation
Maximum influence on peripheral vision	Maximum influence on central vision
Short reaction time (i.e., persistence)	Long reaction time
Short response latency	Long response latency
Ability to inhibit the sustained response	Ability to inhibit the transient response

Dorsal and Ventral Pathways in the Cortex. The M and P systems project from the LGN to the primary visual cortex, area V1 of the occipital cortex. At this point, they branch into three streams. The P pathway divides into two separate processing streams, as cells from parvocellular layers project to both blobs and interblobs of V1. The third stream, sensitive to movement and broad outlines of shape, commences with projections of M cells to layer 4B in V1. The three streams remain distinct as they continue to V2 and higher visual-association areas.

Most of the blob cells, which also receive some input from M cells, are highly sensitive to color and in some cases to brightness. The blobs relay information to the thin stripes in V2, which project onward to the color-sensitive area, V4. Interblobs are sensitive to details of shape; respond to particular orientations, but not to direction of movement. They project to the pale stripes, or interstripes, in V2. The pale stripes, in turn, send out projections to the inferior temporal cortex, which processes form information (Kalat, 1992; Livingstone, 1993). The two pathways, of color processing and form processing, make up the ventral, or "what," cortical vision pathway.

The M stream is essentially the dorsal, or "where," cortical pathway. Cells in area V1 layer 4B, which receive input from magnocellular layers, are selective for orientation and direction of movement. They send information to the thick stripe areas in V2, which are sensitive to movement and stereoscopic depth perception. The thick stripes project to area V3, which is sensitive to shape, and to area V5 in the middle temporal cortex, which is sensitive to speed and direction of movement.

The dorsal M stream ends at the middle temporal cortex (MT area), located in the posterior temporal sulcus (STS). In humans, analogous areas lie near the posterior area, involved in processing of written material (Breitmeyer, 1993). As mentioned, MT is particularly responsive to motion, and its neurons are highly direction selective (Newsome & Wurtz, 1988). Area MT projects to the frontal eye fields and to the inferior parietal cortex via the middle superior temporal area (MST) (Seltzer & Pandya, 1989; Ungerleider & Desimone, 1986). Area MT, along with the areas receiving its projections, is involved in control of spatial attention and eye movements (Newsome & Wurtz, 1988). Additionally, research has shown that the retinal ganglion cells in the magnocellular system, which almost exclusively project to the three pathways, the retinotectal pathway, the geniculo-collicular pathway, and the major geniculo-striate pathway, primarily control eye movements. Connections also exist from the optic nerve to the superior colliculus (SC), which to some extent duplicate the functions of the LGN. The SC contributes to pattern perception in general (visual, auditory, and tactile), eye and head movements, and visuomotor coordination. For these reasons, the SC is also associated with the location-related, or "where," aspect of processing.

Conclusions. The two visual pathways already described, the magnocellular and the parvocellular systems, are crucial to visual perception in general, and to reading in particular. The two systems activate information in disparate manners and speeds; therefore, a successful reading process requires parallel activation of both visual pathways, which need to match in time and content (Lovegrove, 1993a). Processing speed, then, is particularly important to understanding the connection between visual processing and reading, both regular and impaired.

Speed of Processing in the Visual System

One implication of multiple divisions or stages of activation in the visual modality has been the necessary coordination in space and time. Various studies have focused on the speed of activation in various visual areas.

When single units were recorded in anesthetized macaques using flashing visual stimuli (Schmolesky et al., 1998), the earliest visual responses were in the magnocellular layers of the dorsal LGN (LGNd), with a very narrow latency spread, about 33 ± 3.8 ms ($M \pm SD$). Cells in the parvocellular layers of the LGNd exhibited longer, more varied latencies, ranging from 31 ms to 76 ms (50 $\pm$ 8.7 ms). The modal latencies of M and P cells did not overlap and were, in fact, removed 10 ms from one another (M cell 25–75 percentile = 31–34 ms; P cell 25–75 percentile = 44–56 ms).

The shortest latencies in the visual cortex, as short as 34 ms, were found in layer 4Cα of area V1, which receives magnocellular input. These were significantly shorter than in layer 4Cβ, where input is parvocellular. Thus, the latency difference between the M and P LGNd layers is maintained in the geniculo-recipient layers of V1. Overall, the latencies of V1 cells ranged from 34 ms to 97 ms (66 ± 10.7 ms).

Data indicates (Thorpe, Fize, & Marlot, 1996) that the ventral pathway is longer and exhibits more varied latencies. V2 cells had latencies with an average of 82 ms and a large variance (SD, 21.1 ms). Previous research had shown that V2 latencies increase from thick to pale to thin stripes. V4 cells had the longest and most varied latencies in this study (104 ± 23.4 ms).

The dorsal pathway is shorter and exhibits more uniform latencies. The latencies of V3 cells ranged from 55 ms to 101 ms (72 ± 8.6 ms). The average MT latencies were the same (72 ± 10.3 ms). However, Maunsell and Newsome (1987) reported much shorter latencies (39 ms on average), probably because of lack of anesthesia and use of different stimuli (high-contrast square wave gratings) in their experiment.

Current data is in agreement with data reported by Raiguel, Lagae, Gulyas, and Orban (1989). Cells in the medial superior temporal (MST) area exhibited latencies essentially equivalent to V3, averaging 74 ± 16.1 ms. Frontal eye field (FEF) cells showed an average of 75 ± 13.0 ms, in agreement with awake monkey data reported by Schall (1991) and K. G. Thompson, Hanes, Bichot, and Schall (1996). Based on response onset latency, the results suggest a functional sequence in the ventral stream; LGNd P layers, V1, V2, and V4 demonstrate successively longer latencies. In contrast, although the dorsal stream does show progressively longer latencies from LGNd M cells to V1, and to V2, a simultaneous onset of firing is displayed in V3, MT, MST, and FEF. Consequently, the M stream conducts faster than the P stream.

The rapid information transfer in the M stream is most likely contributed by the heavy myelination and relatively wide fiber diameter of axons projecting to dorsal stream areas (e.g., V1 to MT). Due to the rapid transfer of information throughout the dorsal stream, most cells in middle-tier cortical areas exhibit nearly complete overlap of latencies. Comparatively, onset firing in ventral stream cortical areas portrays a classical hierarchical progression, from V1 to V2 to V4. The onset latencies determined for several inferotemporal (IT) cells are in sequential progression. Not enough data is available from additional ventral stream areas to draw any strong conclusions. In many cases, short latencies in

higher tier areas can be accounted for only if multiple processing tiers are entirely bypassed during transfer of information from V1 (e.g., an anatomically
supported bypass route from V1 to MT to FEF). When evoked response potentials (ERPs) in humans were recorded using a go/no-go visual categorization
task (Thorpe et al., 1996), a specific "no-go" activity was displayed at 150 ms, in
frontal recording sites. This implies that a great deal of visual processing had
probably been completed prior to that time.

LOW-LEVEL VISUAL PROCESSES AND DYSLEXIA

The role visual processing deficits play in dyslexia remains unclear, and continues to stir controversy. Disagreement is particularly pronounced in respect to
the existence of low-level deficits, and whether these have direct affects on
reading. A number of researchers maintain that specific low-level visual-
perceptual dysfunctions have a significant role in the etiology of dyslexia (Hill
& Lovegrove, 1993; Goolkasain & King, 1990; Koenig, Kosslyn, & Wolff,
1991; Solman & May, 1990; Stein, 1991). Others, however, remain uncon-
vinced (Aaron, 1993; Calfee, 1983; Velluntino, 1987).

Whereas a clear-cut answer concerning the relation of early visual perception and reading ability has yet to be reached, a variety of hypotheses have been
proposed. These interpretations closely resemble those offered for the auditory
domain. One hypothesis states that early visual perceptual deficits may have a
direct causal role in the discrimination and analysis of visual features of letters
and words (Willows, Kruk, & Corcos, 1993). Another hypothesis renders such
deficits as a reflection of basic processing discrepancies between dyslexic and
regular readers, such as speed of information processing (Di Lollo, Hansen, &
McIntyre, 1983) or attentional processes (Willows et al., 1993). Yet another
theory proposes that both visual processing deficits and reading disorders are
symptoms of a common neurological disorder (Smith, Early, & Grogan, 1990).

Generally speaking, a variety of studies indicate visual processing distinc-
tions between regular and disabled readers; both linguistic and nonlinguistic
processes are implicated, as dyslexics exhibit letter reversals and spelling mistakes due to visual confusion, as well as serial and temporal processing problems
(Stein & Walsh, 1997). These studies have employed such a wide range of tasks
and subject groups that integrative conclusions about the nature of low-level visual deficits in dyslexia are hard to draw. In the following sections, evidence
from a variety of linguistic and nonlinguistic tasks is presented, in an attempt to
reveal the real relation between lower level visual processing and reading dis-

ability. Following this review is a presentation of a leading integrative theory, which associates dyslexia with deficits in the transient visual system.

Evidence of Lower Level Visual Deficits in Dyslexia

Discovery and Identification of a Single Stimulus. Discovery of a single stimulus requires judgment on its presence or absence, whereas identification refers to the complex evaluation of location, length, or identity of the stimulus. Many studies have revealed that dyslexics do not differ from regular readers on these tasks. Hayduk, Bruck, and Cavanaugh (1996) did not find differences in recognition of letters, exposed for 20–130 ms, between college students who read well and college students with poor reading abilities. Blackwell, McIntyre, and Murray (1983) reported that learning disabled children aged 8–13 performed similarly to regular readers when asked to locate and identify a single letter, presented for 150 ms. R. Klein, Berry, Briand, D'Entremont, & Farmer (1990) found that dyslexics aged 13–18 did not differ from regular readers in their ability to recognize a single letter presented for 17 ms. Thus, there is evidence that dyslexic readers, in varying ages, do not show difficulties in location or recognition of single visual stimuli, even when presented briefly.

Separation Between Two Stimuli. There are two types of tasks that require separation, and involve measures of "visual persistence" (i.e., the continued perception of a stimulus after it has been physically removed). In fusion tasks, the first type, subjects are presented with two identical stimuli at the same location, separated temporally by an alternating time interval. The subject has to indicate whether one stimulus or two stimuli were seen. The fastest rate at which two visual stimuli, presented in rapid succession, can be distinguished is known as the "flicker fusion rate" (Galaburda & Livingstone, 1993); it has been found abnormally slow at low spatial frequencies and low spatial contrasts, in about 75% of dyslexic children (Lovegrove, F. Martin, & Slaghuis, 1986; F. Martin & Lovegrove, 1987).

Di Lollo et al. (1983) used two vertical lines, appearing in succession at different time intervals, in order to examine the separation ability of dyslexic children and regular readers aged 8–14 years. The subjects were required to report when two vertical lines, each presented for 20 ms with a varying interval, appeared, and when only one line, presented for 40 ms, appeared. Dyslexics required a significantly longer interstimulus interval (ISI) than regular readers to perform the task with 75% accuracy (115 ms as opposed to 69 ms). In a similar task, O'Neill and Stanley (1976) found that dyslexic children aged 12 also required a longer ISI than regular children (45 ms as opposed to 30 ms) to reach a 75% accuracy level. Comparatively, Lovegrove et al. (1986) found that reading disabled children aged 8–12 consistently required longer ISIs than regular readers to separate grating lines that appeared at intervals of increasing length. Subjects were required to report when the permanent stimulus transformed into a flashing stimulus. The difference in minimal ISI, for a flashing stimulus, between dyslexic and regular subjects was exhibited only for stimuli with low spatial frequency.

The second type of task, which requires separation, involves temporal integration. In these tasks, the subject is presented with two different stimuli, which together comprise a complete stimulus. The stimuli are presented respectively at the same location, but are separated temporally. The minimal ISI, at which the subject perceives a complete stimulus, and not two separate parts, is measured.

Stanley and Hall (1973) presented subjects aged 8–12 with two arms of a cross, each presented for 20 ms, with an alternating interval between them. They found that dyslexics required longer intervals than regular readers in order to separate the two stimuli (140 ms as opposed to 102 ms). In addition, researchers found that to recognize stimuli, dyslexics required an interval of 327 ms, whereas regular readers required only 182 ms. In another study, Winters, Patterson, and Shontz (1989) reported that adult dyslexics aged 18–37 were less sensitive than regular readers to a temporal separation task that presented two sides of a square. At each stage of the experiment, two sides of a square were illuminated, each side for 3 ms. The sides were simultaneously illuminated in half of the stages, and an alternating interval was presented in the other half. In another set, opposite sides were illuminated in half of the stages, and adjacent sides in the other half. The researchers found that dyslexic subjects require a relatively longer interval than regular readers to perform the task with 75% accuracy. However, this difference only appeared when adjacent sides were illuminated, rather than opposite sides. These researchers interpreted this as evidence of a problem within the transient system, which operates in conditions of rapid motion.

In contrast to the studies described previously, Arnett and Di Lollo (1979) did not find performance differences, on a temporal integration task, between regular readers, aged 7–13, and readers with difficulties. The task utilized two matrices missing random points, which were presented at varying intervals. If the matrix points are illuminated in a rapid enough sequence, then the presentation appears simultaneous. However, as the illumination intervals between the first and last points increase, the first points seem to disappear and are confused with the missing points. The lack of differences in this study may be due to the fact that the poor readers were not reading disabled per se. They had a 1-year gap from their expected reading level, and that gap may have been insufficient to find qualitative differences between the groups.

Boden and Brodeur (1999) evaluated whether deficits in visual temporal processing were specific to written words or reflect a basic perceptual deficit; they used verbal and nonverbal stimuli. They examined reading disabled children aged 12–17 and controls matched for age and reading level. They used backward masking with ISIs of 45–270 ms between target and masker, and temporal integration with the same ISIs. All stimuli were presented for 30 ms. The researchers incorporated reaction time and accuracy into one efficiency score. Responses were more efficient in the nonverbal conditions, and participants' efficiency increased with ISI in all groups. Impairment was most evident in the complex conditions, and deficits in verbal processing were evident in both tasks, whereas deficits in nonverbal conditions were evident only in the temporal integration task. In addition, the efficiency of the reading-disabled group was affected most adversely by the complex nonverbal stimuli, supposedly because these stimuli were less familiar than the complex verbal stimuli, and required more time for visual processing.[1] Thus, it seems that both young and adult dyslexics find it difficult to separate two stimuli that require temporal resolution. This study provides support for the existence of a deficit in the visual processing of verbal material, and for the fact that adolescents with reading disabilities may experience difficulties with nonverbal material, as well.

Judgment of Correlation Between Stimuli.   In correlation tasks, subjects are required to judge whether two stimuli appearing in rapid succession are identical or different. Di Lollo et al. (1983) used this procedure with letter stimuli. The letters were presented for one msec, at alternating intervals, to regular and disabled readers, aged 8–14. Subjects were requested to press the appropriate key, based on whether the target stimulus was similar to or different from the first stimulus. The results showed that disabled readers required a longer interval (118 ms as opposed to 63 ms) from the beginning of the first stimulus to the appearance of the next stimulus (stimulus onset asynchrony) to perform the task with 75% accuracy.

Judgment of Temporal Order of Stimuli.   In this type of task, two different stimuli are presented, with a time interval between them. The subject must decide which of the two stimuli appeared first. In order to make a decision regard-

---

[1]The familiarity effect is documented in the literature (LaBerge & Samuels, 1977).

ing the temporal order of stimuli, the subject must first identify the single stimuli as single. In a study by M. A. Reed (1989), each stimulus appeared for 83 ms with an increasing ISI (50, 150, 300, and 400 ms). M. A. Reed (1989) did not find significant differences between regular and disabled readers aged 8–10. These results may be related to the selection of subjects; the reading disabled subjects were defined as such by their schools only.

Temporal order judgment may be done without the need to recognize single stimuli. This is done by presenting stimuli at different locations, and asking the subject to recognize the location where a stimulus first appeared. Brannan and Williams (1987) used three-letter words (FOX or BOX) or sequences of three symbols (& or #) as stimuli. Good and poor readers aged 8, 10, and 12 saw two stimuli at each stage, one to the right and one to the left of a fixation point. The first stimulus was presented for 900 ms, and the second stimulus with an alternating SOA (stimulus onset asynchrony, or length of stimuli presentation) of 40–160 ms). Subjects were requested to point to the screen side where the first stimulus appeared, and the minimal SOA at which the subject performed the task with 75% accuracy was measured. Significant differences were found between the two groups of readers at each age level, with the poor readers requiring longer intervals between stimuli to recognize their order. A significant difference was also found between age groups, with younger readers needing longer intervals to perform the task. Additionally, poor readers had difficulty in performing the task with both word and symbol sequences, whereas good readers experienced difficulty only with symbol sequences.

May, Williams, and Dunlap (1988) asked good and poor readers aged 8–10 to report which of two adjacent words appeared first, and which of two locations appeared first. Words appeared one above or alongside the other with an SOA of 30–90 ms. The results showed that poor readers required an SOA of about 83 ms to recognize the word that appeared first, as opposed to regular readers, who required only 45 ms. To recognize the first location, poor readers required 68 ms as compared to good readers, who required 52 ms. These were significant differences. It seems, therefore, that even when stimulus recognition is not necessary, reading disabled children have difficulty deciding on the appearance order of stimuli. It should be noted that the two latter studies pertained to reading disabled subjects chosen with a gap of at least 1 year between their chronological age and their reading age; this gap does not necessarily meet the dyslexia criteria.

In another study, Kinsborne et al. (1991) examined adult dyslexic and regular readers, who were asked to recognize the appearance order of flashes at different locations, with an alternating SOA beginning at 20 ms. They found significant differences between the two groups. According to one view, problems with judgments of temporal order are part of a general deficit of temporal processing in dyslexia. Indeed, results from research on lower level visual perceptual deficits converge to some extent with findings on lower level auditory perceptual deficits, indicating that temporal processing deficits of dyslexic readers are not confined to the auditory sphere (see chap. 8).

A central finding in recent literature is that dyslexics perform significantly worse than regular readers on tasks of rapid visual processing, as opposed to tests based on static displays. Measures assessing temporal resolution in the visual system include tests of visual persistence, flicker sensitivity, temporal order judgment, and metacontrast (Galaburda & Livingstone, 1993; Lovegrove et al., 1986; Lovegrove & Williams, 1993; Williams & LeCluyse, 1990). Dyslexics' difficulties on these tests apparently persist into adulthood (Hayduk, Bruck, & Cavanagh, 1993).

Some optometric problems, which are common to dyslexia, may be related to temporal processing deficits. These include poor binocular stability and localization, convergence insufficiency, and accommodative dysfunction (Eden, Stein, & Wood, 1993; Evans, Drasdo, & Richards, 1993; Newman, Wadsworth, Archer, & Hockley, 1985; Reddington & Cameron, 1991; Stein, Riddle, & Fowler, 1987). Many investigators maintain that these deficits are not present at the retinal level, but rather occur in later stages of information processing, in the visual cortex (Lovegrove et al., 1986; Rayner & Pollatsek, 1989).

Visual Masking. Among the visual masking paradigms, backward visual masking tasks are those frequently used, and provide a measure of the rate of information pickup in the initial stages of visual information processing (Rayner & Pollatsek, 1989). In backward masking tasks, the onset of one visual stimulus is immediately followed by the onset of another stimulus (the masker) displayed in close spatial proximity. Backward masking occurs when the perception of the first stimulus is impaired by the closely following stimulus. Typically, the subject must decide if the target and masker are the same or different at varying SOAs (stimulus onset asynchronies, or time intervals between the onset of the target and the masker).

Research has shown that on such tasks, disabled readers process visual information in a slower manner (i.e., their critical SOA is longer) than regular readers (Di Lollo et al., 1983; Mazer, McIntyre, Murray, Till, & Blackwell, 1983; Williams, LeCluyse, & Bologna, 1990). Williams et al. (1990), for instance, employed a masking of pattern paradigm to measure visual integration and persistence of regular and disabled readers. Disabled readers showed prolonged masking compared to regular readers, suggesting that visual processing among disabled readers is characterized by longer integration times or longer visual persistence.

Other investigators have employed metacontrast masking tests and have obtained similar results. In these tests, a target is briefly presented and then followed, at various delays, by a spatially adjacent masking stimulus. Accuracy in target detection is measured as a function of the delay between target and masker. Using this paradigm, data has revealed that visual processing in dyslexics is characterized by longer integration times and slower processing rates for both nonlinguistic and word-like stimuli (Williams & LeCluyse, 1990; Williams, Molinet, & LeCluyse, 1989).

Lower Level Visual Linguistic Patterns.   Farmer, R. Klein, and Bryson (1992) assessed dyslexic readers' ability to reproduce visual letter patterns relative to age-matched and reading-level matched controls. These researchers found that dyslexic children performed as well as age-matched controls when four simultaneous letters were presented, at various locations in a 4 × 4 matrix, for a short duration (200 ms). This was not the case when letters were presented in rapid sequence, either in the same or in different locations, at a rate of 100–400 ms per letter. Dyslexic readers could not reproduce the correct sequence of letters, or identify them as well as controls, when the patterns were presented rapidly. Dyslexic readers' performance was worst when required to recall both identity and location of the letters. An earlier study by Fisher and Frankfurter (1977) had similar findings with an identical simultaneous-presentation paradigm, in which four letters appeared for 200 ms.

In another type of study, Koenig, Kosslyn, and Wolff (1991) found that young adult dyslexic readers had greater difficulty than regular readers in generating mental images of multipart letter patterns, but not of novel shapes. In that study, subjects memorized simple line patterns inside a grid, and subsequently judged, on an empty grid, whether an "X" would have fallen on the given pattern. The results of the study suggested that dyslexics have difficulty integrating visual information, which is stored in long-term memory.

Other studies have reported that dyslexic readers perform poorly on tests, in which they must identify embedded letters (Bouma & Legein, 1977, 1980; Enns, Bryson, & Roes, 1995; Legein & Bouma, 1981; Mason, 1980). Mason (1980), for instance, found that poor readers were less accurate at identifying a letter in an array of nonletters, but only when the letter position was not precued. Enns et al. (1995) reported similar findings. These investigators found that dyslexic readers had difficulty reporting the location of a probe letter in an array, as compared to regular readers. This was true regardless of the temporal position of the array (i.e., before, at the same time, or after the probe letter.) They concluded that dyslexic readers have difficulty in segmenting arrays of letters into spatial-temporal sequences.

In a recent study carried out by Boden and Brodeur (1999), dyslexic readers identified letters more slowly than regular readers. These researchers found this phenomenon in processing of visual stimuli at various levels of complexity (e.g., geometric shapes, letters, and words). These findings suggest that speed of visual processing may be slower among dyslexic readers. Additionally, this lends support to the suggestion that speed factors, as represented in naming tasks, as well as phonological abilities, may be linked to problems in establishing memory representations of letter sequences in words or word parts (Wimmer, Mayringer, & Landerl, 1998).

The Transient Deficit

The source of some of the visual problems found in dyslexia, it has been suggested, is a transient system deficit (Evans et al., 1993). One current theory proposes that transient deficits may impede reading by inhibiting the processing and integration of both temporal information and pattern information across fixation-saccade sequences (Hill & Lovegrove, 1993; Willows et al., 1993). One outcome of such an impairment may be the superimposition of words from successive fixations, caused by partial temporal overlap of retinal sustained activity (Hill & Lovegrove, 1993). Another outcome may be deficient within fixation orthographic processing (i.e., processing of letter order and position) associated with disturbed spatial localization (Goolkasian & King, 1990; Koenig, Kosslyn, & Wolff, 1991; Solman & May, 1990; Stein, 1991).

Much of the evidence cited supports the idea of a transient visual system deficit in dyslexia, as described in the previous section. Particular emphasis has been placed on poor performance of dyslexics on tasks of separation, or visual persistence, and visual masking, both believed to rely on transient system functions. Additional support for the transient deficit hypothesis comes from findings on various abnormalities in ocular functioning in dyslexia, and on anatomical deficits in the M system, which are both described in the following sections.

Ocular Functioning and Dyslexia

Eye Movements.   Reading, like any visual scanning of the environment, requires processing and integration across fixation-saccade sequences (Hill & Lovegrove, 1993). Sustained activity, required for analysis of fine patterns and stationary stimuli, is more concentrated in the central or foveal field, whereas transient system components relay global information about overall shape and spatial location, and predominate peripheral vision (Breitmeyer, 1993).

During fixations and saccades, sustained and transient systems are activated, respectively. The two systems act in a mutually inhibitory manner. During fixations, detailed information about the word focused on the fovea is transmitted. Slowly decaying activity in the sustained channel, occurring during fixations, is suppressed by transient activity, which is generated by abrupt and rapid image displacements accompanying the saccades. When the eye's focus shifts, new information is fixated, and the sustained response terminates the transient response. In this manner, information from prior fixations cannot persist across the saccade interval into successive saccades. These system interactions result in a series of temporally segregated frames of sustained activity, which correspond to the information obtained in a given fixation (Breitmeyer, 1993).

Efficient visual processing during reading requires a properly functioning sustained pathway for processing patterns during fixations, and a properly functioning transient pathway, which provides saccadic suppression. Theoretically, abnormalities in either pathway would impair reading. For instance, superimposition of words from successive fixations may occur if sustained messages from a previous fixation are not suppressed by the transient system. It has been suggested that the blurring of text, reported by many dyslexic readers, may be the result of superimposition, which causes a type of retinal image "smear" (Breitmeyer, 1993; Hill & Lovegrove, 1993). It has also been hypothesized that impairment of visual direction constancy, as well as visual instability, are results of impaired transient activity (Stein, 1991, 1993).

Stein (1993) hypothesized that slight defects in transient system operation may lead to the unsteady fixations exhibited by many dyslexics. Stein maintained that the M system controls eye movement because it provides the motion signals essential for its guidance. In addition, the M system is responsible for processing binocular disparity signals; hence, when the integrity of the M system is compromised, unstable visual perception, poor visual direction sense, and visual confusion may result.

Considerable research has shown that dyslexics have different eye movement patterns when decoding text, compared to regular readers. In contrast to the eye movements of regular or retarded readers, eye movements of dyslexics are erratic, exhibit unusual patterns, and show variability of duration; these movements are not altered with age. Dyslexics display more fixations, longer average fixation durations, frequent regressions and mislocations, shorter saccades, and an increased number of reversed saccades (Olson, Conners, & Rack, 1991; Pavlidis, 1985; Rayner & Pollatsek, 1989).

Although abnormal eye movements of dyslexic readers during reading have been well documented, there has been strong disagreement concerning the nature of this relation. Some researchers contend that abnormal eye movements merely reflect the difficulty dyslexics have in decoding the meaning of text (Rayner, 1978), and others have obtained evidence against this hypothesis (Pavlidis, 1985). Research carried out using nonreading tasks further supports the argument that abnormal eye movements may characterize dyslexics, even outside of reading. In a recent study carried out by Fischer, Biscaldi, and Otto (1993), eye movements of adult dyslexics were tracked during a noncognitive visual task of serially presented squares. Results indicated poorer target fixation, smaller amplitudes, more forward saccades, and shorter fixations among these readers.

The previous study involved serial processing, which may be a critical feature affecting ocular functioning. Repeated documentation has indicated the existence of serial processing deficits among dyslexic readers, across sensory modalities and experimental procedures. Experimental studies indicate that dyslexic children differ from regular readers in temporal resolution and serial-order perception of both linguistic and linguistically neutral auditory and visual events (Dodgen & Pavlidis, 1990; Lovegrove, Garzia, & Nicholson, 1990; Livingstone et al., 1991; Tallal, Stark, & Mellits, 1985; Wolff, 1993). Conceivably, difficulties with serial processing may underlie both dyslexia-related phenomena and abnormal eye movements.

Two variables have particular significance, according to the literature, in assessing dyslexics' sequential processing deficits: the rapidity of stimuli presentation and the variability in presentation rate. Hence, the link between aberrant eye movements and dyslexia may be a specific difficulty with rapid, variable temporal processing (Dodgen & Pavlidis, 1990). Other researchers have proposed alternative third factors, which may account for both aberrant eye movement patterns and dyslexia. Olson et al. (1991), for instance, suggested that both phenomena result from impaired selective attention of the visual modality, in the parietal cortex. At present, both hypotheses remain within the realm of speculation, and a connection between the two is conceivable.

Visual-Spatial Attention. Facoetti, Paganoni, Turatto, Marzola, and Macetti (2000) investigated two aspects of visual attention, orientation and focus, in dyslexic children using various cues and SOAs. Their main findings revealed that dyslexics were generally slower than regular children, and were unable to automatically shift attention in response to peripheral visual cues. Dyslexics were capable of using information provided to the fovea, but only at longer stimulus onset asynchrony (SOA). It seems reasonable that this automatic-orienting deficit hampers the planning of ocular movements (saccades), which are crucial for correct and rapid decoding, in children with dyslexia (Rayner & Morris, 1991).

Facoetti et al. (2000) also revealed that dyslexics show limited control over their focus of attention over time, a finding also reported by Sharma, Halperin, Newcorn, and Wolf (1991) and Williams and Bologna (1985).

Dyslexics' limited focusing time may be related to difficulties in suppressing information that flanks an observed word, during reading (Geiger, Lettvin, & Fahle, 1994; Rayner & Pollatsek, 1989), as suggested by the transient deficit hypothesis. It should be noted, however, that some studies do not support such an explanation. For example, Hayduk et al. (1996) examined the existence of a deficient transient system among dyslexics. Twenty adult dyslexics were asked to report on the appearance or lack of appearance of a grating under static conditions with high spatial frequency or under transient conditions with high temporal frequency and low spatial frequency. No discrepancies were found between dyslexics and regular readers in this study.

Peripheral Vision. Several investigators have found evidence of dissimilarities in peripheral vision between regular and dyslexic readers, and have suggested that the differences are related to deficient transient processing.

In one study, Geiger and Lettvin (1987) examined simultaneous lateral masking among dyslexic and regular readers, and found that dyslexics showed a smaller magnitude of lateral masking in the peripheral field. These investigators hypothesized that dyslexic individuals may learn to read outside the foveal field, as a result of their visual processing characteristics.

Compatible with this finding are the results of studies by Williams et al. (1989, 1990). The first was a metacontrast study that compared foveal and peripheral visual processing in regular and dyslexic readers. Evidence obtained supported a slower rate of foveal visual processing in disabled readers. In contrast, their peripheral vision appeared better than that of regular readers, as shown by an absence of metacontrast masking in peripheral presentations for disabled readers. In the latter study, similar results were obtained; dyslexics exhibited enhancement effects (i.e., the masker made the target easier to see) when stimuli were presented to the peripheral retina. These results suggest that peripheral visual processing is characterized by disinhibition of sustained pattern information, perhaps due to reduced inhibitory effects of transient channels.

A more recent study by Geiger, Lettvin, and Zegarra-Moran (1992) further supports the previous results. In this study, evidence indicated that unlike regular readers, adults with severe dyslexia, native speakers of either Hebrew or English, had better recognition of letters further into the peripheral visual field, in the direction of reading (toward the right for English and toward the left for Hebrew.) When letters were presented in aggregates, dyslexics showed marked lateral masking in and near the center of the visual field. These results support the earlier suggestion by Geiger and Lettvin (1987) that dyslexic individuals may learn to read outside the foveal field. Geiger et al. (1992) were able to demonstrate that training in peripheral reading greatly improved dyslexics' reading performance. However, these reading techniques proved difficult to maintain; the newly acquired skill quickly regressed when subjects stopped practicing the technique.

It should be noted that a later study replicated the experimental paradigm used by Geiger et al. (1992), but failed to confirm their findings; the study merely found that dyslexics had longer reaction times for single and embedded letters, in a wide array of spatial positions (Bjaalid et al., 1993).

Vergence Control. Stein and colleagues (Eden et al., 1993; Stein, 1989, 1993; Stein & Fowler, 1985) demonstrated that many dyslexic children experience difficulties with localizing small targets, such as letters, and often complain that letters seem to blur or move around during reading. Stein showed that these symptoms are frequently associated with impaired vergence control, unstable binocular fixation, and inadequate visual direction sense. According to Stein, vergence control allows readers to stably fixate letters and therefore locate them reliably. If this ability is impaired, then letters will seem to move. Stein hypothesized that unstable vergence control, particularly poor fixation, may be caused by abnormal transient system development. He maintained that the output of the magnocellular, transient processing system plays an important role in the control of eye movements.

Anatomical Deficits in the Magnocellular System Among Dyslexics

Jenner, Rosen, and Galaburda (1999) obtained evidence that M layers in the LGN of dyslexics are anatomically less organized, contain magno cells that are about 27% smaller, and are more varied than in nondyslexic brains. Conversely, P layers do not differ; Parvo cells are similar in both dyslexic and regular readers (Livingstone et al., 1991). Galaburda and Livingstone (1993) suggested that because magnocellular geniculate neurons in dyslexics are smaller than parvocellular neurons, they expectedly have thinner axons with slower conduction velocities. However, this observation alone cannot explain the delays, early

VEP or late ERP, found in their study. A 30% decrease in magnocellular axon diameter would result in only a 1-ms delay in geniculo-cortical conduction time, and even a two- or threefold decrease would result in a delay of only a few milliseconds. This provides additional support for the notion that the magnocellular system is affected in dyslexia at many levels, resulting in cumulative processing abnormalities.

VISUAL-ORTHOGRAPHIC PROCESSING AND DYSLEXIA

Orthographic processing is the ability to recognize visually presented words in a rapid, holistic manner, without relying on their phonology. The identification of a written word is accomplished using structural patterns, consisting of letter shapes and their unique order. When learning to read, children must retain a visual image of the letters of the alphabet, and then process a sequence of these letters over a series of rapid eye fixations (Boden & Brodeur, 1999; Rayner & Pollatsek, 1989). Orthography is essential to word recognition mostly in advanced stages of reading acquisition, when the reading process is faster and relies on recognition of complete words without phonological decoding (Ehri, 1991). Research indicates a positive connection between difficulties in word recognition and difficulties with orthographic processes (Bowers et al., 1994, Reitsma, 1989). Orthographic recognition is a process in which perceived items, represented as a group of features, are compared to a stored representation in memory (Bartha, R. C. Martin, & Jensen, 1998).

A number of studies indicate deficits in the visual-orthographic processing system among dyslexics. These deficits are expressed in accuracy and slow reaction time on tasks that examine orthographic skills. Several researchers have speculated that the orthographic deficits found among dyslexic readers may be related to difficulties in automatic induction of orthographic patterns. That is, these readers may have difficulty establishing unitized orthographic codes (Bowers, 1993; Bowers & Wolf, 1993; Reitsma, 1989; Stanovich, 1988) and consequently do not acquire automatic word recognition skills (Bowers et al., 1994). Relevant research has shown that poor readers differ from good readers in their ability to unitize words. This ability enables readers to retrieve a word, upon seeing a complex letter string, as quickly as if identifying a single unit or letter (Bowers & Wolf, 1993). Poor readers, it appears, require more exposure to an unfamiliar word in order to recognize it by its visual, orthographic pattern (Bowers et al., 1994; Ehri & Wilce, 1983; Manis, 1985; Reitsma, 1983, 1989).

It has been speculated that dyslexics' problems with orthographic representations involve basic difficulties with speed of recognition (Bowers et al., 1994). Research showing that dyslexic children do not differ from normal readers in accuracy, on tasks of lexical decision or homonym verification, support this view (see Rack et al., 1992, for a review). However, these tasks focus on whole word orthographic codes, and may not directly tap letter-cluster knowledge. Hence, tests that require judgments on "word-likeness" of nonwords, differing in orthographic structures of letter clusters, may be more discriminative (Bowers & Wolf, 1993). Support for this contention is obtained by showing that knowledge of subword orthographic patterns (i.e., letter clusters) is associated with reading skills. Berninger (1987) and Berninger, Yates, and Lester (1991) found that the ability to detect the presence or absence of a letter cluster in a given word was a good predictor of reading proficiency.

Other research has shown that dyslexics do not read by orthographic analogy. Studies by Lovett, Warren-Chaplin, Ransby, and Borden (1990) and Lemoine, Levy, and Hutchinson (1993) demonstrated that even after extensive practice and study of word patterns in certain words, dyslexic children did not transfer knowledge of orthographic subword patterns to new words with identical orthographic structure. Zecker (1991) found that dyslexics were slower than regular readers in their ability to use orthographic knowledge to decide whether two words were orthographically different or similar, rhymed or not rhymed. Regular readers responded more quickly when an orthographic similarity existed, and dyslexics did not. Manis et al. (1988) examined the different factors of dyslexia. They concluded that processing time measures characterized dyslexics with orthographic difficulties better than processing accuracy. These researchers noted that dyslexics are slow at retrieving orthographic information from memory, but overcome this obstacle when the task has no time restrictions.

Bjaalid et al. (1993) examined the differences between dyslexic and nondyslexic high school students on an orthographic lexical decision task. The subjects, who were shown a sequence of letters on a computer screen, had to discern whether or not the letter sequence was a word. The average response time among the dyslexics was 1.47 s per word, as opposed to .38 s per word among the regular readers.

According to Wolf, Vellutino, and Gleason (1998), global word shapes are extracted within 60 ms to 80 ms. In a word recognition task, words were presented for 60 ms to allow sole use of orthographic knowledge for recognition.

Adult dyslexics recognized merely 14 out of 52 words, compared with the control group, which recognized 34.3 words on average. In addition, on a lexical decision task, dyslexics had an average reaction time of 1, 161 ms, as compared to 690 ms in the control group (Leinonen, Leppänen, Aro, Ahonen, & Lyytinen, 2001). These studies show that dyslexics have problems in using orthographic knowledge, and their attempts to access this knowledge take longer. Dyslexics' apparent inability to effectively utilize rapid orthographic-lexical processes to recognize words is manifested in slow text reading speed (Leinonen et al., 2001).

CONCLUSIONS

This chapter described the manner in which the visual system processes information. The visual system in the brain has a long pathway with a high number of different activation stages. The reading activity begins with the activation of this system by the written symbol stimulus, which must successfully pass through the different stages of the system. Moreover, in order to accommodate the cognitive limitations imposed on information processing, the stimulus must pass through the visual route with high quality and at a fast rate. If ineffective quality or rate of processing occurs at any stage, then the quality of reading will be affected. Moreover, effective visual perception in reading requires a high degree of synchronization in terms of speed and location of the incoming information between the different stages along the visual pathway. The reading impairments of dyslexic readers may reflect a less than optimal synchronization, which may slow down the speed of information processing along this pathway. Chapters 9, 10, and 11 focus at length on this issue.

8

Auditory-Phonological Processing: Regular and Dyslexic

During the reading process, written symbols perceived and processed by the visual system must eventually be translated by the brain into sounds representing language. Thus, the auditory system, which is responsible for receiving, filtering, and storing sounds, becomes a likely contributor to both normal and abnormal reading processes and constitutes a significant factor in the study of these processes. Similar to the visual system, discussed in the previous chapter, the auditory system is a complex, sequential, hierarchical pathway involving many subsystems and processing stages and requiring integration at astounding levels of precision. Here, too, there are many "way stations" through which information must necessarily pass, each characterized by its own processing formats and speeds. Unlike the visual system, however, we have very little information concerning the unique functions and specific subsystems of the pathway leading from the ears to the high auditory association areas of the brain. Although research continues in the field, we are still far from understanding the auditory system as a whole.

Still, a fair amount of research has been carried out relating the auditory system to the reading process, particularly in terms of the possible contribution of auditory deficits to dyslexia and other reading problems. This chapter reviews evidence that has been collected regarding the course of auditory processing and the divisions within it. This review serves as a basis for a discussion of the theoretical and empirical support for the contribution of an auditory system deficit to abnormal fluency in reading.

THE STRUCTURE OF THE AUDITORY MODALITY

When auditory information, or sound, is presented in the external environment, the involvement of the auditory system begins with perception of that information by the ears, whose role it is to enhance sound waves from the environment and relay them to auditory receptors. These receptors mark the beginning of the auditory nerve pathway (cranial nerve VIII), which continues on to the cochlear nuclei of the medulla, and then branches out into a number of ascending routes that meet again at the inferior colliculus. From the inferior colliculus, axons reach a number of destinations, among them the medial geniculate nucleus of the thalamus and subsequently the auditory cortex. Whereas there is significantly less information about auditory pathways leading to the cortex than there is about their visual counterparts, there is some evidence that the auditory system also involves processing along separate dorsal and ventral streams.

In most cerebral locations in which sound is processed along the auditory pathway, neurons are organized according to a tonotopic scheme, meaning that each has a characteristic frequency to which it reacts optimally, and they are all set in the neural tissue in a manner that reflects a gradual increase in the frequencies to which the system responds. Thus, in the auditory nerve, the manner of pulse transfer is such that pure tones at low amplitudes arouse specific single fibers, and nonpure tones arouse a number of nerve cells with each one causing arousal according to its characteristic frequency (Schmidt, 1985). As the level of a neuron in the auditory pathway increases, a more complex sound pattern is required to arouse it (Schmidt, 1985). Some respond to a wider frequency range, according to specific characteristics, such as a specific amplitude or frequency change. Other cells only respond to the beginning of a sound stimulus or to its end. Some neurons, even at lower levels (in the cochlear nucleus), are delayed by auditory input.

From the Ears to the Cortex

Auditory receptor cells, known as hair cells, start in the inner ear or cochlea. Based on the vibration patterns, these cells transmit to a collection of neurons known as the spiral ganglion, whose axons form the auditory nerve. Spiral ganglion neurons send output to one of two nuclei in the medulla, the dorsal and ventral cochlear nuclei, with each nucleus receiving input from the cochlea of the ipsilateral ear. The multiple pathways beginning at the dorsal and ventral cochlear nuclei result in more complex and less understood auditory routes.

One pathway begins in the ventral cochlear nucleus and goes on to the superior olives, found on either side of the brain stem. At this stage, the axons branch out and send information to the superior olives on both sides of the brain, such that from this point on auditory nuclei receive bilateral input. From the superior olive, tracts ascend along the lateral lemniscus, which leads to the inferior colliculus of the midbrain. Many afferent neurons of the dorsal cochlear nucleus follow a similar route, bypassing the superior olive. Although there are others, all ascending auditory pathways converge at the inferior colliculus.

Neurons in the inferior colliculus send out axons to the medial geniculate nucleus (MGN) of the thalamus, which in turn helps synchronize and coordinate auditory information to and from the auditory cortex. The MGN is also involved in the extensive feedback system between the auditory cortex and the other areas in the brain. Other routes from the inferior colliculus include projections to the superior colliculus, where the integration of auditory and visual information occurs, and to the cerebellum.

Auditory Cortex

The primate auditory cortex is subdivided into three areas (i.e., the core, belt, and parabelt) on the basis of their cochleotopic organization, connectional relationships, and architectonic features. Connections between the parabelt, heteromodal, and supramodal regions of the temporal, frontal, and parietal cortices form a distributed network for auditory cognition.

The main processing stream begins in the central nucleus of the inferior colliculus (ICc), goes on to the ventral nucleus of the medial geniculate complex (MGv) of the thalamus, and then reaches the auditory cortex. This is known as the "MGv ➔ core ➔ belt ➔ parabelt" pathway. A parallel stream involves the dorsal (ICd) and pericentral (ICp) divisions of the inferior colliculus, the dorsal (MGd) and medial (MGm) divisions of the medial geniculate complex, and the belt complex. A possible third stream consists of superior colliculus (SC) projections to parts of the medial pulvinar (PM), suprageniculate (Sg), and limitans (Lim) nuclei of the thalamus, which project further to the parabelt cortex. From there on, processing converges in the superior temporal gyrus (STG), superior temporal sulcus (STS), and prefrontal cortex.

The Core Region.   The core region exhibits features of primary sensory cortex, and contains three cochleotopically organized fields, all of which receive dense input from the ventral division of the medial geniculate complex (MGv):

- AI—the largest, most caudal field
- RT—the smallest, most rostral field
- R—intermediate in size and position

It is suggested that auditory information is processed serially from the MGv to the core and in parallel within the three core fields. The core probably has a function in sound detection. AI neurons exhibit better temporal resolution than neurons in surrounding areas.

The Belt Region.   The belt region surrounds the core, and can be thought of as a secondary auditory cortex. It receives most of its afferent input from the core area and the dorsal (MGd) and medial (MGm) divisions of the medial geniculate complex, with a minor contribution from MGv. Seven or eight fields are defined, named according to their relative position along the superior surface of the STG:

- The anterolateral (AL), caudolateral (CL), caudomedial (CM), and middle lateral (ML) fields are cochleotopically organized.
- The rest, including the lateral rostrotemporal (RTL), medial rostrotemporal (RTM), and rostromedial (RM) fields, are not.

Lateral belt neurons are more sensitive to species-specific vocalizations than to pure tones.

The Parabelt Region.   The parabelt region lies adjacent to the lateral belt fields along the lateral surface of the STG, and has strong connections with the belt and minor connections with the core. Two parts have been identified:

- Rostral part of the parabelt (RP or RPB)—receives input from the rostral belt. Neurons are sensitive to white noise but not to pure tones.
- Caudal (CP or CPB)—receives input from the caudal belt. Neurons respond to sounds in the contralateral space, pure tones, motion, and direction. Some cells are heteromodal, visual, or somesthetic.

In parallel, the parabelt also processes direct thalamic input from MGd and MGm, along with strong input from the medial pulvinar, suprageniculate, and limitans nuclei.

Auditory Processing Beyond the Auditory Cortex. Auditory processing extends to specific regions of the adjacent temporal cortex, medial temporal cortex, prefrontal, and parietal cortex. Many cells in these regions are heteromodal and participate in cognitive aspects of auditory processing.

The parabelt has connections with nearby parts of the temporal lobe, including RPB connections with the rostral parts of the superior temporal gyrus (STGr). This is still considered within the third level of processing.

The Fourth Level: Prefrontal Regions. RPB and CPB have overlapping reciprocal connections with the dorsal prearcuate cortex, which is also called area 8A or the frontal eye field (FEF), whereas STGr does not have such connections. RPB and CPB also have connections with the dorsal bank of the principal sulcus cortex (RPB, largely to the rostral region, and CPB, to the caudal part). It has been shown that the caudal principal sulcus region receives topographic sensory inputs from the auditory, somatosensory, visual, and polysensory cortex, whereas the rostral principal sulcus is the major target of projections from auditory and limbic cortices. RPB and STDr have connections with the orbitofrontal cortex, but CPB does not.

Auditory-related prefrontal regions, specifically the auditory-related principal sulcus regions and arcuate sulcus, are interconnected. It has been shown that the dorsal principal sulcus and dorsal prearcuate cortex are interconnected, each showing substantial connections with the premotor cortex, but restricted connections with the ventral prefrontal and orbital cortex. Input to FEF from the principal sulcus may mediate regulatory control over gaze.

In the prearcuate region, neurons are more sensitive to auditory stimuli during auditory localization tasks, and electrical stimulation of this cortex produces large saccadic eye movements into the contralateral visual hemifield. It has been proposed that auditory input to the prearcuate cortex is important for directing attention and gaze toward peripheral auditory stimuli. The adjacent principal sulcus region is considered essential for spatial and nonspatial tasks based on delayed responses, which require short-term or working memory.

Ablation studies suggest that the ventrolateral prefrontal cortex subserves working memory for nonspatial tasks, such as stimulus recognition, whereas inferior orbitofrontal cortex is associated with the reward system, and the emotive and motivational aspects of behavior. This processing is also contributed to by auditory input. More than one half of the neurons in the orbitofrontal cortex are bimodal, and show auditory-visual interactions (inhibition).

Dorsal and Ventral Auditory Pathways

In the belt region, the anterolateral area (AL) connects to more rostral and ventral regions in the temporal lobe, whereas the caudolateral area (CL) makes more caudal and dorsal connections (Romanski et al., 1999). Thus begin the ventral and dorsal streams of the auditory cortex. AL sends further projections to distinct frontal regions, including the frontal pole (BA10), rostral principal sulcus (BA46), and ventral prefrontal regions (BA12 and 45), areas that are implicated in nonspatial functions. CL, on the other hand, projects to the caudal principal sulcus (BA46) and FEF (area 8A). These areas are implicated in spatial processing.

Corresponding projections occur in the parabelt. RPB and STGr receive input from AL and then send major input to the same frontal regions as AL itself. CPB and STGc follow a similar pattern, receiving projections from CL and sending major input to the frontal regions to which it projects. Thus, processing in the auditory cortex is not strictly serial. There may be a third stream, originating from the middle belt area ML, which has frontal connections overlapping with those of AL and CL, and may have an intermediate function.

Conclusions

It is evident that in addition to the external auditory signal in spoken language, the internal auditory signal, which must be matched to the visual signal from printed material in written language, must also pass through many subsystems along the auditory pathway. Clearly, each is characterized by a different manner of activation, possibly dictating a different speed of processing (SOP) at each substage. It is plausible that correct matching between the visual and auditory-acoustic aspects of the alphabetic code can be seen as a result not only of the manner but also of the SOP of activation of these various subsystems. Among other things, reading impairments can be seen as resulting from slow SOP within one or more of these subsystems, or from the speed at which information is transferred between the different subsystems of the auditory-acoustic modality. When considering the contribution of the auditory system to reading and reading impairment, it is useful to separate the lower level perceptual processes discussed previously from higher, linguistic level phonological processes involving meaningful speech. Different theories regarding auditory system deficits in dyslexia have implicated each of these levels of processing. The next section considers the possibility of an auditory perceptual deficit in dyslexia. Later in the chapter, auditory linguistic processes and their role in reading impairment are discussed.

LOWER LEVEL AUDITORY DEFICITS

Auditory perception is the immediate interpretation of sound stimulation. It involves recognition of a sound pattern as the same or different from patterns previously discriminated and stored (Robeck & Wallace, 1990). Those in close contact with people suffering from deep dyslexia often claim that they report difficulties with different aspects of sensory perception. For instance, with respect to the sense of sight, many dyslexics feel that letters "float" on the page and switch around, and they have difficulty distinguishing between form and background. With respect to the auditory channel, dyslexics tend to switch sounds, experience difficulty locating where sounds comes from, have increased difficulty locating sounds due to distracting noises, and find it hard to concentrate at all noise levels (Richardson & Stein, 1993).

At the level of auditory perception, a division can be made based on the quality of the perceived stimuli, namely, if they are purely nonverbal or phonologically meaningful (i.e., speech sounds). Research has revealed that dyslexics differ from normal readers on perceptual tasks using both linguistically neutral and verbally meaningful auditory and visual stimuli (Livingstone et al., 1991; Lovegrove et al., 1990; Tallal et al., 1985).

Today, the prevailing hypothesis implicating lower level deficits in dyslexia proposes problems in the processing of temporal information. This hypothesis is described, followed by a review of the evidence in support of a lower level auditory perceptual deficit in general, and more specifically in relation to temporal processing.

The Temporal Deficit Hypothesis

Much of the current research on the topic of lower level deficits in dyslexia has centered around the hypothesis that dyslexics' perceptual deficits result from problems in the processing of temporal information. The most convincing evidence in support of this contention has come from the work of Tallal (Tallal, 1980; Tallal et al., 1993; Tallal & Stark, 1982), who argued that children with developmental dyslexia may, like language disabled children, suffer from fundamental disturbances in sound perception. The basic tenet of Tallal's theory is that dyslexic (as well as speech disordered) children have difficulty integrating sensory information that converges in rapid succession (within milliseconds) in the central nervous system (Tallal et al., 1993). This deficit appears to influence multiple modalities, and affects motor output within the millisecond time frame.

Although much of her work has been on language impaired children, Tallal viewed reading disability as being on a continuum of language disability that includes widely hetrogeneous groups. Hence, many of her conclusions regarding the language impaired are held to be applicable to the reading disabled. Supporting this view are converging experimental data obtained from language impaired and reading impaired children indicating considerable overlap in the performance profiles of the two groups (Elliot, Hammer, Scholl, & Carrell, 1989; Tallal et al., 1988; Tallal et al., 1993; Tomblin, Freese, & Records, 1992). In the auditory domain, Tallal and colleagues suggested that "a primary temporal processing deficit may result in a form of auditory deprivation that, in turn, alters neuronal mapping and connections across the auditory system with cascading effects on other higher level auditory processes" (Tallal et al., 1993, p. 30). One critical effect is disruption of the phonological processing system, which eventually leads to impairment in speech and/or reading.

The temporal deficit hypothesis has drawn the attention of many researchers and is considered today to be one of the leading hypotheses regarding the source of dyslexia and other learning disabilities. Some researchers claim that a temporal processing deficit among dyslexics exists in all modalities and not only the auditory system. For instance, Farmer and R. Klein (1995) and Merzenich, Schreiner, Jenkins, and Wang (1993) suggested that dyslexics suffer from an overall difficulty with sensory temporal processing.

Hypotheses regarding abnormal temporal processing are difficult to test, because it is hard to empirically distinguish between perceptual and linguistic-cognitive deficits. Still, evidence has accumulated revealing differences between reading impaired and normal readers on temporal processing tasks. This evidence, discussed in the sections that follow, has led to the proposal of various hypotheses regarding the source and development of these temporal processing deficits.

Explaining the Temporal Deficit Hypothesis.   Merzenich et al. (1993) discussed temporal processing in terms of the neural mechanisms underlying temporal integration, segmentation, and input sequence representation, and cited findings according to which temporal-perceptual integration times in the dyslexic population are significantly longer relative to normal readers (Lovegrove, 1993a; Lovegrove et al., 1990; Shapiro, Ogden, & Lind-Blad, 1990; Tallal & Piercy, 1979; Williams & LeCluyse, 1990). In an attempt to understand the source of speech and language deficits characterized by longer than normal temporal integration and segmentation, dyslexia included, Merzenich et al. (1993) suggested two hypotheses. According to the first, temporal processing deficits are learned or acquired, and stem from a sensory processing strategy acquired at birth. When this is the case, Merzenich et al. (1993) claimed that these deficits are most probably correctable as the brain is adaptable to large representation changes even in adulthood and certainly in childhood. However, it is probable that the correction process is long and slow.

According to the second hypothesis raised by Merzenich et al. (1993), there is a physical impairment in the "learning mechanism" among dyslexics, which is manifested globally or locally. This hypothesis makes reference to their claim that temporal integration times at the neuronal level are shortened with development and practice. Many elements participate in this process, and impairment in any one of them may cause the learning process to slow down, prolonging temporal integration. It is possible that there is an impairment focusing on one of these elements, as suggested by focused difficulties characteristic of dyslexics. However, another possibility is that the impairment is general and if so, it will only be expressed in one modality, which will "drag" the others along with it (Merzenich et al., 1993).

Llinas (1993) suggested a hypothesis similar to that of Merzenich et al. (1993), according to which a special inner "clock" exists that controls neural firing rate, and that among language disabled and dyslexic children this "clock" is impaired. He reported that "clock" fluctuations might run at 40 Hz (in other words, one cycle every 25 ms). One hypothesis raised regarding these fluctuations is that they are an essential component involved in entering sensory information into cortico-thalamo-cortical networks. According to Llinas (1993), slow fluctuations and decreased neural firing rate cause a problem with rapidly presented sequential sensory or motor information processing within a range of several milliseconds—exactly the difficulty displayed by language and reading disabled children.

Another hypothesis regarding the nature of the temporal problem among dyslexics is that of Galaburda and Livingston (1993), which is based on neuroanatomic and physiological studies among adult dyslexics. They reported structural and functional differences between dyslexics and normal readers in the magnocellular and thalamo-cortical systems and, in contrast, in the accurateness of the parvocellular system in the visual and auditory modalities (in the medial geniculate nucleus).

In sum, it can be argued that regardless of the source of the temporal impairment among dyslexics, reading, as a temporal activity based on the time and capacity limitations of the information-processing mechanism, is affected by time constraints. Specifically, lengthened temporal processing across reading segments and/or long time gaps between the various segments within a reading task might affect the quality of the process and impair reading effectiveness.

Evidence of Lower Level Auditory Deficits in Dyslexia

Evidence supporting the idea that dyslexics differ from normal readers in auditory perceptual processes that do not involve actual meaningful speech is divided into research on nonverbal stimuli and stimuli composed of phonemic units, or speech sounds. Most, although not all, of this research has been aimed at exploring the temporal processing deficit hypothesis, particularly in studies employing nonverbal stimuli.

Nonverbal Auditory Processing. Whereas the theory that dyslexics may suffer linguistic auditory perceptual difficulties has gained greater acceptance in recent years, the question of whether or not nonlingusitic auditory perception affects reading ability has generated considerable controversy. Some investigators have found evidence of an association between nonverbal processing and reading ability (McCroskey & Kidder, 1980; Nicolson & Fawcett, 1993b), but others have failed to find such an association (B. U. Watson & C. S. Watson, 1993). Research carried out using nonspeech acoustic stimuli is limited, yet the answer to this question is necessary if we are to determine whether dyslexics' difficulties are due to primarily auditory or to more strictly phonetic factors.

The results of a number of studies indicate that dyslexics may have subtle low-level auditory perceptual deficits not normally detected on standard hearing tests. Research has revealed that dyslexic children show problems in the speed of choice reaction time to pure tones (as well as visual flashes; Nicolson & Fawcett, 1993b), in addition to difficulties on tasks of tonal-pattern discrimination (Pinheiro, 1977; Tallal, 1980; B. U. Watson, 1992), gap detection (Ludlow, Cudahy, Bassich, & Brown, 1983), auditory fusion (McCroskey & Kidder, 1980) and discrimination of tone duration (B. U. Watson, 1992).

Evidence of an auditory temporal processing deficit has been obtained through Tallal's research as well as that of other investigators. This deficit appears to center around difficulties with temporal sound processing and sequencing (Nicolson & Fawcett, 1993b). Tallal (1980) reported that reading-impaired children performed more poorly than controls on nonverbal auditory discrimination and temporal order perception tests for two complex computer-generated tones only when the stimuli were presented rapidly. Poor readers were less accurate than normal readers on discrimination and sequencing tasks when two short complex stimuli were presented at short interstimulus intervals (305 ms and less), but not when ISIs were long (428 ms). McCroskey and Kidder (1980) and M. A. Reed (1989) obtained similar results. These results indicate that reading disabled children require significantly longer ISIs than normal students to perceive two complex tones as different. One interpretation of these results is that the perceptual difficulty in distinguishing between sound borders limits dyslexics' phonological abilities, creating the failure considered to be the main factor in dyslexia (Blachman, 1994; Brady & Shankweiler, 1991). This conclusion is based on the fact that the time range of several milliseconds should suffice for phonological processing in speech perception and reading.

The majority of research carried out on nonverbal acoustic perception has used complex tones, based on the notion that dyslexics have trouble perceiving stimuli with rapidly changing acoustic features. Yet, it appears that dyslexics may also perceive pure tones less well than normal readers. In a study carried out by De Weirdt (1988), it was found that both dyslexics and poor first-grade readers performed less well on pure tone same–different discrimination tasks. Later experiments by Nicolson and Fawcett (1993b, 1993c) also used pure tones. These investigators found that although dyslexics responded normally on tests of simple reactions to pure tones, they were significantly slower in selective choice reactions to these stimuli. The authors suggested that these findings may be a result of speed impairments in either perceptual classification or central decision processes.

B. U. Watson (1992) used a wide range of auditory tasks and found differences between dyslexic and normal adult readers on a single-tone duration task. In this task, a standard 1 kHz tone was presented at different durations, ranging from 8 ms to 256 ms. B. U. Watson and Miller (1993) employed identical tasks, again on adult readers, and obtained a somewhat different pattern of results. Both studies indicated a temporal processing deficit among dyslexics, but this later study found that dyslexics performed more poorly than normal readers only on a task assessing ability to discriminate temporal order for tones. In this task, the subjects were required to discriminate the order of two tones with frequencies of 550 Hz and 710 Hz at durations ranging from 20 ms to 200 ms. The tones were presented without gaps between them, and the pairs of tones were followed by a "leader" and a "trailer," consisting of 100 ms 625 Hz tones. The leading and trailing tones changed the task from one limited by the listener's spectral resolving power to one that places greater stress on auditory memory. The reason for the differential findings between the B. U. Watson (1992) and B. U. Watson and Miller (1993) studies is not clear.

Additional studies indicate auditory perceptual problems among dyslexics. For instance, Kinsbourne et al. (1991) presented dyslexic and regular readers with different sounds, in a different ear each time, and requested temporal order judgment. This task was significantly more difficult for the dyslexics relative to the regular readers. Although the finding that the difficulty stemmed from a problem with interhemisphere transfer was disputed, this claim was rejected (May et al., 1988). In another study (McGivern, Berko, Languis, & Chapman, 1991), dyslexic children were examined using a sound sequence discernment test according to rhythm (the Seashore Test). Once again, the task was more difficult for the dyslexics.

In addition to tones, dyslexics appear to perform less well on tasks using clicks as stimuli. Farmer and R. K. Klein (1993) administered a click fusion task and found that dyslexics required longer ISIs than normal readers to perceptually segregate clicks. This finding supports the contention that dyslexics have a temporal processing deficit for any rapidly presented auditory stimuli. Hari and Kiesila (1996) examined adult dyslexics to whom they presented clicks that "jumped" from one ear to another with an alternating ISI (45–500 ms) so that a directional illusion was created. At short ISIs, both groups felt the directional illusion. However, around 90–120 ms the illusion disappeared among the regular readers whereas the dyslexics continued noticing it even at an ISI of 250–500 ms. Hari and Kiesila (1996) suggested that the auditory timing problem might stem from an overly low perceptual clock rate, or in other words, from a temporal perception problem. They claimed that dyslexics do not get a chance to use all the sensory information required, as their information reception rate is relatively slow.

Farmer and R. Klein (1995) claimed that the tasks most indicative of a temporal processing deficit among dyslexics are those requiring serial processing of a number of stimuli, in contrast with processing of a single stimulus (which is, in their opinion, normal among dyslexics). According to Farmer and R. Klein (1995), there is a specific group of dyslexics who suffer from this serial failure, and not all dyslexics are included in it.[1]

The results of studies on nonverbal auditory perception clearly point to the possibility of lower level perceptual deficits largely related to temporal process-

---

[1]In this group, the serial processing failure is found in the visual and auditory modalities and some studies have indeed shown evidence that dyslexic children have difficulty distinguishing visual, and not only auditory, stimuli when they are presented rapidly and are of short lengths (McKeever & Van Deventer, 1975). Thus, there is evidence that the phenomenon is not unique to the auditory sense.

ing among dyslexic readers. However, the precise nature of these deficits needs to be more clearly defined.

Lower Level Phonological Processing. It has been established that auditory perception of phonemic units is directly related to initial reading acquisition (Robeck & Wallace, 1990). Thus, research on the involvement of lower level auditory perception deficits in dyslexia has also employed speech sounds. Clinical observations that dyslexic children typically "hear normally" (i.e., perform normally on standard hearing tests) and understand spoken language may not be sufficient evidence to conclude that they have a normal ability to perceive speech sounds. For some time, the notion has been raised that children with reading disabilities may also have subtle deficits in their perception of the acoustic cues for speech (Shankweiler, 1979; Tallal, 1980, 1984; Tallal & Piercy, 1974, 1975). However, despite increasing consensus that language impairment at the perceptual level may be involved in the etiology of dyslexia, the specific deficits associated with this phenomenon are unclear (Steffens, Eilers, Gross-Glenn, & Jallad, 1992).

It has been hypothesized that the way in which subtle perceptual deficits might affect reading through phonology is through inconsistency in the perception and classification of phonemes, which lead to the development of degraded representations of verbal information in memory. This is thought to interfere with the establishment of stable representations of phonemes in long-term memory. In the absence of consistent, invariant phonemic representations, the process of transforming written script into phonetic units is impeded (Godfrey, Syrdal-Lasky, Millay, & Knox, 1981; Kamhi, Catts, & Mauer, 1990; Mann & Brady, 1988; Stanovich, 1986a; Tallal, 1980, 1993; Torgesen, 1985; B. U. Watson & Miller, 1993).

In tests assessing categorical perception for phonemes, speech degradation is often used to investigate dyslexics' classification of phonemes into phonetic categories in a phoneme boundary shift paradigm. Several researchers have employed identification and discrimination tasks for meaningless synthetic stop consonant continua varying in place of articulation (usually /b-d/ and /d-g/) (Brandt & Rosen, 1980; De Weirdt, 1988; Godfrey et al., 1981). On such tasks, dyslexics have been found to be less able to differentiate phoneme boundaries than good readers.

Vowel perception also seems to be impaired among some dyslexics. In a study by P. Liberman, Meskill, Chatillon and Schupack (1985), both vowel and consonant perception were investigated among adult dyslexics. Their results revealed that whereas some dyslexics did not differ from controls on identification and discrimination tasks, others differed on the perception of consonants, and still others on the perception of vowels. The results of this study suggest sub-types of dyslexics with different perceptual difficulties.

In another study, B. U. Watson (1992) employed a variety of auditory tasks, and found that in addition to other deficits, disabled adult readers per-formed more poorly than normal readers on a syllable sequencing task in which the subjects were required to discriminate the syllables /ta/ka/ from /ka/ ta/ when the two CV syllables were preceded by the syllable /fa/ and followed by the syllable /pa/. That is, the task was to discriminate /fa/, /ta/, /ka/, /pa/, from /fa/, /ka/, /ta/, /pa/. Steffens et al. (1992) also examined syllable perception in adult readers, and found that although adult dyslexics were able to identify and discriminate vowel (/a/-/ /) and CV syllable (/ba/-/da/ and /sta/-/sa/) stimuli, they were less accurate than normal readers, particularly on the syllable tasks. On the vowel task, only dyslexic men revealed greater uncertainty in labeling the stimuli. For the stop-consonant CV syllables (ba/da), both male and female dyslexics were less consistent and accurate in identifying the syllables. An addi-tional finding was that adult dyslexics required greater periods of silence to shift the phonetic boundary from /sa/ to /sta/.

Temporal difficulties have also been shown in a variety of studies employing speech sounds. For example, dyslexics have been found to perform more poorly on tasks of syllable sequencing discrimination. In a study carried out by M. A. Reed (1989), a temporal sequencing task was used to compare reading disabled and control children on their ability to identify the order of two vowels (/e/ and / ae/) and two consonant syllables (/ba/ and /da/). Reading disabled subjects per-formed worse than normal controls when consonant syllables were presented at brief ISIs (300 ms), but not when vowels were presented at the same rate. Reed attributed these results to the rapidly changing acoustic spectra that character-ize the stop consonants but not the vowels. This finding comes together with the evidence from nonverbal processes to support the temporal processing defi-cit hypothesis.

Beyond the Auditory Temporal Deficit Hypothesis

The auditory deficit theory has been highly influential, and many researchers support the view that auditory perceptual dysfunction may be linked to reading through phonological capabilities (Stanovich, 1986a; Tallal, 1980; Torgesen, 1985; B. U. Watson, 1992). Yet, although Tallal's theory that a temporal order or sequencing dysfunction is a major contributor to dyslexia has gained momentum in recent years (Shapiro et al., 1990), there is still no consensus regarding the accuracy of a temporal processing deficit as an explanation for dyslexia (Studdert-Kennedy, 1997), and evidence exists that temporal disorders may not account for all dyslexics' difficulties. Some researchers claim that the source of the phonological deficit is a problem with rapid perception and not temporal perception. In other words, the emphasis is on the rate and not the serial characteristic (Studdert-Kennedy & Mody, 1995). In addition, the emphasis is placed on verbal as opposed to nonverbal material, which dyslexics manage to process easily (Mody, Studdert-Kennedy, & Brady, 1997). Furthermore, although the association between reading and phonological skills is well established, much less is known about the relations between auditory perception, phonological abilities, and reading. It seems that there are as yet many unanswered questions regarding the temporal processing hypothesis.

Evidence from some studies has raised the possibility that deficits in temporal processing exist, but they may only serve as partial explanations. In one early study (Tallal & Stark, 1982), the differences in temporal perception between reading disabled and normal readers were not wholly confirmed. As the dyslexic subjects in this study had adequate phonics abilities (i.e., normal language and articulary skills), it was speculated that poor temporal processing may be more closely related to oral language impairment than to specific reading disability. In order to examine this possibility, a further study was carried out that examined temporal processing in two reading disabled groups, one with concomitant language disorders, and the other without (Tallal et al., 1993). Using a comprehensive battery of sensory and motor tasks designed to assess visual, tactile, cross-modal sensory integration, and rapid sequential motor output, it was found that dyslexic children with oral language disabilities showed significant deficits in nonsense word reading (decoding) and nonverbal temporal processing. Dyslexics with normal oral language scores however, showed neither phonological decoding nor temporal processing deficits in any sensory modality. The reading difficulties of the latter group appear to occur at a higher level of analysis. In short, one possibility is that low-level temporal processing deficits may characterize only a certain type of dyslexic.

Evidence from another direction also suggests that temporal processing deficits at the perceptual level may only partially account for reading impairment. Several investigators have found that the Seashore auditory rhythm test (Seashore, Lewis, & Saetvit, 1956, 1960), which is a paired-comparisons task using patterns of rhythm from five to seven beats, consistently differentiates poor from good readers (Malloch, 1984; McGivern et al., 1991; Newman, Wright, & Fields, 1991; Zurif & Carson, 1970). Substantial correlations have been found between performance on this test and reading ability (Zurif & Carson, 1970).

In an extensive longitudinal study examining a large group of children on a number of cognitive tests commonly associated with dyslexia, Newman et al. (1991) found that in addition to poorer performance on the rhythm test, dyslexic children also performed significantly worse on the pitch section of the Seashore test. Interestingly, neither test involves variations in the rapidity of stimulus presentation. However, both the pitch and rhythm tasks are complex and are based on repeated presentation of stimuli. Newman et al. suggested that these stimulus parameters may serve to "overload" the reading disabled subjects. This view coincides with that of De Weirdt (1988), who proposed that the number of stimulus elements within a response set may play a part in the ability to differentiate stimuli.

Another line of research further supports the proposal that impaired temporal processing may be only one aspect of reading disability. Watson conducted a series of studies designed to investigate the relations between reading and the auditory and phonological domains directly (B. U. Watson, 1992; B. U. Watson & Miller, 1993; B. U. Watson & C. S. Watson, 1993). In the B. U. Watson and Miller (1993) study, evidence was found of a strong relation between speech perception and several of the phonological processes involved in reading. Interestingly, although reading disabled and nondisabled readers differed significantly on a task of assessing temporal order for tones (i.e., a nonspeech measure), no significant relations were found between this or any other nonverbal auditory measure and phonological abilities.

Both the B. U. Watson (1992) and B. U. Watson and C. S. Watson (1993) studies confirmed a specific association between reading disability and auditory temporal processing, but found enough overlap between the performance of reading disabled, math disabled, and normally achieving students to suggest that impaired temporal processing is neither a necessary nor a sufficient cause of specific reading disability. This appears to be true even when the reading disability involves impaired phonics abilities. Supporting this view is an earlier study by Ludlow, Cudahy, Bassich, and Brown (1983), who compared reading disabled, language delayed, and hyperactive boys and found all three clinical subgroups to have significantly longer interstimulus thresholds than normal controls on a temporal order task.

Findings such as these suggest that auditory temporal deficits may not be causally related to language and reading disorders, but instead may be representative of a common neurological disorder such as slower rates of neural transmission (Ludlow et al., 1983). Hence, impaired processing of temporal information could be a general deficit common to various pathologies.

There are also studies that did not find evidence of temporal processing difficulties. Tobey and Cullen (1984) did not find differences between dyslexic and regular readers in temporal processing and, in another study, differences were only found on a single test, word length judgment (B. U. Watson, 1992). In a follow-up study, B. U. Watson and Miller (1993) did not find a difference between groups using the same task, and a statistical analysis made it clear that a model assuming that a phonological deficit is caused by a speech perception difficulty (tasks such as syllabic sequence, sound imitation) was responsible for more variability than a model assuming that auditory temporal processing (tasks such as sound order judgment, sound length judgment) is the cause of a phonological deficit.[2]

Nittrouer (1999) examined temporal processing ability among children from age 8 to 10, both dyslexic and regular readers, using a test requiring the ability to distinguish between stimuli with a very short ISI (20–320 ms), and using a syllabic perception test. The dyslexic children exhibited a relative decrease in phonological ability, verbal working memory, and complex syntax. On temporal tests, all the children in the study made more mistakes when the ISI between stimuli was shorter, and as the stimulus sequence became longer. Even though the dyslexic children made more mistakes than the regular readers in general, the difference was not statistically significant. No differences between groups were found on the speech perception tasks either, so that this study did not support the existence of a temporal processing deficit among dyslexic children.

Another study, using a gap detection task (determining the existence of two sounds with the space between them very short), did not find significant differences between disabled and regular readers in two age groups (fifth and sixth graders and adults; Schulte-Korne, Demiel, Bartling, & Remschmidt, 1998). The correlations between reading and spelling scores and task performance were also negligible. The main purpose of this study was to examine the importance of a temporal processing deficit to reading and spelling. The study actually expressed some reservations about the temporal processing deficit hypothesis in dyslexia (Schulte-Korne et al., 1998).

----

[2]It is possible that the researcher's assumptions in this study regarding the division of tasks between statistical models were incorrect—it can be said that sound order judgment and syllabic sequence are both temporal tasks—and in reality there was a .41 correlation between tasks. One must be careful in judging causality so specifically when simple alternative explanations are available.

In sum, the temporal hypothesis is one of the most studied hypotheses in recent years with regard to dyslexia; however, the findings are not conclusive. There are conflicting results, and a decision has yet to be made regarding the accuracy of the hypothesis and its actual connection to the more prominent phonological hypothesis.

The "Perceptual Center" (P Center) Hypothesis

Another explanation proposing lower level perceptual deficits in dyslexia is the "perceptual center," or "P center," hypothesis, which is related to the temporal processing deficit hypothesis. One basic aspect of auditory temporal processing that may yield the onset time segmentation of the syllable is perceptual center (P center) processing. P centers are perceptual moments of occurrence, that is, points in time at which discrete perceptual event are felt to occur (Morton, Marcus, & Frankish, 1976). In audition, P centers pinpoint the time at which an acoustic experience (produced or perceived, speech or nonspeech) is felt to happen. This perceived moment of occurrence is not the same as the physical onset of the event, and is the probable basis for the perceptual experience of regularity or rhythmic timing in sequences of sounds. P centers theoretically represent the moment of perceived and produced representations across any modality with discrete events having a temporal extent (see Morton et al., 1976). In speech, P centers are the perceptual basis of speech rhythm. The P center of an auditory event is intrinsically linked to the timing and method of production of that event. P centers are most likely computed by the "how" stream of auditory processing, which passes through the temporo-parietal cortex and the planum temporale and is responsible for encoding and storing sound sequences and acting as a sensorimotor interface for mimicry (critical for language acquisition; Wise et al., 2001). This area of the temporo-parietal junction is also the one most usually indicated in neuroimaging studies of developmental dyslexia (Eden & Zeffiro, 1998).

P centers in spoken syllables typically occur between 20 ms and 120 ms into the syllable, depending on the speaker and the sound being made. For example, the P center of a syllable with a long onset (e.g., /la/) will occur later than that of a syllable with a short onset (e.g., /ba/). In acoustic terms, P centers are chiefly determined by the rate of change of the amplitude envelope in lower frequency regions (S. K. Scott, 1998). In the Marcus model of P center determination, P centers are principally determined by the peak increment in mid band spectral energy (corresponding to vowel onset in speech sounds). In the Scott model, this is expressly defined as the onset characteristic of this increment. According to S. K. Scott's (1998) model, P centers are not stored representations of sounds, but a property of the online representation of perceived and produced events. Again, this is interesting with respect to developmental dyslexia. Dyslexic children's difficulties in phonological representation are most clearly indexed by tasks requiring the online comparison or manipulation of spoken words, often produced by unfamiliar speakers.

Goswami (2002) showed significant differences between dyslexic and normally reading children, and between young early readers and normal developers, in P center detection. Further data (Goswami, 2002) show that sensitivity to P centers accounts for 25% of the variance in reading and spelling acquisition even after controlling for individual differences in age, IQ, and vocabulary. Goswami's (2002) hypothesis is that the primary auditory processing deficit in dyslexia is related to P center processing of speech and nonspeech sounds. Rise time contributes to this perceptual primitive, and thus to other observed auditory deficits (e.g., auditory stream segregation, backward masking; Helenius, Uutela, & Hari, 1999; Talcott et al., 1999) that arise because the stimuli used in these judgment tasks have P centers.

LINGUISTIC LEVEL PHONOLOGICAL PROCESSES

Phonological processing refers to the higher order cognitive abilities associated with the awareness, perception, representation, analysis, and manipulation of the sound structure of language, when processing oral and written information (I. Y. Liberman & Shankweiler, 1991). This construct is typically tested using measures of phonological awareness (rhyming, synthesis, and analysis), phonological recoding in lexical access, phonetic recoding in working memory, and rapid naming (Foorman, 1999; Helenius et al., 1999; Snowling, 1995; Wagner & Torgesen, 1987). Many studies support the idea that reading impairment is an outcome of deficits in the auditory-acoustic system at the phonological level (as opposed to the deficits in lower level processes, discussed earlier). The brain areas associated with this system are discussed in this section.

Current research in the neurosciences on phonological processes has shown that the involvement of multiple cortical areas stretching from the frontal lobes all the way back to the cerebellum. Phonology tasks mainly activate (a) the primary auditory and auditory association cortex; (b) temporal lobe regions, that is, the superior temporal gyri, which includes Wernicke's area (see Demb, Poldrack, & Gabrieli, 1999, for review), the middle and inferior (basal) temporal regions (Brunswick et al., 1999; Rumsey et al., 1992; Shaywitz, 1998); (c) areas in the frontal lobe, that is, the frontal-opercular region that includes Broca's area and some parts of the motor and premotor cortex (Demb et al., 1999); and (d) the right hemisphere of the cerebellum (R. B. Scott et al., 2001). Some researchers have found perisylvian activation, for example, in the supramarginal gyrus (see Paulesu, Frith, Snowling, & Gallagher, 1996; Petersen, Fox, Posner, Mintun, & Raichle, 1988; Rumsey et al., 1997a, 1997b, 1997c).

It is important to note that studies have also shown that the brain areas activated in phonological processing appear to vary as a result of different phonological tasks (for review see Joseph, Noble, & Eden, 2001; Pugh, B. A. Shaywitz, S. E. Shaywitz, & Shankweiler, 1997; Pugh et al., 2000, 2001). For example, word-level and sentence-level linguistic information activates Wernicke's area (see Demb et al., 1999, for a review), whereas the planum temporale in the auditory association cortex was found to be activated in phoneme detection tasks (see Pugh et al., 1997, for a review). The anterior areas of the frontal lobe were found to be activated when phonological judgment, such as syllable division and rhyming decision, is required (see discussion in Posner & Raichle, 1995; Rumsey, Nace et al., 1997; S. E. Shaywitz, 1998). Studies have also pointed to activation in Broca's area in a task that requires the phonological assembly of individual sounds (Demonet, Celsis, Nespoulous, & Viallard, 1992; Paulesu et al., 1996; Price, Moore, & Frackowiak, 1994; Pugh et al., 1997; S. E. Shaywitz, 1998; Zatorre, Evans, Meyer, & Gjedde, 1992). Activation occurred in the premotor cortex when the subjects were required to respond to a targeted sound or to other manipulations of phonological information (Demb et al., 1999). In frontal-opercular regions, the insula underneath the Sylvian fissure was found to show activation when phonological processing involved more automatic, rapid temporal changes (see discussion in Posner & Raichle, 1995; Rumsey, Nace et al., 1997; S. E. Shaywitz, 1998).

Imaging studies have also pointed to activation in the cerebellum during a phonological rhyme judgment task for words and for more difficult nonwords (Fulbright et al., 1999). In this study, strong, bilateral activation was found in the cerebellum for the phonological nonword rhyming task, specifically around the posterior superior fissure and two large adjacent areas (simple module and superior semilunar module). D. Klein (Klein, Milner, Zatorre, Meyer, & Evans, 1995) and Rumsey (Rumsey, Nace et al., 1997) also found right hemisphere cerebellum activation in phonological generation and recognition tasks (for more data on the cerebellum, see also Fiez, Petersen, Cheney, & Raichle, 1992; Leggio, Silveri, Petrosini, & Molinari, 2000; Nicolson & Fawcett, 1999; R. B. Scott et al., 2001).

In summary, the neurological structures necessary for auditory and phonological processes activate extensive, multiple regions of the brain. It is conceivable that each area is activated in a different manner and rate, such that reading and phonological processing require parallel-integration and synchronization.

HIGHER LEVEL AUDITORY-PHONOLOGICAL DEFICITS IN DYSLEXIA

The research into linguistic perceptual deficits among dyslexics is more abundant and less controversial. There is greater agreement among investigators in this field regarding the existence of a speech perception impairment in reading disabled individuals. Speech perception is the complex interaction of processes by which spoken language is interpreted (Schwab & Nusbaum, 1986). It is the input process for phonological material, and a necessary first step in all auditory verbal processing tasks (De Weirdt, 1988). The traditional view of speech perception is that the listener receives a spoken word as a sequence of phonemes that is retained in short-term memory until a match is located in the known vocabulary, or lexicon. In this view of word recognition, sequence is important (Robeck & Wallace, 1990).

Auditory perception of speech has become an important topic in the psychology of reading. This has occurred, in part, because both reading and speech comprehension access a common store of words. Different researchers have shown the strong connection between reading activity (word recognition), which constitutes the main difficulty in dyslexia, and understanding heard speech. I. Y. Liberman and Shankweiler (1991) compared the reading process to the speech comprehension process and described the points of similarity between them:

1. Both processes require the decoder to deconstruct words and recognize those using simple linguistic cerebral processes.
2. The information received in the brain is characterized by sight (reading) or sound (speech). However, the occurrences in the brain are not only auditory or visual, but constitute a combination of different mechanisms for decoding information.

Earlier in this chapter, evidence for deficits in the lower level perception of speech sounds was presented. There has also been much research examining higher level processing of meaningful speech.

Many studies indicate the importance of early linguistic abilities in the development of reading and spelling (e.g., Elbro, 1996; Wagner, Torgesen, & Rashotte, 1994), and especially the importance of early sensitivity to the phonological structure of words (e.g., Landerl & Wimmer, 1994; Naslund & Schneider, 1996). The ability to perceive speech accurately is required in order to perform tasks examining phonological awareness (Schulte-Korne et al., 1998). As shown later, different studies have found speech perception deficits among dyslexics. However, there are also studies that contradict this finding (Cornelissen, Hansen, Bradley, & Stein, 1996; Godfrey et al., 1981; Manis, McBride-Chang, Seidenberg, & Keating, 1997; Mody et al., 1997). Studies of speech repetition abilities have shown that poor readers perform more poorly on repetitions of monosyllabic and multisyllabic nonsense words and real words (Brady, Shankweiler, & Mann, 1983; Kamhi & Catts, 1986; Kamhi, Catts, Mauer, Apel, & Gentry, 1988; Kamhi et al., 1990; Snowling, Goulandris, Bowlby, & Howell, 1986; Wolff et al., 1990). However, whether speech repetition is a clean measure of perceptual ability has been debated.

Research examining categorical perception of meaningful speech stimuli has also been carried out. Brady et al. (1983), for instance, employed a degradation paradigm in which meaningful words with either a high or low frequency of occurrence were degraded by noise masking. When these stimuli were masked by amplitude-matched noise, poor readers performed considerably worse. ISI variation also appears to affect discrimination of words. A study by Shapiro et al. (1990) examined the effects of varing ISI on word recognition. In this study, one- and two-syllable words of varying lengths were displayed at short, intermediate, and long durations. Although eye movement patterns were similar in both dyslexics and controls, dyslexic children performed more poorly than controls when reading two-syllable words displayed for a duration long enough to enable two eye fixations (300 ms). Dyslexics did not differ from controls when reading short words requiring one fixation, and long words when display time was insufficient to make a second fixation. The authors suggested that these results may be indicative of a temporal processing deficit (as supported by studies of lower level temporal processing) that may involve either impaired sequential processing ability, or overuse of a simultaneous processing strategy.

Some researchers have questions regarding the contribution of the articulatory system to the dyslexia phenomenon. For instance, Vellutino and Scanlon (1989) claimed that the source of a specific deficit in reading is related to the ability to encode speech. According to them, in order to acquire reading, one must correctly encode information from the auditory channel. They also indicated that the nature of dyslexics' failure is at the linguistic level, and not in the auditory system itself.

Another hypothesis has recently been suggested, according to which dyslexia is caused by a failure to spontaneously use articulation movements (speech expressions) in order to change graphemes to phonemes. This failure creates a phonological awareness deficit. The mechanism considered most vulnerable according to this hypothesis is the motor-articulatory feedback mechanism (Heilman, Voeller, & Alexander, 1996). The hypothesis is based on cases of an acquired disorder of the grapheme–phoneme connection as a result of damage to the anterior perisylvian area in the brain. In addition, it is known from behavioral studies that dyslexics have difficulty articulating long words (T. R. Miles, 1974) and repeating them (Apthorp, 1995; Brady, Poggie, & Rappala, 1989; Catts, 1986, 1989), but not with short words (P. Liberman et al., 1985). Their difficulty in repeating pseudowords is also significant (Stone & Brady, 1995) as is the connection between the rest and lexical knowledge (vocabulary) (Gathercole & Baddeley, 1989, 1990).

CONCLUSIONS

Both the visual and auditory modalities and the orthographic and phonological systems contribute significantly to the quality of reading. As described in chapters 7 and 8, each of these modalities has a different biological structure and a different location in the brain. Moreover, the manner in which each route processes information is different. The reading process requires an exact matching between sounds and symbols, that is, between the graphemes coming from the visual system and the phonemes coming from the auditory system. This, in turn, requires a high degree of synchronization between the systems. Speed of processing is one crucial component of synchronization. The next chapters present evidence from our own research projects regarding speed of processing information within and between the visual-orthographic and auditory-phonological systems and at different stages of information-processing activation.

9

Speed of Processing of Visual and Auditory Modalities: Research Evidence

As indicated in the preceding chapters, no comprehensive study has thus far systematically evaluated processing speed in the visual and auditory modalities of the brain, despite the fact that these modalities are crucial for the onset of word reading processes. Moreover, the literature has not yet provided conclusive answers about whether speed of processing (SOP) in these two modalities is related to effective word reading, and whether and to what extent SOP in these modalities varies between dyslexic and regular readers. In addition, the degree to which and the level of complexity at which nonlinguistic and linguistic SOP relates to efficient word reading have yet to be examined comprehensively. We therefore designed a research plan to address these issues. The aim of the research projects was to verify the contribution of SOP in the visual and auditory modalities to effective word reading in regular and dyslexic readers.

THE STUDY

The research was carried out in two stages:

1. Behavioral Measures Project: Experiments incorporating behavioral measures only.
2. ERP Measures Project: Experiments utilizing both behavioral and ERP measures (see chap. 10).

This chapter discusses the various studies into the behavioral measures project while data obtained in the ERP measures project are described in chapter 10. Speed of processing of the modalities at different levels of activity was examined in the following ways:

1. Investigating regular and dyslexic readers (a within and between subjects design).

2. Controlling and manipulating the experimental tasks from lower level to higher level for both nonlinguistic and linguistic processing, as well as incorporating stimuli at various levels of complexity. At the lower level, tasks included distinguishing between nonlinguistic visual (flashes) and auditory (beeps) stimuli, and distinguishing between linguistic visual (graphemes) and auditory (phonemes) stimuli. At the higher level, subjects were asked to process orthographic and phonological information at the word level (lexical decision and rhyming paradigms).

3. Controlling and manipulating the presentation time of the stimuli according to each experimental design based on pretests.

4. Using behavioral (reaction time, RT, and accuracy, AC) measures and electrophysiological (ERP) measures. Incorporating reaction time, accuracy, and ERP measures allowed us to track information-processing activation at various stages of processing (see chap. 10 for more details).

Subjects

One hundred students participated in the study, including 50 dyslexic and 50 age-matched regular readers. Ages ranged from 19 to 27 years ($x = 24.3$ years, $SD = 1.2$), with 12 females and 38 males in each group. All participants were right-handed native Hebrew speakers and were undergraduate students at the University of Haifa. They all volunteered for the experiment and were paid for their participation. The dyslexics were recruited from the university's Student Support Center for Learning Disabilities. Their reading score was at least one standard deviation below the normal reading achievement score. All were found eligible for receiving learning adjustments. The control group consisted of regular readers who were recruited for the experiment via advertisements and were matched to the dyslexics on SAT scores, gender, and faculty of study.

Several considerations lie behind the decision to use adults, specifically young adult, high functioning (compensated) dyslexic individuals enrolled for university studies, as the target population for this project. To begin with, the reading deficits of university-attending dyslexics are presumably not due to insufficient reading experience, insufficient exposure to print or a developmental lag. In addition, despite the small number of studies on adult dyslexics, there is clear evidence that individuals diagnosed in childhood as dyslexics remain affected by this condition for their entire life (Lefly & Pennington, 1991) even when well "compensated." It is conceivable that most of the reading skills that should have been developed due to print exposure and teaching during school years have already been accomplished, and it can be assumed that the deficits that adult dyslexic readers possess are unaffected by years of print exposure and are strongly related to the core deficits of dyslexia.

Baseline Measures

Validation of the subjects' classification was achieved through a battery of behavioral tests (see Table 9.1).

Measures

I. Behavioral baseline measures.

1) **General Ability**: IQ was assessed using the Raven Standard Progressive Matrices (Raven, 1960).

2) **Reading Ability**: Several tests were used to obtain estimates of reading accuracy, reading time, and comprehension. The first set of tests provided measures of decoding accuracy for real words and pseudowords. The second set assessed reading time in context and evaluated reading comprehension:

a. *Decoding skills*: One Minute Tests (Shatil, 1997). This battery included two subtests in which subjects were asked to read lists as quickly and accurately as possible within the space of 1 minute. The first list contained 100 real words arranged in order of increasing length (one to five syllables) and decreasing frequency, and the second test was comprised of a list of 100 pseudowords arranged in order of increasing length (one to five syllables). Scores were based on the number of words/pseudowords read correctly. In order to obtain a comprehensive decoding score, Z scores were first calculated for each of the tests (i.e., words and pseudowords) and then combined to give a total Z score for decoding performance.

b. *Reading comprehension, accuracy, and speed in context*: The reading performance for text was measured using two texts from the reading test section of the Israeli Psychometric SAT (Center for Psychometric Tests, 1994). Each text contained a short story comprised of 17 sentences (257 words each), which appeared in its entirety on the computer screen. The subject pressed a button

TABLE 9.1

Means and Standard Deviations for Behavioral Baseline Scores

Test	M Dyslexic	SD Dyslexic	M Control	SD Control	F
Oral reading time	120.81	27.09	88.55	15.14	4.99**
Oral reading errors	3.84	2.96	1.38	1.52	4.62**
Oral reading: Comprehension. Time to answer	314.64	132.69	199.05	128.20	2.94*
Oral reading: Comprehension. Correct (out of 5)	4.31	0.82	4.30	0.83	ns
Silent reading time	122.64	34.80	75.38	30.23	4.76**
Silent reading: Comprehension. Time to answer	273.39	138.88	177.78	106.34	2.55*
Silent reading: Comprehension. Correct (out of 5)	2.94	1.177	3.41	0.77	n.s
One-minute word reading test: Correct	69.10	19.84	113.00	17.47	8.03**
One-minute pseudowords: Correct	37.30	11.98	62.62	13.75	6.58**
Verbal fluency: Total words generated for 3 letters	36.95	9.69	47.88	10.54	4.61**
Speed factor (WAIS–3: Coding symbol search SD scores)	7.95	1.35	11.16	1.10	3.91*
Naming speed: Printed letters—time	29.09	14.18	21.57	2.79	3.59*
Naming speed: Numbers—time	21.05	13.93	17.93	2.34	6.33**
Naming speed: Colors—time	36.40	13.92	28.36	5.29	3.66*
Naming speed: Objects—time	45.08	16.03	34.08	6.06	4.22**
Stroop effect score					
Digit span (WAIS–3): Standard score	8.70	2.75	11.29	2.49	4.27**
Working memory: Opposites—total score	5.45	1.46	6.33	1.34	2.08*
Working memory: Completions—total score	4.40	1.46	5.44	1.19	2.62*
Orthography: Parsing—time	340.05	162.34	161.26	39.79	5.31**
Dictation: Errors out of 30	8.30	5.57	2.92	3.21	4.11**
Morphology: Verb generation	61.85	16.52	87.00	18.15	4.76**
Matrices (WAIS–3): Standard score	13.25	2.55	14.25	3.09	ns
Block design (WAIS–3): Standard score	11.25	2.61	12.13	2.15	ns
Similarities (WAIS–3): Standard score	8.95	1.09	9.66	1.14	ns

*$p < .05$. **$p < .01$.

upon beginning to read the story and again upon conclusion. The computer measured reading time for each passage. When the subject had completed reading, the text was automatically erased from the screen and the first of six multiple-choice questions appeared. The subject selected an answer by pressing a number on the keyboard (1–4) corresponding to the answer chosen. Once each question was answered a new one appeared on the screen until all six had been completed. One story was read orally and the other silently. The experimenter recorded decoding errors during oral reading in order to obtain a measure of accuracy. Comprehension scores were based on the total number of correct answers across the two texts. Reading time scores were determined on the basis of the mean reading time across the texts.

3) **Word Recognition Skills**:

a. *Phonology*: Two measures of phonological ability were used.

1. Phoneme Recognition Test for Words and Pseudowords (Ben-Dror & Shani, 1997).

2. Deletion, Omission, and Rhyming (DORT) Test (Shatil, 2001c). Scores were based on the total number of accurate responses and test performance time of the two tests.

b. *Orthography*:

1. Parsing Test (Breznitz, 1997c). This test contained 50 rows of 4 words each. The words were presented as a continuous line of print (i.e., were not separated by blank spaces). The subject was asked to identify the words in each row by drawing a line to indicate where the spaces should be. Scores were based on performance accuracy and total test performance time.

2. Dictation (Shatil, 2001a).

4) **Short-Term (STM) and Working Memory (WM)**:

a. Digit Span subtest (WAIS, 1976).

b. Beads Memory subtest (Stanford-Binet, 1986).

c. Working Memory—Opposites (Shani & Ben-Dror, 1998): This test was comprised of a series of adjectives of approximately the same size, each of which has an opposite (e.g., tall/short, big/small, black/white). The adjective series appeared in sets of two, and were presented in order of increasing length. The number of adjectives in each series of each set ranged successively from two to eight adjectives. Each series of adjectives was read aloud by the examiner, one at a time. When the examiner had completed the series, the subject was required to respond with the opposite of each adjective in the series, in the order in which the adjectives occurred (e.g., the response to "tall–big–black" would be "short–small–white"). The examiner continued until the subject failed two consecutive adjective sequences within the same set. The test was not time limited, and scores were based on the number of correct responses.

d. Working Memory—Completion (Shani & Ben-Dror, 1998): This test was comprised of a set of sentences in which the final word was missing. In this test, the examiner read each sentence aloud, and the subject completed the missing word in the sentence. At the end of all of the sentences in a particular set, the subject was asked to recall the completed words in the order in which they appeared. Each set contained two series of sentences. The number of sentences in each series ranged, in ascending order, from two to five. The examiner continued until the subject failed two consecutive series in the same set. The test was not time limited, and scores were based on the number of correct responses.

5) **Timing Measures**:

a. Rate of retrieval from long-term memory: Word Fluency Test (Breznitz, 1996; designed on the basis of Lezak, 1993). This test assessed the ability to retrieve words from long-term memory according to a specified criterion. Subjects were required to make three separate lists of words. In the first test, subjects listed words beginning with the letter "resh" (r), and in the second words beginning with the letter "shin" (sh) were listed. In the third test, the subject made a list of groceries. One minute was given for each word list. A total fluency score was derived from the sum of words recalled in each of the three separate lists.

b. Rate of processing: WAIS–III Speed of processing factor (comprised out of Digit Symbol and Symbol Search subtests; Wechsler, 1994)

1. Digit Symbol: The subject copies symbols that are paired with numbers. Using a key, the subject draws each symbol under its corresponding number.

2. Symbol Search: The subject visually scans two groups of symbols: a target group (two symbols) and a search group (five symbols) and indicates whether either of the target symbols appears in the search group.

c. Naming tests: Comprised of rapid automatized naming (RAN) tests each containing 50 stimuli from four single categories (after Denckla & Rudel, 1976b; Wolf et al., 1986).

1. Letters: 5 letters (print): ב,כ,ה,ש,ת

2. Digits: 5 digits: 2, 7, 9, 5, 4

3. Colors: 5 colors: blue, yellow, red, green, black

4. Objects: 5 objects: chair, shoe, star, watch, and flower

The naming subtests were given in the traditional RAN form in which the stimuli are arranged randomly in a 10 × 5 matrix.

The subject was required to name the stimuli in each subtest as quickly and accurately as possible. Speed and accuracy for each subtest were measured.

Table 9.1 shows the means and standard deviations of the (one way analysis of variance) (ANOVA) analyses performed on each of the baseline measures in an attempt to verify group differences. As indicated, no between group differences were found for the general ability or oral and silent reading comprehension scores. On all the other measures, the dyslexics were slower and less accurate than the regular readers.

BEHAVIORAL MEASURES PROJECT—INTRODUCTION

Behavioral Experimental Tasks

This project only employed behavioral measures, including choice reaction time (RT), controlled reaction time, and accuracy (AC), during visual and auditory information processing. Each experiment started with a choice RT paradigm. In the visual presentation tasks, the stimulus remained on the computer screen until the subjects made their decision (self-paced RT). In the auditory experiments, the presentation time was based on the length that it took to produce the sound of the stimulus. RT was based on the subjects' self-paced RT (see also Breznitz & Meyler, 2003). In the controlled reaction time, the presentation time of the stimuli were manipulated according to the experimental requirements. The manipulation of the presentation time of the stimuli was based on the distribution of self-paced reaction times of all accurate responses across all subjects. The fastest presentation rate in each experiment was based on the average of the 10% fastest RT achieved and the slowest one on the mean of all subjects RT.

In an attempt to measure SOP in the visual and auditory modalities across the various experiments, stimuli complexity was controlled and manipulated. The battery of tasks tested nonlinguistic and linguistic stimuli processing. The linguistic level consisted of two ranks of complexity, a lower level involving letter and syllable processing, and a higher level that tested processing of words and pseudowords. In all the experiments, the subjects were asked to press the joystick buttons as fast as possible after the disappearance of each stimulus from the computer screen, and according to the specific instructions for each task. Before each experiment began, the subject had a short practice session consisting of five stimuli for each category appearing in the experiment. The two groups were compared on reaction time and accuracy for each task. The mean reaction time (see Tables 9.2, 9.3, and 9.4) for each subject in each experiment was based on scores obtained by deducting stimulus presentation time from the subject's total reaction time.

THE TASKS

Visual Modality

Lower Level

Visual and Motor Reaction Time. The purpose of the experiment was to determine the minimal time required by the subject to respond to the presence of a simple visual stimulus. Subjects were requested to respond as quickly as possible to a square that appeared in the center of the screen for 30 ms. The experiment contained 80 stimuli. In an attempt to eliminate the possibility of habituation, there were random intervals of 800 ms, 1,000 ms, 1,200 ms or 1, 500 ms between stimuli.

Thus, the mean for simple motor RT across the ISIs was about 56 ms longer for the dyslexics than for the regular readers (Fig. 9.1). There is no indication at this point concerning whether the dyslexic readers' relative slowness is a result of slow motor RT, and/or less attention to the task, and/or slowness in perceiving that there is a stimulus on the computer screen. However, data showed that dyslexics are slower than regular readers in RT to visual stimuli that do not require any processing but must be identified on the computer screen.

Single Stimuli Presentation in the Visual Modality. Two experiments were performed using the same time presentations. One experiment used nonlinguistic stimuli and the other linguistic stimuli (letters and syllables).

1. Identification of Single Nonlinguistic Stimuli: The purpose of the experiment was to determine the time required by the subject to identify the direction of nonlinguistic visual stimuli. Each subject was requested to recognize the direction of stimulus lines that appeared on the computer screen. The stimuli were composed of two types of elements, each consisting of three lines. One element contained one long line appearing on its right side, and the other contained a long line appearing on its left side. The two stimulus types were divided into an equal number. The subject was required to press one of two joystick keys as quickly as possible, in accordance with the direction of the long line, one key for the right and the other for the left. A total of 160 stimuli were presented ran-

TABLE 9.2

Reaction Times for Correct Answers for Visual Single Stimulus Presentations

Stimuli	Dyslexics		Controls		F	Sig.
	M	SD	M	SD		
Simple motoric RT	288.11	67.03	231.40	23.17	5.01	.01
Visual non-lingu RT inspection time 40	752.11	152.51	701.80	126.83	7.76	.001
Visual RT inspection time 60	721.85	190.11	627.43	107.12	4.06	.05
Visual RT inspection time 100	696.83	179.95	630.86	114.24	4.70	.03
Visual RT inspection time 200	732.05	254.81	631.08	118.48	3.18	.08
Visual letter identification 40 ꓳꓶ	900.98	197.21	709.08	91.14	25.36	.001
Visual letter identification 60 ꓳꓶ	862.53	240.00	653.67	135.72	4.61	.04
Visual letter identification 100 ꓳꓶ	821.28	265.68	659.05	141.53	4.17	.04
Visual letter identification 200 ꓳꓶ	889.76	296.04	652.65	137.84	7.83	.001
Visual syllables identification 80 HK RK	1176.00	121.71	711.98	87.99	20.11	.001
Visual syllables identification 100 HK RK	1006.21	128.31	717.71	87.44	11.78	.001
Visual syllables identification 200 HK RK	1151.97	121.09	720.09	78.09	9.78	.003
Visual syllables identification 400 HK RK	1267.12	111.21	750.21	91.23	8.56	.001
Lex visual word 100 ms	1127.21	126.53	693.73	114.96	31.72	.001
Lex visual word 300 ms	1236.02	176.97	700.40	129.83	17.96	.001
Lex visual word 500 ms	1221.78	169.21	710.34	143.62	16.50	.001
Lex visual pseudowords 100	1223.31	244.73	732.90	213.26	13.63	.001
Lex visual pseudowords 300	1340.52	196.24	761.04	127.95	16.64	.001
89 lex visual pseudowords 500 ms	1392.75	218.43	759.28	156.31	23.95	.001

TABLE 9.3
Reaction Times for Auditory Stimuli

Stimuli	Dyslexics		Controls		F	Sig.
	M	SD	M	SD		
Motoric reaction time	267.24	66.09	244.79	39.87	3.91	.05
Auditory RT for correct responses to beep sounds	491.93	189.27	363.23	95.46	5.75	.02
Auditory correct responses for beep sounds	49.28	6.85	55.78	2.33	5.01	.03
Letter sound RT for correct responses	436.13	109.93	250.80	62.76	12.33	.002
Letter sound correct responses	47.64	6.78	57.62	4.76	3.96	.05
Syllables discrimination RT for correct responses	725.65	112.80	633.78	69.76	4.79	.03
Syllables discrimination correct	42.43	5.98	51.25	2.99	5.32	.04
Lex auditory words RT	993.49	114.49	655.69	114.21	5.10	.01
Lex auditory words accuracy	56.07	2.55	59.23	1.66	.02	ns
Lex auditory pseudowords	1115.50	119.00	1006.20	64.17	4.95	.03
Lex auditory pseudowords	54.09	1.02	56.11	1.05	.66	ns

TABLE 9.4
Orthographic and Phonological Identification

Stimuli	Dyslexics		Controls		F	Sig.
	M	SD	M	SD		
Pairs of words written the same, RT	1461.32	603.21	1110.00	109.11	7.74	.001
Pairs of words written differently, RT	1268.33	439.42	966.02	129.91	8.67	.006
Pairs of words written the same, AC	52.09	.48	53.12	.23	1.77	ns
Pairs of words written differently, AC	46.11	.41	47.00	.23	2.03	ns
Pairs of words sound the same, RT	1233.30	186.01	1002.09	171.42	4.52	.04
Pairs of words sound different, RT	1288.16	234.87	1189.78	101.22	3.62	.06
Pairs of words sound the same, AC	47.58	17.44	58.40	15.45	3.95	.05
Pairs of words sound different, AC	48.94	17.34	60.00	13.55	4.40	.04
Pseudoword sound like real word, RT	1713.61	345.80	1208.227	190.87	22.30	.001
Pseudoword not sound like real word, RT	1880.09	416.32	1261.09	188.92	14.03	.001
Pseudoword sound like real word, AC	46.33	3.22	54.11	3.08	5.32	.02
Pseudoword not sound like real word, AC	47.56	4.88	57.01	2.98	7.08	.01

domly on the computer screen at 40 ms, 60 ms, 100 ms, and 200 ms. There were 20 stimuli types in each presentation, with a total of 40 stimuli at each rate. See results in Fig. 9.2 for accuracy and Fig. 9.3 for reaction time.

2. Identification of Single Letters: The purpose of the experiment was to determine the time required by the subject to perceive a visual linguistic stimulus. Each subject was asked to recognize which of two similar shape letters (ב and כ)

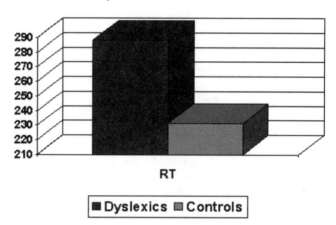

Simple Visual Reaction Time

FIG. 9.1. Simple visual reaction time.

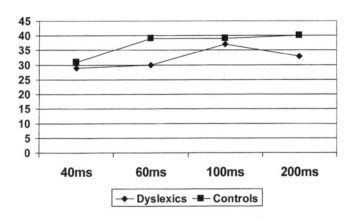

FIG. 9.2. Nonlinguistic visual identification accuracy.

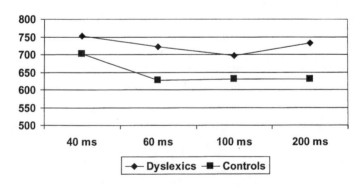

FIG. 9.3. Nonlinguistic visual identification RT.

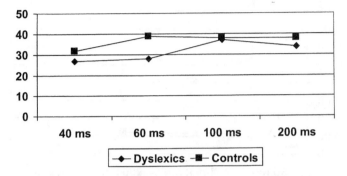

FIG. 9.4.   Visual letter identification accuracy.

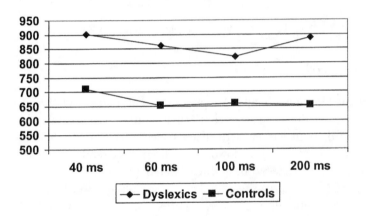

FIG. 9.5.   Visual letter identification RT.

appeared (one letter at a time) on screen. The letters appeared for 40 ms, 60 ms, 100 ms, or 200 ms with 40 stimuli (20 of each letter) in each presentation session, equaling a total of 160 stimuli. The subject was required to press one of two keys as quickly as possible in accordance with the letter that appeared on screen. See results in Figs. 9.4 for accuracy and 9.5 for reaction time.

3. Identification of Syllables: The purpose of the experiment was to determine the time required by the subject to perceive a more complicated visual linguistic stimulus. Each subject was asked to recognize which of two syllables (HK הק and RK רק) appeared (one syllable at a time) on screen. The syllables appeared randomly for 80 ms, 100 ms, 200 ms, or 400 ms with 40 stimuli (20 of each syllable) in each presentation session, equaling a total of 160 stimuli. The subject was required to press one of two keys as quickly as possible in accordance with the letter that appeared on screen. See results of reaction time in Fig. 9.6.

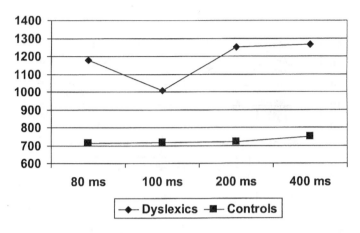

FIG. 9.6.   Visual syllable identification RT.

Higher Level

Lexical Decision—Single Presentation.   The purpose of the experiment was to examine the speed at which the subject distinguished between words and pseudowords (four letters each). Each subject was asked to differentiate between a real word and a pseudoword, which appeared randomly in the center of a computer screen one by one at three different presentation rates: 100 ms, 300 ms, and 500 ms. There were a total of 180 stimuli—90 words and 90 pseudowords with 60 stimuli in each presentation rate—30 words and 30 pseudowords. The type of stimuli and the presentation rate were randomly presented to the subjects on the computer screen. The subject was requested to decide as quickly as possible whether the stimulus was a word or a pseudoword and to respond by pressing the appropriate joystick button. Each response erased the stimulus from the computer screen and triggered the appearance of the next stimulus. See results for accuracy in Fig. 9.7 and for reaction time in Fig. 9.8.

Auditory Modality

Lower Level

Auditory Simple Motor Reaction Time.   The purpose of the experiment was to determine the minimal time required by the subject to respond to the presence of a simple auditory stimulus. Each subject was requested to respond as quickly as possible to a sound played at 1,000 Hz. The experiment contained 80

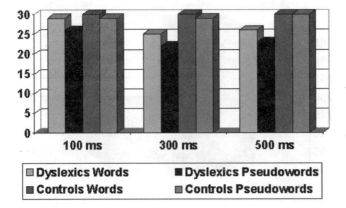

FIG. 9.7.   Visual lexical accuracy decision for words and pseudowords at different presentation times.

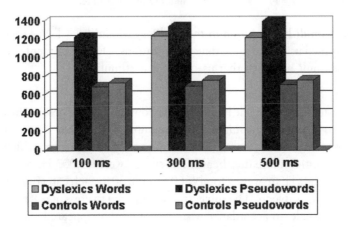

FIG. 9.8.   Visual lexical RT decision for words and pseudowords at different presentation times.

stimuli. In an attempt to eliminate the possibility of habituation, there were random intervals of 800 ms, 1,000 ms, 1,200 ms, or 1,500 ms between stimuli.

As seen in Fig. 9.9, the mean for simple motor RT across the ISI's interval was about 23 ms longer for the dyslexics than for the regular readers. There is no indication at this point concerning whether the dyslexic readers' relative slowness is a result of slow motor RT, and/or less attention to the task, and/or slowness in perceiving the auditory stimulus. However, the data showed that dyslexics are slower than regular readers in RT to auditory stimuli that do not require any processing just recognition of the tone.

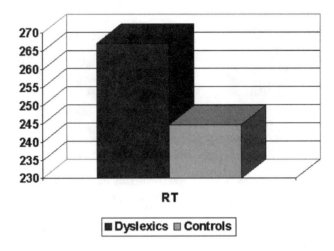

FIG. 9.9.   Simple auditory reaction time.

Single Stimuli Presentation in the Auditory Modality.   Two experiments were performed using the same time presentations. One experiment used nonlinguistic stimuli, and the other used linguistic stimuli.

1. Identification of Single Nonlinguistic Sounds: The purpose of the experiment was to determine the minimal time required by the subject to perceive an auditory nonlinguistic stimulus. Subjects were asked to recognize which of the two nonlinguistic stimuli they heard. The stimuli were a 1,000-Hz sound and a 2,000-Hz sound. There were a total of 60 stimuli, 30 in each category randomly presented to the subjects. The subjects were required to press one of two keys as quickly as possible, in accordance with the sound that appeared via the headphone. The subject's RT controlled the appearance and disappearance of the stimuli.

2. Identification of Single Letters/Phonemes: The purpose of the experiment was to determine the minimal time required by the subject to discriminate between two auditory linguistic phoneme sounds. Subjects were asked to recognize which of two phonemes sounds they heard. The phoneme sounds were ב and פ. A total of 60 phonemes were played, 30 in each category randomly presented to the subjects. The subject was required to press one of two keys as quickly as possible in accordance with the phoneme heard. The subject's RT controlled the appearance and disappearance of the stimuli.

3. Identification of Syllables: The purpose of the experiment was to determine the time required by the subject to perceive a more complicated auditory

linguistic stimulus. Each subject was asked to identify which of two syllables (HK הק and רק) were presented via head phones (one syllable at a time). There where 60 syllables, 30 of each type presented at random to the subjects. The subject was required to press one of two keys as quickly as possible in accordance with the syllable presented via the head phones.

Higher Level

Lexical Decision—Single Presentation. The purpose of this experiment was to examine the speed at which the subject makes a decision regarding the sound of a single word. Each subject was asked to press one joystick button for real words and the other for pseudowords. There was a 1,200 ms interval between stimuli. The experiment contained 30 real words and 30 pseudowords, for a total of 60 stimuli. The subject was requested to respond as quickly as possible. See results for accuracy in Fig. 9.10 and for reaction time in Fig. 9.11.

ORTHOGRAPHIC-PHONOLOGICAL TRANSFORMATION

Phonological-Orthographic Translation

The purpose of the experiment was to determine the speed at which the subject performs phonological-orthographic translation. Each subject was required to judge whether or not two words that were presented via headphones were spelled the same way (orthographically identical). The experiment included a total of 120 stimuli: 45 orthographically identical words (such as צמא-צמא) and 75 orthographically different words. The latter included 25 orthographically different words (such as קנס-פרח), 25 words that were different with respect to their first syllable only (רודף-הודף) and 25 words that were different with re-

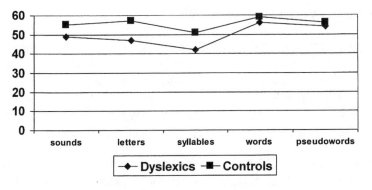

FIG. 9.10. Auditory identification accuracy.

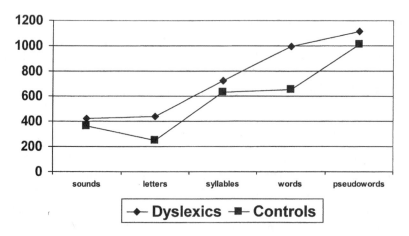

FIG. 9.11.   Auditory accurate identification RT.

spect to their last syllable only (השכיר-השכיל). Each response erased the stimulus and triggered the appearance of the next stimulus.

Results.   Two 2 × 2 RM-Manovas were conducted, Group (Dyslexics × Controls) × Task (Same × Different), one for accuracy and one for RT. Data indicated a main effect of group for accuracy, $F(4, 96) = 6.11, p < .03$. The dyslexics were less accurate than the controls on both tasks. Results also showed a main effect of group for RT, $F(4, 96) = 8.36, p < .001$. The dyslexics were slower than the controls. A main effect of task was also found, $F(2, 96) = 4.12, p < .05$. For both groups, identification of same pairs was longer. A Group × Task interaction was also found, $F(4, 96) = 7.01, p < .01$. The difference in RT between the same and different pairs was larger in the dyslexic group.

Phonological Visual Decision for Word Pairs

The purpose of this experiment was to determine the speed at which the subject phonologically decodes real words. Each subject was required to judge whether or not two words that appeared sequentially on the computer screen sounded alike. The experiment included 60 pairs that sounded alike (e.g., מאיר-מעיר) and 60 words that did not sound alike (e.g., אמיץ-מעיר), for a total of 120 words. The pairs appeared on the computer screen for 400 ms.

Results.   Two 2 × 2 RM-Manovas were conducted, Group (Dyslexics × Controls) × Task (Same × Different), one for accuracy and one for RT. Data indicated a main effect of group for accuracy, $F(4, 96) = 5.62, p < .02$. The dyslexics were less accurate than the controls. Results also indicated a main effect of group for RT, $F(4, 96) = 5.91$, $p < .01$. The dyslexics were slower than the controls. A main effect of task was also found, $F(2, 96) = 4.12$, $p < .05$. For both groups, identification of sound-alike pairs was longer. A Group x Task interaction was also found, $F(4, 96) = 6.55$, $p < .001$. The difference in RT between sound-alike and sound-different pairs was larger in the dyslexic group.

Phonological Visual Decision Tasks for Pseudowords

The purpose of this experiment was to determine the speed at which the subject makes a decision regarding the phonological accuracy of a pseudoword. Each subject was required to decide if the pseudoword presented on the computer screen did or did not sound like a real word. For example, חטול is a pseudoword that sounds like a real word, whereas גאה is a pseudoword that does not sound like a real word. Sixty pseudowords that sounded like real words, and 60 pseudowords that did not sound like real words were presented, for a total of 120 pseudowords. The words were presented on the computer screen for 100 ms. The subjects were requested to make a decision regarding the stimulus as soon as possible, and respond accordingly by pressing a button.

Results. Two 2 × 2 RM-Manovas were conducted, Group (Dyslexics × Controls) × Task (Same × Different), one for accuracy and one for RT. Data indicated a main effect of group for accuracy, $F(4, 96) = 9.12$, $p < .001$. The dyslexics were less accurate than the controls. Results also showed a main effect of group for RT, $F(4, 96) = 11.17$, $p < .001$. The dyslexics were slower than the controls. A main effect of task was also found, $F(2, 96) = 5.43$, $p < .02$. For both groups, identification of sound-alike words was longer. A Group × Task interaction was also found, $F(4, 96) = 7.08$, $p < .001$. The difference in RT between sound-alike and sound-different words was larger in the dyslexic group.

DISCUSSION AND INTEGRATION OF FINDINGS

The results presented in this chapter provide systematic evidence concerning SOP of the modalities and the systems that are activated in reading among dyslexics as compared to age-matched controls. Accuracy differences between the groups were varied according to the experimental tasks. In several experiments, accuracy reached a ceiling effect. In others, the between group differences in performance accuracy ranged between 2 and 10 responses. Significant group differences were found mainly in RT measures. Despite the fact that the dyslexics were all university students, their reaction time in most experimental tasks was significantly slower than that of the control group. This slowness was observed even in two simple experiments where the requirement was only to respond motorically to visual and to auditory signals. The slow RT of the dyslexics was maintained across all experiments.

In the adult groups, in most tasks, processing information in the visual modality was longer than in the auditory modality, both for regular and for dyslexic readers. As the human mind tends to think in words, it is conceivable that visual processing also includes some form of spontaneous (nonconscious) verbal (acoustic) processing, which increases the duration of the visual process. In contrast, auditory-acoustic stimuli are directly presented into the auditory system and remain within this system alone, thereby shortening the duration of the process. Normal information processing appears to imply a longer visual than auditory processing time; a pattern that was observed in the regular readers group. However, this conclusion has to be taken with caution, because the two modalities are biologically different and process information differently. Among regular and dyslexic adults, the direction of RT pattern seems to be similar: Visual information at any level requires more time to be processed than auditory information. However, the differences in reaction time between the dyslexics and the controls were wider in the visual experiments. It is plausible that the visual process incorporates the perception and the identification of the visual patterns as well as the discrimination of its acoustic-phonological matching. Because even among adult dyslexics there is no automaticity in the linguistic processing, the perceived written symbol is activated via the visual and the auditory routes in parallel. This is what lengthens the processing time for dyslexics. In contrast, for the control group the processes are automatic and the performance time is concomitantly shorter. It is important to note that both groups displayed a ceiling effect in most experiments. At the same time, processing time was always significantly longer among dyslexics

The reverse applies in the case of regular and dyslexic young readers (see Breznitz, 2000). The SOP pattern of the young good readers was similar to that of adults, but among the young dyslexic readers processing auditory information took a longer time than processing visual information. It is conceivable that, over the years, some dyslexics learn to speed up the auditory processing such that it becomes faster than the visual one, as a way of compensating for their deficiencies. SOP in the two modalities remained slower in dyslexics than in controls, and the gap between both groups increased with the complexity of the experimental task. Moreover, the within group variances in RT indicated a wider range in between task RT among dyslexics. RT in identifying letters, syllables, words, or pseudowords ranged from 700 ms to 760 ms among controls and from about 900 ms to 1,400 ms among dyslexics. It is conceivable that this wider range of SOP is a result of instability of the linguistic pattern in their mental lexicon.

The fact that increasing task complexity results in longer RT can be seen in the orthographic-phonological transformation tasks. Although the SOP of the dyslexics continued to be significantly slower than that of the controls, RT latencies of both groups increased when compared to the visual and the auditory single modality tasks. In the orthographic-phonological transformation tasks, the tasks involve processing information not only at the level of the stimuli (letters, syllables, or words), but rather the involvement of the two word recognition systems (i.e., the orthographic and phonological systems). This put a profound load on SOP of the information not only among the dyslexics but also among the good readers. However, in all the experiments presented earlier, SOP was measured only by RT at the output stage and the central question is at what stage of the information processing does this slowness in output performance originate? This is tackled in the coming chapters.

Additional interesting findings emerging from our experiments when using visual stimuli were related to the manipulation of the stimuli presentation times. It was observed that a short presentation time of the stimuli, about 40 ms, increased the RT and reduced accuracy of both groups of readers in each experiment. This time of stimuli presentation seems to be too fast for both groups to process information accurately.

The comfortable presentation time range for the good readers group, where accuracy increased and RT decreased, was on average around 80 ms. Interestingly, at presentation time above this level, no changes were observed in the RT and accuracy. Moreover, these results hold across all experiments, regardless of the difficulty of the task.

The dyslexic group displayed similarly interesting results. In their case, a presentation time of about 100 ms, regardless of the task demands and difficulties, was optimal for their performance in terms of RT and accuracy. These findings hold whether the stimuli were letters, syllables, or words and pseudowords. However, below and above this presentation time, RT increased and accuracy decreased among dyslexics. This suggests that although a presentation rate below 100 ms may be too fast for the dyslexics to process the information, a presentation time of above 100 ms may open a "window for distractibility and inattentiveness." The issue of the effectiveness of manipulating the presentation time of linguistic stimuli on the performance of dyslexics is discussed in chapter 12.

10

Event-Related Potentials (ERPs) in the Study of Dyslexia

The main conception on which this book is based is that speed of processing in the modalities and systems activated during reading is crucial for effective reading fluency. This chapter presents data from our research project, which was designed to investigate the speed at which regular and dyslexic readers process information in the modalities and systems that are activated during reading. In all these experiments, only behavioral measures (reaction time, RT, and accuracy, AC) were used. However, as a cognitive activity, reading is based on information-processing mechanisms and requires highly complex information-processing skills. As such, this cognitive activity varies along the different stages of the information-processing system. During the input stage, attention, perception, and discrimination of alphabetic symbols in the visual and acoustic modalities are required. In the processing stage, activation of these symbols in short-term memory (STM) and working memory (WM) is required, as are interpretations and retrieval of the alphabetic representations from long-term memory (LTM) and the mental lexicon (ML). At this stage, the orthographic, phonological, and semantic systems are activated. During the output stage, reading requires activation of various motor systems. This process ends with the reader's responses.

When behavioral measures are used in reading research, information about this entire sequence of cognitive activity is provided only at the conclusion of processing, in the reader's output. This stage only arrives after the completion of sensory, cognitive, and motor processes (Bentin, 1989). As such, behavioral measures cannot specify all the covert component operations that contribute to reading, nor can they determine the relative processing times required by the individual stages. Furthermore, they cannot determine which processes occur serially, which occur in parallel, and which overlap in time (Brandeis & Lehmann, 1994; Johnson, 1995). This makes it difficult to determine, on the basis of behavioral measures alone, the extent to which dysfunction or slowness at any particular stage of processing contributes to reading deficits.

In recent years, a new methodology has been put to use in reading research. This methodology is based on electrophysiological parameters utilizing electro-encephalogram (EEG) data. EEG methods used to assess online processing of cognitive activity focus on the measurement of event-related potentials (ERPs). This method permits direct observation of information processing at different levels of analysis, and can provide crucial information by means of real-time imaging of the neural system's responses to sensory stimulation (Bentin, 1989). Thus, it enables us to trace online the speed at which information is processed during the various cognitive stages of the reading activity. ERPs are extracted from EEG data by averaging brain responses during a number of equivalent trials in a given experiment. ERPs consist of various discrete components, or brain waves, that can be related to different stages of information processing in terms of amplitude and/or latency variations. The components are usually designated by their polarity (P—positive, N—negative) and by the latency of their maximal amplitudes in milliseconds. Areas of brain specialization can be identified by observing variations of amplitude and latency in ERP components across different scalp locations (see Halgren, 1990). ERP components reflect the time course of sensory and cognitive processes with millisecond resolution that cannot be directly inferred from behavior. Nevertheless, the data obtained from behavioral and electrophysiological measures are complementary, as each provides information about the same cognitive activity. Several ERP components have been identified, which according to the literature characterize certain types of brain activity during cognitive processing in general and the reading activity in particular (Regan, 1989):

1. P100-N100 is assumed to represent an exogenic response, or sensory activity, elicited by a stimulus (Johnstone, Barry, J. W. Anderson, & Coyle, 1996; Tonnquist-Uhlen, 1996).

2. P200 is thought to index mechanisms of feature detection (e.g., Luck & Hillyard, 1994), selective attention (e.g., Hackley, Woldorff & Hillyard, 1990), and other early sensory stages of item encoding (B. R. Dunn, D. A. Dunn, Languis, & Andrews, 1998). P200 is not merely an exogenous component, but may also be related to endogenous or cognitive processing variables (Dunn et al., 1998; McDonough, Warren, & Don, 1992).

3. N200 is generally considered to be a processing negativity associated with focused attention, stimulus classification, and discrimination (Näätänen & Picton, 1987; Novak, Ritter, Vaugh, & Wiznitzer, 1990; Ritter, Simson, Vaughan, & Macht, 1982; Vaughan & Kurtzberg, 1992).

4. P300 is a valid index of central information processing during task-related decision making (Palmer, Nasman, & Wilson, 1994). Included among the different processes held to be associated with P300 are the dynamic updating of information held in working memory (Isreal, Chesney, Wickens, & Donchin, 1980; Fitzgerald & Picton, 1983), cognitive resource allocation and task involvement (Kramer, Strayer, & Buckley, 1991), as well as mental effort or workload (Humphrey & Kramer, 1994; Wilson, Swain, & Ullsperger, 1998).

5. N400 is usually regarded as a manifestation of lexical integration and is associated with different aspects of semantic processing (Neville, Coffey, Holcomb, & Tallal, 1993).

6. MMN (mismatch negativity) is a component used for identifying dysfunction in the auditory system.

This chapter reviews the existing research on ERP components in cognitive reading experiments and presents evidence from dyslexic readers. This is followed by a presentation of our studies in this field.

ERP EVIDENCE ON DYSLEXIC READERS

The majority of studies carried out in an attempt to discover differences in the patterns of ERP component activation between dyslexics and regular readers have focused on the P300 component, although there are accumulating reports on earlier and later components. Regarding the early waves, a comparatively large amount of recent work has focused on the P100 component. However, reports on the N100, P200, and N200 are rare.

The P100 Component

This line of investigation has focused on the examination of the magnocellular deficit hypothesis (see chap. 5 as well). Therefore, all reports are on the visual P100. Mixed results have been obtained. Using pattern reversal stimuli, Mecacci, Sechi, and Levi (1983) and Solan, Sutija, Ficarra, and Wurst (1990) reported smaller P100 amplitudes in reading disabled children than in control children. Brannan, Solan, Ficarra, and Ong (1998) also obtained evidence of lower VEP (P100) amplitudes among dyslexic readers in response to sinusoidal checkerboard patterns of spatial frequency arcs at 1 Hz, 4 Hz, and 8 Hz, as well as on an 8 Hz flicker fusion stimulus. These results were obtained in both high and low luminance conditions. Latency differences in P100 have also been reported. Brecelj, Strucl, and Raic (1996), for instance, found a significant prolongation of the P100 wave in dyslexic children when responding to high-contrast, small-checked patterns. On the other hand, Lehmkuhle, Garzia, Turner, and Hash (1993) found that both P100 and N100 latencies of visual evoked potentials among dyslexic children were longer in response to low, but not high, spatial frequency targets. A flickering background for these stimuli was found to increase the latencies and amplitudes of these components among normal readers; however, they only affected amplitudes among reading disabled children. Livingstone et al. (1991) obtained similar results. Visually evoked potentials between 70 ms and 170 ms poststimulus were delayed among dyslexics over the occipital areas when processing rapidly changing patterns with low spatial frequencies and low contrast.

The N100 Component

The scarce data available to date suggest that the N100 component may differ among dyslexic and normal readers, although the direction of this difference is not yet clear. Harter, Anllo-Vento, and Wood (1989) found that reading disabled boys had larger N100s than normal boys on a visual target detection paradigm. Conversely, Hennighausen, Remschmidt, and Warnke (1994) found that a sample of dyslexic children showed lower N100 amplitudes in the left-central region (C3) when fixating on a reversing checkerboard pattern. On the whole, the N100 component was significantly more absent in dyslexic subjects than in controls, but more frequent in dyslexics with low spelling scores. In another study, Neville et al. (1993) observed a lower amplitude and longer latency of N100 in dyslexic as compared to normal readers during simple auditory and visual recognition tasks.

The N100 (or N1) is the most prominent peak of auditory ERPs elicited by simple repetitive stimuli such as tones or syllables. Differences in latency or amplitude of the auditory N100 have been reported in children with reading difficulties (Brunswick & Rippon, 1994; Neville et al., 1993; Pinkerton, Watson, & McClelland, 1989) as well as in children with language impairments (Dawson, Finley, Phillips, & Lewy, 1989; Lincoln, Courchesne, Harms, & Allen, 1995; Neville et al., 1993; Tonnquist-Uhlen, Borg, Persson, & Spens, 1996). Reduction of N100 amplitude was found in a group of 14 boys with difficulties in reading, writing, and spelling (designated "poor readers") as compared to 18 "good readers" (all 8–9 years old) in a study by Pinkerton et al. (1989). Cortical auditory ERPs were recorded in response to 2,000-Hz tone bursts while participants watched silent films. Reduced N100 amplitudes (around 160 ms) in poor readers were observed at three out of four scalp locations. For the whole sample, N100 amplitude was correlated positively with performance IQ, spelling scores, reading accuracy, and comprehension, as well as with arithmetic. In interpreting the data, Pinkerton and colleagues suggested that the decreased N100 magnitude could be associated with impairments in processes mediating selective attention.

Brunswick and Rippon (1994) contrasted 15 dyslexic boys (7–11 years old) with 15 normally reading controls (8–10 years old) on ERPs in response to stop consonant–vowel syllables presented in a dichotic listening paradigm. The participants were asked to report simultaneously presented syllables as accurately as possible. No significant group differences were observed in either the right ear or the left ear responses. However, normally reading children exhibited larger N100 amplitudes at left temporal-electrode sites than the dyslexic children, who showed less lateralized temporal N100 magnitude. The N100 lateralization was also found to be positively related to performance on a phonological awareness task, namely, rhyme oddity detection among words that differed in their final sounds (e.g., pin, win, sit, fin). According to Brunswick and Rippon, the deviations in N100 laterality are associated with abnormal cerebral lateralization of language functions in dyslexia. The failure of the dichotic listening task to discriminate between dyslexic and normal readers despite the N100 laterality differences was interpreted as an indication that laterality does not affect processing of stimuli per se but appears to be associated with later aspects of phoneme analysis. However, in view of the fact that the N100 has been considered a basic index of adequate sensory registration, Leppänen and Lyytinen (1997) proposed that an altered N100 response might reflect inaccurate tuning of sensory information, resulting in less reliable auditory representations that are in turn manifested in poor performance on language tests.

Yingling, Galin, Fein, Peltzman, and Davenport (1986), on the other hand, did not find any differences between 38 severely dyslexic boys (mean age 13.3 years) and 38 nonimpaired peers on ERPs following stimulation with auditory clicks. Bernal et al. (2000) observed no deviations of N100 in response to pure tones in a group of 20 poor readers (10–12 years old), but reported larger amplitudes in two later components, the N200 and the P200, as compared to 20 normally reading children.[1] Molfese (2000) presented evidence that auditory ERPs

---

[1]Unfortunately, Pinkerton et al. (1989), Brunswick and Rippon (1994), and Yingling et al. (1986) did not present any figures depicting grand-average or individual subject ERPs.

recorded within 36 hours of birth discriminated between newborns that would be classified as dyslexic, poor, or normal readers 8 years later. The auditory ERPs analyzed by Molfese included the N100-P200-N200[2] waves elicited by speech and nonspeech syllables with mean peak latencies of 174, 309, and 458 ms, respectively. The left hemisphere N100 latency at birth was found to be shortest for the normally reading children and longest for the poor readers. Neither the dyslexic nor the poor readers displayed a well-defined N100 component. Right hemisphere N200 peak amplitudes were largest for the dyslexic children and smallest for the poor readers. In particular, as suggested by Molfese, the group differences in N100 latency might point to an underlying perceptual mechanism on which some aspects of later developing verbal and cognitive processes are based.

With respect to severe language impairment, or SLI, Dawson et al. (1989) reported atypical hemispheric asymmetry of N100 in response to a simple speech stimulus. In this study, 10 children with SLI ranging from age 6 to 15 years were compared to 10 children with autism and 10 language normal controls (age 8–13 years). Children were presented with a series of auditory stimuli involving 80% clicks, 10% syllables (viz. /da/), and 10% piano chord stimuli. They were asked to indicate whenever the /da/ stimulus occurred. Based on the analysis of right hemisphere minus left hemisphere scores, both the SLI and autistic group showed opposite patterns of N100 asymmetry compared to the pattern that characterized the controls (i.e., smaller left-than-right amplitude and shorter left-than-right latency). Furthermore, in children with autism, language abilities were associated with right hemisphere activity measures. Although performance on three out of six verbal tests correlated positively with the N100 latency, correctness on all six tests was negatively related to the N100 amplitude. In children with SLI, on the other hand, impaired performance on four of the language measures was associated with longer left hemisphere N100 latency. No statistical relation between N100 and language measures was obtained for the control children. According to Dawson and colleagues, the pattern of hemispheric activity found in children with SLI coincides with a deficit in processing sequential information, for which the left hemisphere is thought to be pivotal.

---

[2]It should be noted that the equivalents of the adult components are unclear (Ceponiene, Cheour, & Näätänen, 1998). For example, the N1/N100 component is not consistently present until age 9, although it can be seen more readily when stimulus presentation rate is reduced or multichannel recording techniques are implemented (Bruneau, Roux, Guerin, & Barthelemy, 1997; Ceponiene et al., 1998).

Lincoln et al. (1995) studied children with SLI, autism, and normal language skills (10 in each group, aged 8–14 years) in two experiments. The first experiment involved passive listening to a series of pure tones, which differed in frequency and intensity (1,000 Hz/60dB vs. 70 dB and 3,000 Hz/63 dB vs. 73 dB, all with equal probability). No group differences in latency or amplitude of the auditory N100 were obtained. However, unlike the children with autism or SLI, the control participants did show an increase in N100 amplitude to increases in stimulus intensity. In the second experiment, two pure tones were presented in two different conditions, with the following variation on the so-called oddball paradigm. The active or response condition required the child to press one button as a response to each frequent tone (probability = 70%) and another button in response to each infrequent tone (probability = 30%). In the passive or no-response condition, children simply listened to the stimuli. In both the active and passive conditions, N100 amplitude was found to be generally larger in SLI children as compared to control subjects (and nearly significantly larger compared to autistic children). The N100 latencies were similar in autistic and control children, but differed from the SLI group. Lincoln and colleagues concluded that the N100 deviances are consistent with theories claiming that SLI is related to ineffective regulation of sensory input. They speculated that the duration (50 ms) of the tones employed in their study may have been too short SLI children, which have to allocate further attentional resources, as mirrored by the enhanced N100. Alternatively, it has been suggested that the increased N100 peak is associated with impaired encoding of auditory information in short-term memory. Thus, for some of the SLI children, the 2-second ISI might be too long to maintain the internal reference indicating whether the tone designated the frequent or infrequent stimulus.

Neville et al. (1993) reported N100 deviances in a subset of SLI children who exhibited deficits in auditory temporal processing. Twenty-two SLI children with concomitant reading disability (RD) and 12 controls who displayed normal language development and academic achievement (all 8–10 years old) were compared on auditory and visual ERPs. The auditory paradigm involved an active oddball task in which a 1,000-Hz tone was presented as the target stimulus (10% probability) among 2,000-Hz standard stimuli at one of three ISIs (200 ms, 1,000 ms, and 2,000 ms) and at one of three different stimulus positions (left ear, both ears, and right ear). Because no group differences were obtained for the auditory ERPs to either stimulus, the SLI/RD children were subclassified into two subgroups according to their performance on an auditory rapid sequencing test. SLI/RD children performing below the median level were classified as "low repetition" (i.e., displaying auditory temporal processing problems) while those scoring above were classified as "high repetition."[3] The N140 component to standard tones was significantly diminished over the right hemisphere at the shortest ISI in the low repetition group, as compared to both the language normal controls and the high repetition SLI/RD group. In addition, the latency of the standard N140 was significantly delayed in the low repetition SLI/RD group, especially over temporal and parietal sites of the left hemisphere. Neville and colleagues considered the N140 component to be equivalent to the adult N100. The contralateral (to the stimulated ear) and anterior distribution of the N140 response suggested to them that it reflects activity generated in the superior temporal gyrus, encompassing primary and secondary auditory areas. Hence, these findings were assumed to indicate that the reduced and slowed down activity within the cortical sites of SLI/RD children with auditory temporal processing problems contributed to these children's language symptoms. However, the authors' interpretation ought not to be taken as a single-factor account of the deficits of language and reading impaired children. Various deviations on visual ERPs to both language and nonlanguage stimuli were also reported for either the whole SLI/RD group or only a subset of it.

Finally, Tonnquist-Uhlen et al. (1996) observed significantly delayed N100 latency and a tendency toward higher incidence of unusual topographic maps in 20 children with severe SLI (9–15 years old), when contrasted to an age-matched control group ($n = 20$). Using a passive listening paradigm, pure-tone stimuli of 500 Hz were delivered to the left and right ears separately. The peak latency of the vertex-recorded N100 was longer in the SLI children (on average 110 ms) than in the healthy controls (on average 100 ms) following right-ear stimulation. Both left-ear and right-ear elicited N100 responses tended to decline with increasing age in the control children but not in the SLI group. Whereas the delayed N100 latencies were presumed to be due to slower processing in central auditory pathways, the lack of an age-related latency decrease was seen as indicating that the disturbance persists, rather than reflecting a pure maturational delay. Furthermore, the SLI children showed a trend toward a greater number of deviating or nonfocal topographic maps after left-ear stimulation. According to Tonnquist-Uhlen et al. (1996), atypical N100 topography may be accounted for by a lack of synchronization, that is, due to immature or poor connections between different cortical areas and deeper structures.

Taken together, the auditory ERP studies cited previously indicate differences in N100 features between groups of children designated as SLI, dyslexia,

---

[3]Subgroup sizes are not specified in the article.

or poor readers, and healthy controls. Whereas latency deviances in language-based learning impairments may be associated with a common timing deficit, N100 amplitude differences have been related to attentional factors or inadequate sensory processing. However, large individual variability coupled with recording techniques using only a limited number of electrodes have commonly led to negative results or only nonsignificant trends.

The P200 Component

Very little evidence has been reported on the P200, although the available data suggest that a similar pattern may characterize both young and adult dyslexic readers, at least at the linguistic level in the visual modality. Harter, Deiring, and Wood (1988) found smaller P20040 amplitudes in the left hemisphere as compared to the right among dyslexics and compared to normal children during a letter recognition task (an intralocation selective attention paradigm). Naylor, Wood, and Harter (1995) obtained similar results with adult readers. These researchers obtained evidence of smaller P200s at left central sites among dyslexic adults using the same task. Subjects showed a general reduction in positivity beginning at around 150 ms, until about 500 ms. However, adult dyslexics appear to be characterized by more diffuse, bilateral reductions in electrophysiological responses.

The N200 Component

In general, the scarce studies reporting on the N200 component indicate that N200 latencies may occur later among dyslexic than among normal readers. No group differences in N200 amplitude have been reported. This appears to be true in both the visual and auditory modalities. In the auditory domain, Fawcett et al. (1993) found evidence of later N200s among dyslexic readers in response to target tones in an oddball paradigm. Comparatively more studies have examined this component using visual stimuli. M. J. Taylor and Keenan (1990) found later N200 latencies among dyslexics with a visual processing impairment in response to both linguistic (letters, words, and nonwords) and nonlinuistic (symbols) stimuli. Neville et al. (1993) reported attenuated N200 latencies among language disabled dyslexic readers. Taylor and Keenan (1999) examined dyslexic children with auditory processing deficits and normal children on three visual target detection tasks: orthographic (targets were letters with closed loops), phonological (targets were letters that rhymed with v), and semantic

(three-letter animal names). N200 latencies tended to be longer in the semantic task among dyslexic as compared to normal children.

The P300 Component

P300 components of smaller amplitudes and longer latencies among dyslexic
readers have been reported by many investigators, in response to both linguistic
and nonlinguistic auditory and visual stimuli (Barnea, Lamm, Epstein, & Pratt,
1994; Duncan et al., 1994; Erez & Pratt, 1992; Fawcett et al., 1993; Harter,
Anllo-Vento, Wood, & Schroeder, 1988; Harter, Deiring, & Wood, 1988;
Holcomb, Ackerman, & Dykman, 1985, 1986; Johannes, Mangun, & Muente,
1994; Taylor & Keenan, 1990, 1999). Nevertheless, not all studies have found
evidence of differences on both parameters concurrently in a particular task. In
the auditory domain, for instance, several investigators have found evidence of
smaller but not longer P300s among dyslexic children when using simple auditory stimuli (Holcomb et al., 1986; Lovrich & Stamm, 1983). Others have
found the reverse pattern. For instance, Fawcett et al. (1993) observed longer
P300 latencies but no differences in P300 amplitudes to target tones among dyslexic adolescents performing a selective choice reaction (oddball) task. Studies
employing visual stimuli tend to produce similar results. Neville et al. (1993)
found that language impaired, reading disabled children had significantly
smaller P300 amplitudes relative to normal children in response to visual stimuli in target detection tasks. Duncan et al. (1994) obtained evidence of reductions in visual P300s among dyslexic as compared to normal men with
increasing task demands. However, additional analyses revealed that dyslexic
readers who displayed many symptoms of attention deficit hyperactivity disorder (ADHD) in childhood accounted for group differences.
    Other researchers have reported evidence of differences in P300 latencies.
Johannes et al. (1994) examined visual P300s among dyslexic and normal children using a simple visual discrimination task. They found that although P300
amplitude did not differ between the two groups, the latencies of P300 were longer among dyslexic readers. Furthermore, the distribution of this component
over the two hemispheres was almost symmetrical among dyslexic readers, but
appeared primarily in the left hemisphere among normal readers. Taylor and
Keenan (1990) found evidence that dyslexics with visual processing deficits
had longer latency P300s to nonlinguistic symbols, letters, and words in an oddball task. In a subsequent study, Taylor and Keenan (1999) found that dyslexic
children had longer P300 latencies on phonological and semantic tasks, but not

on orthographic tasks. P300 appeared to be located at a more posterior brain site among dyslexic readers across the three tasks.

Differences in processing linguistic versus nonlinguistic stimuli have also been reported using different types of tasks. Generally, nonlinguistic visual stimuli (symbols) have been found to elicit P300s of greater amplitudes and longer latencies than linguistic visual stimuli (words) in dyslexic readers (Barnea et al., 1994; Holcomb et al., 1985). Barnea et al. (1994) compared ERPs in dyslexic and normal children during a short-term memory task for lexical (digits) and nonlexical (characters) visual stimuli and found smaller P300 amplitudes to lexical stimuli among dyslexics. In addition, response to probes was more prominent over the right scalp in dyslexics and over the left scalp in normal readers. Silva-Pereyra et al. (2001) compared P300s on verbal and nonverbal working memory tasks among dyslexic and normal readers in the third grade. On the verbal task (Sternberg's task), the P300 latency was longer among the dyslexic children, with no significant difference in amplitude. On the nonverbal task, smaller P300s were found among poor readers over occipital regions and larger amplitudes over central regions. The poor reader groups had longer latencies than the controls. The authors concluded that the dyslexics showed later P300s on both linguistic and nonlinguistic tasks, due to difficulty in temporal visual processing. Higher amplitudes on the linguistic task may reflect a higher degree of difficulty for dyslexics on this task. Lastly, researchers have also compared verbal and nonverbal auditory stimuli. Erez and Pratt (1992) compared dyslexic and normal children on target detection tasks and observed both smaller P300 amplitudes and longer P300 latencies in response to verbal (nonsense monosyllables) as compared to nonverbal (pure tones) stimuli. P300 apex orientation tilted to the right among dyslexics, but to the left among normal readers. Barnea and colleagues (1994) suggested that this general pattern of results might indicate that dyslexic readers relate more to physical features of stimuli, whereas normal readers may rely more on linguistic features.

The N400 Component

There is extensive evidence of differences between dyslexic and normal readers on the N400 component. Lovrich, Cheng, Velting, and Kazmerski (1997) compared normal and reading impaired college students on auditory rhyme decision and semantic decision tasks, and found a relatively larger negativity at around 480 ms for reading disabled as compared to normal readers during word rhyming tasks. This was particularly pronounced at C3. No differences in N400 were found between the groups when they were required to make semantic decisions.

However, within group analyses revealed that N480 amplitude was larger for semantic tasks than for rhyme tasks among normal readers, but not among impaired readers. Similar findings were reported by Lovrich, Cheng, and Velting (1996), based on a comparison of dyslexic and normal children. Ackerman et al. (1994) found that compared to slow readers and children with ADD, dyslexic children exhibited an attenuated N450 peak when performing a visual rhyme decision task in which the first of two sequentially presented stimuli was a real word, and the second was either an orthographically similar word or a nonword. Reading disabled children did not show the N400 reduction for rhyming stimuli characteristic of normal children.

McPherson et al. (1996) examined dyslexic adolescents in a paradigm that required them to decide if two sequentially presented pictures were objects with names that rhymed. Phonetic dyslexics (better decoders) showed an N400 priming effect, but dysphonetics (poorer decoders) did not. (The priming effect was calculated on the basis of the mean N450 of the rhyming targets subtracted from the nonrhyming targets.) McPherson, Ackerman, Holcomb, and Dykman (1998) examined disabled and normal readers on visual and auditory rhyme decision tasks using single syllable real words. They found that phonetic dyslexics exhibited reduced auditory priming for the N450, whereas dysphonetic dyslexics displayed reduced visual priming. J. Miles and Stelmack (1994) also used a priming paradigm and found that reading disabled children did not display the usual left hemisphere asymmetry in frontal N450 amplitude to unprimed spoken words. However, the same was true of arithmetic disabled and combined reading/arithmetic disabled subgroups. Studies using sentence paradigms have also reported differences in N400. Brandeis, Vitacco, and Steinhausen (1994) found delayed N400 among dyslexic as compared to normal children during silent reading of correct and incorrect sentence endings. Neville et al. (1993) reported that dyslexic readers exhibited both higher amplitude and later N400s in response to unexpected words at the end of sentences. Robichon, Besson, and Habib (2002) found a larger N400 among dyslexic as compared to normal adults while reading sentences that appeared word by word on a computer screen at a rate of 100 ms a word, in congruous and incongruous conditions. They did not find any differences in the P300 component and assumed that adult dyslexics have not just a pure sensory deficit, but actually experience difficulties integrating the meaning of words into a sentence.

Plante, Van-Petten, and Senkfor (2000) studied the differences between adult learning disabled (reading and language disabilities) and normal adult readers by using a cross-modal experiment with one visual and one auditory stimulus, which were connected or not connected semantically. There were pairs of words and pairs of nonverbal stimuli (picture and sound). No differences were found in the early components. The N400 amplitude was smaller among the learning disabled group, and it appeared only after the nonverbal stimuli in this group. In addition, there was a different scalp distribution for the component. Higher amplitudes were displayed in the right hemisphere for the learning disabled group on verbal and nonverbal stimuli. For the controls, the right hemisphere was dominant for words and the left for nonverbal stimuli. Even though there were no differences in behavioral data, it was assumed that the two groups use different physiological mechanisms to accomplish the task of semantic associations.

The MMN Component

The MMN has recently been applied to the study of phonological and auditory dysfunctions in dyslexia, with promising results (Kujala & Näätänen, 2001). Schulte-Korne et al. (1998) examined the differences in processing of tones and syllables among adolescent dyslexic and normal readers. They found no differences with the nonverbal stimuli. With ¬he syllables (/ba/ - deviant and /da/ - standard) they found that the MMN amplitude was smaller among the dyslexic readers. The authors interpreted this result as reflecting a phonological deficit and not a general failure in processing auditory information. Other studies, such as Baldeweg, Richardson, Watkins, Foale, and Gurzelier (1999), found differences in tone discrimination as well (1,000 Hz—standard; 1,015, 1,030, 1,060 Hz—deviation). Among adult dyslexics, the MMN amplitudes were lower and less accurately behaviorally discriminated. In addition, the MMN and discrimination performance correlated with the degree of phonological skill impairment. Csepe, Szucs, and Osman-Sagi (2000) showed that dyslexics have difficulty processing small rather than big stimulus differences, as reflected by the discrimination of stop-consonants separated from each other by acoustically minor sound differences.

Schulte-Koerne, Bartling, Deimel, and Remschmidt (1999) found that changes in the temporal order of pattern elements also elicited smaller MMNs among dyslexic as compared to normal readers. This might imply that sound elements are masked or interfered with by surrounding sounds of sound sequences in dyslexics. Kujala, Belitz, Tervaniemi, and Näätänen (2003) found that dyslexic subjects had diminished MMNs in response to tone order reversal, which strengthens this assumption. Differences in MMN have been found in genetically high-risk children who have a family member with dyslexia (Pennington, 1995), as compared to children with no family-based risk of dyslexia. Leppänen, Pihko,

Eklund, and Lyytinen (1999) found several differences between the groups. Duration changes elicited different MMNs in amplitude and scalp distribution between the two groups. The amplitude was lower over the left hemisphere among the at-risk children. A small difference in duration elicited an MMN in control but not in at-risk children. These results indicate that with MMN, dysfunctions of phonological/auditory processing in dyslexia can be determined in infants as young as 6 months old. Kujala et al. (2001) showed that children who underwent a phonological training program and improved their phonological processing experienced changes in MMN amplitude that correlated with their improvement on reading skill measures. Heim et al. (2000) showed similar results with language impaired children whose MMNs looked more like those of the control group after a phonological training program.

Conclusions

In sum, electrophysiological research has revealed differences between dyslexic and regular readers in several ERP components. However, this research has revealed a substantial degree of variability in results. It has been suggested that this variance is largely due to differences in sample selection (e.g., different subtypes of dyslexic readers) and a lack of precision concerning the relation between the deficit and the experimental tasks used (see Hagoort & Kutas, 1995, for a discussion). Most of these studies attempted to explore brain activity differences between dyslexic and regular readers using ERP methodology and focused mainly on ERP amplitudes. The few studies that have reported differences between these two groups of readers in terms of ERP latencies have found that the latencies were elicited later in dyslexic readers. The focus of the present book is speed of processing in the modalities and systems that are activated during reading at various stages of information processing. Therefore a comprehensive research project was designed that systematically investigated the speed at which dyslexic and regular readers process information in the visual and auditory modalities, separately as well as simultaneously, and in the orthographic and phonological systems. This project is described in the following section.

OUR STUDIES

Overview

Speed of processing of the modalities and systems at different levels of activity was examined by:

- Investigating the same groups of regular and dyslexic readers in all the experiments (a within and between subject design).
- Controlling the sample selection of the dyslexics.
- Controlling and manipulating the experimental tasks from lower level to higher level for both nonlinguistic and linguistic processing, as well as incorporating stimuli at various levels of complexity. At the lower level, tasks included distinguishing between nonlinguistic visual (flashes-shapes) and auditory (beeps-tones) stimuli, and distinguishing between linguistic visual (graphemes) and auditory (phonemes) stimuli. All were presented in each of the modalities alone. At the higher level, subjects were asked to process orthographic and phonological information at the level of words-pseudowords (lexical decision paradigm) and sentences.
- Using electrophysiological measures (latencies and amplitudes of ERP components) as well as behavioral measures of reaction time (RT) and accuracy (AC).

Subjects

Two samples of subjects participated in the ERP studies:

1. The same 100 adult subjects that participated in our behavioral research project (see chapter 7), including 50 dyslexics and 50 regular readers. All subjects were free of hard neurological signs (APA, 1994).

2. 80 young, right-handed, male readers, including 40 dyslexics and 40 regular age-matched readers with a mean age of 10 years and 7 months ($SD = 1.23$ months). All subjects were from a middle-class background. The regular readers where from two different schools, and were matched to the dyslexics on nonverbal IQ scores (Raven Standard Progressive Matrices; Raven, 1965).

The dyslexics were recruited from the University of Haifa Clinic for Learning Disabilities. All were diagnosed by an intake battery, which included an evaluation of reading skills. All subjects in the dyslexics group met the Israeli criterion for dyslexia, which requires them to be in the 16th percentile or below on the reading achievement test (Breznitz, 2000).

Instrumentation

For each of the computerized tasks, stimuli were presented on an IBM-PC terminal. Visual stimuli were presented in white over a gray background on a computer display located 1.5 m in front of the subject. Auditory stimuli were
presented either over the PC speaker (tones) or via headphones (consonant
sounds). For each task, subjects responded by pressing one of two buttons on a
joystick. Prior to data collection in each task, subjects were instructed to respond immediately after stimulus occurrence. Twenty-two channels of electro-
encephalogram (EEG) were recorded using a Bio-Logic Brain Atlas III
computer system with brain mapping capabilities. This system uses a band pass
of 0.1–70 Hz interfaced with a 20-channel, 12-bit A/D converter. The EEGs
were sampled at a rate of 250 Hz (dwell time = 4.0 ms) beginning 100 ms before
stimulus onset. A full array of electrodes was placed according to the International 10/20 system (Jasper, 1958) utilizing an Electro-cap (a nylon cap fitted
over the head with 9 mm tin electrodes sewn within). Nineteen scalp electrodes
were used, corresponding to standard 10/20 system locations: PF1, PF2, F7, F3,
FZ, F4, F8, T3, C3, CZ, C4, T4, T5, P3, PZ, P4, T6, O1, and O2. All were refer-
enced to an electrode on CVII (the seventh vertebra) and grounded to Fpz. In
addition, one electrode was applied diagonally below the left eye to monitor eye
movements. During data collection electrode impedance was kept below 5K
Ohms by first prepping scalp areas with a mildly abrasive cleanser (Omni-Prep)
and then using an electrolyte gel (Electro-gel). Trial onset was marked on the
Oz channel of EEG via a positive polarity 5 millivolt pulse delivered from an
IBM-PC 486 computer. Signal averaging of the raw EEG data was performed
offline. EEG data was separated into discrete trials. After rejections of the trials
containing eye movement, averages of the individual trials in each experiment
were determined for each subject.

Each subject had approximately 5 to 6 hours of testing sessions. During the
experimental tests in which electrophysiological data were collected, the subjects were seated in a sound-attenuated room in front of an IBM-PC computer
screen. Experimental task presentation was semi-random, in that the four oddball tasks were always administered first (although the order of presentation
across the four oddball tasks was counterbalanced). This was because these
tasks were the simplest, and it was important to habituate the subjects to the
testing situation. Subjects were connected to an Electro-cap (requiring about
30–40 min of preparation). ERPs were obtained for each subject in each experimental condition. Only single trials free from eye movements and associated
with correct responses were averaged to obtain the event-related potentials.

Grand averages over conditions and subjects were then performed for each experiment for each of the 19 scalp electrodes. ERP peaks were first identified and then validated by a machine-scoring algorithm. Latencies were measured from stimulus onset and amplitudes were measured relative to the mean voltage of each channel during the prestimulus baseline. All stimuli were presented via computer and reaction time, measured from stimulus onset until button press response, and accuracy (percentage of correct responses) were recorded.

The Tasks

Nonlinguistic and linguistic tasks employing flashes and shapes, beeps and tones, letter, syllable, word-pseudoword, and sentence conditions were presented in the visual and auditory modalities separately.

Lower Level Processing (Child and Adult Subjects). In each task, a series of 120 stimuli were randomly presented. Of these, 50 were targets and 70 were nontargets. Stimulus duration was 170 ms and the ISI was 1,000 ms. Subjects were asked to press a button in response to target stimuli and to ignore nontarget stimuli. The stimuli were presented in each modality separately and in both modalities simultaneously:

Auditory tasks:
1. Nonlinguistic stimuli were target tones of 1,000 Hz and nontarget tones of 2,000 Hz. Tones were played over the PC speaker placed behind the subject.
2. Linguistic stimuli were consonant sounds. The target was /d/ and the nontarget was /b/. Stimuli were presented via headphones.

Visual tasks:
1. Nonlinguistic stimuli were two meaningless shapes ¼ mm high presented in the center of the computer screen, one for the target and one for the nontarget.
2. Linguistic stimuli were two Hebrew letters presented in the center of the computer screen. The target was the letter "bet" (/b/, ב) and the nontarget was the letter "chaf" (/ch/, כ).

Higher Level Processing

Orthographic-phonological processing among children and adults was examined using the following tasks:

Lexical Decision Task (Breznitz, 1998). A random series of 60 words and 60 pseudowords (total 120) was presented on a computer screen. The stimuli appeared horizontally in the center of the screen, and subjects were instructed to look at the stimuli and to press one button of a joystick in response to the words with the corresponding thumb, and the other button with the other thumb in response to the pseudowords. Performance on words is conceptualized as a measure of higher level orthographic decision processes, whereas performance on pseudowords is perceived as a measure of higher level phonological processing. The stimuli were comprised of Hebrew letters that were ¼ inch in diameter each. Each stimulus contained five letters. Presentation duration of each stimulus was 300 ms and the ISI between stimuli was 2,000 ms. Response hand was counterbalanced across subjects.

Sentence Tasks (Adults Only). Sentences with expected/unexpected endings were presented in the visual and auditory modalities. A total of 240 Hebrew sentences composed of four words each were presented separately to the subjects. Each test contained two types of sentences: 80 sentences in which the last word was not related to the preceding text (unexpected) and 40 sentences in which the last word was related to the context (expected). Unexpected and expected sentences were distributed randomly among the two experimental conditions. One condition presented 120 sentences visually on the computer screen and the other 120 were presented in the auditory modality via headphones.

Results

In most of our experiments, two pronounced ERP components were identified for all groups of subjects: an early P200 component and a later P300 component (see also Breznitz & Meyler, 2003; Breznitz & Misra, 2003). In the sentences study, P200 and N400 components were identified. Amplitudes in all experiments ranged from −1 to 2.1 Vy. However, as the focus of this book is SOP, only data from ERP latencies are reported (for additional data on amplitudes, see Breznitz, 2001a; Breznitz & Meyler, 2003; Breznitz & Misra, 2003; Leiken & Breznitz, 1999). The most pronounced components appeared at the CZ electrodes on most of the tasks. Consequently, Figs. 10.1 to 10.5 present the peak latency times at the CZ electrode in each experiment for adults and children. Tables 10.1 to 10.5 display the means and standard deviations of the peak latency times (at CZ electrode) and reaction time from all the experiments.

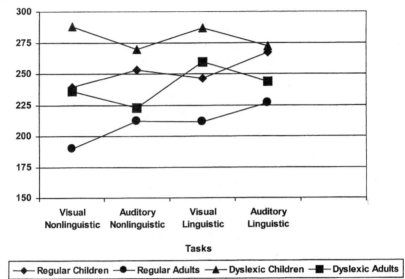

FIG. 10.1.   P200 latency lower level tasks: Regular vs. dyslexic readers (adults and children).

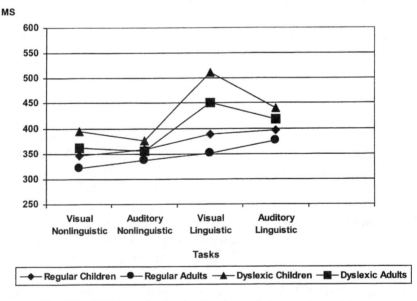

FIG. 10.2.   P300 lower level tasks: Regular vs. dyslexic readers (adults and children).

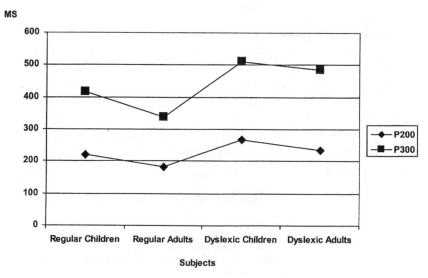

FIG. 10.3. Comparison of P200 and P300 words.

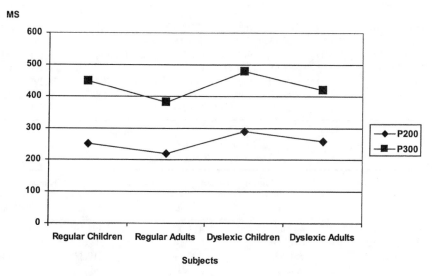

FIG. 10.4. Comparison of P200 and P300 pseudowords.

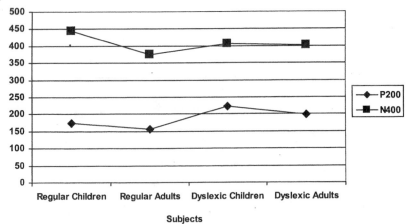

FIG. 10.5. Comparison of P200 and N400 sentence latencies.

TABLE 10.1
Lower Level Tasks ERP Data

M (SD)	Regular Readers				Dyslexics			
	Young		Adult		Young		Adult	
	P200	P300	P200	P300	P200	P300	P200	P300
Visual	239.33	346.19	190.02	321.13	287.91	394.11	236.32	361.31
nonlinguistic	(54.62)	(73.14)	(69.16)	(71.28)	(46.01)	(41.01)	(51.87)	(49.45)
Auditory	253.15	359.23	212.31	337.15	269.51	376.17	222.00	356.18
nonlinguistic	(54.01)	(75.78)	(42.23)	(37.11)	(66.67)	(84.56)	(64.17)	(51.28)
Visual linguis-	246.17	387.81	231.66	351.21	286.87	511.82	259.65	451.32
tic	(49.01)	(66.19)	(54.14)	(43.78)	(68.92)	(87.90)	(76.29)	(68.01)
Auditory lin-	267.18	396.15	246.67	376.16	272.18	439.38	243.49	417.36
guistic	(61.09)	(32.01)	(36.43)	(36.72)	(36.72)	(55.01)	(61.89)	(21.09)

TABLE 10.2
Lower Level Reaction Time

M (SD)	Regular Readers		Dyslexics	
	Young	Adult	Young	Adult
Visual	447.43	421.00	599.19	462.25
nonlinguistic	(23.21)	(49.90)	(38.01)	(67.19)
Auditory	366.53	300.44	419.32	387.44
nonlinguistic	(45.34)	(29.01)	(38.00)	(34.18)
Visual	455.23	401.15	569.67	479.56
linguistic	(67.01)	(56.23)	(54.29)	(65.21)
Auditory	431.67	422.87	479.65	433.59
linguistic	(41.56)	(39.01)	(45.39)	(27.19)

TABLE 10.3
Latencies of P200 and P300 in Words–Pseudowords Processing

	Regular Readers				Dyslexics			
	Young		Adult		Young		Adult	
M								
(SD)	P200	P300	P200	P300	P200	P300	P200	P300
Words	219.01	416.15	181.01	338.67	266.11	510.66	234.32	484.36
	(34.12)	(63.34)	(49.26)	(61.98)	(36.01)	(62.10)	(41.87)	(39.45)
Pseudowords	252.15	447.33	220.16	379.28	288.18	477.67	257.16	419.35
	(44.01)	(65.78)	(32.23)	(47.11)	(36.67)	(74.56)	(54.17)	(71.28)

TABLE 10.4
Sentences Processing

	Regular Readers				Dyslexics			
	Young		Adult		Young		Adult	
M								
(SD)	P200	N400	P200	N400	P200	N400	P200	N400
Sentences	175.11	444.61	156.21	374.34	222.23	405.21	198.22	401.12
Latencies	(69.4)	(72.9)	(29.0)	(37.9)	(44.8)	(38.5)	(71.9)	(69.0)
Sentences	2.24	−2.94	1.77	−2.62	3.90	−4.13	2.34	−1.69
Amplitudes	(1.1)	(0.2)	(1.5)	(1.8)	(1.4)	(1.2)	(1.1)	(1.1)

TABLE 10.5
Mean RT and (SD) for Sentences, Word–Pseudowords Tasks

	Regular readers		Dyslexics	
Mean (SD)	Young	Adult	Young	Adult
Sentences RT	736.56	571.09	819.88	643.03
	(368.09)	(187.30)	(192.40)	(395.04)
Words	1001.13	854.17	1578.10	1189.66
	(188.01)	(87.91)	(359.00)	(190.13)
Pseudowords	1389.54	881.33	2117.15	1440.13
	(378.56)	(123.06)	(831.11)	(671.32)

Results indicate a consistent slowness among young as well as adult dyslexic readers, as compared to regular readers, when processing information in the visual and auditory modalities. This slowness was evident on all tasks and at all levels and stages of activation. It appeared from the lower level of nonlinguistic and linguistic tasks to the higher level of processing words/pseudowords and sentences. In addition, young readers, whether or not they were dyslexic, appear to process information at a slower rate than adults. Our data also showed that the gap in SOP between the dyslexic and regular readers was somewhat smaller among children than among adult subjects, although SOP was slower at all ages when processing higher level tasks. Moreover, the between group SOP gap increased in reaction time, as compared to speed measures at the perceptual stage (P200).

CONCLUSIONS

Examination of the cerebral SOPs of young and adult dyslexic and regular readers using behavioral measures (see chap. 9 as well) and evoked potential methodology indicates the following data among the two types of subjects:

1. The sensory systems involved in reading process information at different rates. This variance was observed in each of the information-processing stages, and was expressed in the attention and perception stages via P200 latency and in the updating and memory processing stages via P300 latency. This variance was also expressed through the differential reaction times of these subjects, which changes in accordance with the modality and system involved in perceiving and processing stimuli.

2. SOP also changes in accordance with task complexity from faster speeds on simple tasks to slower speeds on more complex tasks.

3. Young subjects have slower SOP than adult readers on most of the research tasks. This slowness was observed during visual and auditory-acoustic processing as well as in orthographic-phonological processing. The differences between young and adult readers were wider on higher level linguistic tasks at the word–pseudoword and sentence level. Thus, our data support Kail's (1994) claim that SOP has a developmental aspect.

4. Young and adult dyslexic readers were slower than their regular reading counterparts on visual, auditory-acoustic, orthographic, and phonological processing tasks. The gap between dyslexic and regular readers in SOP increased with task complexity. The main gap was observed when reading words/pseudowords and sentences.

A comparison of the SOPs of dyslexic and regular readers at different stages in the information-processing system revealed a large gap between these two groups, which was mainly expressed in P300 latency. This finding appeared in most of the research tasks and was especially strong in the higher linguistic tasks. Thus, it seems that SOP among dyslexics is slower than that of regular readers from the onset of the nonlinguistic and linguistic processing processes. This slower pace persists and increases throughout all stages of information processing. This slowness increases gradually as tasks become more complex. However, a significant correlation was found in all groups of subjects between the latencies of ERPs and a score that represents the rate of word decoding ability that refers, according to the notion of this book, to "word decoding fluency." The rate of this fluency measure was derived from a comprised score that was based on the number of words and pseudowords the subjects decode accurately in a minute (the Hebrew version of the 1-minute test for words and 1-minute test for pseudowords; Shatil, 1997). This suggests that the SOP of perception (P200) and processing (P300) affects word decoding fluency. As the data indicated, during the normal course of reading among young and adult regular readers, the perception stage as exhibited by P200 latency in the lexical decision task was correlated the highest with this fluency score. The correlation in the young group was $r = .43, p < .001$ and $r = .51, p < .001$ in the adult group. In contrast, in the dyslexic groups, the word fluency score correlated significantly with P300 latency in the lexical decision task, $r = .48, p < .001$, in the young group, and, $r = .68, p < .001$, in the adult group. These data support the suggestion that the regular automatic word decoding fluency process relies on the perception stage. Hence, most of the work is accomplished at the early stage of processing, during the perception and stimulus identification stages. In the young or adult dyslexic readers, however, nonautomatic slow dysfluent word decoding process is connected to the brain activity in the working memory stage. It is conceivable that for a fluent (fast and accurate) word decoding process to occur, the perception stage is not sufficient among dyslexics. This is because the latter are less able to identify the patterns of the words and thus require more brain activation and sources of information, such as memory (including the possibility of meaning) processes. These higher order memory systems may serve as a compensation mechanism for the dyslexics and may contribute to the enhancement of the word decoding process.

Whether it is perception or memory processing that is crucial for effective fluent word decoding, evidence indicates that SOP exhibited by ERP latencies affects the quality of fluent words decoding in a regular and deviant process. The data also support the theory that the comparative slowness exhibited by young and adult dyslexics in processing information does not only appear at the early stage of perception and stimulus identification but continues to the output stage. Moreover, this slowness is also exhibited at the lower level when processing the simple visual and auditory nonlinguistic tasks as well as in reading related tasks such as naming (see chap. 5). This slowness increases as tasks become more complex. On the one hand, these findings support the notion that SOP can be perceived as a trait of the information processor and it affects the quality of the information being processed. On the other hand, it is important to note that a developmental dimension of SOP was also found among regular and dyslexic readers. Adult readers are faster than children, possibly supporting the claim that SOP is affected by control over reading abilities, such that SOP can also be seen as state dependent. Skill and maturation affect performance accuracy and speed.

Moreover, despite the differential slowness between various age groups, a glance at the SOP curve at the perceptual level as expressed by P200 latency and at the processing level as expressed by the P300 latency across different research tasks indicates a similar pattern of differences when comparing the two groups of young subjects and the two groups of adult subjects. This picture changes somewhat with respect to the reaction time measure. The gap between the adult groups and the children increases on the more complex linguistic tasks. Unlike young readers, adult regular readers were faster than the dyslexics during reading of words, pseudowords, and sentences. This finding may be explained by the developmental dimension, as the young regular readers were still at the stage of establishing their reading abilities and may not yet have achieved full automaticity. Consequently, the SOP gap between the young dyslexic readers was smaller. On the other hand, the decoding words of adult regular readers have been well trained over time and have become automatic and stable. Adult dyslexic readers have improved their word decoding skills to a certain degree in comparison with young dyslexics, but not compared to age-matched regular reading peers.

One important aspect arising from our results is that the gap between visual and auditory processing speed (as exhibited at each stage of activation by the ERP latencies and reaction times) varies between the regular and dyslexic readers. The differences in SOP between the modalities appear in the two age groups. Decoding words requires precise and uncompromising grapheme-to-phoneme conversion. Graphemes are perceived via the visual-orthographic system and phonemes rely on auditory-phonological processing. Thus, reading requires intersensory and intersystem integration. Consequently, accurate word reading activity requires synchronization in time between the different cerebral systems involved in the process. It is thus conceivable that a wide gap between the modalities and/or systems impairs word decoding effectiveness and leads to slow-dysfluent reading (see Breznitz, 2000, and Breznitz & Misra, 2003, as well). Chapter 12 focuses on this hypothesis.

11

Cross-Modal Integration

There is a wide consensus that a successful reading process is based, among other things, on correct integration between the graphemic and phonemic information of the written symbol. Researchers also agree that dyslexic readers experience difficulties in carrying out the integration needed for word decoding. The debate in the literature focuses on the stage at which this impairment begins and what it stems from. In light of the fact that processing of graphemes and phonemes relies on the visual and auditory-acoustic modalities, the question occupying many researchers is if the failure to perform the necessary integration stems from impaired intersensory integration ability in general or if it is specific to the language domain. This question is important for our understanding of the underlying factors of the integration deficit.

THE CONNECTION BETWEEN READING
ABILITY AND CROSS-MODAL INTEGRATION

The theory and research related to the connection between intersensory integration ability and the dyslexia phenomenon began in the 1960s with the work of Birch and Belmont (1964), who suggested that dyslexic readers have difficulty integrating information arriving from the different sensory modalities that are activated in reading. They claimed that dyslexics exhibit a lack of coordination between visual-orthographic and auditory-phonological channels already at the nonlinguistic level. To investigate this assumption, researchers examined the extent to which information provided to one sensory module has to become available to other modules in order for proper integration to occur (e.g., Belmont et al., 1968; Birch & Belmont, 1964, 1965; Blank & Bridger, 1966; Muehl & Kremenak, 1966). L. Belmont, Birch, and I. Belmont (1968) compared poor and regular readers with respect to their ability to coordinate between auditory and visual patterns. The auditory patterns were a series of drumbeats separated by half-second or one-second time intervals and the visual patterns were dots separated by small or large spatial intervals. Subjects were requested to choose the correct visual pattern out of three alternatives to match the auditory pattern to which they were exposed. Poor readers achieved significantly lower scores than regular readers in accurately matching auditory to visual and visual to auditory patterns. The audiovisual sensory integration score was positively correlated with reading achievement in grades one and two and was found to be sensitive to the development of reading skills (see Berry, 1967; Kahn & Birch, 1968; Muehl & Kremenak, 1966; Sterritt & Rudnick, 1966, for similar results). These results suggest that there is a connection between general cross-modal integration ability, which does not refer specifically to the linguistic domain, and reading skills at the acquisition stage.

However, P. A. Katz and Deutsch (1964) found that although intersensory integration was important in acquiring reading in the second, third, and fifth grades, disturbed auditory perception was the main characteristic of readers with difficulties. In contrast, Kuhlman and Wolking (1972) showed that for second graders, visual perception was more essential than intersensory integration. A number of studies have shown that intersensory integration skills vary depending on the task used to measure them. For example, Botuck and Turkewitz (1990) found that presentation of the visual pattern before the auditory pattern facilitates the ability to coordinate between them, while presenting the auditory pattern first leads to a greater number of errors. Others pointed out that integration tasks require other skills besides intersensory integration itself, for example, short-term memory and visual differentiation. They claimed that there is no way of determining the relative contributions of each of these component skills (Whiton, Singer, & Cook, 1975). Similarly, Birch and Belmont (1964) and others have been criticized for not controlling for the effect of an intramodule deficit that may have been the source of the intermodule difficulties they reported (Vellutino, Bentley, & Phillips, 1978).

In recent years, the introduction of the connectionist theory of word reading (Seidenberg & McClelland, 1989) and the rise of the PDP (Seidenberg & McClelland, 1989) model of word reading have renewed interest in integration theories. It has been claimed that skilled reading is dependent on fast, automatic, and interactive integration of information coming from visual-ortho-graphic and auditory-phonological sources concerning written materials (Booth et al., 1999). The basic research question in this field is whether a task requiring intersensory integration implies that the relevant systems are acti-vated simultaneously or serially (see the dual route model; Coltheart, Curtis, Atkins, & Haller, 1993; Coltheart & Rastle, 1994).

Upholding the PDP model of processing information in word identification, Booth et al. (1999) suggested that the phonological presentation of written symbols was already activated at the pre-lexical level when the readers began to visually identify the written symbol. According to these researchers, the phono-logical and orthographic activation occurred in parallel. Furthermore, Dijkstra, Frauenfelder, and Schreuder (1993) examined whether graphemes and pho-nemes are activated in parallel or whether they inhibit one another during bi-modal word identification. They suggested that there is mutual, bidirectional activation occurring quickly and automatically between representations of graphemes and phonemes of the written symbol. In their data, no evidence of inhibition between the visual and auditory processing modules were found. This led them to conclude that phoneme–grapheme effects do not require lexi-cal mediation (words). In addition, they found evidence supporting the hypoth-esis that graphemic representations play a role in auditory word identification and that phonemic representations are important in visual word identification. Frost and L. Katz (1989) reached similar conclusions regarding the bidirec-tionality of cross-modal activation.

Whatmough, Arguin, and Bub (1999) also examined whether phonological representations directly activate or inhibit orthographic representations. They used a lexical decision task in which an auditory stimulus (auditory priming) was presented almost simultaneously with a visual stimulus. To encourage deci-sions based solely on orthography, the visual stimuli were a word and a homophonic nonword (e.g., height/hite), such that decisions could not be based on phonology or meaning. The task was performed under two conditions: with and without auditory priming. The subjects were three brain damaged adults with surface dyslexia, who were compared to 12 university students with normal reading skills. Reaction times of dyslexic subjects were significantly shorter in the auditory priming condition, except when original reaction times were less than one second, in which case auditory priming did not shorten them. Among normal readers, auditory priming had an inhibitory effect, lengthening reaction times in comparison to the nonpriming condition, when words of high frequency in the language were presented. Whatmough et al. (1999) suggested that speed at which readers process visual orthographic information influences the involvement of the auditory processing in word identification. If the visual identification of the word is notably slow (over 1 s), then there will be facilitation to the auditory modality, whereas in very fast visual word identification processes there will be inhibition for auditory information.

Moreover, Yap and Van der Leij (1994) suggested that among developmental dyslexics, the joint activation between phonological and orthographic systems is violated due to difficulties in phonological processing. The dyslexic reader compensates for these difficulties by reading words holistically. This often leads to incorrect decoding of new words, due to the inability to break down words into their component phonemes.

The use of advanced technologies for measuring brain activity (PET, fMRI, ERP, and MEG) during cross-modal integration has begun to show systematic evidence regarding the neuronal networks involved in these cross-modal operations. Specific roles are increasingly defined for the superior temporal sulcus, the inferior parietal sulcus, regions of the frontal cortex, the insula, and the claustrum (see Calvert, 2001, for a review). Giard and Peronnet (1999) found that subjects were more accurate and rapid during identification of objects presented multimodally rather than unimodally. They suggested that multisensory integration is mediated by flexible, highly adaptive physiological processes that can take place very early during sensory processing and operate in different ways in sensory-specific and nonspecific cortical structures. Using imaging technology to examine neural activity in multisensory cortical regions in normal and learning disabled readers, Hayes et al. (2003) discovered altered patterns of connectivity among primary sensory and multisensory processing areas in learning disabled subjects (see Pugh et al., 2000, as well). This led them to suggest that reading deficits in these individuals may be caused by deficits in the integration of multisensory information.

At present, there are two dominant theories regarding the integration of sensory input (see Olson, Gatenby, & Gore, 2002). The site-specific integration model suggests that special purpose regions of the cortex process specific combinations of sensory input. This model is supported by neuroanatomical and neurophysiological evidence, which identify association areas of the brain that only process specific stimulus combinations (Olson et al., 2002).

In contrast, the communication relay model suggests that neural areas that process single unimodal stimuli also process multisensory stimuli, and each modality accesses the other modality through a subcortical relay area. Olson et al. (2002) examined the two competing hypotheses using fMRI to examine activation patterns of subjects integrating audiovisual stimuli (audiovisual speech) under temporally synchronized and desynchronized conditions. The findings lent support to the communication relay model. Synchronized audiovisual stimuli activated many of the same sensory-specific brain areas that were activated by desynchronized stimuli. This was taken to indicate that these areas matter both for unimodal and for multimodal processing. Integrated sight and sound also activated the claustrum/putamen, indicating that this area may be a potential sensory relay area.

Raij, Uutela, and Hari (2000) recorded the neuromagnetic cortical response to auditorily, visually, and audiovisually presented single letters, which have auditory (phonemic) and visual (graphemic) qualities. The auditory and visual activation initially converged at around 225 ms after stimulus onset, followed by interaction predominantly in the right temporo-occipito-parietal junction (280–345 ms) and the left (380–535 ms) and right (380–540 ms) superior temporal sulci. These multisensory brain areas are believed to play a role in audiovisual integration of phonemes and graphemes. Brain areas that participate in audiovisual integration are expected to show signs of convergence. This means that activation evoked by stimulation from two modalities jointly differs from the sum of unimodal activations stemming from either of the modalities separately. The aim was to study the audiovisual integration mechanisms of the brain for letters. Subjects were requested to identify letters of the Roman alphabet based on auditory, visual, or audiovisual presentations. Audiovisual letters were presented under both matched and randomly paired (nonmatching) conditions, and meaningless auditory, visual, and audiovisual stimuli were used as controls. The results show that for audiovisual stimuli, the sensory-specific auditory and visual projection areas were first activated strongly at 60–120 ms, and these activations were forwarded to multisensory areas that received maximal input from both modalities around 225 ms. For matching letters, which are known to have been associated through previous learning, a suppressive interaction around 380–150 ms was observed, which was significantly weaker for control stimuli and nonmatching letters. Raij et al. (2000) suggested that convergence and interaction of the auditory and visual activations led to integration of phonemes and graphemes. Audiovisual interaction was prominent in the following brain areas. Left frontoparietal and right frontal regions showed early interaction that did not differentiate between letters and control stimuli. Interaction in the right temporo-occipito-parietal junction and the left and right superior temporal sulcus occurred later and was stronger for letters than for controls. This suggests that the learned association between phonemes and graphemes results in an organizational change in these brain areas. The left posterior STS, part of Wernicke's area, showed notable integration in all subjects. The left STS has also been implicated in auditory processing of visually presented letters (Sergent, Zuck, Levesque, & MacDonald, 1992) and in visual imagery of auditorily presented letters (Raij, 1999).

OUR CROSS-MODAL STUDIES

The connectionist model of reading (PDP) (Seidenberg & McClelland, 1989) portrays word reading as a process that relies on parallel processing in the visual-orthographic, auditory-phonological, and semantic systems. Seidenberg and McClelland (1989) suggested that the amount of activation in each system is an outcome of the level and quality of the reading process. Breznitz (2003b) and Breznitz and Misra (2003) put forward an additional idea suggesting that the speed at which information is processed within and between the three systems is one of the underlying factors of the quality of word recognition. This hypothesis was based on the notion that each of these three systems is located in a different brain site and processes information in different manners and at different speeds. The visual-orthographic system processes information holistically, whereas the auditory-phonological system does so sequentially. In addition, at the cognitive level, reading and reading-related information is processed at different stages of activation. First, the printed stimuli must be discriminated at the perceptual stage. After this, they must move along for processing in short-term memory and working memory systems. Once they have been recognized semantically, they are stored in the mental lexicon in long-term memory. The printed stimuli involved in this process include different forms of representation (visual, acoustic, and semantic). Moreover, at the end of the process, the information from the different modalities and systems must be integrated in order to form an exact word pattern. As each grapheme has only one phoneme, information regarding the printed material to be decoded must arrive in a precise and timely fashion. The data presented in chapters 9 and 10 point to speed of processing differences in the visual-orthographic and auditory-phonological systems between dyslexic readers and regular readers. The dyslexic readers processed information in the two modalities at significantly slower rates than the regular readers. It was hypothesized that this slowness might affect cross-modal integration, thereby impairing word reading effectiveness.

The following research project was designed in an attempt to systematically measure cross-modal integration in dyslexic and regular readers. We used the same subjects that participated in the project that measured speed of processing of the visual and auditory modalities (see chaps. 9 and 10). Participants were 50 dyslexic and 50 regular reading university students. Tasks included nonlinguistic (flashes and tones) and linguistic (letters, syllables and words-pseudowords) stimuli, presented in the visual and auditory modalities simultaneously. Behavioral (reaction time and accuracy) and electrophysiological measures using ERP methodology were incorporated.

CROSS-MODALITY TASKS BEHAVIORAL EXPERIMENTS

Threshold of Simultaneous Identification

In order to determine each subject's baseline for identifying whether two stimuli presented in each modality (auditory and visual) are simultaneous or sequential, the following procedure was administered. The first step of the cross-modality integration was to determine the threshold at which subjects identified which modality came first, the visual or the auditory, and when they saw and heard visual and auditory stimuli simultaneously. For this purpose, four experiments were designed. In each task, two stimuli were presented to the subject at a time, one in the visual modality and the other in the auditory. The tasks were as follows:

1. The first task included nonlinguistic visual flashes and auditory beeps as stimuli.
2. The second task included the visual syllable (hak) and its corresponding auditory phoneme "hak."
3. The third task included visual and auditory presentations of a one-syllable word—" לי" (means "me," pronounced "li").
4. The fourth task included visual and auditory presentations of a one-syllable pseudoword—"ל י" (pronounced "il").

The stimuli in each task were presented in the visual and auditory modalities at different time intervals of 0–1,000 ms in 50-ms increments in three different conditions. In condition 1, the visual stimulus came before the auditory stimulus. In condition 2, the auditory came before the visual. And, in condition 3, they were presented simultaneously. The conditions were presented randomly to the subjects at the various time intervals. The subject was requested to press one of three keyboard buttons corresponding to each condition.

Results. As indicated in Tables 11.1 and 11.2, a between-groups *t*-test analysis was performed on each condition in each experiment. There were two parameters in each experiment. In each parameter, there were two measures:

TABLE 11.1
Threshold Decision Time

		M	SD	F	P
I. Nonlinguistic	Dyslexic	414.28	259.40	13.05	.001
Auditory minimal threshold time	Regular	233.78	154.134		
I. Nonlinguistic	Dyslexic	428.57	231.13	7.76	.007
Visual minimal threshold time	Regular	285.71	196.50		
I. Syllable	Dyslexic	425.71	271.80	4.86	.031
Auditory minimal threshold time	Regular	288.05	191.62		
I. Syllable	Dyslexic	412.85	89.10	4.38	.033
Visual minimal threshold time	Regular	347.22	78.48		
I. Word	Dyslexic	395.71	220.41	8.54	.005
Auditory minimal threshold time	Regular	270.27	136.14		
I. Word	Dyslexic	364.70	273.45	6.97	.010
Visual minimal threshold time					
I. Nonword	Dyslexic	391.42	206.68	7.27	.009
Auditory minimal threshold time	Regular	269.44	173.31		
I. Nonword	Dyslexic	455.71	294.25	15.87	.000
Visual minimal threshold time	Regular	172.97	132.59		

a. Visual and auditory "Minimum Threshold Time" for each subject represents the minimum time gap required between the two stimuli for the subject to identify the order of presentation (Table 11.1).
  1. The threshold time for the subject to identify three consecutive times that the visual stimulus appeared before the auditory stimulus.
  2. The threshold time for the subject to identify three consecutive times that the auditory stimulus appeared before the visual stimulus.
b. The minimum time gap required for the subject to perceive that the visual and auditory stimuli appeared simultaneously (Table 11.2):
  1. The threshold time for the subject to identify when the visual and the auditory stimuli appeared simultaneously when the visual stimuli came before the auditory one.
  2. The threshold time for the subject to identify when the visual and the auditory stimuli appeared simultaneously when the auditory stimuli came before the visual one. As indicated by the results in Table 11.1 and Figs. 11.1–11.3, significant between group differences were found in the threshold times of all research parameters. The gaps in all threshold times were wider in the dyslexic group.

Table 11.1 indicates that the average minimal threshold time (MTT) required in order to discern which modality comes first is about 400 ms for the dyslexics and about 250 for the controls. This modalities time gap appears to be

TABLE 11.2
Minimum Time Gap

			M	SD	F	P
II. Nonlinguistic	Auditory-visual	Dyslexic	247.14	147.10	11.10	.001
Simultaneous perception (auditory first)		Regular	112.16	89.29		
II. Nonlinguistic	Auditory-visual	Dyslexic	258.57	180.46	6.98	.010
Simultaneous perception (visual first)		Regular	102.70	123.57		
II. Syllable	Simultaneous	Dyslexic	268.57	177.02	9.86	.002
Auditory-visual perception (auditory first)		Regular	122.50	97.37		
II. Syllable	Simultaneous	Dyslexic	354.28	221.08	9.38	.003
Auditory-visual perception (visual first)		Regular	119.44	142.56		
II. Word	Simultaneous	Dyslexic	255.71	157.54	3.55	.052
Auditory-visual perception (auditory first)		Regular	117.29	110.52		
II. Word	Simultaneous	Dyslexic	252.85	202.89	3.62	.051
Auditory-visual perception (visual first)		Regular	123.67	136.22		
II. Nonword	Simultaneous	Dyslexic	295.71	171.22	3.94	.051
Auditory-visual perception (auditory first)		Regular	129.72	104.38		
II. Nonword	Simultaneous	Dyslexic	302.85	236.37	8.38	.005
Auditory-visual perception (visual first)		Regular	137.97	132.59		

necessary for each group regardless of whether the visual or the auditory stimulus comes first and regardless of the complexity of the task.

Table 11.2 indicates that when two stimuli from the visual and the auditory modalities were presented separately with variable time gaps between them, it took a smaller time gap for controls than for dyslexics to make them state that the stimuli appeared simultaneously. Regardless of whether the visual or the auditory stimulus appeared first and regardless of the difficulty of the tasks, the between modalities average time gap for dyslexics to perceive the stimuli as simultaneous was between 250 ms and 350 ms, whereas it was about 100 ms for the controls. This indicates that a minimal threshold time and a minimal between modalities time gap is required for cross-modal identification and synchronization in the two groups of readers. Neither the controls nor the dyslexics identified the cross-modal tasks accurately when the two stimuli really appeared simultaneously in the two modalities. The minimal time gap was larger among the dyslexics because it was based on a wider time asynchrony between the visual and the auditory information.

Modalities Matching Tasks

The purpose of these experiments was to examine the subjects' ability to match auditory and visual linguistic information arriving from the two modalities at different time gaps. The experiment included syllable, word, and pseudoword stimuli.

Syllables. The purpose of these experiments was to examine the subjects' ability to integrate linguistic information between the auditory and visual channels. Each subject heard a syllable and saw a syllable and had to decide if the two syllables were different or identical. The subject saw the first syllable on a computer screen and heard the second syllable through a computer sound blaster. There were a total of 80 stimuli pairs. Half of these began with the visual stimulus and half with the auditory. Half the pairs were identical and half were different. Reaction time and accuracy for each stimulus pair was measured during two experiments.

1. In the first experiment, the ISI between stimuli was manipulated with half of the stimuli having an ISI of 40 ms and half of 120 ms. The presentation time for the visual stimuli was 200 ms, whereas presentation time for the auditory stimuli was syllable dependent.

Results: Accuracy was almost perfect for both groups, but there was a main time effect between groups, $F(8, 92) = 5.66, p < .002$. The dyslexics were slower than the controls by about 25%. A main effect of stimulus type was also obtained, $F(8, 92) = 3.91, p < .04$. RT was longer for different stimuli types. A group by stimuli type effect was also found, $F(8, 92) = 5.01, p < .02$. RT for the dyslexics was longer. There was no main effect of ISI.

2. In the second experiment, the presentation time of the visual stimuli was manipulated with the presentation time of half the pairs set at 200 ms, and that of the other half at 50 ms. The auditory presentation time was syllable dependent. The ISI between the two stimuli was 120 ms.

Results: Accuracy was almost perfect for both groups. There was a main time effect of group, $F(8, 92) = 5.87, p < .002$. The dyslexics were slower than the controls on most tasks. A main effect of stimuli type was also obtained, $F(8, 92) = 4.21, p < .03$. RT was longer for different stimulus types. A group by stimulus type effect was also found, $F(8, 92) = 5.01, p < .02$. RT for the dyslexics was longer. No main effect of ISI was found.

Words. The purpose of these experiments was to examine the subjects' ability to integrate linguistic information (verbal) between the auditory and visual channels. Each subject heard and saw one-syllable words and had to decide if the two were different or identical. The subject saw the word on a computer screen and heard the second word through a computer sound blaster. There were a total of 80 stimuli pairs. Half of them began with the visual stimuli and half with the auditory stimuli. Half the pairs were identical and half were different. Two experiments were conducted:

1. In one experiment the ISI between stimuli was manipulated with half of the stimuli having an ISI of 40 ms, and the other half of 120 ms. The presentation time of the visual stimuli was 300 ms and the presentation time of the auditory stimuli was word dependent.

Results: As indicated in Table 11.3, accuracy was almost perfect for both groups on all tasks. A main effect of group was found for RT, $F(8, 92) = 8.11, p < .00$. The dyslexics were slower on all tasks than the controls. A main effect of modality in RT was also obtained, $F(8, 92) = 5.23, p < .002$. RT was longer in both groups when the words were presented first in the visual modality, as compared to the auditory modality. No main effects of stimulus type or ISI were found. For both groups, RT for different and identical words for ISIs of 40 ms or 120 ms was similar.

2. In the other experiment, the presentation time of the visual stimuli was manipulated with the presentation time of half the pairs set at 100 ms and that

TABLE 11.3
Cross-Modality Integration

	Dyslexics		Controls			
Cross-Modality Integration	M	SD	M	SD	F	Sig.
Pairs of words written the same, RT	1461.32	603.21	1110.00	109.11	7.74	.001
Pairs of words written differently, RT	1268.33	439.42	966.02	129.91	8.67	.006
Pairs of words written the same, AC	52.09	.48	53.12	.23	1.77	ns
Pairs of words written differently, AC	46.11	.41	47.00	.23	2.03	ns
Pairs of words sound the same, RT	1233.30	186.01	1002.09	171.42	4.52	.04
Pairs of words sound different, RT	1288.16	234.87	1189.78	101.22	3.62	.06
Pairs of words sound the same, AC	47.58	17.44	58.40	15.45	3.95	.05
Pairs of words sound different, AC	48.94	17.34	60.00	13.55	4.40	.04
Pseudoword sound like real word, RT	1713.61	345.80	1208.227	190.87	22.30	.001
Pseudoword not sound like real word, RT	1880.09	416.32	1261.09	188.92	14.03	.001
Pseudoword sound like real word, AC	46.33	3.22	54.11	3.08	5.32	.02
Pseudoword not sound like real word, AC	47.56	4.88	57.01	2.98	7.08	.01

of the other half at 300 ms. The auditory presentation time was word dependent. The ISI time between the two stimuli was 120 ms. Reaction time and accuracy for each stimulus pair was measured during these experiments.

Results: As indicated in Table 11.3, accuracy was almost perfect for both groups on all tasks. A main effect of group for RT, $F(8, 92) = 2.97, p < .01$, was found. The dyslexics were slower on all tasks than the controls. A main effect of modality in RT was also obtained, $F(8, 92) = 4.33, p < .02$. RT was longer for the two groups when the words were presented first in the visual modality as compared to the auditory. No main effect of stimulus type or presentation time was found. For both groups, RT for different and identical words for an ISI of 100 ms or 300 ms was similar.

Stage 2: ERP Measures

The second stage of cross-modal integration studies included EEG measures with ERP methodology (see chap. 8 for a detailed description). Both nonlinguistic (beeps and flashes) and linguistic (graphemes and phonemes) stimuli were used.

The Tasks

Nonlinguistic. A visual, auditory, and cross-modal processing task (Meyler & Breznitz, 2003) was administered. This task consisted of 150 stimuli, including 50 beeps occurring alone (1,000 Hz), 50 flashes occurring alone, and 50

TABLE 11.4
Lower Level Nonlinguistic Tasks ERP Data

	Controls			Dyslexics		
	P200	P300	RT	P200	P300	RT
Cross-modalities integration	250.11 (66.01)	381.29 (63.56)	421.62 (29.01)	261.34 (34.76)	463.21 (72.12)	601.62 (38.09)

beeps and flashes occurring simultaneously. The subject pressed one button of the joystick when either the beep or the flash occurred separately (x100) and another button when they occurred simultaneously (x50). Offline analysis differentiated between the auditory, visual, and simultaneous segments.

Analysis of the ERP data identified two brain wave components: P200, which represents perception, and P300, which represents processing. As Table 11.4 and Figs. 11.1 and 11.2 indicate, cross-modal processing time at the perception stage (P200) was similar for dyslexics and controls. Significant differences appeared at the processing stage (P300) and in reaction time (RT) at the output stage. The dyslexics were slower than the controls in both stages of activation.

Linguistic. Another visual, auditory (see chap. 8), and cross-modal processing task (Meyler & Breznitz, 2003) was administered. This task consisted of 150 letter "bet" (/b/, ב) stimuli, of which 50 were presented via headphones

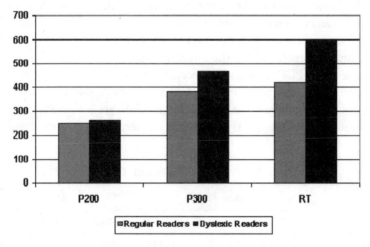

FIG. 11.1. Cross-modality nonlinguistic integration: Comparison of adult regular and dyslexic readers.

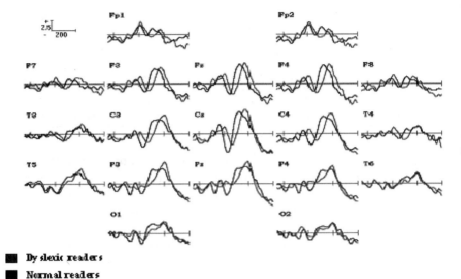

Dyslexic readers

Normal readers

FIG. 11.2.   Cross-modality integration: A comparison between dyslexic and normal readers.

alone, 50 were presented on the computer screen alone, and 50 were presented simultaneously via the two modalities. The subjects pressed one button of the joystick when either the sound or the sight of the letter occurred separately (x100) and another button when they occurred simultaneously (x50). Offline analysis differentiated between the auditory, visual, and simultaneous segments. As can be seen from Table 11.5 and Fig. 11.3, the dyslexics were slower than the controls on most of the cross-modal tasks.

In sum, the central role of the integration process in word reading was revived due to the PDP model, which portrays word reading as a process that relies on various sources of information that are activated simultaneously, and to the use of imaging techniques, which identify brain areas where activation occurs during word reading. As in previous studies, our data consistently con-

TABLE 11.5
Linguistic Level Tasks ERP Data

	Regular Readers			Dyslexics		
	P200	P300	RT	P200	P300	RT
Cross-modalities integration	198.21 (79.32)	405.39 (59.01)	489.38 (33.19)	296.54 (58.34)	561.17 (45.71)	821.76 (77.10)

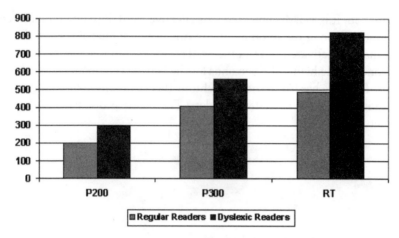

FIG. 11.3.   Cross-modality linguistic integration: Comparison of regular and dyslexic readers.

firmed the slowness of dyslexics in performing bimodal tasks compared to unimodal tasks. The RT was significantly longer and the latencies of P2 and P3 ERP components appeared later in the dyslexics group than in the controls in all of the experimental tasks. The slowness of the dyslexics when processing nonlinguistic information arriving simultaneously from the visual and the auditory modalities appears in the working memory stage (P3) where the decision concerning the type of the stimulus has to take place. This slowness continues on to the output stage (RT). When processing linguistic tasks, this slowness appears already as early as the perception stage (P2) and is maintained in the working memory (P3) and the output stages (RT). Processing linguistic information is the center of the problems of dyslexics.

Moreover, we have found that for the dyslexic readers the identification of which modality presents the stimulus first relies on a wider time gap in the appearance of the stimuli from the two modalities. The dyslexics require a between modalities time gap of about 400 ms and the controls one of only about 100 ms in order to identify which modality presents the stimulus first. The decision of when the visual and auditory stimuli were heard and seen simultaneously also required time gap between their appearances, of about 200–300 ms for dyslexics and about 100 ms for the controls. As the effectiveness of decoding word requires a simultaneous processing of the grapheme and the phoneme forms of the word, any delay might impair the process of word decoding accuracy. The wider between modalities time gap exhibited by dyslexics, together with their slowness in performing cross-modal and unimodal tasks, may affect their ability to synchronize in time any information arriving from more than one source of information. It is well documented that effective word decoding requires temporal integration of the information arriving from the modalities and the systems that are activated in the process. The wider the SOP gap between the components, the higher the demands for the between components synchronization. This idea has led to the "asynchrony theory" as an explanation of word decoding impairment in dyslexic readers. The theory is discussed in the next chapter.

12

The Synchronization Phenomenon

The synchronization hypothesis (Breznitz, 2001a, 2003b; Breznitz & Misra, 2003) proposes that accurate integration of information in decoding words can occur only when the modalities and brain systems are in synchronization with each other. Breznitz (2001a) and Breznitz and Misra (2003) proposed that a successful synchronization is based not only on the content of the information, but also on the speed at which the information is processed and transferred within and between the various systems activated in the process. Conversely, the asynchrony phenomenon stems from a lack of speed coordination in the modalities and brain systems. Thus, this phenomenon can only exist if the following criteria are met: (a) More than one system and/or stage of cognitive operation is involved in the processing task. (b) There are differences in the speeds at which each entity processes information. (c) The SOP of the various entities is not sufficiently coordinated to allow effective integration.

Chapters 9, 10, and 11 present data from a systematic research project aimed at measuring the speed of processing of the visual and auditory modalities as well as cross-modal integration in regular and dyslexic readers when processing nonlinguistic and linguistic information at different levels of complexity. The experiments used behavioral and electrophysiological measures, which enabled us to trace the speed (SOP) at which each modality processes various levels of information, from the stimulus perception stage (indicated by P200 latency at CZ electrodes) to the short-term (STM) and working memory (WM) stages (indicated by P300 latency at CZ electrodes) to the output stage (reaction time and accuracy) of the single modality activity.

We have consistently observed a relative slowness of dyslexics as compared to regular age-matched readers in processing information in the visual, auditory, and cross-modal integration. This slowness appeared when processing both lower level nonlinguistic and linguistic information and higher level linguistic information. The slowness was displayed at the various stages of information processing, from the perception (P2) to the working memory (P3) and output stage (RT). Moreover, cross-modal integration processing in the dyslexic readers appeared to require a wider time gap between the information arriving from the visual and the auditory modalities, which might cause asynchrony between two modalities in processing information.

RESEARCH ON THE ASYNCHRONY HYPOTHESIS

In an attempt to study the asynchrony hypothesis, several "cross-modality gap scores" were computed from the three sets of single-modality experiments that were presented in chapter 10. The subjects were young and adult dyslexic and regular readers. In each experiment, three gap scores were computed: P2 gaps, P3 gaps, and RT gaps. This allowed us to calculate the scores for the different stages of information-processing activation. The scores were computed for each subject based on subtraction of the measures in the visual experiments from those in the auditory experiments. These scores were as follows: a lower level nonlinguistic gap score (visual minus auditory), a lower level linguistic gap score (visual minus auditory), and a higher level gap score in the lexical decision task (orthographic/words minus phonological/pseudowords). The new ERP-gap scores were calculated according to the peak amplitudes of the P200 and P300 ERP components at the Cz electrode for each type of stimulus. The RT gap scores were calculated according to RT of each experiment.

The patterns of the mean gap scores in P200, P300, and RT for the dyslexics and controls in the young and adult groups are presented in Figs. 12.1–12.5. Dyslexic and normal readers significantly differed in terms of their lower level nonlinguistic and linguistic gap scores. The same was true of the higher level pseudowords and words gap score for the P200, P300 latency, and RT. In each of the comparisons, the gap scores were significantly larger in the dyslexic group than in the control group. However, Figs. 12.1–12.5 indicate that despite these cross-modal time gap differences, the patterns of gaps were similar across both types of readers at each stage of activation.

The relations between the word decoding fluency score (which consisted of words and pseudowords read accurately in a minute—see chap. 11; Breznitz, 2002; Breznitz & Misra, 2003) and gap scores were measured for each group of

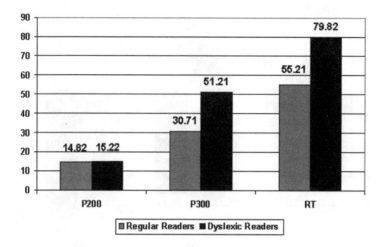

FIG. 12.1. Gap score auditory minus visual nonlinguistic: Comparison of young regular and dyslexic readers.

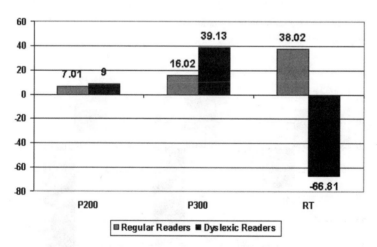

FIG. 12.2. Gap score auditory minus visual nonlinguistic: Comparison of adult regular and dyslexic readers.

subjects separately. In the young dyslexics group, the gap score of P300 on the linguistic lower level task (graphemes–phonemes) was most highly correlated with the word decoding fluency score ($r = .67, p < .001$). In the adult dyslexic group, the highest correlation was with the P300 gap score of the pseudowords minus the words ($r = .62, p < .001$). In the young and adult regular reader groups, no significant correlation was found with any of the gap scores. However, as our previous data indicated (Breznitz, 2002; Breznitz & Misra, 2003), in

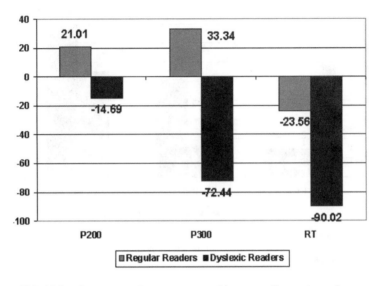

FIG. 12.3.   Gap score auditory minus visual linguistic: Comparison of young regular and dyslexic readers.

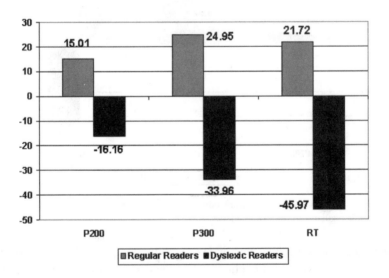

FIG. 12.4.   Gap score auditory minus visual linguistic: Comparison of adult regular and dyslexic readers.

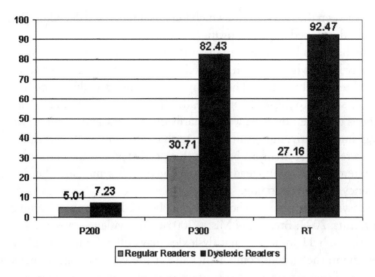

FIG. 12.5.   Gap score pseudowords minus words: Comparison of adult regular and dyslexic readers.

the young regular readers group the word decoding fluency score correlated with the P300 latency in the linguistic (phoneme discrimination) auditory task ($r = .42, p < .001$) and in the adult regular readers group it correlated with the P200 latency in the same linguistic auditory task at the level of phoneme discrimination ($r = .51, p < .001$).

These data suggest that, at least for the type of tasks performed in this study, in normal processing the early sensory stages of processing at the level of feature detection–perception (i.e., Luck & Hillyard, 1994) and item encoding (i.e., B. R. Dunn et al., 1998) in the auditory modality are vital for word decoding fluency. Whereas for the young regular readers group most of the activity occurs in the processing stage (P300), among regular adult readers most of the activity takes place in the early sensory processing stage (P200). For normal readers, SOP in the auditory modality is crucial for a fluent word decoding process. However, for the young and adult dyslexics, the cross-modal time gap in the processing stage (P300) was found to be crucial for fluent word decoding to occur.

Among young dyslexics, dysfluency in word decoding relates to a larger time gap score at the lower linguistic level (phonemes minus graphemes). However, among adult dyslexics, decoding dysfluency relates to larger time gap scores at the higher linguistic level (pseudowords minus words). Thus, the larger time gap score observed for adult dyslexics (but not for regular readers) between the orthographic and phonological systems may reflect lower degrees of synchronization between the two systems, which impairs fluent word decoding. This idea is further developed in the following section.

Note that the adult subjects in the study were compensated adult dyslexics at university level, who had been exposed for years to printed materials and had received remedial training. These subjects recorded decoding accuracy levels that were similar to those of normal readers (see chap. 9). This lends support to the thesis that their dyslexia was primarily due to slow and dysfluent word decoding. Importantly, our results indicate that dysfluent word decoding can be seen as a result of asynchrony between the speed of processing of the modalities and systems involved in reading. Larger gap scores increase the degree of dysfluency in word decoding.

The asynchrony phenomenon has been observed in young and adult dyslexics (Breznitz, 2002; Breznitz & Misra, 2003). The evidence presented in chapters 9 through 11 indicates that dyslexics may suffer from slow information processing in the various components and at the various stages of activation. However, this slowness is not consistent in the two modalities and in the two systems. In some tasks, the visual modality is faster than the auditory, whereas in others the opposite is the case.

Our data pointed to a between modalities gap in processing time in the regular reader groups. We suggest that there is a natural SOP gap score that characterizes normal readers. There is a normal between modalities gap score resulting from the biological constraints of the modalities and systems. This natural gap is also a function of task-specific requirements and of the age of the subjects. In other words, dysfluency in word decoding can be caused for different reasons in different age groups. Word decoding fluency among young dyslexics is based on the lower level grapheme/phoneme speed of correspondence, whereas among adults decoding fluency is an outcome of synchronization at the higher phonological and orthographic levels. This raises the issue of why the asynchrony phenomenon was found among adult dyslexics only at higher level processing stages (i.e., at the word level). Breznitz and Misra (2003) suggested that because the language components (graphemes and phonemes) are limited in number, adult dyslexics over the years may have been exposed to the same alphabetic codes long enough to store them as patterns to be retrieved automatically when needed. But there is a large number of words in any given language, and the number of times that the reader meets the same word is limited. Together with the general time limitations of dyslexics when processing information, this may prevent them from developing fluent word decoding skills.

In addition, Breznitz (2000) and Breznitz and Misra (2003) pointed out that synchronization in word reading may also be based on the time that elapses be-

TABLE 12.1
Within Task Latency Differences (Temporal Gap)
Between P200 and P300 ERP Components at Cz

Test	Control		Dyslexic		Group Comparison
	M	SD	M	SD	t(2,78)
Auditory nonlinguistic	129.15	16.12	134.16	33.27	ns
Visual nonlinguistic	166.98	21.13	241.7*	56.33	6.16**
Auditory linguistic	110.11	27.98	135.89	43.23	ns
Visual linguistic	147.66	17.11	212.35	47.81	8.41**
Words	165.34	12.37	189.01	15.33	ns
Pseudowords	172.32	26.65	267.56	55.15	12.02**

*$p < .01$. **$p < .001$.

tween the perception of the stimuli (the peak latency of P200) and the processing stage (peak latency of P300). Our data showed a longer gap between the two processing stages for dyslexics than for regular readers in both age groups. Breznitz (2000) and Breznitz and Misra (2003) suggested that this time gap between the perception and processing stages may be another source of asynchrony in the information-processing activity and may impair word reading. The evidence presented in Table 12.1 supports this thesis.

Table 12.1 indicates that, among dyslexics, neither the lower levels nor the higher levels of word decoding processing may have ended at the early sensory stage, and dyslexics may need additional time and resources to complete this processing. The long between stage gap scores may point to deeper effort of the brain to solve the problem, particularly for more difficult tasks. The higher order cognitive processes at the stimulus evaluation and categorization stage (as manifested by longer P300 latencies) may thus result from slowness among adult dyslexics. This speed gap score between the processing stages within the task indicates that there is another reason behind the information-processing slowness of dyslexics, which affects fluent word decoding process.

In sum, it can be concluded that dyslexics are slower at processing reading and reading-related information. The slowness is expressed specifically whenever it is necessary to integrate information from different brain sources. The combination of a longer transformation time between the cognitive stages and an asynchrony between the processing time of the visual and auditory modalities and the orthographic and phonological systems ought to be viewed as a core determinant of fluent word decoding.

13

Reading Fluency, Training, and Dyslexia

The central nervous system changes developmentally and as an outcome of experiences in a lifetime. Changes occur at various levels of cerebral organization, at the molecular-synaptic level, in cortical mapping, and among systems (i.e., plasticity between modalities). Functional changes in cerebral organization can occur at any developmental stage, and they range from slight changes in boundaries of functional areas to cross-hemispherical changes (Papanicolaou et al., 2001; Poldrack, 2000). Plasticity has a central function in the normal development of the nervous system. The nervous system is a mechanism that enables adaptation and responsiveness of the central nervous system to exogenous and endogenous inputs. After completion of cerebral development, plasticity becomes less dominant in neural functions, even though it remains active in the mature system. Brain damage inflicted in childhood has been found to cause less behavioral and cognitive deficits than similar damage in adulthood (Stiles, 2000). This indicates that the developing brain can rearrange patterns and networks of connections better than the adult brain. Nonetheless, damaged adult brains may be capable of rearrangement to compensate for neurological deficits (Stiles, 2000).

TRAINING AND BRAIN PLASTICITY

Learning a skill through training is one of the results of plasticity. It alters relevant cerebral representations and increases cerebral activity according to a given task. Today, imaging methods allow us to examine the remapping of the representations that result from training within a wide time frame (Karni, 1996). Conversely, in some cases, decreased cerebral activity occurs as a result of training. A number of explanations have been offered for this phenomenon. One hypothesis proposes that the decrease in intensity of cerebral activity occurs as a result of the sharpening of responses in a specific neural network. In other words, following training, a few neurons in the network fire with high intensity in response to a task stimulus, but most neurons in the network fire with low intensity in response to the same stimulus (Poldrack, 2000). This has been observed in most studies employing short-term training with a limited number of repetitions. Another theory holds that changes in control processes occur as a result of long-term training, which may cause a decrease in activity levels in areas that are functionally connected to supervisory mechanisms. As training progresses, less effort is required. Thus, the need for supervision gradually decreases, until the task is performed automatically.

The prefrontal lobe is a cerebral area associated with executive supervision (J. D. Cohen, Braver, & O'Reilly, 1996). The right prefrontal area is related to suppression of irrelevant responses (Garavan, Ross, & Stein, 1999), whereas the left prefrontal area is involved in the selection of verbal responses from a range of possible responses (Thompson-Schill, D'Esposito, Aguirre, & Farah, 1997). The involvement of each of these areas decreases with training. Supervision of errors is an additional aspect of task supervision. The anterior cingulate gyrus is specifically involved in the detection of errors during task performance (Carter et al., 1998). As a task requires less supervision of errors, the areas involved in this process exhibit decreased activity.

Training tends to be related to increases in cerebral activity, or expansion of activity areas. Many studies have found that these increases occur as a result of long-term training, which involves multiple repetitions. There are a number of possible explanations. The increase in cerebral activity may stem from enlistment of additional cortical units following training. Such increases occur in tasks that require distinction between stimuli characteristics, such as frequency in the auditory cortex or somatosensory location in the motor cortex. These stimuli characteristics are presented in topographical brain maps.

Examining brain plasticity of the motor system, Karni et al. (1998) used fMRI to show how training causes expansion of cerebral activity. Three weeks of daily training, in which subjects were trained to react to a given vowel sequence, produced a wider area of activity in the primary motor region (M1) during performance, as compared to a control sequence. The same response was recorded 3 weeks after training had ended.

An additional theory holds that increased cerebral activity occurs as a result of increased synchronization. Long-term training may cause an increase in connectivity between various cerebral areas, leading to better synchronization between them. This synchronization is reflected in an increase in synaptic activity (Chawla, Lumer, & Friston, 1999).

Other imaging studies have similarly found changes in activity areas as a result of training, which reflect new cortical representations. Posttraining examinations were conducted for periods ranging from a number of hours after training to a number of days. The results, which varied with the duration of training, were related to consolidation processes (Karni, 1996). Imaging methods also showed changes in patterns of cerebral activity during task performance (Karni et al., in press).

LANGUAGE AND BRAIN PLASTICITY

Research on language and associated brain plasticity following training has been carried out on two main topics: acquired language disorders (i.e., aphasias) and developmental dyslexia.

Acquired Language Disorders

C. K. Thompson (2000) recognized that reorganization of cortical networks, related to language, is best carried out by undamaged portions in the left hemisphere, or homologous areas in the right hemisphere (i.e., frontal areas around Broca's, the prefrontal area, or both). Current imaging techniques allow researchers to observe neuroanatomical changes resulting from training, alongside improvements in behavioral performances. Tracking such changes, Musso et al. (1999) trained four patients suffering from Wernicke's aphasia, following a stroke in the temporoparietal area of the left hemisphere (TMP). They focused on linguistic comprehension during training, which included 11 sessions of 8 minutes each, a short token test (sTT), and a PET scan. The results indicated that short-term rehabilitation of linguistic performance correlated with rapid changes in activation patterns of cortical networks. Improved performance on the sTT test was correlated with activation in two cerebral areas: the right posterior super temporal gyrus (pSTG), an area parallel to Wernicke's area, and the posterior section of the precuneus in the left hemisphere.

C. K. Thompson (2000) presented similar results after 32 weeks of linguistic processing training in a patient with agrammatical aphasia. Before training, most cerebral activity during processing of sentences occurred in the right Wernicke's area (BA 22) and the right dorsolateral prefrontal cortex. After training, activity expanded around the right Wernicke's area to areas BA 21 and BA 37, and encompassed the right Broca's area. These changes in activation were accompanied by significant improvements in behavioral task performance.

Developmental Dyslexia

A number of researchers have also begun tracing cerebral changes that occur among developmentally dyslexic readers following training. Two hypotheses have been proposed regarding cortical changes following training (Simos, Breier, Fletcher, Bergman, & Papanicolaou, 2000):

1. The normalization hypothesis: Intervention can assist in "correcting" the reading pathway among dyslexic readers, by creating an identical pathway to the one created naturally among regular readers in reading acquisition.
2. The compensation hypothesis: Intervention creates a new reading pathway among dyslexics that does not exist in regular readers.

Most dyslexic readers have difficulty performing phonetic analyses due to phonological awareness deficits, as observed in both imaging and histological studies (Rosenberger & Rottenberg, 2002). Various training methods have therefore been developed to promote reading among dyslexic readers. These have focused on dyslexics' difficulties in decoding graphemes into phonemes. Several researchers (Simos et al., 2000) have claimed that a faulty pattern of functional connections among language areas underlies differences between regular and dyslexic readers in word reading. Dyslexic readers exhibit deviant activation profiles in tasks that require phonological decoding. These profiles are characterized by significantly lower activation in the left TMP area, combined with higher activation in the homologous area of the right hemisphere (i.e., reverse dominance).

Simos et al. (2002) examined effects of training on activation patterns of dyslexic readers during reading. Eight dyslexic readers were given daily training for 8 weeks, focusing on their decoding and phonological processing abilities. The control group consisted of regular readers who had never received training. To compare activation profiles, a magnetic source imaging (MSI) scan, done on a rhyming task with pseudowords, was performed for both groups before and after training. In addition, all subjects were given the Woodcock–Johnson (WJ–III) behavioral diagnosis before and after training. At the behavioral level, no differences were found in the control group for achievement on the reading tests. However, all dyslexic subjects exhibited a significant improvement in reading skills and improved their achievements to within the normal range. The imaging results indicated changes in activation profiles of the dyslexic subjects, which corroborated the normalization hypothesis. After training on word reading time, more activity was observed in the left posterior superior temporal gyrus (pSTG) than in the right homologous area (i.e., reversal to correct dominance) among dyslexic subjects. But such differences were not found in the control group. From a temporal perspective, the activated left pSTG area worked slower in dyslexic subjects compared to control subjects. This suggests that cerebral reading circuitry in dyslexic subjects, although gaining accuracy, may remain less efficient.

Further support for the normalization hypothesis was reported by Tallal (1993), who trained 20 dyslexic subjects for 8 weeks, using a computer program that trained subjects in skills that are important for reading, including auditory attention, auditory discrimination, memory, phonological processing, and listening comprehension. At the behavioral level, improvement on the reading tests (words, nonwords, and text) led to performance at regular levels. The fMRI scans that were administered following training supported the normalization hypothesis. Training caused increased activity in the left TMP area during performance of rhyming tasks. This area is adjacent to active areas in regular readers. Another normalization effect was observed in Broca's area. Before training, cerebral activity among dyslexic subjects was focused in the frontal sections of Broca's area, whereas in the control group most of the activity was focused in the posterior sections (BA 6, 44). For the dyslexic group, the activity in Broca's area moved to posterior sections after training, achieving closer similarity to activations in control subjects. However, other data arising from the latter study supported the compensation hypothesis. Following training on a rhyming task, the experimental group showed increases in the intensity of activity in areas of the right hemisphere that are homologous to language areas in the left hemisphere, such as the left Broca's area. In the control group, these areas were not active during performance of the task. These findings constitute evidence for the development of compensation mechanisms as a result of training. In addition, they are consistent with those of studies on subjects with left hemisphere damage, for example C. K. Thompson (2000), who showed rehabilitation of language skills along with increased activity in these areas.

The normalization hypothesis has received additional support with reference to morphological processing (Aylward et al., 2003). Two groups of children, regular and dyslexic readers, were given a series of behavioral tests and an fMRI scan, performed during phonological and morphological tasks both before and after training. The dyslexic readers were trained for 3 weeks on various reading components: linguistic awareness, alphabetic principles, fluency, and comprehension. At the behavioral level, the control group exhibited significant improvement on the Woodcock word reading test, on a morphological mapping test, and on a vocal reading test of words with and without affixes. Moreover, the investigators found confirmation for the normalization hypothesis in the scan results. Consistent with Aylward et al. (2003), training among dyslexic readers enhanced the intensity of activity in cerebral pathways that are involved in reading, as was the case with the control subjects. Among other areas, increased activity levels were observed in the left parietal lobe and fusiform gyrus, and in the inferior, superior, and middle frontal lobes. Regarding the first two areas, no differences in intensity of activity were found after training. The researchers emphasized that training led to cerebral activity patterns that were closer to regular patterns. They also noted that the effects of training were differentiated, apparently affecting each reading component separately.

Richards et al. (2000) traced changes in lactic acid shortages among regular and dyslexic readers following training, using proton echo-planar spectroscopic imaging. The experimental group received phonological training during 3 weeks, with each session lasting 2 hours. Training included construction and deconstruction of syllables and words into phonemes, word decoding using syllable patterns, and vocal reading of texts that contain these words. Moreover, all subjects had imaging scans administered before and upon completion of training. During imaging, subjects performed linguistic tasks, such as lexical decision and rhyming judgment, with listening to words as the baseline, as well as nonlinguistic tasks, such as listening to different tones and same–different judgments, with listening to noise as the baseline. After training, all subjects in the experimental group, except two, exhibited regular phonological awareness for their age. On the Woodcock phonological decoding test, performance ranged between average and below average levels. Additionally, significant improvement was observed in phonological memory ability, as compared to pretraining evaluations. The imaging results indicated some functional changes in metabolic activity.

Before training, high lactic acid activity was observed among dyslexic subjects in widespread areas of the left frontal quadrant of the brain in contrast with regular readers, during performance of a phonological judgment task. This cerebral region, related to motor aspects of speech, contains sections of the frontal opercolumn, Broca's area, and the front temporal lobe, as well as areas within the frontal lobe associated with executive functions. After training, dyslexics' lactate levels in the previous region, now less dispersed, were not different from those of the control group. The control group's pattern of activity did not change between examinations.

Not all studies used phonological methods for training subjects with reading or language difficulties. Temple et al. (2000) offered support for the "rapid processing hypothesis," which proposes that phonological processing difficulties among dyslexic readers reflect a basic deficit in processing and integration of rapid signal sequences. According to this hypothesis, difficulties in processing rapid acoustic signals impair the ability to distinguish between acoustic clues, which are essential for phoneme discrimination. This impairment prevents the development of clear, stable phonological representations among dyslexic readers, causing difficulties in phonological processing. In this experiment, differences in brain activity patterns of regular and dyslexic readers were investigated with a rapid, nonlinguistic acoustic stimulus and a slow stimulus. To examine the neurological changes that occur as a result of training, three subjects were trained with a computer program, which improves rapid, sequential processing using linguistic and nonlinguistic stimuli. The training included 100 minutes of daily training for an average of 33 days.

The results indicated that, among regular readers, the left prefrontal cortex (especially BA 46/10/9) was sensitive to rapid changes of nonlinguistic acoustic stimuli. This area exhibits increased activity during processing of rapid stimuli, as opposed to slow stimuli. Among dyslexic subjects, no increases in activity were observed in this area following the processing of rapid acoustic stimuli. Two of the three dyslexic subjects showed behavioral improvement on auditory comprehension tests and rapid auditory processing, along with an increase in the level of activation of the prefrontal cortex. In the third subject who underwent training, no increase in degree of activation was observed in the prefrontal area, and there was no significant improvement on the behavioral tests.

Kujala et al. (2001) examined the effect of training of nonlinguistic stimuli on dyslexic subjects in the first grade. The purpose was to examine whether perceptual training, which does not involve the phonological system, influences reading skills. The training program involved practice of an audiovisual matching game, which contained a series of sounds and rectangles presented on a computer screen. The sounds differed in volume, duration, and tone. These characteristics were represented visually by thickness, length, and location of the rectangles, respectively. The subjects were trained to match the rectangle series that appeared on the screen to the sound series that they heard; this is analogous to matching a grapheme to its corresponding phoneme, only in a nonlinguistic fashion. Aside from the audiovisual game results, participants' reading skills were evaluated by a word reading test, and their ability to discriminate presentation order of sound pairs was measured electrophysiologically by a mismatch negativity component (MMN). The training continued for 7 weeks, with a total of 14 sessions, lasting 10 minutes each.

Following training, differences between the groups were observed in all examinations conducted. On the word reading test, only the trained group significantly improved on measures of accuracy and reading speed. In the audiovisual game test, the training group improved on accuracy and reaction time measures. The effects of training were also seen in the electrophysiological measurements. Although the MMN results did not indicate differences between groups prior to training, the measurement signal changed morphologically in the training group posttraining. The amplitude of the signal significantly increased after training, relative to the control group. In addition, the researchers found a correlation between the MMN amplitude change and the change on the reading tests, which exposed a connection between cortical discrimination of nonlinguistic sound elements and reading skills.

All of the aforementioned studies have claimed to support the idea that difficulties in dyslexia are based, at least partially, on a general dysfunction in sensory discrimination, rather than on a specific phonological processing deficit. Nonlinguistic training apparently led to plasticity changes in the neural base of sound discrimination, and thus to improvement of reading skills. According to these researchers, the higher amplitude observed after training indicates the formation of more accurate acoustic representations in the cortex.

CAN WORD READING FLUENCY BE IMPROVED THROUGH TRAINING?

As already discussed, there is primary evidence indicating that training affects the quality of cerebral activity. However, most training studies have focused on phonology. Research results demonstrate that direct intensive training in phonemic awareness improves decoding and word identification in poor readers, but yields only minimal gains in reading fluency (Lyon & Moats, 1997; for a review see Meyer & Felton, 1999). A central question thus arises: Can reading fluency be improved through training as well?

Reading Acceleration Training

As reading rate is a basic component of reading fluency, it was hypothesized that it can benefit from training by acceleration manipulation under time constraints (Breznitz & Itzhak, in preparation). The study described next examined if developmental dyslexics' word reading improves following acceleration training, and if this improvement is expressed in changes in brain activity. These questions were examined using behavioral and electrophysiological (EEG) measures. As indicated in chapter 2, the acceleration phenomenon has only been tested in a single session, after which subsequent self-paced reading of all participants returned to premanipulation levels (for reviews see Breznitz, 2001a, 2002). Solid evidence suggests that accelerated reading may prompt the dyslexic brain to process graphemic information more effectively (Breznitz, 2003b). Consequently, we set out to document a complete training experiment on accelerated reading rates of dyslexic readers in order to measure the effect on reading effectiveness.

DESCRIPTION OF THE STUDY

Subjects

Fifteen dyslexic university students participated in this study, ranging from 21 to 25 years of age (mean age 23 years, 5 months; $SD = .10$). All were native Hebrew speakers from a middle-class background, were right-handed, and displayed normal or corrected-to-normal vision in both eyes. None of the participants had a history of neurological or emotional disorders and all were paid volunteers. The subjects were recruited through the University Student Support Service, which aids students with learning disabilities. They had all been diagnosed with dyslexia in childhood and were classified as impaired readers by the Student Support Service, according to recently proposed criteria, defined by a score of 1.5 or more standard deviations below the mean on the Word Decoding Test (Ministry of Education, 2000; see Table 13.1). To control for gender differences in elements of evoked response potentials (ERP) (Hoffman & Polich, 1999; Lambe, 1999), only male participants with IQs within the normal range were selected as participants.

Several considerations underlie the decision to use adult dyslexic individuals enrolled for university studies as the target population for this project. First, the reading deficits of university-attending dyslexics are presumably not due to insufficient reading experience, lack of exposure to print, or a developmental lag. Second, even though there are fewer studies on adult dyslexics, it is clear that individuals diagnosed as dyslexics in childhood remain affected by this condition for their entire lives (Leiken & Breznitz, forthcoming). One can assume that the deficits of adult dyslexics, similar to developmental dyslexics, are unaffected by years of exposure to print. Finally, the deficits of these individuals, both on behavioral and ERP measures, tend to follow a consistent pattern, more so than similar measures in children (Leiken & Breznitz, 1999).

TABLE 13.1
Behavioral Baseline Measures

	Dyslexic (n = 15)	
Tests	M	SD
Raven Matrices (raw scores)	51.65	3.81
Decoding, Z scores (words, pseudowords, and connected text)	−1.52	1.66
Reading time—connected text (in seconds)	101.1	30.01
Comprehension connected text (out of 6)	5.01	1.71
Phonological accuracy (out of 40)	24.2	15.87
Phonological time (in seconds)	146.2	7.36
Orthographic processing: Parsing test—accuracy (out of 50)	36.77	4.07
Orthographic processing: Parsing test—time (in seconds)	276.84	23.16
Working memory completion (out of 10)	4.33	.75
Working memory opposites (out of 10)	4.95	.91
Total word production fluency	33.65	6.43
RAN letters time	31.12	7.67
RAN objects time	47.01	14.19
% WAIS Digit Symbols (percent accuracy)	78%	8.65
WAIS–III Symbol Search (speed)	46.76	9.66

Experimental Measures

Behavioral Measures. The behavioral battery included measures of general ability and reading ability. General ability, or IQ, was tested using the Raven Standard Progressive Matrices (Raven, 1960). Measures of reading ability included the following:

1. Decoding skills: 1-minute tests for words, pseudowords, and connected texts (Shatil, 1997) measured accuracy and reading time.
2. Reading comprehension, accuracy, and speed in context (Center for Psychometric Tests, 1994).
3. Word recognition skills: tests of phonological, orthographic, and morphological processing (Ben-Dror & Shani, 1997; Breznitz, 1996).
4. Spelling skills: the word list and connected-text spelling tests.
5. Memory: short-term memory tasks (Digit Span WAIS–III) and working memory tasks (Ben-Dror & Shani, 1997).
6. Speed of processing: linguistic and nonlinguistic speed of processing tasks, including the processing speed index (Digit-Symbol Coding and

Symbol Search subtests of WAIS–III), the Word Fluency Test (Breznitz, 1996, designed on the basis of Lezak, 1993), RAN naming test for letters and objects (adapted from Wolf & Obregon, 1997).

7. The reading acceleration test "Acceleration Manipulation" was performed during ERP data collection, before and after training.

The Reading Acceleration Paradigm.   The stimuli used in the reading acceleration paradigm were sentences (i.e., connected texts) composed of words that were selected by length and frequency in Hebrew (Balgor, 1980). Each test item consisted of 7–12 words, with each word 2–6 letters long. Each item was presented only once within a single set of sessions, and no more than twice throughout the training program. The mean letter height on screen was 5 mm. The words were black on a gray background, presenting 60% contrast, and the viewing distance was 60 cm. Any one test item was no longer than two lines of text with 18 mm vertical spacing between lines. A sentence bank contained sentences that were constructed according to the previous rules and subjectively rated by regular readers ($N = 66$, Haifa University students, native Hebrew speakers) for ease of comprehension in silent reading. Only those sentences that rated as easy-moderate (1,500 items) were included as stimuli.

Training and Testing

Training Regime

Each individual had 8 hours of training in four 20-minute sessions weekly over a 6-week period. In order to preserve consistency in all sessions, subjects read the items orally. Each session consisted of 50 items. Participants were prompted to answer a two-choice question (2AFC) for each item to ascertain comprehension (e.g., "What color word appeared in the item?" or "Did the farmer support the candidate following the debate?"). The items appeared one at a time on a computer screen, and participants were instructed to begin reading each item immediately upon its appearance on screen. After reading an item, the subject pressed the spacebar, the text consequently disappeared, and was followed by a comprehension question that appeared on the computer screen with four multiple-choice answers. The subjects were requested to choose the correct answer by pressing the corresponding computer key.

The Reading Acceleration Paradigm

Two forms of reading acceleration test were used, one before and one after training (Breznitz & Leiken, 2000a). In each form, three versions of the reading tasks were presented to each subject, both before and after the training sessions.

Self-Paced, Full-Screen Presentation (Without Electrophysiological Measures. In the first self-paced condition, one set of the reading forms was administered in order to obtain a measure of normal, self-paced reading rate. In this condition, each item appeared in its entirety on the computer screen. Reading times and comprehension for each of the 17 items were recorded for each participant.

Self-Paced, Window Presentation (with Electrophysiological Measures). In the second self-paced condition, another parallel set of 17 items was presented. In this condition, sentences appeared word by word, and were then followed by full-screen multiple-choice questions. This manner of presentation was adopted in order to reduce eye movements by focusing the participant's gaze on the center of the computer screen. Word presentation rate was calculated for each participant, as follows. The reading time for each sentence in the first self-paced condition was divided by the number of words in that item, yielding a per-word average reading time. Next, a combined average was calculated for the 17 per-word averages. This served as the presentation rate for the words in each sentence in the window paradigm. As these rates were calculated for each individual reader, subsequent presentation rates differed across participants. To eliminate ERP overlap between words, the SOA (presentation time for each word in a sentence and the ISI between words) was 1,200 ms. ISIs varied according to the presentation rate of each word in each sentence for each participant.

Fast-Paced, Window Presentation (with Electrophysiological Measures). In this condition, a third parallel set of 17 items was presented. The words in each sentence appeared word by word in the center of the screen. However, words were presented at the fastest average per-word rate exhibited in the first self-paced condition. That is, of the 17 original per-word averages, the fastest average was selected. As in the self-paced condition, the SOA was 1,200 ms and ISIs varied according to the presentation rate of each word in a sentence for each participant.

Instrumentation.   All stimuli were presented on an IBM-PC terminal. Visual stimuli were presented in white over a gray background on a computer display situated 1.5 m in front of the participant.

Training Procedure and Equipment and Software for Electrophysiological Measures

Each training session began with a test of self-paced sentence reading rate for each individual. Next, a block of 50 items was presented, with the letters in each item disappearing one by one, starting at the beginning of the target sentence, and based on the subject's best per-letter average reading time, as calculated in the self-paced condition. The per-letter "disappearance rate" was increased in steps of 4% (Breznitz, 1996, 1997a, 1997b). A staircase-like procedure was used. The "disappearance rate" increased only if the subject's answers to the probe questions were correct on six consecutive sentences. At any given time during the session, subjects could decelerate the presentation rates of items on the screen.

The study was carried out in five stages:

1. **Subject selection**: Selection of subjects according to established criteria for dyslexia. Administration of the behavioral battery to determine individuals' level of reading-related skills.
2. **Pretraining measurements**: Behavioral and ERP measures were obtained during sentence reading at self- and fast-paced reading rates. Data were collected prior to training, in order to inspect acceleration effects. ERP data analysis was performed in stage 3.
3. **Training sessions**: There were 50 easy-to-moderate sentences presented per training session. Training lasted 6 weeks for the 15 subjects.
4. **Post-training measurements**: These included (a) reading sentences at self-paced and accelerated rates, while measuring reading time, comprehension, accuracy, and ERP data; and (b) collecting data from behavioral 1-minute tests for words and pseudowords, as well as data from oral and silent reading in context.
5. **Analysis of ERP and behavioral data.**

Equipment.   Electrophysiological activity was recorded using a 19-channel EEG (Bio-Logic) system. PC terminals were used for acceleration training and testing, as well as for stimuli presentation during ERP studies. A PC-implemented Visual Basic software package, modified from the Breznitz acceleration paradigm (Leiken & Breznitz, 2001), was set up for training purposes. Two main ERP components were identified: P200 and P300.

Results

Baseline Measures. Results showed that dyslexic readers achieved lower scores on most baseline tests (see Table 13.1) in comparison with normative scores (Breznitz & Berman, 2003; Breznitz & Misra, 2003).

Behavioral Training Measures. Results of *t*-test analyses between per-word reading time, decoding errors, comprehension time in connected text, and 1-minute tests for words and pseudowords, prior and posttraining, yielded significant differences. Generally speaking, reading and comprehension times were shorter, decoding errors decreased in number, and there were more correct words and pseudowords in posttraining measures. No significant differences were found between pre- and posttraining comprehension questions (see Table 13.2).

Figure 13.1 indicates that, on average, subjects systematically improved their reading times up to day 23 of training. From day 23 to day 30, no improvements were noted. Moreover, there were considerable decreases in per-word reading time from day 1 to day 13 for all subjects, within 30 ms. From day 13 to day 30, an average improvement of only 10 ms was observed, and only among 11 subjects.

Electrophysiological Measures. To examine whether reading acceleration training led to changes in brain activity patterns of the subjects, within subject comparisons of latency and amplitude of ERP components were performed. Sentences were read at self-paced reading rates both before and after training.

TABLE 13.2
The Effects of Training on Reading:
Oral Reading of Words–Pseudowords and Connected Text

	Pretraining		Posttraining		
	M	SD	M	SD	T
Per-word reading time of connected text (ms)	0.58	0.13	0.51	0.0	3.11**
Decoding errors in connected text	6.18	4.64	4.36	5.29	3.05**
Comprehension time	372.96	162.95	161.28	71.94	3.97**
Number of correct answers	3.01	1.02	3.06	1.28	ns
Correct words per minute	78.18	13.79	84.15	13.46	3.66**
Correct pseudowords per minute	33.18	18.43	42.63	13.42	3.71**

Note. **$p < .001$.

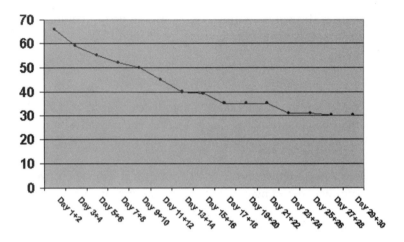

FIG. 13.1. Mean learning curves during accelerated reading training: Oral reading (mean per word reading time, ms).

Reading time and reading comprehension were measured for each sentence. The data indicated two ERP components on EEG brain waves P200 and P300. No significant differences were found in any pre- or posttraining amplitude, on P200 or P300. However, significant differences between pre- and posttraining conditions were found in the latencies of P200 and P300. The two components were elicited significantly earlier in posttraining testing. A main effect of sessions was obtained for P200, $F(2, 13) = 5.11, p < .02$, and for P300, $F(2, 13) = 7.42, p < .001$.

The most prominent ERP component, in all sessions, was observed on the CZ electrode; reported means and standard deviations refer to latencies taken from this electrode. The latency of P200 in the pretraining condition was $X = 309.21$ ($SD = 97.11$) and for the posttraining condition $X = 257.86$ ($SD = 112.06$). The latency of P300 in the pretraining condition was $X = 521.24$ ($SD = 87.58$) and for the posttraining condition $X = 388.25$ ($SD = 96.19$).

CONCLUSIONS

The study described examined the effects of reading training on dyslexic university students. The behavioral measures employed indicated that these readers read accurately but display slow reading in and out of context, as well as slow reading of pseudowords. We attempted to train these subjects in order to increase reading rate, by means of the acceleration phenomenon. To prevent information-processing overload, training was based on reading easy-to-moderate sentences. The subjects read the passages orally at each training session in order to practice their phonological pattern building skills as well. The training program was based on each subject's personal self-paced reading rate, which constituted the starting point for training. Each subject underwent 30 training sessions, 30 minutes each, reading 50 sentences within each session.

The results showed that all subjects improved their reading rates by 30 ms per word, at least until day 13. From day 13 of training onward, and until day 23, this improvement continued for 11 subjects, at an average of 10 m per word. From day 23 to day 30, no training effect was observed for any of the subjects (see Fig. 13.1). Reading rates were differential at the start (each subject had a different starting rate), and training effects varied. However, all 15 subjects clearly accelerated their personal reading rates. It is likely that the 4 subjects who did not continue to improve their reading rates after day 13 had reached an asymptote in their reading. The same may be true for the remaining subjects after day 23. Reading acceleration training has been successfully transferred, as displayed in improved decoding quality and decreased reading times for material not included in the training program. The data also point to improvements in speed of information processing, as manifested in earlier latencies of ERP components posttraining.

Most evidence available to date offers support for the hypothesis that phonological deficits are the main cause for word reading impairment in dyslexics (i.e., Torgesen, 2000). Dyslexics' self-paced reading is slow, sequential, nonautomatic, and involves acoustic-phonological processing. As previously argued (Breznitz, 1997b), acceleration has an enhancing effect on word reading in dyslexic readers. This may be because, under time constraints, the brain is barred, at least partly, from processing information via the impaired phonological system. Instead, it is compelled to divert words via direct retrieval from the mental lexicon, which is based on holistic, orthographic word patterns. As a result of numerous years of poor reading habits, this process cannot be self-activated by the dyslexic brain. Rather, this bypass can be utilized only when forced under direct manipulation. Acceleration training teaches the dyslexic brain to use an alternative and more effective processing route. Bypassing the impaired phonological route may lead to effective and fluent word reading in dyslexic readers.

Further support for the positive effects of the acceleration phenomenon on the brain activity of dyslexic readers can be seen in our recent fMRI study (Karni et al., 2001). Differences in brain activity between dyslexic and regular readers were observed when the two groups read items at their self-paced reading rates. At self-paced rates, regular readers showed increased activity, and dyslexic readers decreased activity, in Wernicke's area (see also E. S. Shaywitz et al., 1998), whereas the activation in Broca's area was decreased in regular readers but stayed constant in dyslexics. However, in the fast-paced reading condition, the two groups did not differ in the extent of activation in Broca's area. Moreover, during fast-paced reading, activation in Wernicke's area increased among dyslexic readers. It was therefore suggested that brain activation patterns of adult dyslexics become more similar to those of regular readers during accelerated reading.

The results of this study may provide a basis for a new approach to remediation of developmental dyslexia. Our study suggests new methodology for reading training, which could be subsequently applied to improving reading in readers of all ages, with or without reading impairments. It may also provide an empirical base for comparing different training regimes and the effectiveness of various training materials (e.g., methods targeting single words, connected text, or nonwords). Furthermore, continued research in this field may provide new insights into the pathophysiology of dyslexia—the neural substrates of reading skills among adult dyslexic individuals. In so doing, it may lead to a better understanding of dyslexia, and hence to better remediation.

14

Conclusion: The Key Role of SOP Within the Orchestration of Reading

Reading is a cognitive skill that starts exclusively with the decoding of printed materials. A successful word decoding process frees cognitive resources for reading comprehension. For years, researchers have focused on *inaccuracy* in word decoding as the basis of dyslexia. In recent years, the idea of a lack of *fluency* as an additional and separate component of dyslexia has opened new directions for the understanding of this phenomenon. The aim of this book has been to determine the underlying factors of fluency, and the specific causes of dysfluency in word decoding during reading.

What makes fluency such an important factor in word decoding? Given the time constraints imposed on the reading processes by the information processing system, fluency in word decoding is a crucial requirement for the enhancement of reading. Moreover, the high demand for rapid and accurate decoding in our technology- and knowledge-based societies gives an extra impetus to the necessity of focusing on the factors that influence fluency in word reading. Clearly, fluency is a time-based term. But how do we define fluent word reading? It is obvious that given the aforementioned constraints, successful word reading requires fast decoding of written material. Based on the arguments presented in this book, I suggest that we can simplify our definition of fluency by defining it as the rate of word decoding. In our experiments we refer to this as reading rate.

Why reading rate? Reading rate already incorporates a wide range of time-based features that are crucial to the reading process. As compared to other word decoding measures, the aspect of time appears only in word reading rate. Unlike other word reading skills, reading rate operates on a time scale with a wide range. This makes it superior to other reading measures such as comprehension and decoding rate, as it is more precise and more objective. Thus far, it has been viewed as a dependent variable, which is affected by the quality of word recognition skills and by decoding accuracy and comprehension. Consequently, reading rate can be seen as a diagnostic measure as well. However, since reading rate itself impacts the quality of reading, it should also be viewed as an independent variable. Our central focus should therefore shift to the way in which reading rate affects accuracy and comprehension.

Having defined word decoding fluency as word decoding rate, we can now inquire into its *causes*. What are the determinants of word decoding rate?

As we proposed in this book, word decoding rate is determined by two crucial factors:

1. The characteristics of the information processing system.
2. Speed of processing of the modalities and the systems involved in reading.

What are the implications of this? First, to overcome the time constraints imposed by the information processing mechanism, the activation in the systems that are involved in word reading needs to be *fast enough*—in other words, at a sufficiently high SOP. Second, as word reading requires an exact grapheme/phoneme correspondence, the information arriving from the different systems regarding printed symbols must be *synchronized in time for appropriate integration*.

Regarding within-systems SOP, we have shown that in a regular, fluent, and accurate word decoding process, the SOP in each modality and system is relatively fast. However, in impaired word decoding, the SOP in each modality and system is slower. Furthermore, among regular readers in most tasks and activation stages (perception, working memory, and output) the auditory modality is slower than the visual. Among dyslexics an opposite pattern was found. Regarding between-systems SOP, we have shown that regular readers typically have a relatively narrow between-modalities time gap, which does not affect their word decoding effectiveness. In contrast, this time gap is much wider among dyslexic readers, and is highly related to the word decoding rate.

At which processing stage does SOP contribute most to the effectiveness of word decoding rate? Our results suggest a fundamentally different pattern of SOP contribution for dyslexic and regular readers in the processing of linguistic tasks. Regression analyses incorporating all of our research parameters (see Breznitz, 2000; Breznitz & Misra, 2003) indicated that it is SOP at the perception stage of phonemes (P200 latency) which explains most of the variance in fluent word decoding among regular readers. As word reading is automatic among regular readers, the perception stage in the speech based system suffices for successful word decoding. In other words, in a regular course of fluent word decoding it is enough for the visual symbol to be matched with its phoneme at the initial stage of stimuli discrimination (possibly the pre-lexical stage). This is not the case for dyslexic readers. The latter were found to be significantly slower than regular readers at each stage of activation in the word decoding process in each modality and system. However, regardless of the slow information processing in the perceptual, working memory, and output stages (possibly the lexical stage), it was the SOP in working memory (P300 latency) during visual processing of words that was the first explanatory factor for the dyslexics' lack of word reading fluency.

Furthermore, we claimed that dyslexic readers are less able to identify word patterns, as these are not appropriately stored in their mental lexicon. Thus, dyslexics will tend to rely on various sources of information in their brains, in an attempt to compose or piece together the accurate and complete pattern of the word to be decoded. We argue that this, in turn, further slows down their already slow SOP. Second, we propose that since different dyslexic individuals will tend to rely on different information sources in order to retrieve and piece together the correct word patterns, dyslexics can be expected to be not just generally slower, but also to be less unified in the way in which they process information. Some dyslexics will be faster in processing in the auditory-phonology systems, others will be faster in the visual-orthography systems. Consequently, the general slowness in reading of dyslexics is a result of their *differential* domain-specific slowness. In other words, there will be various subtypes of dyslexic readers.

It is clear from our data that dyslexics are suffering from slow processing SOP in the reading related brain systems. This overall slowness can explain reading comprehension deficits but not necessarily word decoding accuracy. Our data showed that it is the SOP time gap between the visual and auditory modalities and between the orthographic and phonological systems which explained the word decoding problems of dyslexic readers. Specifically the time gap between P300 latencies of the grapheme less phoneme in young dyslexics and the P300 latencies of the pseudowords less words in adult dyslexics explained most of the word decoding variances of these groups. This is what we referred to as the "Asynchrony Phenomenon"—the imperfect timing of information flowing between a number of different brain sources. As we have spelled out, fluent word decoding is based on the timely arrival of information from more than one source. As each source operates at a different speed, it requires time synchronization. The wider the time gap between the visual and auditory modalities (the pre-lexical stage), the larger the asynchrony between the orthographic and phonological systems (the lexical stage), and the poorer the word decoding (Breznitz, 2000; Breznitz & Misra, 2003).

What can facilitate appropriate brain synchronization in the word decoding process? We argue that for this synchronization to occur, a specific integration function is needed. A regulator is required that will effectively moderate the incoming information from its different sources according to the task demands. This idea is in some ways related to Llinas's (1993) notion of a clock and Nicholson's (2000) suggestion of a pacer in the cerebellum, or to Wolf and Bower's (1999) precise timing mechanism.

Our idea is that like any good regulator, the reading regulator has to have a number of specific characteristics. First, it has to have the ability to absorb changes in the environment (*flexibility*). Second, it has to be *sensitive* to the task demands and the needs of the reader. Ideally this regulator should have a wide range. Here we would like to suggest that the regulator for word reading could be compared to the conductor of a symphonic orchestra. The musical instruments are the visual and the auditory modalities and the phonological and the orthographic systems that are activated in word reading. Just like each instrument has its own sound, so each of these entities has its own location in the brain and its own manner and speed of processing. In order to achieve harmony, an orchestra conductor synchronizes the overall sound of his many players by flexibly using a musical score. In the same vein, in order to achieve grapheme–phoneme integration for effective word reading, the regulator's task is to synchronize the information that arrives from the different entities.

In the case of word reading, this synchronization is all the more important because each entity processes information at a different speed. We propose that the regulator in word reading operates sequentially, first at the lower level of visual-auditory modalities and then at the higher level of phonological-auditory systems. After the information from the printed material enters the "gate" (Perfetti & Bolger, 2004) of the information processing, the regulator must precisely match the relevant incoming information from the visual modality with the auditory-acoustic sounds associated with the visual symbols. To do so, the regulator must absorb the signals arriving from these two modalities at different speeds, and, like an orchestra conductor, it must flexibly handle these signals and temporize between them. Once this is achieved, the information in the regulator enters a higher level of processing, which is entirely interior to the reader's brain. At this stage, the phonological, orthographic, and semantic systems operate in parallel (PDP model). Each of these higher level systems also operates at its own speed, so speed regulation between the three is again required.

In the case of regular readers, the time gap between the two modalities and subsequently between the three systems is limited (see chaps. 9, 10, 11, 12). As a result, the regulator can handle its synchronization tasks at both levels relatively easily. Such successful synchronization processes will lead to a flexible reading rate, which will enhance the fluency of word decoding. Reading rate is measured objectively on a time scale with a wide range of values. It is determined by the different speeds of processing of the entities at the two processing levels and by the synchronization between these speeds. In the case of regular readers, reading rate can flexibly adjust to changes in the written materials (flexibility) and to the reader's moods and skills (sensitivity). This is why reading rate can also be changed through training (see chap. 13). Whether these changes are cognitive, biological, or both is still an open question. Similarly, it remains to be studied whether training the reading rate leads to changes of speed activation in the thalamus, the cerebellum, or the frontal lobe areas of the brain.

In the case of dyslexic readers, the processing time gap between the lower level modalities and between the higher level systems is wider (see chap. 12). These wider time gaps increase the disruption in the synchronization of the information arriving from the different entities. As a result of this poor synchronization, impaired linguistic patterns are processed, which leads to a slow reading rate and dysfluent and inaccurate word decoding processes. This provokes a number of hypotheses regarding the functioning of the regulator in dyslexic readers' brains. On the one hand, it could be that dyslexics have a stiff and inflexible regulator that cannot accommodate to anomalies in processing speed. On the other hand, it might be that the limited capacity and rapid decay imposed by the information processing system on any cognitive task combine with the speed anomalies specific to dyslexics to make it impossible for their regulator to function above a certain level of time gaps. Future research will need to clarify these issues.

We cannot avoid the fact that inaccuracy in word decoding has for years been the indicator of dyslexia. Inaccuracy refers to the number of decoding errors made when orally reading any reading materials. The reading materials can be at any level of linguistic complexity, i.e., letters, syllables, single words, or connected text. The number of errors made by the reader comprises a diagnostic measure for dyslexia. At the level of causality, it is commonly agreed that the lack of accuracy in word decoding stems from deficits in word recognition skills. There is wide agreement that appropriate activation in the orthographic, phonological, semantic and syntactic systems is crucial for effective word decoding to occur. A long line of research has pointed to phonological processing deficits as the primary source of dyslexic readers' difficulties in word decoding. Other studies have found that fundamental orthographic deficits have accumulated among disabled readers. However, currently accumulative data suggests that adult dyslexics, after years of training, can decode words more accurately and successfully complete various levels of phonological and orthographic tasks. And yet, their reading rate and their performance time on the phonological and orthographic tasks remain significantly slower when compared to average readers.

This raised a central question in our investigation of the factors underlying dyslexia. Why is it that after years of remedial reading training, dyslexics can in part overcome their accuracy deficits, *but not their slow word decoding rate, nor their slow performance in word recognition tasks?* Where does this slowness come from? In an attempt to answer these questions we have argued that among dyslexics the deficits in the word recognition systems are only a part of the explanation of word decoding inaccuracy. Importantly, as the phonological and orthographic processing of written symbols relies on information from the visual and the auditory modalities, it is not just the manner, but also the speed at which each modality processes information that affects word recognition skills. Our theory suggests that speed of processing (SOP) is a fundamental prerequisite for effective activation in the phonological and orthographic systems, which themselves affect word decoding accuracy.

In sum, we suggest that slow SOP is the general underlying cause of dyslexia, in that it affects not just word decoding rate (which can also be named fluency), but also phonology, orthography, and higher linguistic skills. The present SOP theory of dyslexia also provides the basis for a new approach to remediation of developmental dyslexia across all ages and levels of reading. Further research on this factor is likely to yield wide-ranging new insights into the pathophysiology of dyslexia. Thus, a better scientific understanding and concomitant remediation of reading rate may hold the key to our future fine-tuning of the manifold processes that build up the reading process.

CONCLUSION

Reading depends on so many different things that have to happen just right. It is undoubtedly one of the major challenges to our brains. Fortunately, in most instances, it can be effectively mastered with several years of practice, and proper maturation of the complex brain mechanisms that provide the basis for automatic recognition of word patterns. It is only when things go wrong that the enormous complexity of the task reveals itself. This book has argued that a major feature of this complexity is the effective temporal coordination of all the components that participate in the process of translating artificial printed symbols into properly understood meaning. For it is not only that many different things have to happen just right. They also have to happen fast enough, and at precisely the right time. In the absence of proper speed and synchronization, reading continues to be the highly effortful decoding of graphemes, and the miracle of automatic word recognition is never achieved. We have made the case for the centrality of SOP in the understanding of dyslexia. It is conceivable that SOP in its most basic form is a personal characteristic with significant genetic elements. At the same time, we have showed that it is at least partially amenable to systematic training. Increasing the SOP of dyslexic readers was shown to enhance both decoding and comprehension. This provides a ray of hope for effective intervention and treatment.

References

Aaron, P. G. (1993). Is there a visual dyslexia? *Annals of Dyslexia, 43*, 110–124.

Ackerman, P. T., & Dykman, R. A. (1993). Phonological processes, confrontational naming, and immediate memory in dyslexia. *Journal of Learning Disabilities, 26*(9), 597–609.

Ackerman, P. T., Dykman, R. A., & Oglesby, D. M. (1994). Visual event-related potentials of dyslexic children to rhyming and nonrhyming stimuli. *Journal of Clinical and Experimental Neuropsychology, 16*(1), 138–154.

Adams, M. J. (1981). What good is orthographic redundancy? In O.J.L. Tzeng & H. Singer (Eds.), *Perception of print: Reading research in experimental psychology* (pp. 197–221). Hillsdale, NJ: Lawrence Erlbaum Associates.

Adams, M. J. (1990). *Beginning to read: Thinking and learning about print.* Cambridge, MA: MIT Press.

Aksoomoff, N. A., & Courchesne, E. (1992). A new role for the cerebellum in cognitive operation. *Behavioral Neuroscience, 106*(5), 731–738.

American Psychiatric Association. (1994). *Diagnostic and statistical manual of mental disorders* (4th ed.). Washington, DC: Author.

Amir, Y., Harel, M., & Malach, R. (1993). Cortical hierarchy reflected in the organization of intrinsic connections in macaque monkey visual cortex. *Journal of Comparative Neurology, 334*(1), 19–46.

Anderson, J. R. (1992). Automaticity and the ACT* Theory. *American Journal of Psychology, 105*(2), 165–180.

Anderson, M., Reid, C., & Nelson, J. (2001). Developmental changes in inspection time: What a difference a year makes. *Intelligence, 29*(6), 475–486.

Anderson, R. C., Wilkinson, I. A., & Mason, J. M. (1991). A microanalysis of the small-group, guided reading lesson: Effects of an emphasis on global story meaning. *Reading Research Quarterly, 26*(4), 417–441.

Apthorp, H. S. (1995). Phonetic coding and reading in college students with and without learning disabilities. *Journal of Learning Disabilities, 28*(6), 342–352.

Arnett, J. L., & Di Lollo, V. (1979). Visual information processing in relation to age and to reading ability. *Journal of Experimental Child Psychology, 27*(1), 143–152.

Atkinson, R. C., & Shiffrin, R. M. (1971). The control of short-term memory. *Scientific American, 225*(2), 82–90.

Aylward, E. H., Richards, T. L., Berninger, V. W., Nagy, W. E., Field, K. M., Grimme, A. C., Richards, A. L., Thomson, J. B., & Cramer, S. C. (2003). Instructional treatment associated with changes in brain activation in children with dyslexia. *Neurology, 61*, 212–219.

Baddeley, A. (1986). Modularity, mass action and memory. *Quarterly Journal of Experimental Psychology: Human Experimental Psychology, 38*(4A), 527–533.

Baddeley, A. D., Ellis, N. C., Miles, T. R., & Lewis, V. J. (1982). Developmental and acquired dyslexia: A comparison. *Cognition, 11*(2), 185–199.

Baddeley, A., Vallar, G., & Wilson, B. (1987). Sentence comprehension and phonological memory: Some neuropsychological evidence. In M. Coltheart (Ed.), *Attention and performance 12: The psychology of reading* (pp. 509–529). Hillsdale, NJ: Lawrence Erlbaum Associates.

Badian, N. A. (1994). Do dyslexic and other poor readers differ in reading-related cognitive skills? *Reading and Writing, 6*(1), 45–63.

Badian, N. A. (1995). Predicting reading ability over the long-term: The changing roles of letter naming, phonological awareness and orthographic processing. *Annals of Dyslexia: An Interdisciplinary Journal, 45*, 79–86.

Badian, N. A. (1996). Dyslexia: A validation of the concept at two age levels. *Journal of Learning Disabilities, 29*(1), 102–112.

Badian, N. A. (1997). Dyslexia and the double deficit hypothesis. *Annals of Dyslexia, 47*, 69–87.

Baker, L. A., Vernon, P. A., & Ho, H. (1991). The genetic correlation between intelligence and speed of information processing. *Behavior Genetics, 21*(4), 351–367.

Baldeweg, T., Richardson, A., Watkins, S., Foale, C., & Gurzelier, J. (1999). Impaired auditory frequency discrimination in dyslexia detected with mismatch evoked potentials. *Annals of Neurology, 45*(4), 495–503.

Balgor, A. (1980). *The frequency of words in Hebrew.* Hapoalem Library, Tel Aviv, Israel.

Barker, T. A., Torgesen, J. K., & Wagner, R. K. (1992). The role of orthographic processing skills on five different reading tasks. *Reading Research Quarterly, 27*(4), 334–335.

Barnea, A., & Breznitz, Z. (1998). Phonological and orthographic processing of Hebrew words: Electrophysiological aspects. *Journal of Genetic Psychology, 159*(4), 492–504.

Barnea, A., Lamm, O., Epstein, R., & Pratt, H. (1994). Brain potentials from dyslexic children recorded during short-term memory tasks. *International Journal of Neuroscience, 74*, 227–237.

Bartha, M. C., Martin, R. C., & Jensen, C. R. (1998). Multiple interference effects in short-term recognition memory. *American Journal of Psychology, 111*(1), 89–118.

Belmont, L., Birch, H. G., & Belmont, I. (1968). Auditory-visual intersensory processing and verbal mediation. *Journal of Nervous and Mental Disease, 147*(6), 562–569.

Ben-Dror, I., Bentin, S., & Frost, R. (1995). Semantic, phonologic, and morphologic skills in reading disabled and normal children: Evidence from perception and production of spoken Hebrew. *Reading Research Quarterly, 30*(4), 876–893.

Ben-Dror, I., Polatsek, A., & Scarpati, S. (1991). Word identification in isolation and in context by college students. *Brain and Language, 31,* 308–327.

Ben-Dror, I., & Shani, M. (1997). *The working memory test.* Mofet. Tel Aviv, Israel.

Bentin, S. (1989). Electrophysiological studies of visual word perception, lexical organization, and semantic processing: A tutorial review. *Language and Speech, 32,* 205–220.

Bentin, S., Deutsch, A., & Liberman, I. Y. (1990). Syntactic competence and reading ability in children. *Journal of Experimental Child Psychology, 48,* 147–172.

Berman, R. A. (1985). The acquisition of Hebrew. In D. I. Slobin (Ed.), *The crosslinguistic study of language acquisition: Vol. 1. The data: Vol. 2. Theoretical issues* (pp. 255–371). Hillsdale, NJ: Lawrence Erlbaum Associates.

Bernal, J., Harmony, T., Rodriguez, M., Reyes, A., Yanez, G., Fernandez, T., Galan, L., Silva, J., Fernandez-Bouzas, A., Rodriguez, H., Guerrero, V., & Marosi, E. (2000). Auditory event related potentials in poor readers. *International Journal of Psychophysiology, 36*(1), 11–23.

Berninger, V. W. (1987). Global component, and serial processing of printed words in beginning reading. *Journal of Experimental Child Psychology, 43,* 387–418.

Berninger, V. W. (1990). Multiple orthographic codes: Key to alternative instructional methodologies for developing orthographic-phonological connections underlying word identification. *School Psychology Review, 19,* 518–533.

Berninger, V. W. (2001). Understanding the "lexia" in dyslexia: A multidisciplinary team approach to learning disabilities. *Annals of Dyslexia, 51,* 23–48.

Berninger, V. W., Abbott, R. D., & Alsdorf, B. J. (1997). Lexical and sentence level processes in comprehension of written sentences. *Reading and Writing, 9*(2), 135–162.

Berninger, V. W., Yates, C., & Lester, K. (1991). Multiple orthographic codes in reading and writing acquisition. *Reading and Writing: An Interdisciplinary Journal, 3,* 115–149.

Berry, C. (1967). Timing of cognitive responses in naming tasks. *Nature, 215*(5106), 1203–1204.

Biddle, K. R. (1996). *The development of visual naming speed and verbal fluency in average and impaired readers: The implications for assessment, intervention, and theory.* Unpublished doctoral dissertation, Tufts University, Boston, MA.

Biemiller, A. (1978). Relationships between oral reading rates for letters, words, and simple text in the development of reading achievement. *Reading Research Quarterly, 13*(2), 223–253.

Birch, H. G., & Belmont, L. (1964). Auditory-visual integration in normal retarded readers. *American Journal of Orthopsychiatry, 34*(5), 852–861.

Birch, H. G., & Belmont, L. (1965). Auditory-visual integration in brain-damaged and normal children. *Developmental Medicine and Child Neurology, 7*(2), 135–144.

Birnboim, S., Breznitz, Z., Pratt, H., & Aharon, Y. (2002). Automatic and controlled verbal-information processing in patients with frontal lobe lesions. *Genetic, Social and General Psychology Monographs, 128*(1), 29–46.

Bjaalid, I. K., Hoien, T., & Lundberg, I. (1993). Letter identification and lateral masking in dyslexics and normal readers. *Scandinavian Journal of Educational Research, 37*(2), 151–161.

Blachman, B. A. (1984). Relationship of rapid naming ability and language analysis skills to kindergarten and first grade reading achievement. *Reading Research Quarterly, 13,* 223–253.

Blachman, B. A. (1994). What we have learned from longitudinal studies of phonological processing and reading, and some unanswered questions: A response to Torgesen, Wagner, and Roshotte. *Journal of Learning Disabilities, 27*(5), 287–291.

Blackwell, S. L., McIntyre, C. W., & Murray, M. E. (1983). Information processed from brief visual displays by learning-disabled boys. *Child Development, 54*(4), 927–940.

Blank, M., & Bridger, W. H. (1966). Conceptual cross-modal transfer in deaf and hearing children. *Child Development, 37*(1), 29–38.

Blinkhorn, S. F., & Hendrickson, D. E. (1982). Averaged evoked responses and psychometric intelligence. *Nature, 295*(5850), 596–597.

Boden, C., & Brodeur, D. A. (1999). Visual processing of verbal and nonverbal stimuli in adolescents with reading disabilities. *Journal of Learning Disabilities, 32*(1), 58–71.

Boomsma, D. I., & Somsen, R. J. (1991). Reaction times measured in a choice reaction time and a double task condition: A small twin study. *Personality and Individual Differences, 12*(6), 519–522.

Booth, J. R., Perfetti, C. A., & MacWhinney, B. (1999). Quick, automatic and general activation of orthographic and phonological representations in young readers. *Developmental Psychology, 35*(1), 3–19.

Botuck, S., & Turkewitz, G. (1990). Intersensory functioning: Auditory visual pattern equivalence in younger and older children. *Developmental Psychology, 26*(1), 115–120.

Bouma, H., & Legein, Ch. P. (1977). Foveal and parafoveal recognition of letters and words by dyslexics and average readers. *Neuropsychologia, 15*, 69–80.

Bouma, H., & Legein, Ch. P. (1980). Dyslexia: A specific recoding deficit? An analysis of response latencies for letters and words in dyslexics and in average readers. *Neuropsychologia, 18*, 285–298.

Bowers, P. G. (1993). Text reading and re-reading: Determinants of fluency beyond word recognition. *Journal of Reading Behavior, 25*(2), 133–153.

Bowers, P. G. (1995, April). *Re-examining selected reading research from the viewpoint of the "double-deficit hypothesis."* Paper presented at the Society for Research in Child Development, Indianapolis, IN.

Bowers, P. G., Golden, J., Kennedy, A., & Young, A. (1994). Limits upon orthographic knowledge due to processes indexed by naming-speed. In V. W. Berninger (Ed.), *The varieties of orthographic knowledge I: Theoretical and developmental issues* (pp. 173–218). Dordecht, The Netherlands: Kluwer Academic.

Bowers, P. G., Steffy, R. A., & Swanson, L. B. (1986). Naming speed, memory, and visual processing in reading disability. *Canadian Journal of Behavioral Science, 18*, 209–223.

Bowers, P. G., Steffy, R., & Tate, E. (1988). Comparison of the effects of I.Q. control methods on memory and naming speed predictors of reading disability. *Reading Research Quarterly, 23*, 304–309.

Bowers, P. G., Sunseth, K., & Golden, J. (1999). The route between rapid naming and reading progress. *Scientific Studies of Reading, 3*(1), 31–53.

Bowers, P. G., & Swanson, L. B. (1991). Naming speed deficits in reading disability: Multiple measures if a singular process. *Journal of Experimental Child Psychology, 51*, 195–219.

Bowers, P. G., & Wolf, M. (1993). Theoretical links among naming speed, precise timing mechanisms and orthographic skill in dyslexia. *Reading and Writing, 5*, 69–85.

Bowey, J. A. (1985). Contextual facilitation in children's oral reading in relation to grade and decoding skill. *Journal of Experimental Child Psychology, 40*(1), 23–48.

Brady, S. A., & Shankweiler, D. P. (1991). *Phonological processes in literacy: A tribute to Isabelle Y. Liberman.* Hillsdale, NJ: Lawrence Erlbaum Associates.

Brady, S. A., Shankweiler, D. P., & Mann, V. (1983). Speech perception and memory coding in relation to reading ability. *Journal of Experimental Child Psychology, 35*(2), 345–367.

Brady, S., Poggie, E., & Rappala, M. M. (1989). Speech repetition abilities in children who differ in reading skill. *Language and Speech, 32*(Pt. 2), 109–122.

Brandeis, D., & Lehmann, D. (1994). ERP mapping: A tool for assessing language disorders. In H. J. Heinze, T. F. Mante, & G. R. Mangun (Eds.), *Cognitive electrophysiology* (pp. 242–250). Boston: Birkhauser.

Brandeis, D. L., Vitacco, D., & Steinhausen, H. C. (1994). Mapping brain electric microstates in dyslexic children during reading. *Acta Paedopsychiatrica, 56,* 239–247.

Brandt, J., & Rosen, J. J. (1980). Auditory phonemic perception in dyslexia: Categorical identification and discrimination of stop consonants. *Brain and Language, 9,* 324–337.

Brannan, J. R., Solan, H. A., Ficarra, A. P., & Ong, E. (1998). Effect of luminance on visual evoked potential amplitudes in normal and disabled readers. *Optom Visual Science, 75*(4), 279–283.

Brannan, J., & Williams, M. (1987). Allocation of visual attention in good and poor readers. *Perceptual Psychophysics, 41,* 23–28.

Brecelj, J., Strucl, M., & Raic, V. (1996). Do visual neurophysiological tests reflect magnocellular deficit in dyslexic children? *Pfluegers Archive, 431*(6, Suppl. 2), R299–300.

Breen, K., & Warrington, E. K. (1995). Impaired naming and preserved reading: A complete dissociation. *Cortex, 31*(3), 583–588.

Breitmeyer, B. G. (1993). The roles of sustained and transient channels in reading and reading disability. In S. F. Wright & R. Groner (Eds.), *Facets of dyslexia and its remediation* (pp. 13–32). North-Holland: Elsevier Science.

Brewer, N., & Smith, G. A. (1989). Developmental changes in processing speed: Influence of speed accuracy regulation. *Journal of Experimental Psychology: General, 118*(3), 298–310.

Breznitz, Z. (1981). The role of speed in reading acquisition as perceived by the teachers. Unpublished manuscript, University of Haifa, Israel.

Breznitz, Z. (1987a). Increasing first graders' reading accuracy and comprehension by accelerating their reading rate. *Journal of Educational Psychology, 79,* 236–242.

Breznitz, Z. (1987b). Reducing the gap in reading performance between Israeli lower- and middle-class first-grade pupils. *Journal of Psychology, 121,* 491–501.

Breznitz, Z. (1988). Reading performance of first graders: The effects of pictorial distracters. *Journal of Educational Research, 82,* 47–52.

Breznitz, Z. (1990). Vocalization and pauses in fast-paced reading. *Journal of General Psychology, 117,* 153–159.

Breznitz, Z. (1991). The beneficial effect of accelerating reading rate of dyslexic readers on their reading comprehension. In M. Snowling & M. Thomson (Eds.), *Dyslexia: Integrating theory and practice* (pp. 236–244). London: Whurr Publishers.

Breznitz, Z. (1996). *Word Fluency Test based on Lezak, 1993.* Unpublished test, University of Haifa, Israel.

Breznitz, Z. (1997a). The effect of accelerated reading rate on memory for text among dyslexic readers. *Journal of Educational Psychology, 89,* 287–299.

Breznitz, Z. (1997b). Enhancing the reading of dyslexics by reading acceleration and auditory masking. *Journal of Educational Psychology, 89*, 103–113.

Breznitz, Z. (1997c). *Parsing test*. Unpublished test, University of Haifa, Israel.

Breznitz, Z. (1997d). Reading rate acceleration: Developmental aspects. *Journal of Genetic Psychology, 158*, 427–443.

Breznitz, Z. (1998). *Lexical decision*. Unpublished test, University of Haifa, Israel.

Breznitz, Z. (2000). *Reading achievement test*. Unpublished test, University of Haifa, Israel.

Breznitz, Z. (2001a). The determinants of reading fluency: A comparison of dyslexic and average readers. In M. Wolf (Ed.), *Dyslexia, fluency and the brain* (pp. 245–276). Cambridge, MA: York Press.

Breznitz, Z. (2001b). *Orthographic choice*. Unpublished test, University of Haifa, Israel.

Breznitz, Z. (2002). Asynchrony of visual-orthographic and auditory-phonological word recognition processes: An underlying factor in dyslexia. *Reading and Writing, 15*(1–2), 15–42.

Breznitz, Z. (2003a). *Reading test*. Unpublished test, University of Haifa, Israel.

Breznitz, Z. (2003b). Speed of phonological and orthographic processing as factors in dyslexia: Electrophysiological evidence. *Genetic, Social and General Psychology Monographs, 129*(2), 183–206.

Breznitz, Z. (2005). Brain activity during performance of naming tasks: Comparison between dyslexic and normal readers. *Scientific Studies of Reading, 9*(1), 17–42.

Breznitz, Z., & Berman, L. (2003). Reading rate as a dependent variable: A review. *Educational Psychology Review, 15*(3), 247–265.

Breznitz, Z., DeMarco, T., & Hakerem, G. (1993). Topographic measures of cerebral activity during reading of text at fast-and-slow paced rates. *Brain Topography, 6*, 117–121.

Breznitz, Z., DeMarco, T., Shammi, P., & Hakerem, G. (1994). Self-paced versus fast-paced reading rates and their effect upon comprehension and event-related potentials. *Journal of Genetic Psychology, 155*, 397–407.

Breznitz, Z., & Itzhak, Y. (in press). Training dyslexic readers using the reading acceleration paradigm. M.A. *thesis in preparation*, University of Haifa, Israel.

Breznitz, Z., & Leiken, M. (2000a). Effects of accelerated reading rate on processing words' syntactic functions by normal and dyslexic readers: Event related potentials evidence. *Journal of Genetic Psychology, 162*(3), 276–296.

Breznitz, Z., & Leiken, M. (2000b). Syntactic processing of Hebrew sentences in normal and dyslexic readers: Electrophysiological evidence. *Journal of Genetic Psychology, 161*, 359–380.

Breznitz, Z., & Meyler, A. (2003). Speed of lower-level auditory and visual processing as a basic factor in dyslexia: Electrophysiological evidence. *Brain and Language, 85*(1), 166–184.

Breznitz, Z., & Misra, M. (2003). Speed of processing of the visual-orthographic and auditory-phonological systems in adult dyslexics: The contribution of "asynchrony" to word recognition deficits. *Brain and Language, 85*(3), 486–502.

Breznitz, Z., & Share, D. L. (1992). The effect of accelerated reading rate on memory for text. *Journal of Educational Psychology, 84*, 193–200.

Brickenkamp, R., & Zillmer, E. A. (1995). *Concentration Endurance Test (d2 Test of Attention)*. Odessa, FL: Psychological Assessment Resources.

British Psychological Society. (1999). *Dyslexia, literacy and psychological assessment*. Leicester, UK: British Psychological Society.

Bruck, M. (1990). Word-recognition skills of adults with childhood diagnoses of dyslexia. *Developmental Psychology, 26*, 439–454.

Bruck, M. (1998). Outcomes of adults with childhood histories of dyslexia. In C. Hulme & J. R. Malatesha (Eds.), *Reading and spelling: Development and disorders* (pp. 179–200). Hillsdale, NJ: Lawrence Erlbaum Associates.

Bruneau, N., Roux, S., Guerin, P., & Barthelemy, C. (1997). Temporal prominence of auditory evoked potentials (N1 wave) in 4–8-year-old children. *Psychophysiology, 34*(1), 32–38.

Brunswick, N., McCrory, E., Price, C. J., Frith, C. D., & Frith, U. (1999). Explicit and implicit processing of words and pseudowords by adult developmental dyslexics. *Brain, 122*(10), 1901–1917.

Brunswick, N., & Rippon, G. (1994). Auditory event-related potentials, dichotic listening performance and handedness as indices of lateralisation in dyslexic and normal readers. *International Journal of Psychophysiology, 18*(3), 265–275.

Butterworth, B. (1980). *Language production.* Academic Press: London.

Calfee, R. (1983). The mind of the dyslexic. *Annals of Dyslexia, 33,* 9–28.

Calfee, R. C., & Piontkowski, D. C. (1981). The reading diary: Acquisition of decoding. *Reading Research Quarterly, 16,* 346–373.

Calvert, G. A. (2001). Crossmodal processing in the human brain: Insights from functional neuroimaging studies. *Cerebral Cortex, 11*(12), 1110–1123.

Carroll, P. J., & Slowiaczek, M. L. (1987). Modes and modules: Multiple pathways to the language processor. In J. L. Garfield (Ed.), *Modularity in knowledge representation and natural-language understanding* (pp. 221–247). Cambridge, MA: MIT Press.

Carter, C. S., Braver, T. S., Barch, D. M., Botvinivk, M. M., Noll, D., & Cohen, J. D. (1998). Anterior cingulate cortex, error detection, and the online monitoring of performance. *Science, 280,* 747–749.

Carver, R. P. (1990). *Reading rate: A review of research and theory.* San Diego, CA: Academic Press.

Carver, R. P. (1991). Using letter-naming speed to diagnose reading disability. *RASE: Remedial and Special Education, 12*(5), 33–43.

Carver, R. P. (1997). Reading for one second, one minute, or one year from the perspective of rauding theory. *Scientific Studies of Reading, 1*(1), 3–43.

Cattell, M. (1886). The time it takes to see and name objects. *Mind, 2,* 63–85.

Catts, H. W. (1986). Speech production/phonological deficits in reading-disordered children. *Journal of Learning Disabilities, 19,* 504–508.

Catts, H. W. (1989). Speech production deficits in developmental dyslexia. *Journal of Speech and Hearing Disorders, 54*(3), 422–428.

Catts, H. W., Gillispie, M., Leonard, L. B., Kail, R. V., & Miller, C. A. (2002). The role of speed of processing, rapid naming, and phonological awareness in reading achievement. *Journal of Learning Disabilities, 35*(6), 510–525.

Cavanagh, P. (1991). The contribution of color to motion. In A. Valberg & B. B. Lee (Eds.), *From pigments to perception* (pp. 151–164). New York: Plenum.

Center for Psychometric Tests. (1994). *Comprehension test, Israeli Psychometric Scholastic Aptitude Test,* Tel Aviv.

Ceponiene, R., Cheour, M., & Näätänen, R. (1998). Interstimulus interval and auditory event-related potentials in children: Evidence for multiple generators. *Electroencephalography and Clinical Neurophysiology: Evoked-Potentials, 108*(4), 345–354.

Cerella, J. (1985). Information processing rates in the elderly. *Psychological Bulletin, 98,* 67–83.

Chabot, R. J., Petros, T. V., & McCord, G. (1983). Developmental and reading ability differences in accessing information from semantic memory. *Journal of Experimental Child Psychology, 35*(1), 128–142.

Chabot, R. J., Zehr, H. D., Prinzo, O. V., & Petros, T. V. (1984). The speed of word recognition subprocesses and reading achievement in college students. *Reading Research Quarterly, 19*(2), 147–161.

Chafe, W. (1980). The deployment of consciousness in the production of a narrative. In W. Chafe (Ed.), *The pear stories: Cognitive, cultural, and linguistic aspects of narrative production* (pp. 9–50). Norwood, NJ: Ablex.

Chall, J. S. (1983). *Stages of reading development.* New York: McGraw-Hill.

Chawla, D., Lumer, E. D., & Friston, K. J. (1999). The relationship between synchronization among neuronal populations and their mean activity levels. *Neural Computation, 11,* 1389–1411.

Chi, M. T. (1977). Age differences in the speed of processing: A critique. *Developmental Psychology, 13*(5), 543–544.

Chi, M. T. (1978). Knowledge structures and memory development. In R. S. Siegler (Ed.), *Children's thinking: What develops?* (pp. 73–96). Hillsdale, NJ: Lawrence Erlbaum Associates.

Chi, M. T., & Gallagher, J. D. (1982). Speed of processing: A developmental source of limitation. *Topics in Learning and Learning Disabilities, 2*(2), 23–32.

Chi, M. T., & Klahr, D. (1975). Span and rate of apprehension in children and adults. *Journal of Experimental Child Psychology, 19*(3), 434–439.

Childs, M. K., & Polich, J. M. (1979). Developmental differences in mental rotation. *Journal of Experimental Child Psychology, 27*(2), 339–351.

Chomsky, N. (1978). When you still can't read in third grade: After decoding, what? In S. Samuels (Ed.), *What research has to say about reading instruction* (pp. 13–30). Newark, DE: International Reading Association.

Chomsky, N., & Halle, M. (1968). *The sound pattern of English.* New York: Harper & Row.

Cirilo, R. K., & Foss, D. J. (1980). Text structure and reading time for sentences. *Journal of Verbal Learning and Verbal Behavior, 19*(1), 96–109.

Clark, H., & Clark, E. (1977). *Psychology and language.* New York: Harcourt Brace Jovanovich.

Cohen, J. D., Braver, T. S., & O'Reilly, R. C. (1996). A computational approach to prefrontal cortex, cognitive control, and schizophrenia: Recent developments and current challenges. *Philosophical Transactions of the Royal Society of London Series B (Biological Sciences), 351*(1346), 1515–1527.

Cohen, J. D., Dunbar, K., & McClelland, J. L. (1990). On the control of automatic processes: A parallel distributed processing account of the Stroop effect. *Psychological Review, 97,* 332–361.

Cohen, H., Josee, D., & Mayada, E. (2001). The role of prosody in discourse processing. *Brain and Cognition, 46*(1–2), 73–82.

Collier, R., & Hart, J. 't. (1975). The role of intonation in speech perception. In A. Cohen & S. G. Nooteboom (Eds.), *Structure and process in speech perception* (pp. 107–121). Heidelberg: Springer-Verlag.

Collins, V. L. (1989). *Reading fluency: An examination of its role in the reading process.* Unpublished master's thesis, University of Oregon, Eugene.

Coltheart, M., Curtis, B., Atkins, P., & Haller, M. (1993). Models of reading aloud: Dual-route and parallel-distributed-processing approach. *Psychological Review, 100*(4), 589–608.

Coltheart, M., & Rastle, K. (1994). Serial processing in reading aloud: Evidence for dual-route models of reading. *Journal of Experimental Psychology: Human Perception and Performance, 20*(6), 1197–1211.

Compton, D. L., & Carlisle, J. F. (1994). Speed of word recognition as a distinguishing characteristic of reading disabilities. *Educational Psychology Review, 6*, 115–140.

Compton, D. L., Chayna, J. D., DeFries, D. J., Gayan, J., & Olson, R. K. (2001). Genetic and environmental influences on reading and RAN: An overview of results from the Colorado twin study. In M. Wolf (Ed.), *Dyslexia, fluency and the brain* (pp. 277–303). Cambridge, MA: York Press.

Cornelissen, P. L., Hansen, P. C., Brady, L., & Stein, J. F. (1996). Analysis of perceptual confusions between nine sets of consonant-vowel sounds in normal and dyslexic adults. *Cognition, 59*(3), 275–306.

Cornwall, A. (1992). The relationship of phonological awareness, rapid naming, and verbal memory to severe reading and spelling disability. *Journal of Learning Disability, 25*, 532–538.

Courchesne, E. (1978). Changes in P3 waves with event repetition: Long-term effects on scalp distribution and amplitude. *Electroencephalography and Clinical Neurophysiology, 45*, 754–766.

Cromer, R. F. (1970). "Children are nice to understand": Surface structure clues for the recovery of a deep structure. *British Journal of Psychology, 61*(3), 397–408.

Csepe, V., Szucs, D., & Osman-Sagi, J. (2000). Abnormal mismatch negativity to phonetic deviations in developmental dyslexia (in Hungarian). *Hungarian Psychology Review, 55*, 475–500.

Cunningham, A. E., & Stanovich, K. E. (1990). Assessing print exposure and orthographic processing skill in children: A quick measure of reading experience. *Journal of Educational Psychology, 82*, 733–740.

Cutler, A., & Butterfield, S. (1991). Word boundary cues in clear speech: A supplementary report. *Speech Communication, 10*(4), 335–353.

Cutler, A., Dahan, D., & van Donselaar, W. (1997). Prosody in the comprehension of spoken language: A literature review. *Language and Speech, 40*(2), 141–201.

Cutting, L. E., & Denckla, M. B. (2001). The relationship of rapid serial naming and word reading in normally developing readers: An exploratory model. *Reading and Writing, 14*(7–8), 673–705.

Cycowicz, Y. M., Friedman, D., & Rothstein, M. (1996). An ERP study of repetition priming by auditory novel stimuli. *Psychophysiology, 33*, 680–690.

Daly, E. J., Martens, B. K., Hamler, K. R., Dool, E. J., & Eckert, T. L. (1999). A brief experimental analysis for identifying instructional components needed to improve oral reading fluency. *Journal of Applied Behavior Analysis, 32*, 83–94.

Davidson, R. J., Leslie, S. C., & Saron, C. (1990). Reaction time measures of interhemispheric transfer time in reading disabled and normal children. *Neuropsychologia, 28*(5), 471–485.

Davidson, R. J., & Saron, C. D. (1992). Evoked potential measures of interhemispheric transfer time in reading disabled and normal boys. *Developmental Neuropsychology, 8*(2–3), 261–277.

Davis, A. E., & Wada, J. A. (1977). Hemispheric asymmetries of visual and auditory information processing. *Neuropsychologia, 15*(6), 799–806.

Davis, H., & Anderson, M. (2001). Developmental and individual differences in fluid intelligence: Evidence against the unidimensional hypothesis. *British Journal of Developmental Psychology, 19*(2), 181–206.

Dawson, G., Finley, C., Phillips, S., & Lewy, A. (1989). A comparison of hemispheric asymmetries in speech-related brain potentials of autistic and dysphasic children. *Brain and Language, 37*(1), 26–41.

Deary, I. J. (1993). Inspection time and WAIS–R IQ subtypes: A confirmatory factor analysis study. *Intelligence, 17*(2), 223–236.

Deary, I. J., & Stough, C. (1996). Intelligence and inspection time: Achievements, prospects, and problems. *American Psychologist, 51*(6), 599–608.

Decety, J., Sjoholm, H., Ryding, E., Stenberg, G., & Ingvar, D. H. (1990). The cerebellum participates in mental activity—tomographic measurements of regional cerebral blood flow. *Brain Research, 535,* 313–317.

Dechert, H. (1980). Pauses and intonation as indicators of verbal planning in second language speech production. In H. Dechert & M. Raupach (Eds.), *Temporal variables in speech* (pp. 271–286). The Hague: Mouton.

Dechert, W., & Raupach, M. (Eds.). (1980). *Temporal variables in speech: Studies in honor of Frieda Goldman-Eisler.* The Hague: Mouton.

Decker, S. N. (1989). Cognitive processing rates among disabled and normal reading young adults: A nine year follow-up study. *Reading and Writing, 2,* 123–134.

Deeney, T., Wolf, M., & Goldberg-O'Rourke, A. (2001). "I like to take my own sweet time": Case study of a child with naming-speed deficits and reading disabilities. *Journal of Special Education, 35*(3), 145–155.

Demb, J. B., Poldrack, R. A., & Gabrieli, J.D.E. (1999). Functional neuroimaging of word processing in normal and dyslexic readers. In R. M. Klein & P. A. McMullen (Eds.), *Converging methods for understanding reading and dyslexia. Language, speech, and communication* (pp. 245–304). Cambridge, MA: MIT Press.

Demonet, J. F., Celsis, P., Nespoulous, J. L., & Viallard, G. (1992). Cerebral blood flow correlates of word monitoring in sentences: Influence of semantic incoherence: A SPECT study in normals. *Neuropsychologia, 30*(1), 1–11.

Denckla, M. B., & Rudel, R. G. (1974). Rapid automatized naming of pictured objects, colors, letters and numbers by normal children. *Cortex, 10,* 186–202.

Denckla, M. B., & Rudel, R. G. (1976a). Naming of objects by dyslexic and other learning disabled children. *Brain and Language, 3,* 1–15.

Denckla, M. B., & Rudel, R. G. (1976b). Rapid automatized naming (R.A.N): Dyslexia differentiated from other learning disabilities. *Neuropsychologia, 14,* 471–479.

Deno, S. L., Mirkin, P. K., & Chiang, B. (1982). Identifying valid measures of reading. *Exceptional Children, 49*(1), 36–45.

De Soto, J. L., & De Soto, C. B. (1983). Relationship of reading achievement to verbal processing abilities. *Journal of Educational Psychology, 75*(1), 116–127.

De Weirdt, W. (1988). Speech perception and frequency discrimination in good and poor readers. *Applied Psycholinguistics, 9,* 163–183.

Dijkstra, T., Frauenfelder, U. H., & Schreuder, R. (1993). Bidirectional grapheme phoneme activation in a bimodal detection task. *Journal of Experimental Psychology: Human Perception and Performance, 19*(5), 931–950.

Di Lollo, V., Hanson, D., & McIntyre, J. S. (1983). Initial stages of visual information processing in dyslexia. *Journal of Experimental Psychology: Human Perception and Performance*, 9(6), 923–935.

Dodgen, C. E., & Pavlidis, G. T. (1990). Sequential, timing, rhythmic and eye movement problems in dyslexics. In G. T. Pavlidis (Ed.), *Perspective on dyslexia: Vol. 1. Neurology, neuropsychology and genetics* (pp. 221–252). New York: Wiley.

Doehring, D.G.G. (1976). Acquisition of rapid reading responses. *Monographs of the Society for Research in Child Development, 41*(2), 54.

Dowhower, S. L. (1991). Speaking of prosody: Fluency's unattended bedfellow. *Theory into Practice, 30*, 165–175.

Duffy, F. H., McAnulty, G. B., Wolff, P. H., & Waber, D. P. (1999). *Diminished cortical connectivity during internally paced rhythmic finger tapping in children referred for diagnosis of learning problems.* Unpublished manuscript.

Dugas, J. L., & Kellas, G. (1974). Encoding and retrieval processes in normal children and retarded adolescents. *Journal of Experimental Child Psychology, 17*(1), 177–185.

Duncan, C. C., Rumsey, J. M., Wilkniss, S. M., Denckla, M. B., Hamburger, S. D., & Odou-Potkin, M. (1994). Developmental dyslexia and attention dysfunction in adults: Brain potential indices of information processing. *Psychophysiology, 31*, 386–401.

Dunn, B. R., Dunn, D. A., Languis, M., & Andrews, D. (1998). The relation of ERP components to complex memory processing. *Brain and Cognition, 36*, 355–376.

Dustman, R. E., & Beck, E. C. (1965). Phase of alpha brain waves, reaction time and visually evoked potentials. *Electroencephalography and Clinical Neurophysiology, 18*(5), 433–440.

Eden, G. F., Stein, J. F., & Wood, F. B. (1993). Visuospatial ability and language processing in reading disabled and normal children. In S. F. Wright & R. Groner (Eds.), *Facets of dyslexia and its remediation* (pp. 321–336). North-Holland: Elsevier Science.

Eden, G., Stein, J., Wood, M., & Wood, F. (1995). Verbal and visual problems in reading disability. *Journal of Learning Disabilities, 28*, 272–290.

Eden, G. F., & Zeffiro, T. A. (1998). Neural systems affected in developmental dyslexia revealed by functional neuroimaging. *Neuron, 21*(2), 279–282.

Egan, D. E., & Schwartz, B. J. (1979). Chunking in recall of symbolic drawings. *Memory and Cognition, 7*(2), 149–158.

Ehri, L. C. (1991). Development of the ability to read words. In R. Barr, M. L. Kamil, P. Mosenthal, & P. D. Pearson (Eds.), *Handbook of reading research* (Vol. 2, pp. 385–419). New York: Longman.

Ehri, L. C., & Wilce, L. S. (1983). Development of word identification speed in skilled and less skilled beginning readers. *Journal of Educational Psychology, 75*, 3–18.

Elbro, C. (1996). Early linguistic abilities and reading development: A review and a hypothesis. *Reading and Writing, 8*, 1–33.

Elliot, L. L., Hammer, M. A., Scholl, M. E., & Carrell, T. D. (1989). Discrimination of rising and falling simulated single-formant frequency transitions: Practice and transition duration effects. *Journal of the Acoustical Society of America, 86*(3), 945–953.

Elliott, R. (1970). Simple reaction time: Effects associated with age, preparatory interval, incentive-shift, and mode of presentation. *Journal of Experimental Child Psychology, 9*(1), 86–107.

Elliott, R. (1972). Simple reaction time in children: Effects of incentive, incentive-shift and other training variables. *Journal of Experimental Child Psychology, 13*(3), 540–557.

Ellis, N. C., & Miles, T. R. (1981). A lexical encoding deficiency I: Experimental evidence. In G.T.H. Pavlidis & T. R. Miles (Eds.), *Dyslexia research and its applications to education* (pp. 177–215). Chichester, England: Wiley.

Enns, J. T., Bryson, S., & Roes, C. (1995). Search for letter identity and location by disabled readers. *Canadian Journal of Experimental Psychology, 49*, 357–367.

Epstein, W. (1961). The influence of syntactical structure on learning. *American Journal of Psychology, 74*, 80–85.

Erez, A., & Pratt, H. (1992). Auditory event-related potentials among dyslexic and normal-reading children: 3CLT and midline comparisons. *International Journal of Neuroscience, 63*, 247–264.

Evans, B.J.W., Drasdo, N., & Richards, I. L. (1993). Linking the sensory and motor visual correlates of dyslexia. In S. F. Wright & R. Groner (Eds.), *Facets of dyslexia and its remediation. Studies in visual information processing* (Vol. 3, pp. 179–191). Amsterdam, Netherlands: North-Holland/Elsevier Science.

Eysenck, H. J. (1986). The theory of intelligence and the psychophysiology of cognition. In R. J. Sternberg (Ed.), *Advances in the psychology of human intelligence* (Vol. 3, pp. 1–34). Hillsdale, NJ: Lawrence Erlbaum Associates.

Facoetti, A., Paganoni, A., Turatto, M., Marzola, V., & Macetti, G. G. (2000). Visual-spatial attention in developmental dyslexia. *Cortex, 36*, 109–123.

Farmer, M. E., & Klein, R. K. (1993). Auditory and visual temporal processing in dyslexic and normal readers. In P. Tallal, A. M. Galaburda, R. R. Llinas, & C. von Eurler (Eds.), *Temporal information processing in the nervous system. Annals of the New York Academy of Sciences, 682*, 339–341.

Farmer, M. E., & Klein, R. (1995). The evidence for a temporal processing deficit linked to dyslexia: A review. *Psychonomic Bulletin and Review, 2*(4), 460–493.

Farmer, M. E., Klein, R., & Bryson, S. E. (1992). Computer assisted reading: Effects of whole-word feedback on severe dyslexics. *Journal of Remedial and Special Education, 13*, 50–60.

Fawcett, A. J., Chattopadhyay, A. K., Kandler, R. H., Jarrat, J. A., Nicolson, R. I., & Proctor, M. (1993). Event-related potentials and dyslexia. In P. Tallal, A. M. Galaburda, R. R. Llinas, & C. von Eurler (Eds.), *Temporal information processing in the nervous system. Annals of the New York Academy of Sciences, 682*, 342–345.

Fawcett, A. J., & Nicolson, R. I. (1994). Naming speed in children with dyslexia. *Journal of Learning Disabilities, 27*, 641–646.

Fawcett, A. J., Nicolson, R. I., & Dean, P. (1996). Impaired performance of children with dyslexia on a range of cerebellar tasks. *Annals of Dyslexia, 46*, 259–283.

Felleman, D. J., & Van Essen, D. C. (1991). Distributed hierarchical processing in the primate cerebral cortex. *Cerebral Cortex, 1*(1), 1–47.

Felton, R. H., & Brown, I. S. (1990). Phonological processes as predictors of specific reading skills in children at risk for reading failure. *Reading and Writing: An Interdisciplinary Journal, 2*, 39–59.

Felton, R. H., Naylor, C. E., & Wood, R. B. (1990). Neuropsychological profile of adult dyslexics. *Brain and Language, 39*, 48–497.

Felton, R. H., Wood, F. B., Brown, I. S., Campbell, S. K., & Harter, M. R. (1987). Separate verbal memory and naming deficits in attention deficit disorder and reading disability. *Brain and Language, 31*, 171–184.

Ferreira, F. (1993). Creation of prosody during sentence production. *Psychological Review, 100,* 233–253.

Fiez, J. A., Petersen, S. E. Cheney, M. K., & Raichle, M. E. (1992). Impaired non-motor learning and error detection associated with cerebellar damage. A single case study. *Brain, 115*(Pt. 1), 155–178.

Finkel, D., & Pedersen, N. L. (2000). Contribution of age, genes, and environment to the re-lationship between perceptual speed and cognitive ability. *Psychology and Aging, 15*(1), 56–64.

Fischer, B., Biscaldi, M., & Otto, P. (1993). Saccadic eye movements of adult dyslexic sub-jects. *Neuropsychologia, 31,* 887–906.

Fisher, D. F., & Frankfurter, A. (1977). Normal and disabled readers can locate and identify letters: Where's the perceptual deficit? *Journal of Reading Behavior, 9*(1), 31–43.

Fitzgerald, P. G., & Picton, T. W. (1983). Event-related potentials recorded during the dis-crimination of improbable stimuli. *Biological Psychology, 17,* 241–276.

Fleischer, L. S., Jenkins, J., & Pany, D. (1979). Effects on poor readers' comprehension of training in rapid decoding. *Reading Research Quarterly, 14,* 30–48.

Flowers, D. L. (1995). Neuropsychological profiles of persistent reading disability and read-ing improvement. In C. K. Leong & R. M. Joshi (Eds.), *Developmental and acquired dyslexia* (pp. 61–77). Dordrecht: Kluwer Academic.

Fodor, J. A. (1983). *The modularity of mind.* Cambridge, MA: MIT Press.

Fodor, J. A., & Garrett, M. (1967). Some syntactic determinants of sentential complexity. *Perception and Psychophysics, 2*(7), 289–296.

Foorman, B. (1999). Why direct spelling instruction is important. In *Consortium on Reading Excellence (CORE). (1999). Reading research: Anthology: The why? of reading instruction* (pp. 116–119). Novato, CA: Arena Press.

Ford, M. E., & Keating, D. P. (1981). Developmental and individual differences in long-term memory retrieval: Process and organization. *Child Development, 52*(1), 234–241.

Forster, K. I., & Ryder, L. A. (1971). Perceiving the structure and meaning of sentences. *Journal of Verbal Learning and Verbal Behavior, 10*(3), 285–296.

Fox Tree, J. E., & Meijer, P.J.A. (2000). Untrained speakers' use of prosody in syntactic disambiguation and listeners' interpretations. *Psychological Research, 63,* 1–13.

Frederiksen, J. R., Warren, B. M., & Rosebery, A. S. (1985). A componential approach to training reading skills: II. Decoding and use of context. *Cognition and Instruction, 2*(3–4), 271–338.

Freedman, S. E., & Forster, K. I. (1985). The psychological status of overgenerated sen-tences. *Cognition, 19*(2), 101–131.

Frost, R., & Katz, L. (1989). Orthographic depth and the interaction of visual and auditory processing in word recognition. *Memory and Cognition, 17*(3), 302–310.

Fuchs, L. S., Fuchs, D., Hosp, M. K., & Jenkins, J. R. (2001). Oral reading fluency as an indi-cator of reading competence: A theoretical, empirical, and historical analysis. *Scientific Studies of Reading, 5*(3), 239–256.

Fuchs, L. S., Fuchs, D., & Maxwell, L. (1988). The validity of informal reading comprehen-sion measures. *RASE: Remedial and Special Education, 9*(2), 20–28.

Fulbright, R. K., Jenner, A. R., Mencl, W. E., Pugh, K. R., Shaywitz, B. A., Shaywitz, S. E., Frost, S. J., Skudlarski, P., Constable, R. T., Lacadie, C. M., Marchione, K. E., & Gore, J. C. (1999). The cerebellum's role in reading: A functional MR imaging study. *American Journal of Neuroradiology, 20*(10), 1925–1930.

Galaburda, A., & Livingstone, M. (1993). Evidence for a magnocellular defect in developmental dyslexia. In P. Tallal, A. M. Galaburda, R. R. Llinas, & C. von Eurler (Eds.), *Temporal information processing in the nervous system. Annals of the New York Academy of Sciences, 682,* 70–82.

Galaburda, A. M., Menard, M. T., & Rosen, G. D. (1994). Evidence for aberrant auditory anatomy in developmental dyslexia. *Procedures of the National Academy of Sciences USA, 91,* 8010–8013.

Gallagher, A. M., Laxon, V., Armstrong, E., & Frith, U. (1996). Phonological difficulties in high-functioning dyslexics. *Reading and Writing: An Interdisciplinary Journal, 8,* 499–509.

Garavan, H., Ross, T. J., & Stein, E. A. (1999). Right hemispheric dominance of inhibitory control: An event related functional MRI study. *Proceedings of the National Academy of Sciences USA, 96,* 8301–8306.

Garrett, M. F. (1988). Processes in language production. In F. J. Newmeyer (Ed.), *Language: Psychological and biological aspects. Linguistics: The Cambridge survey* (Vol. 3, pp. 69–96). New York: Cambridge University Press.

Gathercole, S. E., & Baddeley, A. D. (1989). Evaluation of the role of phonological STM in the development of vocabulary in children: A longitudinal study. *Journal of Memory and Language, 28*(2), 200–213.

Gathercole, S. E., & Baddeley, A. D. (1990). The role of phonological memory in vocabulary acquisition: A study of young children learning new names. *British Journal of Psychology, 81*(4), 439–454.

Geary, D. C., Brown, S. C., & Samaranayake, V. A. (1991). Cognitive addition: A short longitudinal study of strategy choice and speed-of-processing differences in normal and mathematically disabled children. *Developmental Psychology, 27*(5), 787–797.

Gee, J., & Grosjean, F. (1983). Performance structure: A psycholinguistic and linguistic appraisal. *Cognitive Psychology, 14,* 411–458.

Geiger, G., & Lettvin, J. Y. (1987). Peripheral vision in persons with dyslexia. *New England Journal of Medicine, 316,* 1238–1243.

Geiger, G., Lettvin, J. Y., & Fahle, M. (1994). Dyslexic children learn a new visual strategy for reading: A controlled experiment. *Vision Research, 34*(9), 1223–1233.

Geiger, G., Lettvin, J., & Zegarra-Moran, O. (1992). Task-determined strategies of visual process. *Cognitive Brain Research, 1,* 39–52.

Geluykens, R., & Swerts, M. (1994). Prosodic cues to discourse boundaries in experimental dialogues. *Speech Communication, 15*(1–2), 69–77.

Gersons-Wolfensberger, D. C., & Ruijssenaars, W. A. (1997). Definition and treatment of dyslexia: A report by the committee on dyslexia of the health council of the Netherlands. *Journal of Learning Disabilities, 30,* 209–213.

Geschwind, N. (1972). Language and the brain. *Scientific American, 226*(4), 76–83.

Giard, M. H., & Peronnet, F. (1999). Auditory-visual integration during multimodal object recognition in humans: A behavioral and electrophysiological study. *Journal of Cognitive Neuroscience, 11*(5), 473–490.

Gladstone, M., & Best, C. T. (1985). Developmental dyslexia: The potential role of interhemispheric collaboration in reading acquisition. In C. T. Best (Ed.), *Hemispheric function and collaboration in the child* (pp. 87–118). New York: Academic Press.

Godfrey, J. J., Syrdal-Lasky, A. K., Millay, K. K., & Knox, C. M. (1981). Performance of dyslexic children on a speech perception test. *Journal of Experimental Child Psychology, 32,* 401–424.

Goffman, L. (1999). Prosodic influences on speech production in children with specific language impairment and speech deficits: Kinematic, acoustic, and transcription evidence. *Journal of Speech, Language, and Hearing Research, 42*, 1499–1517.

Goldberg, E., & Costa, L. D. (1981). Hemisphere differences in the acquisition and use of descriptive systems. *Brain and Language, 14*(1), 144–173.

Goldman-Eisler, F. (1968). *Psycholinguistics: Experiments in spontaneous speech.* New York: Academic Press.

Goldman-Eisler, F. (1972). Pauses, clauses, sentences. *Language and Speech, 15*(2), 103–113.

Goldman-Eisler, F., Skarbek, A., & Henderson, A. (1966). Breath rate and the selective action of chlorpromazine on speech behaviour. *Psychopharmacologia, 8*(6), 415–427.

Goolkasian, P., & King, J. (1990). Letter identification and lateral masking in dyslexic and average readers. *American Journal of Psychology, 103*(4), 519–538.

Goswami, U. (2002). In the beginning was the rhyme? A reflection on Hulme, Hatcher, Nation, Brown, Adams, and Stuart (2002). *Journal of Experimental Child Psychology, 82*(1), 47–57.

Gough, P. B., & Hillinger, M. L. (1980). Learning to read: An unnatural act. *Bulletin of the Orton Society, 30*, 179–196.

Gough, P., & Tunmer, W. (1986). Decoding, reading and reading disability. *RASE: Remedial and Special Education, 7*(1), 6–10.

Greene, B. A., Kincade, K. M., & Hays, T. A. (1994). A research-based modification of a computer program for reading instruction. *Journal of Educational Computing Research, 10*(4), 341–348.

Greene, B. A., & Royer, J. M. (1994). A developmental review of response time data that support a cognitive components model of reading. *Educational Psychology Review, 6*(2), 141–172.

Griffiths, P. (1991). Word-finding ability and design fluency in developmental dyslexia. *British Journal of Clinical Psychology, 30*, 47–60.

Grosjean, F. (1980). Spoken word recognition processes and the gating paradigm. *Perception and Psychophysics, 28*(4), 267–283.

Grosjean, F., & Collins, M. (1979). Breathing, pausing and reading. *Phonetica, 36*(2), 98–114.

Grosjean, F. H., Grosjean, L., & Lane, H. (1979). The patterns of silence: Performance structures in sentence production. *Cognitive Psychology, 11*(1), 58–81.

Hackley, S. A., Woldorff, M., & Hillyard, S. A. (1990). Cross-modal selective attention effects on retinal, myogenic, brainstem, and cerebral evoked potentials. *Psychophysiology, 27*, 195–208.

Hagoort, P., & Kutas, M. (1995). Electrophysiological insights into language deficits. In F. Boller & J. Grafman (Eds.), *Handbook of neuropsychology* (Vol. 10, pp. 105–134). North Holland: Elsevier Science.

Hale, S. (1990). A global developmental trend in cognitive processing speed. *Child Development, 61*(3), 653–663.

Hale, S., Fry, A. F., & Jessie, K. A. (1993). Effects of practice on speed of information processing in children and adults: Age sensitivity and age invariance. *Developmental Psychology, 29*(5), 880–892.

Hale, S., & Jansen, J. (1994). Global processing-time coefficients characterize individual and group differences in cognitive speed. *Psychological Science, 5*(6), 384–389.

Hale, S., Myerson, J., & Wagstaff, D. (1987). General slowing of nonverbal information processing: Evidence for a power law. *Journal of Gerontology, 42*(2), 131–136.

Halgren, E. (1990). Insights from evoked potentials into the neuropsychological mechanisms of reading. In A. B. Scheibel & A. F. Wechsler (Eds.), *Neurobiology of higher cognitive function* (pp. 103–150). New York: Guilford.

Hammond, G. R. (1982). Hemispheric differences in temporal resolution. *Brain and Cognition, 1*(1), 95–118.

Hari, R., & Kiesila, P. (1996). Deficit of temporal auditory processing in dyslexic adults. *Neuroscience Letters, 205*, 138–140.

Harpaz, R., & Breznitz, Z. (1997). *Speed of processing as a factor of quality in the reading of impulsive hyperactive children as compared to dyslexic children.* Unpublished master's thesis, University of Haifa, Israel.

Harris, G. J., & Fleer, R. E. (1974). High speed memory scanning in mental retardates: Evidence for a central processing deficit. *Journal of Experimental Child Psychology, 17*(3), 452–459.

Harris, T., & Hodges, R. (1995). *The literacy dictionary.* Newark, DE: International Reading Association.

Harter, M. R., Anllo-Vento, L., & Wood, F. B. (1989). Event-related potentials, spatial orienting, and reading disabilities. *Psychophysiology, 26*(4), 404–421.

Harter, M. R., Anllo-Vento, L., Wood, F. B., & Schroeder, M. M. (1988). Separate brain potential characteristics in children with reading disability and attention deficit disorder: Color and letter-relevance effects. *Brain and Cognition, 7*, 115–140.

Harter, M. R., Deiring, S., & Wood, F. B. (1988). Separate brain potential characteristics in children with reading disability and attention deficit disorder: Relevance-independent effects. *Brain and Cognition, 7*, 54–86.

Hayduk, S., Bruck, M., & Cavanagh, P. (1993). Do adult dyslexics show low-level visual processing deficits? In P. Tallal, A. M. Galaburda, R. R. Llinas, & C. von Eurler (Eds.), *Temporal information processing in the nervous system. Annals of the New York Academy of Sciences, 682*, 351–353.

Hayduk, S., Bruck, M., & Cavanagh, P. (1996). Low-level visual processing skills of adults and children with dyslexia. *Cognitive Neuropsychology, 13*(7), 975–1015.

Hayes, E. A., Warrier, C. M., Nicol, T. G., Zecker, S. G., & Kraus, N. (2003). Neural plasticity following auditory training in children with learning problems. *Clinical Neurophysiology, 114*(4), 673–684.

Health Council of the Netherlands. (1995). *Dyslexia. Definition and treatment.* The Hague: Health Council of the Netherlands (Publication No. 1995/15). www.gr.nl

Heath, S. M., Hogben, J. H., & Clark, C. D. (1999). Auditory temporal processing in disabled readers with and without oral language delay. *Journal of Child Psychology and Psychiatry and Allied Disciplines, 40*(4), 637–647.

Heilman, K. M., Voeller, K., & Alexander, A. W. (1996). Developmental dyslexia: A motor-articulatory feedback hypothesis. *Annals of Neurology, 39*(3), 407–412.

Heim, S., Eulitz, C., Kaufmann, J., Fuchter, I., Pantev, C., Lamprecht-Dinnesen, A., Matulat, P., Scheer, P., Borstel, M., & Elbert, T. (2000). Atypical organisation of the auditory cortex in dyslexia as revealed by MEG. *Neuropsychologia, 38*(13), 1749–1759.

Helenius, P., Uutela, K., & Hari, R. (1999). Auditory stream segregation in dyslexic adults. *Brain, 122*(5), 907–913.

Hennighausen, K., Remschmidt, H., & Warnke, A. (1994). Visually evoked potentials in boys with developmental dyslexia. *European Child and Adolescent Psychiatry, 3*(2), 72–81.

Hess, A. M. (1982). An analysis of the cognitive processes underlying problems in reading comprehension. *Journal of Reading Behavior, 14*(3), 313–333.

Hill, R., & Lovegrove, W. (1993). One word at a time: A solution to the visual deficit in the specific reading disabled? In S. F. Wright & R. Groner (Eds.), *Facets of dyslexia and its remediation* (pp. 65–76). North-Holland: Elsevier Science.

Hoffman, J. V., & Isaacs, M. E. (1991). Developing fluency through restructuring the task of guided oral reading. *Theory into Practice, 30,* 185–194.

Hoffman, L. D., & Polich, J. (1999). P300, handedness, and corpus callosal size: Gender, modality, and task. *International Journal of Psychophysiology, 31*(2), 163–174.

Hogaboam, T. W., & Perfetti, C. A. (1978). Reading skill and the role of verbal experience in decoding. *Journal of Educational Psychology, 70*(5), 717–729.

Holcomb, P. J., Ackerman, P. T., & Dykman, R. A. (1985). Cognitive event-related brain potentials in children with attention and reading deficits. *Psychophysiology, 22,* 656–667.

Holcomb, P. J., Ackerman, P. T., & Dykman, R. A. (1986). Auditory event-related potentials in attention and reading disabled boys. *International Journal of Psychophysiology, 3,* 263–273.

Holcomb, P. J., Coffey, S. A., & Neville, H. J. (1992). Visual and auditory sentence processing: A developmental analysis using event-related brain potentials. *Developmental Neuropsychology, 8,* 203–241.

Holtz, K. L. (1993). Information integration and reading disabilities. In S. F. Wright & R. Groner (Eds.), *Facets of dyslexia and its remediation* (pp. 305–320). Amsterdam: Elsevier.

Hudson, R., Mercer, C. D., & Lane, H. (2000). *Exploring reading fluency: A paradigmatic overview.* Unpublished manuscript, University of Florida, Gainesville.

Huey, S. E. (1905). *The psychology and pedagogy of reading.* Cambridge, MA: MIT Press.

Humphrey, D. G., & Kramer, A, F. (1994). Toward a physiological assessment of dynamic changes in mental workload. *Human Factors, 36*(1), 3–26.

Hunt, E. (1980). Intelligence as an information processing concept. *British Journal of Psychology, 71,* 449–474.

Hutner, N., & Liederman, J. (1991). Right hemisphere participation in reading. *Brain and Language, 41*(4), 475–495.

Hynd, G. W., Hall, J., Novey, E. S., Eliopulos, D., Black, K., Gonzalez, J. J., Edmonds, J. E., Riccio, C., & Cohen, M. (1995). Dyslexia and corpus callosum morphology. *Archives of Neurology, 52*(1), 32–38.

Isreal, J. B., Chesney, G. L., Wickens, C. D., & Donchin, E. (1980). P300 and tracking difficulty: Evidence for multiple resources in dual-task performance. *Psychophysiology, 17*(3), 259–273.

Ito, M. (1984). *The cerebellum and neural control.* New York: Raven.

Ito, M. (1990). A new physiological concept on cerebellum. *Revue Neurologique (Paris), 146,* 564–569.

Jackson, M. D., & McClelland, J. L. (1979). Processing determinants of reading speed. *Journal of Experimental Psychology: General, 108*(2), 151–181.

Jaffe, J., & Feldstein, S. (1970). *Rhythms of dialogue.* New York: Academic Press.

Jasper, H. H. (1958). The ten–twenty electrode system of the International Federation. *Electroencephalography and Clinical Neurophysiology, 10,* 371–375.

Jenkins, I. H., Brooks, D. J., Nixon, P. D., Frackowiak, R.S.J., & Passingham, R. E. (1994). Motor sequence learning: A study with positron emission tomography. *Journal of Neuroscience, 14,* 3775–3790.

Jenner, A. R., Rosen, G. D., & Galaburda, A. M. (1999). Neuronal asymmetries in primary visual cortex of dyslexic and nondyslexic brains. *Annals of Neurology, 46*(2), 189–196.

Jensen, A. R. (1982). Level I/level II: Factors or categories? *Journal of Educational Psychology, 74*(6), 868–873.

Jirsa, R. E., & Clontz, K. (1990). Long latency auditory event related potentials in children with auditory processing disorders. *Ear and Hearing, 11*(3), 222–232.

Johannes, S., Mangun, G. R., & Muente, T. F (1994). Developmental dyslexia and cerebral lateralization: Electrophysiological findings. *Nervenarzt, 65*(12), 859–864.

Johnson, R. (1995). Effects of color on children's naming of pictures. *Perceptual and Motor Skills, 80,* 1091–1101.

Johnstone, S. J., Barry, R. J., Anderson, J. W., & Coyle, S. F. (1996). Age-related changes in child and adolescent event-related potential component morphology, amplitude and latency to standard and target stimuli in an auditory oddball task. *International Journal of Psychophysiology, 24,* 223–238.

Joseph, J., Noble, K., & Eden, G. (2001). The neurobiological basis of reading. *Journal of Learning Disabilities, 34*(6), 566–579.

Kaas, J. H., & Morel, A. (1993). Connections of visual areas of the upper temporal lobe of owl monkeys: The MT crescent and dorsal and ventral subdivisions of FST. *Journal of Neuroscience, 13*(2), 534–546.

Kahn, D., & Birch, H. G. (1968). Development of auditory-visual integration and reading achievement. *Perceptual and Motor Skills, 27*(2), 459–468.

Kail, R. (1979). Use of strategies and individual differences in children's memory. *Developmental Psychology, 15*(3), 251–255.

Kail, R. (1985). Development of mental rotation: A speed-accuracy study. *Journal of Experimental Child Psychology, 40*(1), 181–192.

Kail, R. (1986a). The impact of extended practice on rate of mental rotation. *Journal of Experimental Child Psychology, 42*(3), 378–391.

Kail, R. (1986b). Sources of age differences in speed of processing. *Child Development, 57*(4), 969–987.

Kail, R. (1988a). Developmental functions for speeds of cognitive processes. *Journal of Experimental Child Psychology, 45*(3), 339–364.

Kail, R. (1988b). "Developmental changes in speed of processing: Central limiting mechanism or skill transfer?": Reply to Stigler, Nusbaum, and Chalip. *Child Development, 59*(4), 1154–1157.

Kail, R. (1990). More evidence for a common, central constraint on speed of processing. In J. T. Enns (Ed.), *The development of attention: Research and theory. Advances in psychology* (Vol. 69, pp. 159–173). Oxford, England: North-Holland.

Kail, R. (1991a). Developmental changes in speed of processing during childhood and adolescence. *Psychological Bulletin, 109,* 490–501.

Kail, R. (1991b). Processing time declines exponentially during childhood and adolescence. *Developmental Psychology, 27*(2), 259–266.

Kail, R. (1994). A method for studying the generalized slowing hypothesis in children with specific language impairment. *Journal of Speech and Hearing Research, 37*(2), 418–421.

Kail, R. (2000). Speed of information processing: Developmental change and links to intelligence. *Journal of School Psychology, 38*(1), 51–61.

Kail, R., & Hall, L. K. (1994). Processing speed, naming speed and reading. *Developmental Psychology, 30*(6), 949–954.

Kail, R., & Park, Y. (1990). Impact of practice on speed of mental rotation. *Journal of Experimental Child Psychology, 49*(2), 227–244.

Kail, R., & Salthouse, T. A. (1994). Processing speed as a mental capacity. *Acta Psychologica, 86,* 199–225.

Kalat, J. W. (1992). *Biological psychology* (4th ed.). Pacific Grove, CA: Brooks/Cole.

Kame'enui, E. J., Simmons, D. C., Good, R. H., & Harn, B. A. (2001). The use of fluency-based measures in early identification and evaluation of intervention efficacy in schools. In M. Wolf (Ed.), *Dyslexia, fluency and the brain* (pp. 307–331). Cambridge, MA: York Press.

Kamhi, A. G., & Catts, H. W. (1986).Toward an understanding of developmental language and reading disorders. *Journal of Speech and Hearing Disorders, 51*(4), 337–347.

Kamhi, A. G., Catts, H. W., & Mauer, D. (1990). Explaining speech deficits in poor readers. *Journal of Learning Disabilities, 23,* 632–636.

Kamhi, A. G., Catts, H. W., Mauer, D., Apel, K., & Gentry, B. F. (1988). Phonological and spatial processing abilities in language- and reading-impaired children. *Journal of Speech and Hearing Disorders, 53*(3), 316–327.

Kaplan, E., Goodglass, H., & Weintraub, S. (1983). *The Boston Naming Test.* Philadelphia: Lea & Febiger.

Karni, A. (1996). The acquisition of perceptual and motor skills: A memory system in the adult human cortex. *Cognitive Brain Research, 5,* 39–48.

Karni, A., Meyer, G., Rey-Hipolito, C., Jezzard, P., Adams, M. M., Turner, R., & Ungerleider, L. G. (1998). The acquisition of skilled motor performance: Fast and slow experience driven changes in primary motor cortex. *Proceedings of the National Academy of Science USA, 95*(3), 381–868.

Karni, A., Morocz, I. A., Bitan, T., Shaul, S., Kusnir, T., & Breznitz, Z. (in press). An fMRI study of the differential effects of word presentation rates ("reading acceleration") on dyslexic readers' brain activity patterns. *Journal of Neurolinguistics.*

Katz, P. A., & Deutsch, M. (1964). Modality of stimulus presentation in serial learning for retarded and normal readers. *Perceptual and Motor Skills, 19*(2), 627–633.

Katz, L., & Wicklund, D. A. (1971). Word scanning rate for good and poor readers. *Journal of Educational Psychology, 62*(2), 138–140.

Keating, D. P., & Bobbitt, B. (1978). Individual and developmental differences in cognitive-processing components of mental ability. *Child Development, 49,* 155–167.

Kehoe, M. M. (2000). Truncation without shape constraints: The latter stages of prosodic acquisition. *Language Acquisition, 8*(1), 23–67.

Kelly, M. H. (1992). Using sound to solve syntactic problems: The role of phonology in grammatical category assignments. *Psychological Review, 99*(2), 349–364.

Kerr, B., Davidson, J., Nelson, J., & Haley, S. (1982). Stimulus and response contributions to the children's reaction-time repetition effect. *Journal of Experimental Child Psychology, 34*(3), 526–541.

Kershner, J. G., & Graham, N. A. (1995). Attentional control over language lateralization in dyslexic children: Deficit or delay? *Neuropsychologia, 33*(1), 39–51.

Kimball, J. (1973). Seven principles of surface structure parsing in natural language. *Cognition, 2*(1), 15–47.

Kimelman, M.D.Z. (1999). Prosody, linguistic demands, and auditory comprehension in aphasia. *Brain and Language, 69,* 212–221.

Kinsborne, M., Rufo, D. T., Gamzu, E., & Palmer, R. L. (1991). Neuropsychological deficits in adults with dyslexia. *Developmental Medicine and Child Neurology, 33*(9), 763–775.

Kintsch, W., & Monk, D. (1972). Storage of complex information in memory: Some implications of the speed with which inferences can be made. *Journal of Experimental Psychology, 94*(1), 25–32.

Klein, D., Milner, B., Zatorre, R. J., Meyer, E., & Evans, A. C. (1995). The neural substrates underlying word generation: A bilingual functional-imaging study. *Proceedings of the National Academy of Sciences of the United States of America, 92*(7), 2899–2903.

Klein, R., Berry, G., Briand, K., D'Entremont, B., & Farmer, M. (1990). Letter identification declines with increasing retinal eccentricity at the same rate for normal and dyslexic readers. *Perception and Psychophysics, 47*(6), 601–606.

Klein, W. (1980). Verbal planning in route direction. In H. Dechert & M. Raupach (Eds.), *Temporale variables in speech* (pp. 159–169). New York: Mouton.

Knierim, J. J., & Van Essen, D. C. (1992). Neuronal responses to static texture patterns in area V1 of the alert macaque monkey. *Journal of Neurophysiology, 67*(4), 961–980.

Koenig, O., Kosslyn, S. M., & Wolff, P. (1991). Mental imagery and dyslexia: A deficit in processing multipart visual objects? *Brain and Language, 41,* 381–394.

Korhonen, T. (1995). The persistence of rapid naming problems in children with reading disabilities: A nine-year follow-up. *Journal of Learning Disabilities, 28,* 232–239.

Koriat, A., Sreenberg, S. V., & Kreiner, H. (2002). The extraction of structure during reading: Evidence from reading prosody. *Memory and Cognition, 30*(2), 270–280.

Kramer, A. F., Strayer, D. L., & Buckley, J. (1991). Task versus component consistency in the development of automatic processing: A psychophysiological assessment. *Psychophysiology, 28*(4), 425–437.

Kranzler, J. H., & Jensen, A. R. (1989). Inspection time and intelligence: A meta-analysis. *Intelligence, 13*(4), 329–347.

Kuhlman, E. S., & Wolking, W. D. (1972). Development of within- and cross-modal matching ability in the auditory and visual sense modalities. *Developmental Psychology, 7*(3), 365.

Kuhn, M. R., & Stahl, S. A. (2003). Fluency: A review of developmental and remedial practices. *Journal of Educational Psychology, 95,* 3–21.

Kujala, T., Belitz, S., Tervaniemi, M., & Näätänen, R. (2003). Auditory sensory memory disorder in dyslexic adults as indexed by the mismatch negativity. *European Journal of Neuroscience, 17,* 1323–1327.

Kujala, T., Karma, K., Ceponiene, R., Belitz, S., Turkkila, P., Tervaniemi, M., & Näätänen, R. (2001). Plastic neural changes and reading improvement caused by audio-visual training in reading-impaired children. *Proceedings of the National Academy of Sciences, 98,* 10509–10514.

Kujala, T., & Näätänen, R. (2001).The mismatch negativity in evaluating central auditory dysfunction in dyslexia. *Neuroscience and Biobehavioral Reviews, 25*(6), 535–543.

Laasonen, M., Halme, T. J., Nuuttila, L. P., Service, E., & Virsu, V. (2000). Rate of information segregation in developmentally dyslexic children. *Brain and Language, 75*(1), 66–81.

LaBerge, D., & Samuels, S. J. (1974). Toward a theory of automatic information processing in reading. *Cognitive Psychology, 6,* 293–323.

LaBerge, D., & Samuels, S. J. (1977). *Basic processes in reading: Perception and comprehension.* Oxford, England: Lawrence Erlbaum Associates.

Lambe, E. K. (1999). Dyslexia, gender, and brain imaging. *Neuropsychologia, 37*(5), 521–536.

Landerl, K., & Wimmer, H. (1994). Phonological awareness as predictor for reading and spelling abilities after two, three, and four years of reading instruction. *Zeitschrift fuer Paedagogische Psychologie, 8*(3–4), 153–164.

Lashley, K. S. (1951). The problem of serial order in behavior. In L. A. Jeffress (Ed.), *Cerebral mechanisms in behavior; the Hixon Symposium* (pp. 112–146). Oxford, England: Wiley.

Lefly, D. L., & Pennington, B. F. (1991). Spelling errors and reading fluency in compensated adult dyslexics. *Annals of Dyslexia, 41,* 143–162.

Legein, Ch. P., & Bouma, H. (1981). Visual recognition experiments in dyslexia. In G. T. Pavladis & T. R. Miles (Eds.), *Dyslexia: Research and its applications to education* (pp. 165–175). Chichester, England: Wiley.

Leggio, M. G., Silveri, M. C., Petrosini, L., & Molinari, M. (2000). Phonological grouping is specifically affected in cerebellar patients: A verbal fluency study. *Journal of Neurology, Neurosurgery, and Psychiatry, 69*(1), 102–106.

Lehmkuhle, S., Garzia, R. P., Turner, L., & Hash, T. (1993). A defective visual pathway in children with reading disability. *New England Journal of Medicine, 328*(14), 989–996.

Leiken, M. (2002). Processing syntactic functions of words in normal and dyslexic readers. *Journal of Psycholinguistic Research, 31*(2), 145–163.

Leiken, M., & Breznitz, Z. (1999). Syntactic processing in Hebrew sentences: Electrophysiological aspects. *Genetic, Social and General Psychology Monographs, 125*(2), 173–191.

Leiken, M., & Breznitz, Z. (2001). Effects of accelerated reading rate on syntactic processing of Hebrew sentences among normal readers: Electrophysiological evidence. *Genetic, Social and General Psychology Monographs, 127*(2), 193–211.

Leiken, M., & Breznitz, Z. (forthcoming). Contribution of the word syntactic functions to sentence processing of dyslexic and normal readers: A review. *Developmental Neuropsychology.*

Leiner, H. C., Leiner, A. L., & Dow, R. S. (1989). Reappraising the cerebellum: What does the hindbrain contribute to the forebrain? *Behavioural Neuroscience, 103,* 998–1008.

Leiner, H. C., Leiner, A. L., & Dow, R. S. (1993). Cognitive and language functions of the human cerebellum. *Trends in Neuroscience, 16,* 444–447.

Leinonen, S., Leppänen, P., Aro, M., Ahonen, T., & Lyytinen, H. (2001). Heterogeneity in adult dyslexic readers: Relating processing skills to the speed and accuracy of oral text reading. *Reading and Writing, 14*(3–4), 265–296.

Lemoine, H. E., Levy, B. A., & Hutchinson, A. (1993). Increasing the naming speed of poor readers: Representations formed across repetitions. *Journal of Experimental Child Psychology, 55,* 297–328.

Leonard, L. B. (1974). A preliminary view of generalization in language training. *Journal of Speech and Hearing Disorders, 39*(4), 429–436.

Leppänen, P.H.T., & Lyytinen, H. (1997). Auditory event-related potentials in the study of developmental language related disorders. *Audiology and Neuro-Otology, 2*(5), 308–340.

Leppänen, P.H.T., Pihko, E., Eklund, K. M., & Lyytinen, H. (1999). Cortical responses of infants with and without a genetic risk for dyslexia: II. Group Effects. *Neuro Report, 10,* 969–973.

Lesgold, A. M., & Curtis, M. E. (1980). *Learning to read words efficiently.* Report of the National Institute of Education (DHEW), Washington, DC.

Levelt, W.J.M. (1989). *Speaking: From intention to articulation.* Cambridge, MA: MIT Press.

Levine, G., Preddy, D., & Thorndike, R. L. (1987). Speed of information processing and level of cognitive ability. *Personality and Individual Differences, 8*(5), 599–607.

Levitt, J. B., Yoshioka, T., & Lund, J. S. (1994). Intrinsic cortical connections in macaque visual area V2: Evidence for interaction between different functional streams. *Journal of Comparative Neurology, 342*(4), 551–570.

Levy, B. A. (2001). Moving the bottom: Improving reading fluency. In M. Wolf (Ed.), *Dyslexia, fluency and the brain* (pp. 357–379). Cambridge, MA: York Press.

Lezak, M. D. (1993). Newer contributions to the neuropsychological assessment of executive functions. *Journal of Head Trauma Rehabilitation, 8*(1), 24–31.

Liberman, A. M., & Mattingly, I. G. (1985). The motor theory of speech perception revised. *Cognition, 21*(1), 1–36.

Liberman, I. Y., & Shankweiler, D. (1991). Phonology and beginning reading: A tutorial. In L. Reiben & C. A. Perfetti (Eds.), *Learning to read: Basic research and its implications* (pp. 3–17). Hillsdale, NJ: Lawrence Erlbaum Associates.

Liberman, P., Meskill, R. H., Chatillon, M., & Schupack, H. (1985). Phonetic speech perception deficits in dyslexia. *Journal of Speech and Hearing Research, 28,* 480–486.

Lieberman, M., & Prince, A. (1977). On stress and linguistic rhythm. *Linguistic Inquiry, 8,* 249–336.

Lieberman, P. (1969). On the acoustic analysis of primate vocalizations. *Behavior Research Methods and Instrumentation, 1*(5), 169–174.

Lieberman, P. (1975). *Intonation, perception, and language.* Oxford, England: MIT Press.

Lincoln, A. J., Courchesne, E., Harms, L., & Allen, M. (1995). Sensory modulation of auditory stimuli in children with autism and receptive developmental language disorder: Event related brain potential evidence. *Journal of Autism and Developmental Disorders, 25*(5), 521–539.

Livingstone, M. (1993). Parallel processing in the visual system and the brain: Is one subsystem selectively affected in dyslexia? In A. M. Galaburda (Ed.), *Dyslexia and development: Neurobiological aspects of extra-ordinary brains* (pp. 237–256). Cambridge, MA: Harvard University Press.

Livingstone, M. S., & Hubel, D. H. (1987). Psychophysical evidence for separate channels for the perception of form, color, movement, and depth. *Journal of Neuroscience, 7,* 3416–3468.

Livingstone, M. S., & Hubel, D. H. (1988). Segregation of form, color, movement, and depth: Anatomy, physiology, and perception. *Science, 240,* 740–749.

Livingstone, M. S., Rosen, G. D., Drislane, F. W., & Galaburda, A. M. (1991). Physiological and anatomical evidence for a magnocellular deficit in developmental dyslexia. *Proceedings of the National Academy of Sciences, 88,* 7943–7947.

Llinas, R. (1993). Is dyslexia a dyschronia? In P. Tallal, A. M. Galaburda, R. R. Llinas, & C. von Eurler (Eds.), *Temporal information processing in the nervous system. Annals of the New York Academy of Sciences, 682,* 48–56.

Logan, G. D. (1978). Attention in character classification: Evidence for the automaticity of component stages. *Journal of Experimental Psychology: General, 107,* 32–63.

Logan, G. D. (1979). On the use of a concurrent memory load to measure attention and automaticity. *Journal of Experimental Psychology: Human Perception and Performance, 5,* 189–207.

Logan, G. D. (1988a). Automaticity, resources, and memory: Theoretical controversies and practical implications. *Human Factors, 30,* 367–386.

Logan, G. D. (1988b). Toward an instance theory of automatization. *Psychological Review, 95,* 492–527.

Logan, G. D. (1992). Shapes of reaction-time distributions and shapes of learning curves: A test of the instance theory of automaticity. *Journal of Experimental Psychology: Learning, Memory, and Cognition, 20,* 1022–1050.

Logan, G. D. (1997). TI: Automaticity and reading: Perspectives from the instance theory of automatization. *Reading and Writing Quarterly, 13*(2), 123–146.

Lovegrove, W. (1993a). Do dyslexics have a visual deficit? In S. F. Wright & R. Groner (Eds.), *Facets of dyslexia and its remediation* (pp. 33–49). Amsterdam: Elsevier Science.

Lovegrove, W. (1993b). Weakness in the transient visual system: A causal factor in dyslexia? *Annals of the New York Academy of Science, 682,* 57–69.

Lovegrove, W., Garzia, R. P., & Nicolson, S. B. (1990). Experimental evidence for a transient deficit in specific reading disability. *Journal of the American Optometric Association, 61*(2), 137–146.

Lovegrove, W., Martin, F., & Slaghuis, W. (1986). A theoretical and experimental case for a visual deficit in specific reading disability. *Cognitive Neuropsychology, 3,* 225–267.

Lovegrove, W. J., & Williams, M. C. (1993). Visual temporal processing deficits in specific reading disability. In D. M. Willows, R. S. Kruk, & E. Corcos (Eds.), *Visual processes in reading and reading disabilities* (pp. 311–329). Hillsdale, NJ: Lawrence Erlbaum Associates.

Lovett, M. W. (1984). A developmental perspective on reading dysfunction: Accuracy and rate criteria in the subtyping of dyslexic children. *Brain and Language, 22,* 67–91.

Lovett, M. W. (1987). A developmental approach to reading disability: Accuracy and speed criteria of normal and deficient reading skill. *Child Development, 58,* 234–260.

Lovett, M. W. (1995, April). *Remediating dyslexic children's word identification deficits: Are the core deficits of developmental dyslexia amenable to treatment?* Paper presented at Society for Research in Child Development, Indianapolis, IN.

Lovett, M. W., Borden, S. L., DeLuca, T., Lacerenza, L., Benson, N. J., & Brackstone, D. (1994). Treating the core deficits of developmental dyslexia: Evidence of transfer of learning after phonologically- and strategy-based reading training programs. *Developmental Psychology, 30*(6), 805–822.

Lovett, M. W., Steinbach, K. A., & Frijters, J. C. (2000). Remediating the core deficits of developmental reading disability: A double-deficit perspective. *Journal of Learning Disabilities, 33*(4), 334–358.

Lovett, M. W., Warren-Chaplin, P. M., Ransby, M. J., & Borden, S. L. (1990). Training the word recognition skills of reading disabled children: Treatment and transfer effects. *Journal of Educational Psychology, 82,* 769–780.

Lovrich, D., Cheng, J. C., & Velting, D. M. (1996). Late cognitive brain potentials, phono-logical and semantic classification of spoken words, and reading ability in children. *Journal of Clinical and Experimental Neuropsychology, 18*, 161–177.

Lovrich, D., Cheng, J. C., Velting, D. M., & Kazmerski, V. (1997). Auditory ERPs during rhyme and semantic processing: Effects of reading ability in college students. *Journal of Clinical and Experimental Neuropsychology, 19*(3), 313–330.

Lovrich, D., & Stamm, J. S. (1983). Event-related potential and behavioral correlates of at-tention in reading retardation. *Journal of Clinical Neuropsychology, 5*(1), 13–37.

Luciano, M., Wright, M. J., Smith, G. A., Geffen, G. M., Geffen, L. B., & Martin, N. G. (2001). Genetic covariance among measures of information processing speed, working memory, and IQ. *Behavior Genetics, 31*(6), 581–592.

Luck, S. J., & Hillyard, S. A. (1994). Electrophysiological correlates of feature analysis during visual search. *Psychophysiology, 31*, 291–308.

Ludlow, C. L., Cudahy, E. A., Bassich, C., & Brown, G. L. (1983). Auditory processing skills of hyperactive, language impaired and reading disabled boys. In E. Z. Lasky & J. Katz (Eds.), *Central auditory processing disorders* (pp. 163–184). Baltimore: Park Press.

Lundberg, I., & Hoien, T. (1990). Patterns of information processing skills and word recogni-tion strategies in developmental dyslexia. *Scandinavian Journal of Educational Research, 34*(3), 231–240.

Lyon, G. R., & Moats, L. C. (1997). Critical conceptual and methodological considerations in reading intervention research. *Journal of Learning Disabilities, 30*(6), 578–588.

Mackay, D. G. (1982). The problem of flexibility, fluency, and speed-accuracy trade off in skilled behavior. *Psychological Review, 89*, 483–506.

Mackworth, J. F., & Mackworth, N. H. (1974). How children read: Matching by sight and sound. *Journal of Reading Behavior, 6*(3), 295–303.

Maisto, A. A., & Baumeister, A. A. (1975). A developmental study of choice reaction time: The effect of two forms of stimulus degradation on encoding. *Journal of Experimental Child Psychology, 20*(3), 56–464.

Malach, R. (1994). Cortical columns as devices for maximizing neuronal diversity. *Trends in Neurosciences, 17*(3), 101–104.

Malach, R., Amir, Y., Harel, M., & Grinvald, A. (1993). Relationship between intrinsic con-nections and functional architecture revealed by optical imaging and in vivo targeted biocytin injections in primate striate cortex. *Proceedings of the National Academy of Sci-ences of the United States of America, 90*(22), 10469–10473.

Malach, R., Schirman, T. D., Harel, M., Tootell, R. B., & Malonek, D. (1997). Organization of intrinsic connections in owl monkey area MT. *Cerebral Cortex, 7*(4), 386–393.

Malach, R., Tootell, R. B., & Malonek, D. (1994). Relationship between orientation do-mains, cytochrome oxidase stripes, and intrinsic horizontal connections in squirrel mon-key area V2. *Cerebral Cortex, 4*(2), 151–165.

Malloch, F. J. (1984). *Patterns in good and poor grade four readers' rhythm discrimination, atten-tion to language frequencies and pitch discrimination related to listening abilities and literary ex-periences.* Unpublished doctoral dissertation, Ohio State University, Columbus, OH.

Manis, F., Doi, L., & Bhadha, B. (2000). Naming speed, phonological awareness and ortho-graphic knowledge in second graders. *Journal of Learning Disabilities, 33*, 325–333, 374.

Manis, F. R. (1985). Acquisition of word identification skills in normal and disabled readers. *Journal of Educational Psychology, 77*, 78–90.

Manis, F. R., Custodio, R., & Szeszulski, P. A. (1993). Development of phonological and orthographic skill: A 2-year longitudinal study of dyslexic children. *Journal of Experimental Child Psychology, 56*, 64–86.

Manis, F. R., McBride-Chang, C., Seidenberg, M. S., & Keating, P. (1997). Are speech perception deficits associated with developmental dyslexia? *Journal of Experimental Child Psychology, 66*(2), 211–235.

Manis, F. R., Szeszulski, P. A., Holt, L. K., & Graves, K. (1988). A developmental perspective on dyslexic subtypes. *Annals of Dyslexia, 38*, 139–153.

Mann, V. (1984). Review: Reading skill and language skill. *Developmental Review, 4*, 1–15.

Mann, V. A., & Brady, S. (1988). Reading disability: The role of language deficiencies. *Journal of Consulting and Clinical Psychology, 56*, 811–816.

Martin, F., & Lovegrove, W. (1987). Flicker contrast sensitivity in normal and specifically disabled readers. *Perception, 16*, 215–221.

Martin, J. G. (1972). Rhythmic (hierarchical) versus serial structure in speech and other behavior. *Psychological Review, 79*(6), 487–509.

Mason, M. (1980). Reading ability and the encoding of item and location information. *Journal of Experimental Psychology: Human Perception and Performance, 6*(1), 89–98.

Mason, M. (1982). Recognition time for letters and nonletters: Effects of serial position, array size, and processing order. *Journal of Experimental Psychology: Human Perception and Performance, 8*(5), 724–738.

Maunsell, J. H., & Newsome, W. T. (1987). Visual processing in monkey extrastriate cortex. *Annual Review of Neuroscience, 10*, 363–401.

May, J. G., Williams, M. C., & Dunlap, W. P. (1988). Temporal order judgements in good and poor readers. *Neuropsychologia, 26*(6), 917–924.

Mazer, S. R., McIntyre, C. W., Murray, M. E., Till, R. E., & Blackwell, S. L. (1983). Visual persistence and information pick-up in learning disabled children. *Journal of Learning Disabilities, 16*(4), 221–225.

McBride-Chang, C., & Manis, F. R. (1996). Structural invariance in the associations of naming speed, phonological awareness, and verbal reasoning in good and poor readers: A test of the double deficit hypothesis. *Reading and Writing: An Interdisciplinary Journal, 8*, 323–339.

McCauley, C., Kellas, G., Dugas, J., & DeVellis, R. F. (1976). Effects of serial rehearsal training on memory search. *Journal of Educational Psychology, 68*(4), 474–481.

McClelland, J. L. (1985). Putting knowledge in its place: A scheme for programming parallel processing structures on the fly. *Cognitive Science, 9*, 113–146.

McClelland, J. L. (1986). The programmable blackboard model of reading. In J. L. McClelland & D. E. Rumelhart (Eds.), *Parallel distributed processing: Exploration in the microstructure of cognition* (pp. 122–169). Cambridge, MA: MIT Press.

McCroskey, R. L., & Kidder, H. C. (1980). Auditory fusion among learning disabled, reading disabled and normal children. *Journal of Learning Disability, 13*, 18–25.

McDonough, E. B., Warren, C. A., & Don, N. S. (1992). Event related potentials in a guessing task: The gleam in the eye effect. *International Journal of Neuroscience, 66*, 209–219.

McGivern, R. F., Berko, C., Languis, M. L., & Chapman, S. (1991). Detection of deficits in temporal pattern discrimination using the Seashore Rhythm Test in young children with reading impairments. *Journal of Learning Disabilities, 24*, 58–62.

McGue, M., Bouchard, T. J., Lykken, D. T., & Feuer, D. (1984). Information processing abilities in twins reared apart. *Intelligence, 8*(3), 239–258.

McKeever, W. F., & Van Deventer, A. D. (1975). Dyslexic adolescents: Evidence of impaired visual and auditory language processing associated with normal lateralization and visual responsivity. *Cortex, 11*, 361–378.

McPherson, W. B., & Ackerman, P. T. (1999). A study of reading disability using event-related brain potentials elicited during auditory alliteration judgments. *Developmental Neuropsychology, 15*(3), 359–378.

McPherson, W. B., Ackerman, P. T., Holcomb, P. J., & Dykman, R. A. (1998). Event-related brain potentials elicited during phonological processing differentiate subgroups of reading disabled adolescents. *Brain and Language, 62*, 163–185.

McPherson, W. B., Ackerman, P. T., Oglesby, D. M., & Dyckman, R. A. (1996). Event-related brain potentials elicited by rhyming and non-rhyming pictures differentiate subgroups of reading disabled adolescents. *Integrative Physiological and Behavioral Science, 31*, 3–17.

Mecacci, L., Sechi, E., & Levi, G. (1983). Abnormalities of visual evoked potentials by checkerboards in children with specific reading disability. *Brain and Cognition, 2*(2), 135–143.

Merzenich, M. M., Jenkins, W. M., Johnston, P., Schreiner, C., Miller, S. L., & Tallal, P. (1996). Temporal processing deficits of language learning impaired children ameliorated by training. *Science 271*, 77–81.

Merzenich, M. M., Schreiner, C. E., Jenkins, W., & Wang, A. (1993). Neural mechanisms underlying temporal integration, segmentation, and input sequence representation: Some implications for the origin of learning disabilities. In P. Tallal & A. M. Galaburda (Eds.), *Temporal information processing in the nervous system: Special reference to dyslexia and dysphasia. Annals of the New York Academy of Sciences, 682*, 1–22.

Meyer, M. S., & Felton, R. H. (1999). Repeated reading to enhance fluency: Old approaches and new directions. *Annals of Dyslexia, 49*, 283–306.

Meyer, M. S., Wood, F. B., Hart, L. A., & Felton, R. H. (1998). Selective predictive value of rapid automatized naming in poor readers. *Journal of Learning Disabilities, 31*, 106–117.

Meyler, A., & Breznitz, Z. (2003). Processing of phonological, orthographic and cross-modal word representations among adult dyslexic and normal readers. *Reading and Writing, 16*, 785–803.

Meyler, A., & Breznitz, Z. (submitted). Serial pattern processing deficits among dyslexic readers: Evidence from event-related potentials. *Journal of Clinical and Experimental Neuropsychology.*

Miles, J., & Stelmack, R. M. (1994). Learning disability subtypes and the effects of auditory and visual priming on visual event-related potentials to words. *Journal of Clinical and Experimental Neuropsychology, 16*(1), 43–64.

Miles, T. R. (1974). *The dyslexic child.* Hove, England: Priory Press.

Miller, E. M. (1994). Intelligence and brain myelination: A hypothesis. *Personality and Individual Differences, 17*(6), 803–832.

Ministry of Education. (2000). *Reading Achievement Test (RAT).* Jerusalem, Israel.

Misra, M., Katzir, T., Wolf, M., & Poldrack, R. A. (2004). Neural systems for Rapid Automatized Naming in skilled readers: Unraveling the RAN reading relationship. *Scientific Studies of Reading, 8*(3), 241–256.

Misra, M., Katzir, T., Wolf, M., & Poldrack, P. (in press). Neural systems underlying Rapid Automatized Naming (RAN) in skilled readers: An fMRI investigation. *Brain and Language.*

Mody, M., Studdert-Kennedy, M., & Brady, S. (1997). Speech perception deficits in poor readers: Auditory processing or phonological coding? *Journal of Experimental Child Psychology, 64*(2), 199–233.

Molfese, D. L. (2000). Predicting dyslexia at 8 years of age using neonatal brain responses. *Brain and Language, 72*(3), 238–245.

Morice, R., & Slaghuis, W. L. (1985). Language performance and reading ability at 8 years of age. *Applied Psycholinguistics, 6*(2), 141–160.

Morocz, I. A., Bitan, T., Shaul, S., Sterkin, A., Kushnir, T., Breznitz, Z., & Karni, A. (2001, June). *Accelerated reading in developmental dyslexia: Shorter grapheme presentation times result in decreased language area processing?* Paper presented at the Human Brain Mapping Conference, Brighton, UK.

Morton, J., Marcus, S., & Frankish, C. (1976). Perceptual centers (P-centers). *Psychological Review, 83*(5), 405–408.

Mozer, M. C. (1988). *The perception of multiple objects: A parallel distributed processing approach.* San Diego: Institute for Cognitive Science, University of California.

Muehl, S., & Kremenak, S. (1966). Ability to match information within and between auditory and visual sense modalities and subsequent reading achievement. *Journal of Educational Psychology, 57*(4), 230–238.

Musso, M., Weiller, C., Kiebel, S., Muller, S. P., Bulau, P., & Rijntjes, M. (1999). Training-induced brain plasticity in aphasia. *Brain, 122*(Pt. 9), 1781–1790.

Näätänen, R., & Picton, T. W. (1987). The N1 wave of the human electric and magnetic response to sound: A review and an analysis of the component structure. *Psychophysiology, 24,* 375–425.

Naslund, J. C., & Schneider, W. (1996). Kindergarten letter knowledge, phonological skills, and memory processes: Relative effects on early literacy. *Journal of Experimental Child Psychology, 62*(1), 30–59.

Nathan, R. G., & Stanovich, K. E. (1991). The causes and consequences of differences in reading fluency. *Theory into Practice, 30,* 176–184.

Nation, K., Marshall, C. M., & Snowling, M. J. (2001). Phonological and semantic contributions to children's picture naming skill: Evidence from children with developmental reading disorders. *Language and Cognitive Processes, 16*(2), 241–259.

Nation, K., & Snowling, M. (1998). Semantic processing and the development of word-recognition skills: Evidence from children with reading comprehension difficulties. *Journal of Memory and Language, 39*(1), 85–101.

National Institute of Child Health and Human Development. (2000). *Report of the National Reading Panel. Teaching children to read: An evidence-based assessment of the scientific research literature on reading and its implications for reading instruction: Reports of the subgroups* (NIH Publication No. 00-4754). Washington, DC: U.S. Government Printing Office.

Naylor, C. E., Wood, F. B., & Harter, M. R. (1995). Event-related potentials in adults diagnosed as reading disabled in childhood. Special issue: M. Russell Harter memorial issue:

Progress in visual information processing. *International Journal of Neuroscience, 80*(1–4), 339–352.

Neisser, U. (1967). *Cognitive psychology*. East Norwalk, CT: Appleton-Century-Crofts.

Neubauer, A. C., Spinath, F. M., Riemann, R., Borkenau, P., & Angleitner, A. (2000). Genetic and environmental influences on two measures of speed of information processing and their relation to psychometric intelligence: Evidence from the German Observational Study of Adult Twins. *Intelligence, 28*(4), 267–289.

Neville, H. J., Coffey, S. A., Holcomb, P. J., & Tallal, P. (1993). The neurobiology of sensory and language processing in language-impaired children. *Journal of Cognitive Neuroscience, 5*, 235–253.

Newell, A., & Rosenbloom, P. S. (1981). Mechanisms of skill acquisition and the law of practice. In J. R. Andesron (Ed.), *Cognitive skills and their acquisitions* (pp. 1–55). Hillsdale, NJ: Lawrence Erlbaum Associates.

Newman, S. P., Wadsworth, J. F., Archer, R., & Hockley, R. (1986). Ocular dominance, reading, and spelling ability in schoolchildren. *British Journal of Ophthalmology, 69*(3), 228–232.

Newman, S., Wright, S., & Fields, H. (1991). Identification of a group of children with dyslexia by means of IQ-achievement discrepancies. *British Journal of Educational Psychology, 61*, 139–154.

Newsome, W. T., & Wurtz, R. H. (1988). Probing visual cortical function with discrete chemical lesions. *Trends in Neuroscience, 11*(9), 394–400.

Nicholson, T. (1991). Do children read words better in context or in lists? A classic study revisited. *Journal of Educational Psychology, 83*, 444–450.

Nicholson, T., & Tan, A. (1999). Proficient word identification for comprehension. In G. B. Thompson & T. Nicholson (Eds.), *Learning to read: Beyond phonics and whole language* (pp. 150–173). Newark, DE: International Reading Association.

Nicolson, R. I., & Fawcett, A. J. (1990). Automaticity: A new framework for dyslexia research? *Cognition, 35*, 159–182.

Nicolson, R. I., & Fawcett, A. J. (1993a). Children with dyslexia automatize temporal skills more slowly. *Annals of the New York Academy of Sciences, 682*, 390–392.

Nicolson, R. I., & Fawcett, A. J. (1993b). Children with dyslexia classify pure tones slowly. In P. Tallal, A. M. Galaburda, R. R. Llinas, & C. von Eurler (Eds.), *Temporal information processing in the nervous system. Annals of the New York Academy of Sciences, 682*, 387–389.

Nicolson, R. I., & Fawcett, A. J. (1993c). Toward the origin of dyslexia. In S. F. Wright & R. Groner (Eds.), *Facets of dyslexia and its remediation* (pp. 371–391). North-Holland: Elsevier Science.

Nicolson, R. I., & Fawcett, A. J. (1994a). Comparison of deficits in cognition and motor skills among children with dyslexia. *Annals of Dyslexia, 44*, 147–164.

Nicolson, R. I., & Fawcett, A. J. (1994b). Reaction times and dyslexia. *Quarterly Journal of Experimental Psychology—Human Experimental Psychology, 47A*, 29–48.

Nicolson, R. I., & Fawcett, A. J. (1995). Balance, phonological skill and dyslexia: Towards the dyslexia early screening test. *Dyslexia Review, 7*, 8–11.

Nicolson, R. I., & Fawcett, A. J. (1999). Developmental dyslexia: The role of the cerebellum. *Dyslexia: An International Journal of Research and Practice, 5*, 155–177.

Nicolson, R. I., Fawcett, A. J., & Dean, P. (2001). Developmental dyslexia: The cerebellar deficit hypothesis. *Trends in Neurosciences, 24*(9), 508–511.

Nittrouer, S. (1999). Do temporal processing deficits cause phonological processing problems? *Journal of Speech, Language, and Hearing Research, 42*(4), 925–942.

Norman, D. A. (1968). Toward a theory of memory and attention. *Psychological Review, 75*(6), 522–536.

Novak, G. P., Ritter, W., Vaughan, H. G., & Wiznitzer, M. L. (1990). Differentiation of negative event-related potentials in an auditory discrimination task. *Electroencephalography and Clinical Neurophysiology, 75*, 255–275.

Novoa, L. (1988). *Word-retrieval process and reading acquisition and development in bilingual and monolingual children.* Unpublished doctoral dissertation, Harvard University, Cambridge, MA.

Novoa, L., & Wolf, M. (1984). *Word-retrieval and reading in bilingual children.* Paper presented at Boston University Language Conference, Boston, MA.

Obregon, M. (1994). *Exploring naming time patterns by dyslexic and normal readers on the serial RAN task.* Unpublished master's thesis, Tufts University, Boston, MA.

O'Connell, D. C. (1980). Toward an empirical rhetoric: Some comparisons of expressiveness in poetry readings by authors, English professors, and drama professors. *Archiv fuer Psychologie, 133*(2), 117–128.

O'Connell, D. C., Turner, E. A., & Onuska, L. A. (1968). Intonation, grammatical structure, and contextual association in immediate recall. *Journal of Verbal Learning and Verbal Behavior, 7*(1), 110–116.

Ojemann, G. A. (1983). Brain organization for language from the perspective of electrical stimulation mapping. *Behavioral and Brain Sciences, 6*(2), 189–230.

Ojemann, G. A. (1984). Common cortical and thalamic mechanisms for language and motor functions. *American Journal of Physiology, 246*, 901–903.

Olson, I. R., Gatenby, J. C., & Gore, J. C. (2002). A comparison of bound and unbound audio-visual information processing in the human cerebral cortex. *Cognitive Brain Research, 14*(1), 129–138.

Olson, R. K., Conners, F. A., & Rack, J. P. (1991). Eye movements in dyslexic and normal readers. In J. F. Stein (Ed.), *Vision and visual dyslexia* (pp. 243–250). London: Macmillan.

O'Neill, G., & Stanley, G. (1976). Visual processing of straight lines in dyslexic and normal children. *British Journal of Educational Psychology, 46*(3), 323–327.

Ortar, G., & Segev, N. (1970). *Reading comprehension test for grades one and two.* Jerusalem, Israel: Israeli Ministry of Education and Culture.

Palmer, B., Nasman, V. T., & Wilson, G. F. (1994). Task detection difficulty: Effects on ERPs in a same-different letter classification task. *Biological Psychology, 38*(2–3), 199–214.

Papanicolaou, A. C., Simos, P. G., Breier, J. I., Wheless, J. W., Mancias, P., Baumgartner, J. E., Maggioa, W. W., Gormley, W., Constantinou, J. E., & Butler, I. I. (2001). Brain plasticity for sensory and linguistic functions: A functional imaging study using magnetoencephalography with children and young adults. *Journal of Child Neurology, 16*(4), 241–252.

Parks, R. W., Cassens, G., Crockett, D. J., & Herrera, J. A. (1990). Correlation of the Shipley institute of living scale with regional cerebral glucose metabolism as measured by positron emission tomography in dementia. *International Journal of Clinical Neuropsychology, 12*(1), 14–19.

Patterson, K., & Coltheart, V. (1987). Phonological processes in reading: A tutorial review. In M. Coltheart (Ed.), *Attention and performance 12: The psychology of reading* (pp. 421–447). Hillsdale, NJ: Lawrence Erlbaum Associates.

Paulesu, E., Frith, C. D., & Frackowiak, R. J. (1993). The neural correlates of the verbal component of working memory. *Nature, 362,* 342–345.

Paulesu, E., Frith, U., Snowling, M., & Gallagher, A. (1996). Is developmental dyslexia a disconnection syndrome? Evidence from PET scanning. *Brain, 119*(Pt. 1), 43–157.

Pavlidis, G. T. (1985). Eye movement differences between dyslexics, normal, and retarded readers while sequentially fixating digits. *American Journal of Optometry and Physiological Optics, 62*(12), 820–832.

Pennington, B. F. (1995). Genetics of learning disabilities. *Journal of Child Neurology, 10*(Suppl. 1), S69–S77.

Perfetti, C. (1985). *Reading ability.* New York: Oxford University Press.

Perfetti, C. A. (1977). Language comprehension and fast decoding: Some psycholinguistic prerequisites for skilled reading comprehension. In J. T. Guthrie (Ed.), *Cognition, curriculum and comprehension.* Newark, DE: International Reading Association.

Perfetti, C. A., & Bolger, D. J. (2004). The brain might read that way. *Scientific Studies of Reading, 8*(3), 293–304.

Perfetti, C. A., Finger, E., & Hogaboam, T. W. (1978). Sources of vocalization latency differences between skilled and less skilled young readers. *Journal of Educational Psychology, 70*(5), 730–739.

Perfetti, C. A., & Hogaboam, T. (1975). The relationship between single word decoding and reading comprehension skill. *Journal of Educational Psychology, 67,* 461–469.

Petersen, S. E., Fox, P. T., Posner, M. I., Mintun, M., & Raichle, M. E. (1988). Positron emission tomographic studies of the cortical anatomy of single word processing. *Nature, 331,* 585–589.

Pick, A. D., & Frankel, G. W. (1974). A developmental study of strategies of visual selectivity. *Child Development, 45,* 1162–1165.

Pinheiro, M. L. (1977). Tests of central auditory function in children with learning disabilities. In R. W. Keith (Ed.), *Central auditory dysfunction* (pp. 223–256). New York: Grune & Stratton.

Pinkerton, F., Watson, D. R., & McClelland, R. J. (1989). A neurophysiological study of children with reading, writing and spelling difficulties. *Developmental and Medical Child Neurology, 31*(5), 569–581.

Plante, E., Van-Petten, C., & Senkfor, A. J. (2000). Electrophysiological dissociation between verbal and nonverbal semantic processing in learning disabled adults. *Neuropsychologia, 38*(13), 1669–1684.

Poldrack, R. A. (2000). Imaging brain plasticity: Conceptual and methodological issues—a theoretical review. *NeuroImage, 12,* 1–13.

Posner, M. I., & Boies, S. J. (1971). Components of attention. *Psychological Review, 78,* 391–408.

Posner, M. I., Lewis, J. L., & Conrad, C. (1972). Component processes in reading: A performance analysis. In J. F. Kavanagh & I. G. Mattingly (Eds.), *Language by ear and by eye: The relationship between speech and reading* (pp. 59–92). Oxford, England: MIT Press.

Posner, M. I., & Raichle, M. E. (1995). Precise of images of mind. *Behavioral and Brain Sciences, 18*(2), 327–383.

Posner, M. I., & Snyder, C. R. R. (1975). Attention and cognitive control. In R. L. Solso (Ed.), *Information processing and cognition: The Loyola symposium* (pp. 669–681). Hillsdale, NJ: Lawrence Erlbaum Associates.

Posthuma, D., Mulder, E.J.C.M., Boomsma, D. I., & de-Geus, E.J.C. (2002). Genetic analysis of IQ, processing speed and stimulus-response incongruency effects. *Biological Psychology, 61*(1–2), 157–182.

Posthuma, D., Neale, M. C., Boomsma, D. I., & de-Geus, E.J.C. (2001). Are smarter brains running faster? Heritability of alpha peak frequency, IQ, and their interrelation. *Behavior Genetics, 31*(6), 567–579.

Prawat, R. S., & Cancelli, A. A. (1977). Semantic retrieval in young children as a function of type of meaning. *Developmental Psychology, 13*(4), 354–358.

Price, C. J., Moore, C. J., & Frackowiak, R.S.J. (1994). The effect of alternating rate and duration on brain activity during reading. *NeuroImage, 3*, 40–52.

Pugh, K. R., Mencl, W. E., Jenner, A. R., Katz, L., Frost, S. J., Lee, J. R., Shaywitz, B. A., & Shaywitz, S. E. (2001). Neurobiological studies of reading and reading disability. *Journal of Communication Disorders, 34*(6), 479–492.

Pugh, K. R., Mencl, W. E., Shaywitz, B. A., Shaywitz, S. E., Fulbright, R. K., Constable, R. T., Skudlarski, P., Marchione, K. E., Jenner, A. R., Fletcher, J. M., Liberman, A. M., Shankweiler, D. P., Katz, L., Lacadie, C., & Gore, J. C. (2000). The angular gyrus in developmental dyslexia: Task-specific differences in functional connectivity within posterior cortex. *Psychological Science, 11*(1), 51–56.

Pugh, K. R., Shaywitz, B. A., Shaywitz, S. E., & Shankweiler, D. P. (1997). Predicting reading performance from neuroimaging profiles: The cerebral basis of phonological effects in printed word identification. *Journal of Experimental Psychology: Human Perception and Performance, 23*(2), 299–318.

Rabinowitz, M., Ornstein, P. A., Folds-Bennett, T. H., & Schneider, W. (1994). Age-related differences in speed of processing: Unconfounding age and experience. *Journal of Experimental Child Psychology, 57*(3), 449–459.

Rack, J. P., Snowling, M. J., & Olson, R. K. (1992). The nonword reading deficit in developmental dyslexia: A review. *Reading Research Quarterly, 27*, 29–53.

Raiguel, S. E., Lagae, L., Gulyas, B., & Orban, J. A. (1989). Response latencies of visual cells in macaque areas V1, V2 and V5. *Brain Research, 493*(1), 155–159.

Raij, T. (1999). Patterns of brain activity during visual imagery of letters. *Journal of Cognitive Neuroscience, 11*(3), 282–299.

Raij, T., Uutela, K., & Hari, R. (2000). Audiovisual integration of letters in the human brain. *Neuron, 28*, 617–625.

Raney, G. E. (1993). Monitoring changes in cognitive load during reading: An event-related brain potential and reaction time analysis. *Journal of Experimental Psychology: Learning, Memory, and Cognition, 19*(1), 51–69.

Rasinski, T. V. (1990). Effects of repeated reading and listening while reading on reading fluency. *Journal of Educational Research, 83*(3), 147–150.

Raven, J. C. (1960). *Guide to the standard progressive matrices.* London: H. K. Lewis.

Raven, J. C. (1965). *Advanced progressive matrices sets I and II.* London: H. K. Lewis.

Rayner, K. (1978). Eye movements in reading and information processing. *Psychological Bulletin, 85*(3), 618–660.

Rayner, K., & Morris, R. K. (1991). Comprehension processes in reading ambiguous sentences: Reflections from eye movements. In G. B. Simpson (Ed.), *Understanding word and sentence. Advances in psychology, No. 77* (pp. 175–198). Amsterdam: North-Holland.

Rayner, K., & Pollatsek, A. (1989). *The psychology of reading.* Englewood Cliffs, NJ: Prentice-Hall.

Reddington, J. M., & Cameron, K. D. (1991). Visual and auditory information processing in dyslexia: The possibility of subtypes. *International Journal of Disability, Development and Education, 38*(2), 171–203.

Reed, M. A. (1989). Speech perception and discrimination of brief auditory cues in reading disabled children. *Journal of Experimental Child Psychology, 48,* 270–292.

Reed, T. E. (1984). Mechanism for heritability of intelligence. *Nature, 311*(5985), 417.

Regan, D. (1989). *Human brain electrophysiology: Evoked potentials and evoked magnetic fields in science and medicine.* New York: Elsevier.

Reicher, G. M. (1969). Perceptual recognition as a function of meaningfulness of stimulus material. *Journal of Experimental Psychology, 81*(2), 275–280.

Reitsma, P. (1983). Printed word learning in beginning readers. *Journal of Experimental Child Psychology, 36*(2), 321–339.

Reitsma, P. (1989). Orthographic memory and learning to read. In P. G. Aaron & R. M. Joshi (Eds.), *Reading and writing disorders in different orthographic systems* (pp. 51–73). The Netherlands: Kluwer Academic.

Reutzel, D. R., & Hollingsworth, P. M. (1993). Effects of fluency training on second graders' reading comprehension. *Journal of Educational Research, 86*(6), 325–331.

Richards, T. L., Corina, D., Serafini, S., Steury, K., Echelard, D. R., Dager, S. R., Marro, K., Abbott, R. D., Maravilla, K. R., & Berninger, V. W. (2000). Effects of a phonologically driven treatment for dyslexia on lactate levels measured by proton MR spectroscopic imaging. *American Journal of Neuroradiology, 21*(5), 916–922.

Richardson, A. J., & Stein, J. F. (1993). Personality characteristics of adult dyslexics. In S. F. Wright & R. Groner (Eds.), *Facets of dyslexia and its remediation. Studies in visual information processing* (Vol. 3, pp. 411–423). Amsterdam: Elsevier Science.

Ridderinkhof, K. R., & Van der Molen, M. W. (1997). Mental resources, processing speed, and inhibitory control: A developmental perspective. *Biological Psychology, 45*(1–3), 241–261.

Rijsdijk, F. V., & Boomsma, D. I. (1997). Genetic mediation of the correlation between peripheral nerve conduction velocity and IQ. *Behavior Genetics, 27*(2), 87–98.

Rijsdijk, F. V., Boomsma, D. I., & Vernon, P. A. (1995). Genetic analysis of peripheral nerve conduction velocity in twins. *Behavior Genetics, 25*(4), 341–348.

Ritter, W., Simson, R., Vaughan, H. G., & Macht, M. (1982). Manipulation of event-related potential manifestations of information processing stages. *Science, 218*(4575), 909–911.

Risberg, J. (1986). Regional cerebral blood flow in neuropsychology. *Neuropsychologia, 24*(1), 135–140.

Robeck, M. C., & Wallace, R. R. (1990). *The psychology of reading: An interdisciplinary approach* (2nd ed.). Hillsdale, NJ: Lawrence Erlbaum Associates.

Robichon, F., Besson, M., & Habib, M. (2002). An electrophysiological study of dyslexic and control adults in a sentence reading task. *Biological Psychology, 59*(1), 29–53.

Roe, A. W., & Ts'o, D. Y. (1995). Visual topography in primate V2: Multiple representation across functional stripes. *Journal of Neuroscience, 15*(5 Pt. 2), 3689–3715.

Roland, P. E., Eriksson, L., Widen, L., & Stone-Elander, S. (1989). Changes in regional cerebral oxidative metabolism induced by tactile learning and recognition in man. *European Journal of Neuroscience, 1*, 3–18.

Romanski, L. M., Tian, B., Fritz, J., Mishkin, M., Goldman-Rakic, P. S., & Rauschecker, J. P. (1999). Dual streams of auditory afferents target multiple domains in the primate prefrontal cortex. *Nature Neuroscience, 2*(12), 1131–1136.

Rose, S. A., Feldman, J. F., & Jankowski, J. J. (2002). Processing speed in the 1st year of life: A longitudinal study of preterm and full-term infants. *Developmental Psychology, 38*(6), 895–902.

Rose, S. A., Feldman, J. F., Janowski, J. J., & Futterweit, L. R. (1999). Visual and auditory temporal processing, cross-modal transfer and reading. *Journal of Learning Disabilities, 32*(3), 256–266.

Rosenberger, P. B., & Rottenberg, D. A. (2002). Does training change the brain? *Neurology, 58*(8), 1139–1140.

Roth, C. (1983). Factors affecting developmental changes in the speed of processing. *Journal of Experimental Child Psychology, 35*(3), 509–528.

Roth, F. P., & Spekman, N. J. (1989). The oral syntactic proficiency of learning disabled students: A spontaneous story sampling analysis. *Journal of Speech and Hearing Research, 32*(1), 67–77.

Rumsey, J. M., Andreason, P., Zametkin, A. J., Aquino, T., King, C., Hamburger, S. D., Pitkus, A., Rapoport, J. L., & Cohen, R. (1992). Failure to activate the left temporal cortex in dyslexia: An oxygen 15 positron emission tomographic study. *Archives of Neurology, 49*(5), 527–534.

Rumsey, J. M., Donohue, B. C., Brady, D. R., Nace, K., Giedd, J. N., & Andreason, P. (1997). A magnetic resonance imaging study of planum temporale asymmetry in men with developmental dyslexia. *Archives of Neurology, 54*(12), 1481–1489.

Rumsey, J. M., Horwitz, B., Donohue, B. C., Nace, K., Maisog, J. M., & Andreason, P. (1997). Phonological and orthographic components of word recognition: A PET-rCBF study. *Brain, 120*(5), 739–759.

Rumsey, J. M., Nace, K., Donohue, B., Wise, D., Maisog, M., & Andreason, P. (1997). A positron emission tomographic study of impaired word recognition and phonological processing in dyslexic men. *Archives of Neurology, 54*(5), 562–573.

Saccuzzo, D. P., Larson, G. E., & Rimland, B. (1986). Visual, auditory and reaction time approaches to the measurement of speed of information processing and individual differences in intelligence. *Personality and Individual Differences, 7*(5), 659–667.

Salin, P. A., & Bullier, J. (1995). Corticocortical connections in the visual system: Structure and function. *Physiological Reviews, 75*(1), 107–154.

Salthouse, T. A., & Prill, K. (1983). Analysis of a perceptual skill. *Journal of Experimental Psychology: Human Perception and Performance, 9*(4), 607–621.

Salthouse, T. A., & Somberg, B. L. (1982). Time-accuracy relationships in young and old adults. *Journal of Gerontology, 37*(3), 349–353.

Samuels, S. J., & Flor, R. F. (1997). The importance of automaticity for developing expertise in reading. *Reading and Writing Quarterly, 13*, 107–121.

Samuels, S. J., Schermer, N., & Reinking, D. (1992). Reading fluency: Techniques for making decoding automatic. In S. J. Samuels & A. E. Farstrup (Eds.), *What research has to say about reading instruction* (pp. 124–166). Newark, DE: International Reading Association.

Satz, P., Fletcher, J. M., Clark, W., & Morris, R. (1981). Lag, deficit, rate and delay constructs in specific learning disabilities. In A. Ansara, N. Geschwind, M. A. Galaburda, & N. Cartell (Eds.), *Sex differences in dyslexia* (pp. 129–150). Towson, MD: The Orton Dyslexia Society.

Scarborough, H. S. (1991). Early syntactic development of dyslexic children. *Annals of Dyslexia, 41*, 207–220.

Schafer, A. J., Carlson, K., Clifton, C., & Frazier, L. (2000). Focus and the interpretation of pitch accent: Disambiguating embedded questions. *Language and Speech, 43*(1), 75–105.

Schafer, A. J., Speer, S. R., Warren, P., & White, S. D. (2000). Intonational disambiguation in sentence production and comprehension. *Journal of Psycholinguistic Research, 29*(2), 169–182.

Schall, J. D. (1991). Neuronal activity related to visually guided saccades in the frontal eye fields of rhesus monkeys: Comparison with supplementary eye fields. *Journal of Neurophysiology, 66*(2), 559–579.

Schiller, P. H. (1966). Developmental study of color-word interference. *Journal of Experimental Psychology, 72*, 105–108.

Schmidt, S. (1985). Hearing impaired students in physical education. *Adapted Physical Activity Quarterly, 2*(4), 300–306.

Schmolesky, M. T., Wang, Y., Hanes, D. P., Thompson, K. G., Lentgeb, S., Schall, J. P., & Leventhal, A. G. (1998). Signal timing across Macaque visual system. *Journal of Neurophysiology, 79*(6), 3272–3278.

Schneider, W., Dumais, S. T., & Shiffrin, R. M. (1984). Automatic and controlled processing and attention. In R. Parasuraman & R. Davies (Eds.), *Varieties of attention* (pp. 1–27). New York: Academic Press.

Schneider, W., & Fisk, A. D. (1982). Concurrent automatic and controlled visual search: Can processing occur without resource cost? *Journal of Experimental Psychology: Learning, Memory, and Cognition, 8*, 261–278.

Schneider, W., & Fisk, A. D. (1984). Automatic category search and its transfer. *Journal of Experimental Psychology: Learning, Memory, and Cognition, 10*(1), 1–15.

Schreiber, P. (1980). On the acquisition of reading fluency. *Journal of Reading Behavior, 12*, 177–186.

Schretlen, D., Pearlson, G. D., Anthony, J. C., Aylward, E. H., Augustine, A. M., Davis, A., & Barta, P. (2000). Elucidating the contributions of processing speed, executive ability, and frontal lobe volume to normal age-related differences in fluid intelligence. *Journal of the International Neuropsychological Society, 6*(1), 52–61.

Schulte-Korne, G., Bartling, J., Deimel, W., & Remschmidt, H. (1999). Attenuated hemispheric lateralization in dyslexia: Evidence of a visual processing deficit. *Neuroreport, 10*(17), 3697–3701.

Schulte-Koerne, G., Deimel, W., Bartling, J., & Remschmidt, H. (1998). Auditory processing and dyslexia: Evidence for a specific speech processing deficit. *Neuroreport, 9*(2), 337–340.

Schwab, E. C., & Nusbaum, H. C. (1986). *Pattern recognition by humans and machines: Vol. 1. Speech perception.* Orlando, FL: Academic Press.

Schwanenflugel, P. J., & Shoben, E. J. (1983). Differential context effects in the comprehension of abstract and concrete verbal materials. *Journal of Experimental Psychology: Learning, Memory, and Cognition, 9*(1), 82–102.

Schwantes, F. M. (1981). Effect of story context on children's ongoing word recognition. *Journal of Reading Behavior, 13*(4), 305–311.

Scott, R. B., Stoodley, C. J., Anslow, P., Paul, C., Stein, J. F., Sugden, E. M., & Mitchell, C. D. (2001). Lateralized cognitive deficits in children following cerebellar lesions. *Developmental Medicine and Child Neurology, 43*(10), 685–691.

Scott, S. K. (1998). The point of P-centres. *Psychological Research, 61*(1), 4–11.

Seashore, C. E., Lewis, D., & Saetveit, J. G. (1956). *Seashore measures of musical talents.* Oxford, England: Psychological Corporation.

Seashore, C. E., Lewis, D., & Saetveit, J. G. (1960). *Seashore measures of musical talents—revised.* New York: Psychological Corporation.

Segal, D., & Wolf, M. (1993). Automaticity, word retrieval, and vocabulary development in children with reading disabilities. In L. Meltzer (Ed.), *Cognitive, linguistic, and developmental perspectives on learning disorders* (pp. 141–165). Boston: Little & Brown.

Seidenberg, M. S., & McClelland, J. L. (1989). A distributed developmental model of word recognition and naming. *Psychological Review, 96*, 523–568.

Selkirk, E. (1980). The role of prosodic categories in English word stress. *Linguistic Inquiry, 11*, 563–606.

Seltzer, B., & Pandya, D. N. (1989). Intrinsic connections and architectonics of the superior temporal sulcus in the rhesus monkey. *Journal of Comparative Neurology, 290*(4), 451–471.

Sergent, J., Zuck, E., Levesque, M., & MacDonald, B. (1992). Positron emission tomography study of letter and object processing: Empirical findings and methodological considerations. *Cerebral Cortex, 2*(1), 68–80.

Seymour, P.H.K. (1986). *Cognitive analysis of dyslexia.* International library of psychology. New York: Routledge.

Shani, M., & Ben-Dror, I. (1998). *Working memory—completion test.* Tel Aviv: Mofet.

Shankweiler, D. (1979). The speech code and learning to read. *Journal of Experimental Psychology: Human Learning and Memory, 5*(6), 531–544.

Shankwieler, D., & Crain, S. (1986). Language mechanisms and reading disorder: A modular approach. *Cognition, 24*, 139–168.

Shapiro, K. L., Ogden, N., & Lind-Blad, F. (1990). Temporal processing in dyslexia. *Journal of Learning Disabilities, 23*(2), 99–107.

Share, D. L. (1999). Phonological recoding and orthographic learning: A direct test of the self-teaching hypothesis. *Journal of Experimental Child Psychology, 72*(2), 95–129.

Sharma, V., Halperin, J. H., Newcorn, J. N., & Wolf, L. E. (1991). The dimension of focused attention: Relationship to behavior and cognitive functioning in children. *Perceptual and Motor Skills, 72*(3, Pt. 1), 787–793.

Shatil, E. (1997). *One-minute test for words and pseudowords.* Unpublished test, University of Haifa, Israel.

Shatil, E. (2001a). *Dictation test.* Unpublished test, University of Haifa, Israel.

Shatil, E. (2001b). *Morphological test.* Unpublished test, University of Haifa, Israel.

Shatil, E. (2001c). *Phonological test battery.* Unpublished tests, University of Haifa, Israel.

Shaul, S., & Breznitz, Z. (in press). Speed of auditory and visual processing: a comparison between young and adult dyslexics by means of electro-physiological measures. *Journal of Genetic Psychology*.

Shaywitz, E. S., Shaywitz, B. A., Pugh, K. R., Fulbright, R. K., Constable, R. T., Mencl, W. E., Shankweiler, D. P., Liberman, A. M., Skudlarski, P., Fletcher, J. M., Katz, L., Marchione, K. E., Lacadie, C., Gatenby, C., & Gore, J. C. (1998). Functional disruption in organization of the brain for reading in dyslexia, *Neurobiology, 95*, 2636–2641.

Shaywitz, S. E. (1998). Current concepts: Dyslexia. *New England Journal of Medicine, 338*(5), 307–312.

Shiffrin, R. M., & Schneider, W. (1977). Controlled and automatic human information processing: II Perceptual learning, automatic attending, and a general theory. *Psychological Review 84*, 127–190.

Shinn, M. R., Good, R. H., Knutson, N., Tilly, W. D., & Collins, V. L. (1992). Curriculum-based measurement of oral reading fluency: A confirmatory analysis of its relation to reading. *School of Psychology Review, 21*, 459–479.

Siegel, L. (1988). Development of grammatical sensitivity, phonological and short term memory skills in normally achieving and learning disabled children. *Developmental Psychology, 24*(1), 28–37.

Siegler, R. S. (1987). Some general conclusions about children's strategy choice procedures. *International Journal of Psychology, 22*(5–6), 729–749.

Siegman, A. W. (1978). The meaning of silent pauses in the initial interview. *Journal of Nervous and Mental Disease, 166*(9), 642–654.

Silva-Pereyra, J., Fernandez, T., Harmony, T., Bernal, J., Galan, L., Diaz-Comas, L., Fernandez-Bouzas, A., Yanez, G., Rivera-Gaxiola, M., Rodriguez, M., & Marosi, E. (2001). Delayed P300 during Sternberg and color discrimination tasks in poor readers. *International Journal of Psychophysiology, 40*(1), 17–32.

Simos, P. G., Breier, J. I., Fletcher, J. M., Bergman, E., & Papanicolaou, A. C. (2000). Cerebral mechanisms involved in word reading in dyslexic children: A magnetic source imaging approach. *Cerebral Cortex, 10*(8), 809–816.

Simos, P. G., Fletcher, J. M., Bergman, E., Breier, J. I., Foorman, B. R., Castillo, E. M., Davis, R. N., Fitzgerald, M., & Papanicolaou, A. C. (2002). Dyslexia-specific brain activation profile becomes normal following successful remedial training. *Neurology, 58*(8), 1203–1213.

Sinatra, G. M., & Royer, J. M. (1993). Development of cognitive component processing skills that support skilled reading. *Journal of Educational Psychology, 85*(3), 509–519.

Sinatra, R. (1989). Verbal/visual processing for males disabled in print acquisition. *Journal of Learning Disabilities, 22*(1), 69–71.

Sliwinski, M., & Buschke, H. (1999). Cross-sectional and longitudinal relationships among age, cognition, and processing speed. *Psychology and Aging, 14*(1), 18–33.

Sloboda, J. A. (1976). Decision times for word and letter search: A holistic word identification model examined. *Journal of Verbal Learning and Verbal Behavior, 15*(1), 93–101.

Sloboda, J. A. (1977). The locus of the word-priority effect in a target-detection task. *Memory and Cognition, 5*(3), 371–376.

Smith, A. T., Early, F., & Grogan, S. C. (1986). Flicker masking and developmental dyslexia. *Perception, 15*(4), 473–482.

Smith, F. (1979). *Reading without nonsense.* New York: Teacher's College Press.

Smith, F., & Holmes, D. L. (1970–1971). The independence of letter, word and meaning identification in reading. *Reading Research Quarterly, 6,* 394–415.

Snowling, M. J. (1980). The development of grapheme-phoneme correspondence in normal and dyslexic readers. *Journal of Experimental Child Psychology, 29,* 294–305.

Snowling, M. J. (1995). Phonological processing and developmental dyslexia. *Journal of Research in Reading, 18*(2), 132–138.

Snowling, M. (2000). *Dyslexia* (2nd ed.). Malden, MA: Blackwell.

Snowling, M., Goulandris, N., Bowlby, M., & Howell, P. (1986). Segmentation and speech perception in relation to reading skill: A developmental analysis. *Journal of Experimental Child Psychology, 41*(3), 489–507.

Snyder, L. S., & Downey, D. M. (1995). Serial rapid naming skills in children with reading disabilities. *Annals of Dyslexia, 45,* 31–49.

Sokolov, J. L. (1988). Cue validity in Hebrew sentence comprehension. *Journal of Child Language, 15*(1), 129–155.

Solan, H. A., Sutiji, V. G., Ficarra, A. P., & Wurst, S. A. (1990). Binocular advantage and visual processing in dyslexic and control children as measured by visual evoked potentials. *Optometry and Vision Science, 67,* 105–110.

Solman, R. T., & May, J. G. (1990). Spatial localization discrepancies: A visual deficiency in poor readers. *American Journal of Psychology, 103,* 243–263.

Southwood, M. H., & Chatterjee, A. (1999). Simultaneous activation of reading mechanisms: Evidence from a case of deep dyslexia. *Brain and Language, 67,* 1–29.

Southwood, M. H., & Chatterjee, A. (2000). The interaction of multiple routes in oral reading: Evidence from dissociations in naming and oral reading in phonological dyslexia. *Brain and Language, 72,* 14–39.

Spear, L. C., & Sternberg, R. J. (1987). An information processing framework for understanding reading disability. In S. J. Ceci (Ed.), *Handbook of cognitive, social and neuropsychological aspects of learning disabilities* (pp. 3–31). Hillsdale, NJ: Lawrence Erlbaum Associates.

Speer, S., Crowder, R., & Thomas, L. (1993). Prosodic structure and sentence recognition. *Journal of Memory and Language, 32,* 336–358.

Sperber, R. D., Davies, D., Merrill, E. C., & McCauley, C. (1982). Cross-category differences in the processing of subordinate-superordinate relationships. *Child Development, 53*(5), 1249–1253.

Spring, C., & Capps, C. (1974). Encoding speed, rehearsal, and probed recall of dyslexic boys. *Journal of Educational Psychology, 66*(5), 780–786.

Spring, C., & Davis, J. (1988). Relations of digit naming speed with three components of reading. *Applied Psycholinguistics, 9,* 315–334.

Stanley, G., & Hall, R. (1973). Short-term visual information processing in dyslexics. *Child Development, 44*(4), 841–844.

Stanovich, K. E. (1981). Relationships between word decoding speed, general name-retrieval ability, and reading progress in first-grade children. *Journal of Educational Psychology, 73*(6), 809–815.

Stanovich, K. E. (1985). Explaining the variance in reading ability in terms of psychological processes: What have we learned? *Annals of Dyslexia, 35,* 67–96.

Stanovich, K. E. (1986a). Cognitive processes and the reading problems of learning disabled children: Evaluation the assumption of specificity. In J. K. Torgesen & B.Y.L. Wong (Eds.), *Psychological and educational perspectives on learning disabilities* (pp. 87–131). Orlando, FL: Academic Press.

Stanovich, K. E. (1986b). Mathew effects in reading: Some consequences of individual differences in the acquisition of literacy. *Reading Research Quarterly, 21*, 360–406.

Stanovich, K. E. (1988). Explaining the differences between word decoding speed, general name retrieval ability, and reading progress in first grade children. *Journal of Experimental Child Psychology, 73*, 809–815.

Stanovich, K. E. (1990). Concepts in developmental theories of reading skill: Cognitive resources, automaticity, and modularity. *Developmental Review, 10*(1), 72–100.

Stanovich, K. E. (1993). A model for studies of reading disability. *Developmental Review, 13*(3), 225–245.

Stanovich, K. E. (1991). Word recognition: Changing perspectives. In *Handbook of reading research* (Vol. 2, pp. 418–452). Hillsdale, NJ: Lawrence Erlbaum Associates.

Stanovich, K. E., Cunningham, A. E., & Feeman, D. J. (1984). Relation between early reading acquisition and word decoding with and without context: A longitudinal study of first-grade children. *Journal of Educational Psychology, 76*(4), 668–677.

Stanovich, K. E., Nathan, R. G., & Vala-Rossi, M. (1986). Developmental changes in the cognitive correlates of reading ability and the developmental lag hypothesis. *Reading Research Quarterly, 21*(3), 267–283.

Stanovich, K. E., & West, R. F. (1989). Exposure to print and orthographic processing. *Reading Research Quarterly, 24*, 402–433.

Steffens, M. L., Eilers, R. E., Gross-Glenn, K., & Jallad, B. (1992). Speech perception in adult subjects with familial dyslexia. *Journal of Speech and Hearing Research, 35*, 192–200.

Stein, J. (2001). The neurobiology of reading difficulties. In M. Wolf (Ed.), *Dyslexia, fluency and the brain* (pp. 3–21). Cambridge, MA: York Press.

Stein, J. F. (1989). Unfixed reference, monocular occlusion, and developmental dyslexia—a critique. *British Journal of Ophthalmology, 73*(4), 319–320.

Stein, J. F. (Ed.). (1991). *Vision and visual dysfunction: Vol. 13. Visual dyslexia.* London: Macmillan.

Stein, J. F. (1993). Visuospatial perception in disabled readers. In D. M. Willows, R. S. Kruk, & E. Corcos (Eds.), *Visual processes in reading and reading disabilities* (pp. 331–346). Hillsdale, NJ: Lawrence Erlbaum Associates.

Stein, J. F., & Fowler, S. (1985). Effect of monocular occlusion on visuomotor perception and reading in dyslexic children. *The Lancet, 2*, 69–73.

Stein, J. F., & McAnally, K. (1995). Auditory temporal processing in developmental dyslexics. *Irish Journal of Psychology, 16*(3), 220–228.

Stein, J. F., Riddell, P. M., & Fowler, M. S. (1987). Fine binocular control in dyslexic children. *Eye, 1*(Pt. 3), 433–438.

Stein, J. F., Riddell, P. M., & Fowler, M. S. (1988). Disordered vergence control in dyslexic children. *British Journal of Ophthalmology, 72*, 162–166.

Stein, J., & Talcott, J. (1999). Impaired neuronal timing in developmental dyslexia—the magnocelluar hypothesis. *Dyslexia, 5*(2), 59–77.

Stein, J., & Walsh, V. (1997). To see but not to read; the magnocellular theory of dyslexia. *Trends in Neurosciences, 20*(4), 147–152.

Sternberg, S. (1966). High-speed scanning in human memory. *Science, 153*(3736), 652–654.

Sterritt, G. M., & Rudnick, M. (1966). Auditory and visual rhythm perception in relation to reading ability in fourth grade boys. *Perceptual and Motor Skills, 22*(3), 859–864.

Stiles, J. (2000). Neural plasticity and cognitive development. *Developmental Neuropsychology, 18*(2), 237–272.

Stone, B., & Brady, S. (1995). Evidence for phonological processing deficits in less-skilled readers. *Annals of Dyslexia, 45*, 51–78.

Straub, K. A. (1997). *The production of prosodic cues and their role in the comprehension of syntactically ambiguous sentences.* Unpublished doctoral dissertation, University of Rochester, Rochester, NY.

Stringer, R., & Stanovich, K. E. (1998, March). *On the possibility of cerebellar involvement in reading disability.* Paper presented at the fourth conference of the Society for Scientific Studies of Reading, San Diego.

Stringer, R., & Stanovich, K. E. (2000). The connection between reaction time and variation in reading ability: Unravelling covariance relationships with cognitive ability and phonological sensitivity. *Scientific Studies of Reading, 4*(1), 41–53.

Studdert-Kennedy, M. G. (1997). Deficits in phoneme awareness do not arise from failures in rapid auditory processing. *Symposium on basic neural mechanisms in cognition and language with special reference to phonological problems in dyslexia.* Stockholm, Sweden.

Studdert-Kennedy, M. G., & Mody, M. (1995). Auditory temporal perception deficits in the reading impaired: A critical review of the evidence. *Psychonomic Bulletin and Review, 2*, 508–514.

Sunseth, K., & Bowers, P. G. (1997, March). *The relationship between digit naming speed and orthography in children with and without phonological deficits.* Paper presented to the meetings of the Society for the Scientific Study of Reading, Chicago.

Swanson, L. B. (1989). *Analyzing naming speed-reading relationships in children.* Unpublished doctoral dissertation, University of Waterloo, Waterloo, Ontario, Canada.

Swerts, M., & Geluykens, R. (1994). Prosody as a marker of information flow in spoken discourse. *Langauge and Speech, 37*, 21–43.

Talcott, J. B., Witton, C., McClean, M., Hansen, P. C., Rees, A., Green, G.G.R., & Stein, J. F. (1999). Can sensitivity to auditory frequency modulation predict children's phonological and reading skills? *Neuroreport, 10*(10), 2045–2050.

Tallal, P. (1980). Auditory temporal perception, phonics, and reading disabilities in children. *Brain and Language, 9*, 182–198.

Tallal, P. (1984). Temporal or phonetic processing deficit in dyslexia? That is the question. *Applied Psycholinguistics, 5*(2), 167–169.

Tallal, P. (1993). Neurobiological basis of speech: A case for the preeminence of temporal processing. In P. Tallal, A. M. Galaburda, R. R. Llinas, & C. von Eurler (Eds.), *Temporal information processing in the nervous system. Annals of the New York Academy of Sciences, 682*, 421–423.

Tallal, P., Curtiss, S., & Kaplan, R. (1988). The San Diego longitudinal study: Evaluating the outcomes of preschool impairment in language development. In S. E. Gerber & G. T.

Mencher (Eds.), *International perspectives on communication disorders* (pp. 86–126). Washington, DC: Gallaudet University Press.

Tallal, P., Miller, S., & Fitch, R. H. (1993). Neurobiological basis of speech: A case of the preeminence of temporal processing. In P. Tallal, A. M. Galaburda, R. R. Llinas, & C. von Eurler (Eds.), *Temporal information processing in the nervous system. Annals of the New York Academy of Sciences, 682*, 421–423.

Tallal, P., Miller, S., & Fitch, R. H. (1995). Neurobiological basis of speech: A case for the preeminence of temporal processing. *Irish Journal of Psychology, 16*(3), 194–219.

Tallal, P., & Piercy, M. (1974).Developmental aphasia: Rate of auditory processing and selective impairment of consonant perception. *Neuropsychologia, 12*(1), 83–93.

Tallal, P., & Piercy, M. (1975). Developmental aphasia: The perception of brief vowels and extended stop consonants. *Neuropsychologia, 13*(1), 69–74.

Tallal, P., & Piercy, M. (1979). Defects of auditory perception in children with developmental dysphasia. In M. A. Syke (Ed.), *Developmental dysphasia* (pp. 63–84). Orlando, FL: Academic Press.

Tallal, P., & Stark, R. E. (1982). Perceptual/motor profiles of reading impaired children with or without concomitant oral language deficits. *Annals of Dyslexia, 32*, 163–176.

Tallal, P., Stark, R., Kallman, C., & Mellits, D. (1981). A reexamination of some nonverbal perceptual abilities of language-impaired and normal children as a function of age and sensory modality. *Journal of Speech and Hearing Research, 24*(3), 351–357.

Tallal, P., Stark, R. E., & Mellits, D. (1985). Identification of language-impaired children on the basis of rapid perception and production skills. *Brain and Language, 25*(2), 314–322.

Tan, A., & Nicholson, T. (1997). Flashcards revisited: Training poor readers to read words faster improves their comprehension of text. *Journal of Educational Psychology, 59*, 276–288.

Taylor, M. J., & Keenan, N. K. (1990). Event related potentials to visual and language stimuli in normal and dyslexic children. *Psychophysiology, 27*, 318–327.

Taylor, M. J., & Keenan, N. K. (1999). ERPs to orthographic, phonological, and semantic tasks in dyslexic children with auditory processing impairment. *Developmental Neuropsychology, 15*(2), 307–326.

Temple, E., Poldrack, R. A., Protopapas, A., Nagarajan, S., Salz, T., Tallal, P., Merzenich, M., & Gabrieli, J.D.E. (2000). Disruption of the neural response to rapid acoustic stimuli in dyslexia: Evidence from functional MRI. *Proceedings of the National Academy of Sciences USA, 97*(25), 13907–13912.

Thompson, C. K. (2000). The neurobiology of language recovery in aphasia. *Brain and Language, 71*(1), 245–248.

Thompson, K. G., Hanes, D. P., Bichot, N. P., & Schall, J. D. (1996). Perceptual and motor processing stages identified in the activity of Macaque frontal eye field neurons during visual search. *Journal of Neurophysiology, 76*(6), 4040–4055.

Thompson-Schill, S. L., D'Esposito, M., Aquirre, G. K., & Farah, M. J. (1997). Role of left inferior prefrontal cortex in retrieval of semantic knowledge: A reevaluation. *Proceedings of the National Academy of Sciences USA, 94*, 14792–14797.

Thorndike, R. L., Hagen, E. P., & Sattler, J. M. (1986). *Stanford–Binet Intelligence Scale* (4th ed.). Itasca, IL: Riverside Publishing.

Thorpe, S., Fize, D., & Marlot, C. (1996). Speed of processing in the human visual system. *Nature, 381*(6582), 520–522.

Tobey, E. A., & Cullen, J. K. (1984). Temporal integration of tone glides by children with auditory-memory and reading problems. *Journal of Speech and Hearing Research, 27*(4), 527–533.

Tomblin, J. B., Freese, P. R., & Records, N. L. (1992). Diagnosing specific language impairment in adults for the purpose of pedigree analysis. *Journal of Speech and Hearing Research, 35*(4), 832–843.

Tonnquist-Uhlen, I. (1996). Topography of auditory evoked long-latency potentials in children with severe language impairment: The P2 and N2 components. *Ear and Hearing, 17*(4), 314–326.

Tonnquist-Uhlen, I., Borg, E., Persson, H. E., & Spens, K. E. (1996). Topography of auditory evoked cortical potentials in children with severe language impairment: The N1 component. *Electroencephalography and Clinical Neurophysiology: Evoked Potentials, 100*(3), 250–260.

Tootell, R. B., Hamilton, S. L., & Silverman, M. S. (1985). Topography of cytochrome oxidase activity in owl monkey cortex. *Journal of Neuroscience, 5*(10), 2786–2800.

Torgesen, J. K. (1985). Memory processes in reading disabled children. *Journal of Learning Disabilities, 18*(6), 350–357.

Torgesen, J. K. (2000). Individual differences in response to early interventions in reading: The lingering problem of treatment resisters. *Learning Disabilities Research and Practice, 15*(1), 55–64.

Torgesen, J., Rashotte, C., & Alexander, A. (2001). The prevention and remediation of reading fluency problems. In M. Wolf (Ed.), *Dyslexia, fluency and the brain* (pp. 333–355). Cambridge, MA: York Press.

Torgesen, J., Rashotte, C., & Wagner, R. (1997, November). *Research on instructional interventions for children with reading disabilities.* Paper presented at the International Dyslexia Association Conference, Chicago.

Travis, F. (1998). Cortical and cognitive development in 4th, 8th, and 12th grade students: The contribution of speed of processing and executive functioning to cognitive development. *Biological Psychology, 48*, 37–56.

Tunmer, W. E. (1989). The role of language-related factors in reading disability. In D. Shankweiler & I. Y. Liberman (Eds.), *Phonology and reading disability: Solving the reading puzzle. International Academy for Research in Learning Disabilities monograph series, No. 6* (pp. 91–131). Ann Arbor, MI: University of Michigan Press.

Tunmer, W. E., Pratt, C., & Herriman, M. L. (Eds.). (1984). *Metalinguistic awareness in children. Theory, research and implications.* Berlin: Springer-Verlag.

Tyler, C. W. (1990). A stereoscopic view of visual processing streams. *Vision Research, 30*(11), 1877–1895.

Tzeng, O., & Wang, W. S. (1984). Search for a common neurocognitive mechanism for language and movements. *American Journal of Physiology, 246*, 904–911.

Ungerleider, L. G., & Desimone, R. (1986). Cortical connections of visual area MT in the macaque. *Journal of Comparative Neurology, 248*(2), 190–222.

Van Daal, V., & Van der Leij, A. (1999). Developmental dyslexia: Related to specific or general deficits. *Annals of Dyslexia, 49*, 71–104.

Van den Bos, K. (1998). IQ, phonological awareness, and continuous-naming speed related to Dutch children's poor decoding performance on two word identification tests. *Dyslexia, 4,* 73–89.

Van den Bos, K. P., Zijlstra, B.J.H., & Spelberg, H. C. (2002). Life-span data on continuous-naming speeds of numbers, letters, colors, and pictured objects, and word-reading speed. *Scientific Studies of Reading, 6*(1), 25–49.

Van der Leij, A., & Van Daal, V.H.P. (1999). Automatization aspects of dyslexia: Speed limitations in word identification, sensitivity to increasing task demands, and orthographic compensation. *Journal of Learning Disabilities, 32*(5), 417–428.

Van Essen, D. C., Felleman, D. J., DeYoe, E. A., Olavarria, J., & Knierim, J. (1990). Modular and hierarchical organization of extrastriate visual cortex in the macaque monkey. *Cold Spring Harbor Symposia on Quantitative Biology, 55,* 679–696.

Vaughan, H. G., Jr., & Kurtzberg, D. (1992). Electrophysiologic indices of human brain maturation and cognitive development. In M. R. Gunnar & C. Nelson (Eds.), *Minnesota Symposia on Child Psychology* (Vol. 24, pp. 1–36). Hillsdale, NJ: Lawrence Erlbaum Associates.

Vellutino, F. R. (1987). Dyslexia. *Scientific American, 256* (March), 20–27.

Vellutino, F. R., Bentley, W. L., & Phillips, F. (1978). Inter- versus intra-hemispheric learning in dyslexic and normal readers. *Developmental Medicine and Child Neurology, 20*(1), 71–80.

Vellutino, F. R., & Scanlon, D. (1989). Auditory information processing in poor and normal readers. In J. J. Dumont & H. Nakken (Eds.), *Learning disabilities: Vol. 2. Cognitive, social and remedial aspects* (pp. 19–46). Amsterdam: Swets & Zeitlinger.

Vernon, P. A. (1987). New developments in reaction time research. In P. A. Vernon (Ed.), *Speed of information-processing and intelligence* (pp. 1–20). Westport, CT: Ablex.

Vernon, P. A. (1989). The heritability of measures of speed of information-processing. *Personality and Individual Differences, 10*(5), 573–576.

Vernon, P. A. (1990). An overview of chronometric measures of intelligence. *School Psychology Review, 19*(4), 399–410.

Vernon, P. A. (1993). Intelligence and neural efficiency. In D. K. Detterman (Ed.), *Individual differences and cognition: Current topics in human intelligence* (Vol. 3, pp. 171–187). Westport, CT: Ablex.

Vernon, P. A., & Mori, M. (1992). Intelligence, reaction times, and peripheral nerve conduction velocity. *Intelligence, 16*(3–4), 273–288.

Vernon, P. A., Nador, S., & Kantor, L. (1985). Reaction times and speed-of-processing: Their relationship to timed and untimed measures of intelligence. *Intelligence, 9*(4), 357–374.

Vigneau, F., Blanchet, L., Loranger, M., & Pepin, M. (2002). Response latencies measured on IQ tests: Dimensionality of speed indices and the relationship between speed and level. *Personality and Individual Differences, 33*(1), 165–182.

Vogel, S. A. (1983). A qualitative analysis of morphological ability in learning disabled and achieving children. *Journal of Learning Disabilities, 16*(7), 416–420.

Waber, D. P. (2001). Aberrations of timing in children with impaired reading: Cause or effect? In M. Wolf (Ed.), *Dyslexia, fluency and the brain* (pp. 103–125). Cambridge, MA: York Press.

Wagner, R. K., & Torgesen, J. K. (1987). The nature of phonological processing and its causal role in the acquisition of reading skills. *Psychological Bulletin, 101,* 192–212.

Wagner, R. K., Torgesen, J. K., Laughon, P. L., Simmons, K., & Rashotte, C. A. (1993). Development of young readers phonological processing abilities. *Journal of Educational Psychology, 85*, 83–103.

Wagner, R. K., Torgesen, J. K., & Rashotte, C. A. (1994). Development of reading-related phonological processing abilities: New evidence of bidirectional causality from a latent variable longitudinal study. *Developmental Psychology, 30*, 73–87.

Walsh, D., Price, G., & Gillingham, M. (1988). The critical but transitory importance of letter naming. *Reading Research Quarterly, 23*, 108–122.

Watson, B. U. (1992). Auditory temporal acuity in normally achieving and learning-disabled college students. *Journal of Speech and Hearing Research, 35*, 148–156.

Watson, B. U., & Miller, T. K. (1993). Auditory perception. phonological processing, and reading ability/disability. *Journal of Speech and Hearing Research, 36*, 850–863.

Watson, B. U., & Watson, C. S. (1993). Auditory perception, phonological processing and reading ability/disability. In P. Tallal, A. M. Galaburda, R. R. Llinas, & C. von Eurler (Eds.), *Temporal information processing in the nervous system. Annals of the New York Academy of Sciences, 682*, 421–423.

Webster, P. E. (1994). Linguistic factors in reading disability: A model for assessing children who are without overt language impairment. *Child Language Teaching and Therapy, 10*(3), 259–281.

Wechsler, D. (1994). *Wechsler Intelligence Scale for Adults (WAIS–3)*. Winsor: NFER.

Wechsler, D. (1974). *Wechsler Intelligence Scale for Children—Revised (WISC–R)*. Winsor: NFER.

Weiler, M. D., Forbes, P., Kirkwood, M., & Waber, D. (2003). The development course of processing speed in children with and without learning disabilities. *Journal of Experimental Child Psychology, 85*(2), 178–194.

Weiler, M. D., Harris, N. S., Marcus, D. H., Bellinger, D., Kosslyn, S., & Waber, D. P. (2000). Speed of information processing in children referred for learning problems as measured by a visual filtering test. *Journal of Learning Disabilities, 33*, 538–550.

Whatmough, C., Arguin, M., & Bub, D. (1999). Cross-modal priming evidence for phonology-to-orthography activation in visual word recognition. *Brain and Language, 66*(2), 275–293.

White, S. (1995). Listening to children read aloud: Oral fluency. *NAEPFacts*. National Center for Education Statistics, U.S. Department of Education.

Whitney, P. (1986). Developmental trends in speed of semantic memory retrieval. *Developmental Review, 6*(1), 57–79.

Whiton, M. B., Singer, D. L., & Cook, H. (1975). Sensory integration skills as predictors of reading acquisition. *Journal of Reading Behavior, 7*(1), 79–89.

Wickens, C. D. (1974). Temporal limits of human information processing: A developmental study. *Psychological Bulletin, 81*(11), 739–755.

Wiegel-Crump, C. A., & Dennis, M. (1986). Development of word-finding. *Brain and Language, 27*(1), 1–23.

Wiig, E. H., Semel, E. M., & Crouse, M. A. (1973). The use of English morphology by high-risk and learning disabled children. *Journal of Learning Disabilities, 6*(7), 457–465.

Wiig, E. H., Zureich, P., & Chan, H.N.H. (2000). A clinical rationale for assessing rapid automatized naming in children with language disorders. *Journal of Learning Disabilities, 33*(4), 359–374.

Williams, M., LeCluyse, K., & Bologna, N. (1990). Masking by light as a measure of visual integration time and persistence in normal and disabled readers. *Clinical Vision Science, 5,* 335–343.

Williams, M., Molinet, K., & LeCluyse, K. (1989). Visual masking as a measure of temporal processing in normal and disabled readers. *Clinical Visual Science, 4,* 137–144.

Williams, M. C., & Bologna, N. B. (1985). Perceptual grouping in good and poor readers. *Perception and Psychophysics, 38*(4), 367–374.

Williams, M. C., & LeCluyse, K. (1990). Perceptual consequences of a temporal processing deficit in reading disabled children. *Journal of American Optometric Association, 61*(2), 111–121.

Willows, D. M., Kruk, R., & Corcos, E. (1993). Are there differences between disabled and normal readers in their processing of visual information? In D. M. Willows, R. S. Kruk, & E. Corcos (Eds.), *Visual processes in reading and reading disabilities* (pp. 265–285). Hillsdale, NJ: Lawrence Erlbaum Associates.

Wilson, G. F., Swain, C. R., & Ullsperger, P. (1998). ERP components elicited in response to warning stimuli: The influence of task difficulty. *Biological Psychology, 47,* 137–158.

Wimmer, H. (1993). Characteristics of developmental dyslexia in a regular writing system. *Applied Psycholinguistics, 14,* 1–33.

Wimmer, H. (1996). The nonword reading deficit in developmental dyslexia: Evidence from children learning to read German. *Journal of Experimental Child Psychology, 61*(1), 80–90.

Wimmer, H., Mayringer, H., & Landerl, K. (1998). Poor reading: A deficit in skill-automatization or a phonological deficit? *Scientific Studies of Reading, 2*(4), 321–340.

Wingfield, A., Lindfield, K. C., & Goodglass, H. (2000). Effects of age and hearing sensitivity on the use of prosodic information in spoken word recognition. *Journal of Speech, Language, and Hearing Research, 43,* 915–925.

Winters, R. L., Patterson, R., & Shontz, W. (1989). Visual persistence and adult dyslexia. *Journal of Learning Disabilities, 22,* 641–645.

Wise, R.J.S., Scott, S. K., Blank, S. C., Mummery, C. J., Murphy, K., & Warburton, E. A. (2001). Separate neural sub-systems within "Wernicke's area." *Brain, 124*(1), 83–95.

Wolf, M. (1982). The word retrieval process and reading in children and aphasics. In K. Nelson (Ed.), *Children's language* (pp. 437–493). Hillsdale, NJ: Lawrence Erlbaum Associates.

Wolf, M. (1986). Rapid alternating stimulus naming in the developmental dyslexias. *Brain and Language, 27,* 360–379.

Wolf, M. (1991). Naming speed and reading: The contribution of the cognitive neurosciences. *Reading Research Quarterly, 26,* 123–141.

Wolf, M. (1997). A provisional, integrative account of phonological and naming-speed deficits in dyslexia: Implications for diagnosis and intervention. In B. Blachman (Ed.), *Foundations of reading acquisition and dyslexia* (pp. 67–92). Hillsdale, NJ: Lawrence Erlbaum Associates.

Wolf, M. (1999). What time may tell: Towards a new conceptualization of developmental dyslexia. *Annals of Dyslexia, 49,* 3–27.

Wolf, M. (2001). *Dyslexia, fluency and the brain.* Cambridge, MA: York Press.

Wolf, M., Bally, H., & Morris, R. (1986). Automaticity, retrieval processes, and reading: A longitudinal study in average and impaired readers. *Child Development, 57,* 988–1000.

Wolf, M., & Biddle, K. (1997). The double-deficit hypothesis for developmental dyslexia: The role of timing in the reading process. *Learning Disabilities Network Exchange, 15*, 1–5.

Wolf, M., & Bowers, P. G. (1999). The double-deficit hypothesis for the developmental dyslexias. *Journal of Educational Psychology 91*, 415–438.

Wolf, M., & Bowers, P. (2000). The question of naming-speed deficits in developmental reading disability: An introduction to the double-deficit hypothesis. *Journal of Learning Disabilities, 33*, 322–324.

Wolf, M., Bowers, P. G., & Biddle, K. (2000). Naming-speed processes, timing, and reading: A conceptual review. *Journal of Learning Disabilities, 33*(4), 387–407.

Wolf, M., & Goodglass, H. (1986). Dyslexia, dysnomia, and lexical retrieval: A longitudinal investigation. *Brain and Language, 28*, 154–168.

Wolf, M., & Katzir-Cohen, T. (2001). Reading fluency and its intervention. *Scientific Studies of Reading, 5*(3), 211–238.

Wolf, M., Miller, L., & Donnelly, K. (2000). Retrieval, automaticity, vocabulary elaboration, orthography (RAVE-O): A comprehensive, fluency-based reading intervention program. *Journal of Learning Disabilities, 33*(4), 375–386.

Wolf, M., & Obregon, M. (1989, April). *Eighty eight children in search of a name: A 5 year investigation of rate, word retrieval, and vocabulary in reading development and dyslexia.* Paper presented at the meeting of the Society for Research in Child Development, Kansas City, MO.

Wolf, M., & Obregon, M. (1992). Early naming deficits, developmental dyslexia, and a specific deficit hypothesis. *Brain and Language, 42*, 219–247.

Wolf, M., & Obregon, M. (1997). Naming-speed deficits and the "double deficit" hypothesis: Implications for diagnosis and practice in reading disabilities. In L. Putnam & S. Stahl (Eds.), *Readings on language and literacy* (pp. 177–210). Cambridge, MA: Brookline.

Wolf, M., Vellutino, F., & Gleason, J. B. (1998). A psycholinguistic account of reading. In J. B. Gleason & N. Bernstein Ratner (Eds.), *Psycholinguistics* (2nd ed., pp. 409–451). New York: Harcourt Brace.

Wolff, P. H. (1993). Impaired temporal resolution in developmental dyslexia. In P. Tallal, A. M. Galaburda, R. R. Llinas, & C. von Eurler (Eds.), *Temporal information processing in the nervous system. Annals of the New York Academy of Sciences, 682*, 87–103.

Wolff, P. H. (2000a). Impaired temporal resolution in developmental dyslexia. *Annals of the New York Academy of Sciences, 682*, 87–103.

Wolff, P. H. (2000b). Timing precision and rhythm in developmental dyslexia. *Reading and Writing, 15*(1–2), 179–206.

Wolff, P. H., Michel, G. F., & Ovrut, M. (1990). The timing of syllable repetitions in developmental dyslexia. *Journal of Speech and Hearing Research, 33*, 281–289.

Wood, F. B., & Felton, R. H. (1994). Separate linguistic and developmental factors in the development of reading. *Topics in Language Disorders, 14*, 42–57.

Yap, R., & Van der Leij, A. (1993a). Rate of elementary symbol processing in dyslexics. In S. F. Wright & R. Groner (Eds.), *Facets of dyslexia and its remediation* (pp. 337–348). Amsterdam: Elsevier.

Yap, R., & Van der Leij, A. (1993b). Word processing in dyslexics. An automatic decoding deficit? *Reading and Writing, 5*, 261–279.

Yap, R. L., & Van der Leij, A. (1994). Testing the automatization deficit hypothesis of dyslexia via a dual—task paradigm. *Journal of Learning Disabilities, 27*(10), 660–665.

Yingling, C. D., Galin, D., Fein, G., Peltzman, D., & Davenport, L. (1986). Neurometrics does not detect "pure" dyslexics. *Electroencephalography and Clinical Neurophysiology, 63*(5), 426–430.

Young, A., & Bowers, P. (1995). Individual differences and text difficulty determinants of reading fluency and expressiveness. *Journal of Experimental Child Psychology, 60,* 428–454.

Young, A., Bowers, P., & MacKinnon, G. (1996). Effects of prosodic modeling and repeated reading on poor readers' fluency and comprehension. *Applied Psycholinguistics, 17,* 59–84.

Zaidel, E. (1983). A response to Gazzaniga: Language in the right hemisphere, convergent perspectives. *American Psychologist, 38*(5), 542–546.

Zaidel, E., & Schweiger, A. (1985). Right hemisphere reading: A case of "deja vu." *Behavioral and Brain Sciences, 8*(2), 365–367.

Zatorre, R. J., Evans, A. C., Meyer, E., & Gjedde, A. (1992). Lateralization of phonetic and pitch discrimination in speech processing. *Science, 256*(5058), 846–849.

Zbrodoff, N. J., & Logan, G. D. (1986). On the autonomy of mental processes: A case study of arithmetic. *Journal of Experimental Psychology: General, 115,* 118–130.

Zecker, S. G. (1991). The orthographic code: Developmental trends in reading-disabled and normally-achieving children. *Annals of Dyslexia, 41,* 178–192.

Zurif, E. B., & Carson, G. (1970). Dyslexia in relation to cerebral dominance and temporal analysis. *Neuropsychologia, 8,* 351–361.

Author Index

Note: The letter *n* following a page number denotes a footnote.

A

Aaron, P. G., 112
Abbott, R. D., 67, 223
Ackerman, P. T., xiii, 67, 79, 81, 179, 180, 181
Adams, M. J., xiii, 17, 35, 36, 42, 83, 99
Adams, M. M., 219, 233
Aharon, Y., 27
Ahonen, T., 126
Aksoomoff, N. A., 47
Alexander, A. W., 5, 149
Allen, M., 173, 176
Alsdorf, B. J., 67
Amir, Y., 106, 107
Anderson, J. R., 40
Anderson, J. W., 171
Anderson, M., 97, 99
Anderson, R. C., 3
Andreason, P., 145, 146
Andrews, D., 171, 215
Angleitner, A., 91, 95, 97
Anllo-Vento, L., 173, 179
Anslow, P., 146
Apel, K., 139, 148
Apthorp, H. S., 149

Aquino, T., 145, 146
Aquirre, G. K., 219
Archer, R., 117
Arguin, M., 197
Armstrong, E., xii, xiii, xiv
Arnett, J. L., 114
Aro, M., 126
Atkins, P., 197
Atkinson, R. C., 90
Aylward, E. H., 222, 223

B

Baddeley, A. D., 11, 62, 81, 149
Badian, N. A., xii, xiv, 67
Baker, L. A., 97
Baldeweg, T., 182
Balgor, A., 228
Bally, H., 45, 67, 69, 155
Barch, D. M., 219
Barker, T. A., xii
Barnea, A., 179, 180
Barry, R. J., 171
Bartha, M. C., 124
Barthelemy, C., 175*n*

Bartling, J., 143, 148, 182
Bassich, C., 136, 142, 143
Baumeister, A. A., 94
Baumgartner, J. E., 218
Belitz, S., 182, 183, 224
Belmont, I., 196
Belmont, L., 195, 196
Ben-Dror, I., xii, xiv, 11, 154, 155, 227
Bentin, S., xii, 87, 170, 171
Bentley, W. L., 196
Bergman, E., 221
Berko, C., 138, 141
Berman, L., xiv, 9, 231
Berman, R. A., 26
Bernal, J., 174, 180
Berninger, V. W., 8, 43, 66, 125, 222, 223
Berry, C., 196
Berry, G., 113
Besson, M., 181
Best, C. T., 102, 103
Bhadha, B., xiv, 79, 80, 124
Bichot, N. P., 111
Biddle, K. R., xiii, xiv, 67, 73, 86, 101
Biemiller, A., 9, 10, 13
Birch, H. G., 195, 196
Birnboim, S., 27
Biscaldi, M., 121
Bitan, T., 220
Bjaalid, I. K., xii, 123, 125
Blachman, B. A., 43, 137
Black, K., 85
Blackwell, S. L., 113, 117
Blanchet, L., 95
Blank, M., 196
Blinkhorn, S. F., 96
Bobbitt, B., 95
Boden, C., 115, 119, 124
Bois, S. J., 37
Bolger, D. J., 238
Bologna, N., 117, 122
Boomsma, D. I., 91, 95, 96, 97
Booth, J. R., 11, 197
Borden, S. L., 125
Borg, E., 173, 177
Borkenau, P., 91, 95, 97
Borstel, M., 183

Botuck, S., 196
Botvinivk, M. M., 219
Bouchard, T. J., 97
Bouma, H., 118
Bowers, P. G., xii, xiii, xiv, 1, 5, 15, 42, 43, 45, 67, 68, 77, 78, 79, 80, 82, 83, 84, 85, 100, 101, 124, 125, 238
Bowey, J. A., 11, 12
Bowlby, M., 148
Brady, D. R., 146
Brady, L., 148
Brady, S. A., 137, 139, 141, 148, 149
Brandeis, D. L., 171, 181
Brandt, J., 139
Brannan, J. R., 116, 172
Braver, T. S., 219
Brecel, J., 173
Breen, K., 76
Breier, J. I., 218, 221
Breitmeyer, B. G., 101, 108, 120
Breznitz, Z., xi, xii, xiii, xiv, xv, 1, 3, 4, 8, 9, 13, 17, 18, 20, 21, 22, 23, 25, 26, 27, 28, 29, 30, 33, 35, 59, 60, 63, 84, 87, 88, 99, 101, 102, 104, 154, 155, 156, 168, 184, 187, 194, 200, 206, 207, 211, 212, 213, 215, 216, 217, 220, 225, 226, 227, 228, 229, 230, 231, 233, 236, 238
Briand, K., 113
Bridger, W. H., 196
Brodeur, D. A., 115, 119, 124
Brooks, D. J., 47
Brown, G. L., 136, 142, 143
Brown, I. S., 75, 76
Brown, S. C., 94
Bruck, M., xii, xiv, 1, 113, 117, 122
Bruneau, N., 175n
Brunswick, N., xiv, 145, 173, 174, 174n
Bryson, S. E., 118
Bub, D., 197
Buckley, J., 172
Bulau, P., 220
Bullier, J., 107
Butler, I. I., 218
Butterfield, S., 55
Butterworth, B., 56

C

Calfee, R. C., 43, 112
Calvert, G. A., 198
Cameron, K. D., 117
Campbell, S. K., 75
Cancelli, A. A., 95
Carlisle, J. F., 10, 11, 99
Carlson, K., 53, 54
Carrell, T. D., 134
Carroll, P. J., 51, 55, 59, 62
Carson, G., 142
Carter, C. S., 219
Carver, R. P., xii, 9, 16, 99
Cassens, G., 96
Castillo, E. M., 221
Cattell, M., 2
Catts, H. W., 99, 139, 148, 149
Cavanagh, P., 108, 113, 117, 122
Ceponiene, R., 175n, 183
Cerella, J., 91
Chabot, R. J., xiii, 11
Chafe, W., 64
Chall, J. S., 2
Chan, H. N. H., 69, 70
Chapman, S., 138, 141
Chatillon, M., 139, 149
Chatterjee, A., 76
Chattopadhyay, A. K., 178, 179
Chawla, D., 220
Chayna, J. D., xiv
Cheney, M. K., 146
Cheng, J. C., 180, 181
Cheour, M., 175n
Chesney, G. L., 172
Chi, M. T., 97, 98, 99
Chiang, B., 3, 13
Childs, M. K., 97
Chomsky, N., 50, 53
Cirilo, R. K., 15
Clark, E., 55
Clark, H., 55
Clark, W., 70
Clifton, C., 53, 54
Coffey, S. A., 172, 173, 176, 178, 179, 181
Cohen, H., 51, 61
Cohen, J. D., 39, 40, 219
Cohen, M., 85
Cohen, R., 145, 146
Collier, R., 55
Collins, M., 64
Collins, V. L., 3, 5
Coltheart, M., 197
Coltheart, V., 62
Compton, D. L., xiv, 10, 11, 99
Conners, F. A., 120, 121
Conrad, C., 6
Constable, R. T., 146, 198, 234
Constantinou, J. E., 218
Cook, H., 196
Corcos, E., 112, 119
Corina, D., 223
Cornelissen, P. L., 148
Cornwall, A., 76, 77
Costa, L. D., 102, 103
Courchesne, E., 47, 173, 176
Coyle, S. F., 171
Crain, S., 10
Cramer, S. C., 222, 223
Crockett, D. J., 96
Cromer, R. F., 14
Crouse, M. A., xii
Crowder, R., 57
Csepe, V., 182
Cudahy, E. A., 136, 142, 143
Cullen, J. K., 143
Cunningham, A. E., xii, 15
Curtis, B., 197
Curtis, M. E., 15
Curtiss, S., 100, 134
Custodio, R., 5
Cutler, A., 55, 58

D

Dager, S. R., 223
Dahan, D., 58
Davenport, L., 174, 174n
Davidson, J., 94
Davidson, R. J., 102, 103
Davies, D., 95
Davis, A. E., 102

Davis, H., 99
Davis, J., 67, 72, 75, 82
Davis, R. N., 221
Dawson, G., 173, 175
de-Geus, E. J. C., 91, 95, 96, 97
De Soto, C. B., 3, 14
De Soto, J. L., 3, 14
De Vellis, R. F., 98
De Weirdt, W., 137, 139, 142, 147
Dean, P., 46, 47, 86
Deary, I. J., 95
Decety, J., 47
Dechert, H., 63
DeFries, D. J., xiv
Deimel, W., 143, 148, 182
Deiring, S., 178, 179
DeMarco, T., 18, 25
Demb, J. B., 145, 146
Denckla, M. B., 45, 66, 67, 155, 179
Dennis, M., 12
Deno, S. L., 3, 13
D'Entremont, B., 113
Desimone, R., 110
D'Esposito, M., 219
Deutsch, A., xii
Deutsch, M., 196
DeYoe, E. A., 107
Di Lollo, V., 112, 113, 114, 115, 117
Diaz-Comas, L., 180
Dijkstra, T., 197
Dodgen, C. E., 121
Doehring, D. G. G., 2, 10, 11, 12, 15
Doi, L., xiv, 79, 80, 124
Don, N. S., 171
Donchin, E., 172
Donnelly, K., 44
Donohue, B. C., 146
Dow, R. S., 47, 48
Dowhower, S. L., 51, 59
Downey, D. M., 5, 67
Drasdo, N., 117, 119
Drislane, F. W., 101, 121, 123, 133, 173
Dugas, J. L., 98
Dumais, S. T., 37
Dunbar, K., 39, 40
Duncan, C. C., 179

Dunlap, W. P., 116
Dunn, B. R., 171, 215
Dunn, D. A., 171, 215
Dykman, R. A., xiii, 67, 79, 81, 179, 180, 181

E

Early, F., 112
Echelard, D. R., 223
Eden, G. F., 117, 123, 144, 146
Edmonds, J. E., 85
Egan, D. E., 98
Ehri, L. C., 2, 5, 43, 124, 125
Eilers, R. E., 139, 140
Eklund, K. M., 183
Elbert, T., 183
Elbro, C., 148
Eliopulos, D., 85
Elliott, L. L., 98, 134
Ellis, N. C., 11, 82
Enns, J. T., 118
Epstein, R., 179, 180
Epstein, W., 58, 62, 63
Erez, A., 179, 180
Eriksson, L., 47
Eulitz, C., 183
Evans, A. C., 146
Evans, B. J. W., 117, 119
Eysenck, H. J., 97

F

Facoetti, A., 121, 122
Fahle, M., 122
Farah, M. J., 219
Farmer, M. E., xiv, 84, 85, 101, 113, 118, 133, 138
Fawcett, A. J., xii, xiv, 45, 46, 47, 48, 70, 79, 86, 100, 136, 137, 146, 178, 179
Feeman, D. J., 15
Fein, G., 174, 174n
Feldman, J. F., 91
Feldstein, S., 60
Felleman, D. J., 106, 107

Felton, R. H., xii, xiii, xiv, 4, 5, 69, 70, 75, 76, 225
Fernandez, T., 174, 180
Fernandez-Bouzas, A., 174, 180
Ferreira, F., 56
Feur, D., 97
Ficarra, A. P., 172
Field, K. M., 222, 223
Fields, H., 142
Fiez, J. A., 146
Finger, E., 68, 69
Finkel, D., 95, 97
Finley, C., 173, 175
Fischer, B., 121
Fisher, D. F., 118
Fisk, A. D., 37, 39
Fitch, R. H., 100, 133, 134, 141
Fitzgerald, M., 221
Fitzgerald, P. G., 172
Fize, D., 111, 112
Fleer, R. E., 98
Fleischer, L. S., 14
Fletcher, J. M., 70, 146, 198, 221, 234
Flor, R. F., 43
Foale, C., 182
Fodor, J. A., 24, 55
Folds-Bennett, T. H., 97
Foorman, B. R., 145, 221
Ford, M. E., 95
Forster, K. I., 15, 55, 56
Foss, D. J., 15
Fowler, M. S., 117, 123
Fox, P. T., 146
Fox Tree, J. E., 54
Frackowiak, R. S. J., 47
Frankel, G. W., 98
Frankfurter, A., 118
Frankish, C., 144
Frauenfelder, U. H., 197
Frazier, L., 53, 54
Frederiksen, J. R., 10, 12
Freedman, S. E., 15
Freese, P. R., 133
Frijters, J. C., xiv
Friston, K. J., 220
Frith, C. D., xiv, 47, 145

Frith, U., xii, xiii, xiv, 145, 146
Fritz, J., 132
Frost, R., xii, 197
Frost, S. J., 146
Fry, A. F., 94
Fuchs, D., 3, 4, 13, 14
Fuchs, L. S., 3, 4, 13, 14
Fuchter, I., 183
Fulbright, R. K., 146, 198, 234

G

Gabrieli, J. D. E., 145, 146, 224
Galaburda, A. M., 85, 101, 113, 117, 121, 123, 133, 135, 173
Galan, L., 174, 180
Galin, D., 174, 174n
Gallagher, A. M., xii, xiii, xiv, 146
Gallagher, J. D., 98, 99
Gamzu, E., 70, 116, 138
Garrett, M. F., 55, 63
Garzia, R. P., 121, 133, 134, 173
Gatenby, C., 234
Gatenby, J. C., 198
Gathercole, S. E., 149
Gayan, J., xiv
Geary, D. C., 94
Gee, J., 53
Geffen, G. M., 95, 97
Geffen, L. B., 95, 97
Geiger, G., 122, 123
Geluykens, R., 56
Gentry, B. F., 139, 148
Gersons-Wolfensberger, D. C., xii, 36
Geschwind, N., 66
Giard, M. H., 198
Giedd, J. N., 146
Gillingham, M., 68
Gillispie, M., 99
Gjedde, A., 146
Gladstone, M., 102, 103
Gleason, J. B., 125
Godfrey, J. J., 139, 148
Goffman, L., 52
Goldberg, E., 102, 103

Golden, J., 78, 80, 124, 125
Goldman-Eisler, F., 56, 59, 63, 64
Goldman-Rakic, P. S., 132
Gonzalez, J. J., 85
Good, R. H., xiii, 5, 7
Goodglass, H., 57, 67, 72, 80
Goolkasian, P., 112, 119
Gore, J. C., 146, 198, 234
Gormley, W., 218
Goswami, U., 145
Gough, P. B., 9, 25
Goulandris, N., 148
Graham, N. A., 103
Graves, K., xii, 125
Green, G. G. R., 145
Greenberg, S. V., 59
Greene, B. A., 9, 10, 11
Greimme, A. C., 222, 223
Grinvald, A., 107
Grogan, S. C., 112
Grosjean, F. H., 53, 63, 64
Grosjean, L., 53
Gross-Glenn, K., 139, 140
Guerin, P., 175n
Guerrero, V., 174
Gulyas, B., 111
Gurzelier, J., 182

H

Habib, M., 181
Hackley, S. A., 171
Hagoort, P., 183
Hakerem, G., 18, 25
Hale, S., 90, 91, 92, 93, 94
Haley, S., 94
Halgren, E., 171
Hall, J., 85
Hall, L. K., 71
Hall, R., 114
Halle, M., 53
Haller, M., 197
Halme, T. J., 101
Halperin, J. H., 122
Hamburger, S. D., 145, 146, 179
Hamilton, S. L., 107

Hammer, M. A., 134
Hammond, G. R., 102
Hanes, D. P., 110, 111
Hansen, P. C., 145, 148
Hanson, D., 112, 113, 115, 117
Harel, M., 106, 107
Hari, R., 138, 145, 199
Harmony, T., 174, 180
Harms, L., 173, 176
Harn, B. A., xiii, 7
Harpaz, R., 23
Harris, G. J., 98
Harris, T., 48
Hart, J. 't, 55
Hart, L. A., 5, 69
Harter, M. R., 75, 173, 178, 179
Hash, T., 173
Hayduk, S., 113, 117, 122
Hayes, E. A., 198
Hays, T. A., 9, 10, 11
Heilman, K. M., 149
Heim, S., 183
Helenius, P., 145
Hendrickson, D. E., 96
Hennighausen, K., 173
Herrera, J. A., 96
Herriman, M. L., xii
Hess, A. M., 12, 15
Hill, R., 112, 119, 120
Hillyard, S. A., 171, 215
Ho, H., 97
Hockley, R., 117
Hodges, R., 48
Hoffman, J. V., 3
Hoffman, L. D., 226
Hogaboam, T. W., 4, 11, 12, 14, 38, 68, 69
Hoien, T., xii, 11, 123, 125
Holcomb, P. J., 79, 172, 173, 176, 178, 179,
   180, 181
Hollingsworth, P. M., 3, 4
Holmes, D. L., 13
Holt, L. K., xii, 125
Horwitz, B., 146
Hosp, M. K., 4
Howell, P., 148
Hubel, D. H., 108

Hudson, R., 4
Huey, S. E., 2
Humphrey, D. G., 172
Hutchinson, A., 125
Hutner, N., 103
Hynd, G. W., 85

I

Ingvar, D. H., 47
Isaacs, M. E., 3
Israel, J. B., 172
Ito, M., 47, 48
Itzhak, Y., 225

J

Jackson, M. D., 10, 11
Jaffe, J., 60
Jallad, B., 139, 140
Jankowski, J. J., 91
Jansen, J., 93, 94
Jarrat, J. A., 178, 179
Jasper, H. H., 185
Jenkins, I. H., 47
Jenkins, J. R., 4, 14
Jenkins, W. M., 85, 134, 135
Jenner, A. R., 123, 146, 198
Jensen, A. R., 92, 95
Jensen, C. R., 124
Jessie, K. A., 94
Jezzard, P., 219, 233
Johannes, S., 179
Johnson, R., 171
Johnston, P., 85
Johnstone, S. J., 171
Josee, D., 51, 61
Joseph, J., 146

K

Kaas, J. H., 107
Kahn, D., 196
Kail, R. V., 71, 90, 91, 92, 93, 94, 99, 192

Kalat, J. W., 108, 109
Kallman, C., 100
Kame'enui, E. J., xiii, 7
Kamhi, G. A., 139, 148
Kandler, R. H., 178, 179
Kantor, L., 95
Kaplan, E., 67
Kaplan, R., 100, 134
Karma, K., 183
Karni, A., 219, 220, 233
Katz, L., 15, 146, 197, 198, 234
Katz, P. A., 196
Katzir, T., 86
Katzir-Cohen, T., xiv, 7
Kaufmann, J., 183
Kazmerski, V., 180
Keating, D. P., 95
Keating, P., 148
Keenan, N. K., 178, 179
Kehoe, M. M., 52
Kellas, G., 97, 98
Kelly, M. H., 55
Kennedy, A., 78, 124, 125
Kerr, B., 94
Kershner, J. G., 103
Kidder, H. C., 136, 137
Kiebel, S., 220
Kiesila, P., 138
Kimball, J., 55
Kimelman, M. D. Z., 51, 56
Kincade, K. M., 9, 10, 11
King, C., 145, 146
King, J., 112, 119
Kinsborne, M., 70, 116, 138
Kintsch, W., 16
Klahr, D., 98
Klein, D., 146
Klein, R. K., xiv, 84, 85, 101, 113, 118, 133, 138
Klein, W., 64
Knierim, J. J., 106, 107
Knox, C. M., 139, 148
Knutson, N., 5
Koenig, O., 112, 118, 119
Korhonen, T., xiv, 70
Koriat, A., 59

Kosslyn, S. M., 112, 118, 119
Kramer, A. F., 172
Kranzler, J. H., 95
Kraus, N., 198
Kreiner, H., 59
Kremenak, S., 196
Kruk, R., 112, 119
Kuhlman, E. S., 196
Kuhn, M. R., 59
Kujala, T., 182, 183, 224
Kurtzberg, D., 172
Kusnir, T., 220
Kutas, M., 183

L

Laasonen, M., 101
LaBerge, D., 2, 6, 36, 38, 40, 42, 43, 69, 115n
Lacadie, C. M., 146, 198, 234
Lagae, L., 111
Lambe, E. K., 226
Lamm, O., 179, 180
Lamprecht-Dinnesen, A., 183
Landerl, K., xiv, 47, 79, 119, 148
Lane, H., 4, 53
Languis, M. L., 138, 141, 171, 215
Lashley, K. S., 62
Laughon, P. L., 76, 148
Laxon, V., xii, xiii, xiv
LeCluyse, K., 117, 118, 122, 134
Lee, J. R., 146
Lefly, D. L., xiv, 1, 152
Legein, Ch. P., 118
Leggio, M. G., 146
Lehmann, D., 171
Lehmkuhle, S., 173
Leiken, M., xiv, 3, 6, 18, 25, 26, 27, 187, 226, 229, 231
Leiner, A. L., 47, 48
Leiner, H. C., 47, 48
Leinonen, S., 126
Lemoine, H. E., 125
Lentgeb, S., 110
Leonard, L. B., 58, 62, 99
Leppänen, P. H. T., 126, 174, 182
Lesgold, A. M., 15

Leslie, S. C., 103
Lester, K., 125
Lettvin, J. Y., 122, 123
Levelt, W. J. M., 63
Leventhal, A. G., 110
Levesque, M., 200
Levi, G., 172
Levine, G., 92
Levitt, J. B., 107
Levy, B. A., xiv, 125
Lewis, D., 141
Lewis, J. L., 6
Lewis, V. J., 11
Lewy, A., 173, 175
Lezak, M. D., 155
Liberman, A. M., 146, 198, 234
Liberman, I. Y., xii, xiii, 145, 147
Liberman, P., 139, 149
Lieberman, M., 53, 64
Liederman, J., 103
Lincoln, A. J., 173, 176
Lind-Blad, F., 134, 141
Lindfield, K. C., 57
Livingstone, M. S., 101, 108, 109, 113, 117, 121, 123, 133, 135, 173
Llinas, R., 86, 102, 103, 135
Logan, G. D., 37, 38, 41
Loranger, M., 95
Lovegrove, W. J., 101, 110, 112, 113, 114, 117, 119, 120, 121, 133, 134
Lovett, M. W., xiv, 45, 77, 78, 125
Lovrich, D., 179, 180, 181
Luciano, M., 95, 97
Luck, S. J., 171, 215
Ludlow, C. L., 136, 142, 143
Lumer, E. D., 220
Lund, J. S., 107
Lundberg, I., xii, 11, 123, 125
Lykken, D. T., 97
Lyon, G. R., xiii, 225
Lyytinen, H., 126, 174, 183

M

MacDonald, B., 200
Macetti, G. G., 121, 122

Macht, M., 172
Mackay, D. G., 39, 40
MacKinnon, G., 43
Mackworth, H. N., 10, 11
Mackworth, J. F., 10, 11
MacWhinney, B., 11, 197
Maggioa, W. W., 218
Maisog, J. M., 146
Maisto, A. A., 94
Malach, R., 106, 107
Malloch, F. J., 141
Malonek, D., 107
Mancias, P., 218
Mangun, G. R., 179
Manis, F. R., xii, xiv, 5, 73, 79, 80, 124, 125, 148
Mann, V. A., 82, 139, 148
Maravilla, K. R., 223
Marchione, K. E., 146, 198, 234
Marcus, S., 144
Marlot, C., 111, 112
Marosi, E., 174, 180
Marro, K., 223
Marshall, C. M., 80
Martin, F., 113, 117
Martin, J. G., 58, 61, 62
Martin, N. G., 95, 97
Martin, R. C., 124
Marzola, V., 121, 122
Mason, J. M., 3
Mason, M., 10, 118
Matulat, P., 183
Mauer, D., 139, 148
Maunsell, J. H., 108, 111
Maxwell, L., 3, 13, 14
May, J. G., 112, 116, 119
Mayada, E., 51, 61
Mayringer, H., xiv, 47, 79, 119
Mazer, S. R., 117
McAnally, K., 99, 101
McBride-Chang, C., 73, 148
McCauley, C., 95, 97–98
McClean, M., 145
McClelland, J. L., xi, 10, 11, 25, 39, 40, 84, 196, 200
McClelland, R. J., 173, 174n

McCord, G., 11
McCrory, E., xiv, 145
McCroskey, R. L., 136, 137
McDonough, E. B., 171
McGivern, R. F., 138, 141
McGue, M., 97
McIntyre, C. W., 113, 117
McIntyre, J. S., 112, 113, 115, 117
McKeever, W. F., 138n
McPherson, W. B., 79, 181
Mecacci, L., 172
Meijer, P. J. A., 54
Mellits, D., 100, 121, 133
Menard, M. T., 85
Mencl, W. E., 146, 198, 234
Mercer, C. D., 4
Merrill, E. C., 95
Merzenich, M. M., 85, 134, 135, 224
Meskill, R. H., 139, 149
Meyer, E., 146
Meyer, G., 219, 233
Meyer, M. S., xii, xiii, xiv, 4, 5, 69, 225
Meyler, A., 13, 87, 99, 101, 156, 187, 206, 207
Michel, G. F., 67, 69, 70, 75, 85, 100
Miles, T. R., 11, 82, 149
Millay, K. K., 139, 148
Miller, C. A., 99
Miller, E. M., 92, 96
Miller, L., 44
Miller, S. L., 85, 100, 133, 134, 141
Miller, T. K., 137, 139, 142, 143
Milner, B., 146
Mintun, M., 146
Mirkin, P. K., 3, 13
Mishkin, M., 132
Misra, M., 86, 87, 101, 102, 187, 194, 200, 211, 212, 213, 215, 216, 217, 231, 236, 238
Mitchell, C. D., 146
Moats, L. C., xiii, 225
Mody, M., 141, 148
Molfese, D. L., 174
Molinari, M., 146
Molinet, K., 118, 122
Monk, D., 16

Morel, A., 107
Mori, M., 96
Morice, R., xii
Morocz, I. A., 220
Morris, R. K., 45, 67, 69, 70, 122, 155
Morton, J., 144
Mozer, M. C., 25
Muehl, S., 196
Muente, T. F., 179
Mulder, E. J. C. M., 91, 95, 97
Muller, S. P., 220
Murray, M. E., 113, 117
Musso, M., 220
Myerson, J., 92

N

Näätänen, R., 172, 175n, 182, 183, 224
Nace, K., 146
Nador, S., 95
Nagarajan, S., 224
Nagy, W. E., 222, 223
Naslund, J. C., 148
Nasman, V. T., 172
Nathan, R. G., 10, 11, 13, 14
Nation, K., xii, 80
Naylor, C. E., 70, 75, 178
Neale, M. C., 96
Neisser, U., 53
Nelson, J., 94, 97
Neubauer, A. C., 91, 95, 97
Neville, H. J., 172, 173, 176, 178, 179, 181
Newcorn, J. N., 122
Newell, A., 40, 98
Newman, S. P., 117, 141, 142
Newsome, W. T., 108, 110, 111
Nicholson, T., 14, 40, 41, 238
Nicol, T. G., 198
Nicolson, R. I., xii, xiv, 45, 46, 47, 48, 70, 79,
    86, 100, 136, 137, 146, 178, 179
Nicolson, S. B., 121, 133, 134
Nittrouer, S., 143
Nixon, D., 47
Noble, K., 146
Noll, D., 219
Norman, D. A., 6

Novak, G. P., 172
Novey, E. S., 85
Novoa, L., xiv
Nusbaum, H. C., 147
Nuuttila, L. P., 101

O

Obregon, M., 67, 74, 78, 80, 81, 228
O'Connell, D. C., 58, 62, 64
Odou-Potkin, M., 179
Ogden, N., 134, 141
Oglesby, D. M., xiii, 181
Ojemann, G. A., 86
Olavarria, J., 107
Olson, I. R., 198
Olson, R. K., xiii, xiv, 120, 121, 125
O'Neill, G., 113
Ong, E., 172
Onuska, L. A., 58, 62
Orban, J. A., 111
O'Reilly, R. C., 219
Ornstein, P. A., 97
Ortar, G., 17
Osman-Sagi, J., 182
Otto, P., 121
Ovrut, M., 67, 69, 70, 75, 85, 100

P

Paganoni, A., 121, 122
Palmer, B., 172
Palmer, R. L., 70, 116, 138
Pandya, D. N., 110
Pantev, C., 183
Pany, D., 14
Papanicolaou, A. C., 218, 221
Park, Y., 93
Parks, R. W., 96
Passingham, R. E., 47
Patterson, K., 62
Patterson, R., 114
Paul, C., 146
Paulesu, E., 47, 146
Pavlidis, G. T., 120, 121

Pedersen, N. L., 95, 97
Peltzman, D., 174, 174n
Pennington, B. F., xiv, 1, 152, 182
Pepin, M., 95
Perfetti, C. A., 3, 4, 7, 10, 11, 12, 14, 17, 35, 38, 42, 43, 68, 69, 197, 238
Peronnet, F., 198
Persson, H. E., 173, 177
Petersen, S. E., 146
Petros, T. V., xiii, 11
Petrosini, L., 146
Phillips, F., 196
Phillips, S., 173, 175
Pick, A. D., 98
Picton, T. W., 172
Piercy, M., 134, 139
Pihko, E., 182
Pinheiro, M. L., 136
Pinkerton, F., 173, 174n
Piontkowski, D. C., 43
Pitkus, A., 145, 146
Plante, E., 181
Poggie, E., 149
Polatsek, A., xii, xiv, 11
Poldrack, R. A., 86, 145, 146, 218, 219, 224
Polich, J. M., 97, 226
Pollatsek, A., 117, 120, 122, 124
Posner, M. I., 6, 37, 39, 146
Posthuma, D., 91, 95, 96, 97
Pratt, C., xii
Pratt, H., 27, 179, 180
Prawat, R. S., 95
Preddy, D., 92
Price, C. J., xiv, 145
Price, G., 68
Prill, K., 94
Prince, A., 53
Prinzo, O. V., xiii
Proctor, M., 178, 179
Protopapas, A., 224
Pugh, K. R., 146, 198, 234

R

Rabinowitz, M., 97
Rack, J. P., xiii, 120, 121, 125

Raic, V., 173
Raichle, M. E., 146
Raiguel, S. E., 111
Raij, T., 199, 200
Ransby, M. J., 125
Rapoport, J. L., 145, 146
Rappala, M. M., 149
Rashotte, C. A., xiv, 5, 76, 148
Rasinski, T. V., 50
Rastle, K., 197
Raupach, M., 63
Rauschecker, J. P., 132
Raven, J. C., 152, 184, 227
Rayner, K., 117, 120, 121, 122, 124
Records, N. L., 133
Reddington, J. M., 117
Reed, M. A., 96, 116, 137, 140
Reed, T. E., 96
Rees, A., 145
Regan, D., 171
Reicher, G. M., 11
Reid, C., 97
Reinking, D., 50
Reitsma, P., 124, 125
Remschmidt, H., 143, 148, 173, 182
Reutzel, D. R., 3, 4
Rey-Hipolito, C., 219, 233
Reyes, A., 174
Riccio, C., 85
Richards, A. L., 222, 223
Richards, I. L., 117, 119
Richards, T. L., 222, 223
Richardson, A. J., 133, 182
Riddell, P. M., 117
Ridderinkhof, K. R., 93
Riemann, R., 91, 95, 97
Rijntjes, M., 220
Rijsdijk, F. V., 96
Rippon, G., 173, 174, 174n
Risberg, J., 96
Ritter, W., 172
Rivera-Gaxiola, M., 180
Robeck, M. C., 133, 139, 147
Robichon, F., 181
Rodriguez, H., 174
Rodriguez, M., 174, 180

Roe, A. W., 107
Roes, C., 118
Roland, P. E., 47
Romanski, L. M., 132
Rose, S. A., 91
Rosebery, A. S., 10, 12
Rosen, G. D., 85, 101, 121, 123, 133, 173
Rosen, J. J., 139
Rosenberger, P. B., 221
Rosenbloom, P. S., 40, 98
Roth, C., 93, 97, 98
Roth, F. P., xii
Rottenberg, D. A., 221
Roux, S., 175n
Royer, J. M., 10, 12
Rudel, R. G., 45, 66, 67, 155
Rudnick, M., 196
Rufo, D. T., 70, 116, 138
Ruijssenaars, W. A., xii, 36
Rumsey, J. M., 145, 146, 179
Ryder, L. A., 55, 56
Ryding, E., 47

S

Saetveit, J. G., 141
Salin, P. A., 107
Salthouse, T. A., 92, 94
Salz, T., 224
Samaranayake, V. A., 94
Samuels, S. J., 2, 6, 36, 38, 40, 42, 43, 50, 69, 115n
Saron, C. D., 102, 103
Satz, P., 70
Scanlon, D., 148
Scarborough, H. S., xii
Scarpati, S., xii, xiv, 11
Schafer, A. J., 53, 54
Schall, J. D., 111
Schall, J. P., 110
Scheer, P., 183
Schermer, N., 50
Schiller, P. H., 38
Schirman, T. D., 107
Schmidt, S., 128
Schmolesky, M. T., 110

Schneider, W., 37, 39, 40, 97, 148
Scholl, M. E., 134
Schreiber, P., 4, 6
Schreiner, C., 85, 134, 135
Schreuder, R., 197
Schroeder, M. M., 179
Schulte-Korne, G., 143, 148, 182
Schupack, H., 139, 149
Schwab, E. C., 147
Schwanenflugel, P. J., 15
Schwantes, F. M., 12
Schwartz, B. J., 98
Schweiger, A., 103
Scott, R. B., 146
Scott, S. K., 144, 145
Seashore, C. E., 141
Sechi, E., 172
Segal, D., 67
Segev, N., 17
Seidenberg, M. S., xi, 84, 148, 196, 200
Selkirk, E., 53, 56
Seltzer, B., 110
Semel, E. M., xii
Senkfor, A. J., 181
Serafini, S., 223
Sergent, J., 200
Service, E., 101
Shammi, P., 18, 25
Shani, M., 154, 155, 227
Shankweiler, D. P., xii, xiii, 10, 137, 139, 145, 146, 147, 148, 198, 234
Shapiro, K. L., 134, 141
Share, D. L., xiii, 29, 30
Sharma, V., 122
Shatil, E., 152, 154, 193, 227
Shaul, S., xv, 1, 220
Shaywitz, B. A., 146, 198, 234
Shaywitz, E. S., 234
Shaywitz, S. E., 145, 146, 198
Shiffrin, R. M., 37, 39, 40, 90
Shinn, M. R., 5
Shoben, E. J., 15
Shontz, W., 114
Siegel, L., 25
Siegler, R. S., 97
Siegman, A. W., 63, 64

Silva, J., 174
Silva-Pereyra, J., 180
Silveri, M. C., 146
Silverman, M. S., 107
Simmons, D. C., xiii, 7
Simmons, K., 76, 148
Simos, P. G., 218, 221
Simson, R., 172
Sinatra, G. M., 10, 12
Singer, D. L., 196
Sjoholm, H., 47
Skudlarski, P., 146, 198, 234
Slaghuis, W. L., xii, 113, 117
Sloboda, J. A., 10
Slowiaczek, M. L., 51, 55, 59, 62
Smith, A. T., 112
Smith, F., 13
Smith, G. A., 95, 97
Snowling, M. J., xii, xiii, 25, 36, 80, 125, 145,
    146, 148
Snyder, C. R. R., 37, 39
Snyder, L. S., 5, 67
Sokolov, J. L., 26
Solan, H. A., 172
Solman, R. T., 112, 119
Somberg, B. L., 92
Somsen, R. J., 97
Southwood, M. H., 76
Spear, L. C., 42
Speer, S. R., 53, 57
Spekman, N. J., xii
Spelberg, H. C., 73
Spens, K. E., 173, 177
Sperber, R. D., 95
Spinath, F. M., 91, 95, 97
Spring, C., 67, 72, 75, 82
Stahl, S. A., 59
Stamm, J. S., 179
Stanley, G., 113, 114
Stanovich, K. E., xii, 10, 11, 13, 14, 15, 21,
    24, 40, 41, 43, 47, 68, 69, 94, 99, 124,
    139, 140
Stark, R. E., 100, 121, 133, 141
Steffens, M. L., 139, 140
Steffy, R. A., 67, 77, 82
Stein, J. F., xiv, 99, 101, 112, 117, 119, 120,
    123, 133, 145, 146, 148

Steinbach, K. A., xiv
Steinhausen, H. C., 181
Stenberg, G., 47
Sternberg, R. J., 42
Sternberg, S., 95, 96, 98
Sterritt, G. M., 196
Steury, K., 223
Stiles, J., 218
Stone, B., 149
Stone-Elander, S., 47
Stoodley, C. J., 146
Stough, C., 95
Straub, K. A., 53
Strayer, D. L., 172
Stringer, R., 47, 99
Strucl, M., 173
Studdert-Kennedy, M. G., 141, 148
Sugden, E. M., 146
Sunseth, K., 80
Sutiji, V. G., 172
Swain, C. R., 172
Swanson, L. B., 45, 68, 77, 82, 83
Swerts, M., 56
Syrdal-Lasky, A. K., 139, 148
Szeszulski, P. A., xii, 5, 125
Szucs, D., 182

T

Talcott, J. B., 145
Tallal, P., xiv, 82, 85, 100, 102, 121, 133,
    134, 136, 139, 140, 141, 172, 173,
    176, 178, 179, 181, 222, 224
Tan, A., 14, 40, 41
Tate, E., 67, 77
Taylor, M. J., 178, 179
Temple, E., 224
Tervaniemi, M., 182, 183, 224
Thomas, L., 57
Thompson, C. K., 220, 222
Thompson, K. G., 110, 111
Thompson-Schill, S. L., 219
Thomson, J. B., 222, 223
Thorndike, R. L., 92
Thorpe, S., 111, 112
Tian, B., 132

Till, R. E., 117
Tilly, W. D., 5
Tobey, E. A., 143
Tomblin, J. B., 133
Tonnquist-Uhlen, I., 173, 177
Tootell, R. B., 107
Torgesen, J. K., xii, xiii, xiv, xv, 5, 76, 139, 140, 145, 148, 233
Travis, F., 93
Ts'o, D. Y., 107
Tunmer, W. E., xii, 9, 25
Turatto, M., 121, 122
Turkewitz, G., 196
Turkkila, P., 183
Turner, E. A., 58, 62
Turner, L., 173
Turner, R., 219, 233
Tyler, C. W., 108
Tzeng, O., 86

U

Ullsperger, P., 172
Ungerleider, L. G., 110, 219, 233
Uutela, K., 145, 199

V

Vala-Rossi, M., 10, 11
Vallar, G., 62
Van Daal, V. H. P., xiv, 45, 46
Van den Bos, K. P., xiv, 73
Van der Leij, A., xii, xiv, 43, 45, 46, 100, 198
Van der Molen, M. W., 93
Van Deventer, A. D., 138n
van Donselaar, W., 58
Van Essen, D. C., 106, 107
Van-Petten, C., 181
Vaughan, H. G., Jr., 172
Vellutino, F. R., 112, 125, 148, 196
Velting, D. M., 180, 181
Vernon, P. A., 94, 95, 96, 97
Vigneau, F., 95
Virsu, V., 101
Vitacco, D., 181

Voeller, K., 149
Vogel, S. A., xii

W

Waber, D. P., xiv
Wada, J. A., 102
Wadsworth, J. F., 117
Wagner, R. K., xii, xiv, 76, 145, 148
Wagstaff, D., 92
Wallace, R. R., 133, 139, 147
Walsh, D., 68
Walsh, V., 112
Wang, A., 134, 135
Wang, W. S., 86
Wang, Y., 110
Warnke, A., 173
Warren, B. M., 10, 12
Warren, C. A., 171
Warren, P., 53
Warren-Chaplin, P. M., 125
Warrier, C. M., 198
Warrington, E. K., 76
Watkins, S., 182
Watson, B. U., 136, 137, 139, 140, 142, 143
Watson, C. S., 136, 142
Watson, D. R., 173, 174n
Webster, P. E., xii
Wechsler, D., 95, 155
Weiller, C., 220
Weintraub, S., 67
West, R. F., xii
Whatmough, C., 197
Wheless, J. W., 218
White, S. D., 3, 5, 13, 53
Whitney, P., 94
Whiton, M. B., 196
Wickens, C. D., 91, 172
Wicklund, D. A., 15
Widen, L., 47
Wiegel-Crump, C. A., 12
Wiig, E. H., xii, 69, 70
Wilce, L. S., 2, 5, 43, 125
Wilkinson, I. A., 3
Wilkniss, S. M., 179
Williams, M. C., 116, 117, 118, 122, 134

Willows, D. M., 112, 119
Wilson, B., 62
Wilson, G. F., 172
Wimmer, H., xiv, 47, 77, 79, 119, 148
Wingfield, A., 57
Winters, R. L., 114
Wise, D., 146
Witton, C., 145
Wiznitzer, M. L., 172
Woldorff, M., 171
Wolf, L. E., 122
Wolf, M., xii, xiii, xiv, 5, 7, 13, 42, 43, 44, 45,
    67, 68, 69, 72, 74, 78, 79, 80, 83, 84,
    85, 86, 100, 101, 124, 125, 155, 228,
    238
Wolff, P. H., xiv, 67, 69, 70, 75, 85, 100, 102,
    112, 118, 119, 121, 148
Wolking, W. D., 196
Wood, F. B., 5, 69, 75, 117, 123, 173, 178, 179
Wood, R. B., 70, 75
Wright, M. J., 95, 97
Wright, S., 141, 142
Wurst, S. A., 172
Wurtz, R. H., 110

Y

Yanez, G., 174, 180
Yap, R., xii, xiv, 43, 45, 46, 100, 198
Yates, C., 125
Yingling, C. D., 174, 174n
Yoshioka, T., 107
Young, A., xii, xiv, 1, 15, 43, 78, 124, 125

Z

Zaidel, E., 103
Zametkin, A. J., 145, 146
Zatorre, R. J., 146
Zbrodoff, N. J., 37
Zecker, S. G., xii, 125, 198
Zeffiro, T. A., 144
Zegarra-Moran, O., 122, 123
Zehr, H. D., xiii
Zijlstra, B. J. H., 73
Zuck, E., 200
Zureich, P., 69, 70
Zurif, E. B., 142

Subject Index

A

Acceleration phenomenon, 18
  cognitive mediation of, 28–34
  detection of, 20–21
  developmental perspective on, 22–23
  in dyslexic readers, 23–27
  and reading performance of adult readers, 25–28
  among young regular and impaired readers, 21–25
Acceleration training, reading, 225–226, 228–234
Acquisition, reading
  stages of, 23
ACT theory, 40
Ambiguous sentences, 54
Aphasia, 56, 220–221
Articulation difficulty, naming deficits in dyslexics and, 81–82
Asynchrony hypothesis, research on, 212–217
Asynchrony phenomenon, 210–211, 216, 237
Attention, acceleration phenomenon and, 29–30

Auditory cortex, 129
  auditory processing beyond the, 131
  belt region, 130
  core region, 129–130
  parabelt region, 130–131
Auditory deficits, lower level, 133, 140–145, see also Auditory temporal deficit hypothesis
  evidence of, in dyslexia, 136–140
Auditory masking, 33
Auditory modality, structure of, 128–132, 149
Auditory-phonological deficits in dyslexia, higher level, 147–149
Auditory processing, 149
  nonverbal, 136–139
Auditory simple motor reaction time, 162–165, 167–169
Auditory temporal deficit hypothesis, 133–134, 137–139
  beyond the, 140–144
  explaining the, 134–136
Automatic decoding, see also Decoding skills; Word decoding
  importance of, 43–45

Automatic processing, 39, *see also*
    Automaticity
Automaticity, 48–49
    characteristics of, 37–38, 48–49
    as continuum vs. dichotomous activity, 39
    dyslexia and, 45–47
        cerebral involvement, 47–48
    fluency and, 48–49
    model of, 2
    reading and, 42–43
    theories of
        limited capacity, 38–40
        modularity, 40–42
Automatization, xii
    defined, 36–37

B

Belt region of auditory cortex, 130
Bottleneck theory, 3–4, 14
Brain plasticity, 218
    acquired language disorders and, 220–221
    in dyslexics, 221–225
        hypotheses regarding cortical changes
            following training, 221
    language and, 220–225
    training and, 218–221

C

Cerebellum, 47–48
Cerebral hemispheres and information proc-
    essing, 102–103
Cerebral impairment and dyslexia, 47–48
Cognitive expectancies, two-process model
    of, 39
Communication relay model, 198–199
Comprehension, *see also specific topics*
    automatic word identification skills and,
        38–39
    fluency and, 6, 16
    reading time, decoding accuracy, and,
        17–18, 20–28
    word recognition and, 6
Connected text

rate of reading words in, 13–16
    reading subskills for, 7
Connectionist model of reading, 200, *see also*
    Parallel-distributed processing (PDP)
    model
Controlled processing, 39
Cross-modal integration, *see also* Asynchrony
    hypothesis
    and reading ability, 195–200
        in dyslexics, 195–198, 202–210
    theories regarding, 198–199
Cross-modality tasks behavioral experiments
    ERP measures, 206–210
    modalities matching tasks, 204
        syllables, 204–205
        words, 205–206
    threshold of simultaneous identification,
        201–204
Curriculum-based materials (CBM), 13–14
Curriculum-based measurement (CBM), 3

D

Declarative knowledge, 40
Decoding skills, 14, 17, 152, *see also* Auto-
    matic decoding; Word decoding
    reading rate and, 18
Distractibility and acceleration phenomenon,
    29–30
Dorsal auditory pathways, 132
Dorsal lateral geniculate nuclei (LGNd),
    110–111
Dorsal pathways in cortex, 109–110
Dyslexia, *see also specific topics*
    definition, 36
    developmental, xi–xiii
Dyslexic automatization deficit (DAD), 46–47

E

Episodic memory and automaticity, 41
ERP components that characterize reading
    activity, 171–172, *see also* ERP evi-
    dence on dyslexic readers

ERP evidence on dyslexic readers, 172, 183,
    187–194
  MMN component, 182–183
  N100 component, 173–178
  N200 component, 178–179
  N400 component, 180–182, 190
  P100 component, 172–173
  P200 component, 178, 188–191, 217
  P300 component, 179–180, 188–189, 191,
    217
ERPs (event-related potentials), 171–172
Expectancies, cognitive
  two-process model of, 39
Eye movements, 119–121

F

Flicker fusion rate, 113
Fluency, xii, see also specific topics
  definitions and meanings, 1, 4–8, 17, 235
  description of, xvi
  determinants of, xvi, 239
  developmental perspective on, 7–8
  linguistic perspective on, 5–7
  nature of, 14
  as outcome of quality of oral reading skills,
    4–5
  theoretical systems analysis approach to, 8
  use of, in the literature, 2–4
Frontal lobe head injury patients, 27

G

General ability (G factor), 91, 104
Global trend hypothesis, 93
Grammatical functions of words, identifying,
    26

H

Head injury patients, acceleration phenome-
    non in, 27
Hemispheres, cerebral
  and information processing, 102–103

I

Impulsive-hyperactive children, 23–24
Information processing, see also Processing
  modes of, 39
Information-processing theory, 6
Inspection time (IT), 97
Intelligence and speed of processing, 95–97,
    104
Interhemispheric transfer time (IHTT), 103
Interhemispheric transient deficit hypothesis,
    101, 103
Intersensory integration, see Cross-modal in-
    tegration
Interstimulus interval (ISI), 113–116,
    137–138, 143, 148, 204–205

K

Knowledge, declarative vs. production rule,
    40

L

Latency, reading, xiii, 12
Lateral geniculate nuclei (LGN), 105–108,
    110–111
  magnocellular and parvocellular layers,
    108–109
"Learning mechanism," physical impairment
  in
  among dyslexics, 135
Learning processes, 40
Letter reading skills, 7
Lexical decision task, 187, 189–192
Linguistic components of reading, 5–8
Linguistic levels, 5–8

M

Magnocellular (M) system, 108–109
  anatomical deficits in, among dyslexics,
    123–124

Masking
  auditory, 33
  visual, 117–118
Medial geniculate complex (MGv), 129–130
Medial geniculate nucleus (MGN), 129
Memory, *see also* Semantic memory; Short-
    term memory; Working memory
  episodic, and automaticity, 41
  prosody and, 52
  for wording and word order, 30–31
  for wording vs. semantic information, 31
Mistiming hypothesis, 100–101
Motor-articulatory feedback mechanism, 149
Motor reaction time, 157–165, 167–169

N

Naming
  axes defining the relations between reading
      and, 73
  discrete vs. sequential, 67–71
Naming speed, 66, *see also* Rapid automatized
      naming
  developmental differences in, 70–74
  and difficulty creating orthographic pat-
      terns, 83–84
  and reading ability, 66–67, 83
  reading disability and, 83–89
  representing general temporal processing,
      84–86
Naming speed deficits among dyslexics, 70,
      74–75
  explanations for, 75–83
    deficit model, 70–71
    developmental lag model, 70
    double deficit hypothesis, 78–79

O

Object naming, 72, *see also* Naming
Ocular functioning and dyslexia, 119–123
Orthographic-phonological processing,
      186–187
Orthographic-phonological transformation,
      165–167, 169

Orthographic processing and dyslexia,
      124–126
Orthographic surplus, model of, 83–84

P

Parallel-distributed processing (PDP) model,
      39–40, 196–197, 200
Parvocellular (P) system, 108–109
"Perceptual center" (P center) hypothesis,
      144–145
Perceptual learning, stages of, 42
Peripheral vision, 122–123
Phonological awareness deficit, 149
Phonological impairment, overcoming, 33
Phonological-orthographic translation,
      165–166, 169
Phonological output lexicon (POL), 76
Phonological processes, linguistic level,
      145–147
Phonological processing, 45, *see also* Ortho-
      graphic-phonological processing
  defined, 145
  in dyslexics, 33, 45, 75–80, 82–83
  fluency as result of effectiveness of, xiii–xv
  lower level, 139–140
Phonological visual decision for word pairs,
      166–167
Phonological visual decision task for
      pseudowords, 167
Phonology tasks, brain areas activated by,
      145–147
Plasticity, *see* Brain plasticity
Prefrontal regions, 131, 224
Processing, higher vs. lower order, 42
Production rule knowledge, 40
Prosodic reading, markers of, 59
Prosodic representation and reading process,
      61–64
Prosody, 50, 64–65
  acquisition of, 52–54
  conceptions of, 51
  as consisting of auditory temporal patterns,
      61–62
  defined, 50
  nature of, 49–51

in reading, 58–61, 64–65
and structure in speech comprehension
process, 55–58
Pseudowords, 167, 187, *see also* Word and
pseudoword processing
Punctuation and prosody, 61

R

Rapid alternating stimulus (RAS) test, 67–68
Rapid automatized naming (RAN), 66
Rapid automatized naming (RAN) processes,
89
speed of processing hypothesis for, 86–89
Rapid automatized naming (RAN) slowness
in dyslexic readers, source of, 87–89
Rapid automatized naming (RAN) tasks,
67–68, 71–72, 79, 81
Rapid processing hypothesis, 224
"Rauding theory," 16
Reaction time (RT), 11, 87, *see also* Motor reaction time; Visual reaction time
in dyslexics, 167–169
Reading acceleration training, *see* Acceleration training
Reading duration, xiii
Reading performance vs. reading ability,
21–22
Reading rate, xiii, 9–17, 34–35, 235–236, *see
also* Acceleration phenomenon;
Automaticity, characteristics
as dependent variable, 9–17
as independent factor, 17–19, 26
and memory for wording and word order,
30–31
self- vs. fast-paced, 30–33
and short-term memory, 30–32
and temporal features of reading, 33–34
Reading rate manipulation, basic, 18–19
and reading performance, 20–28
Reading rate theory, Carver's, 16–17
Reading regulator, 238–239
Reading skill development, criteria for measuring, 43–44
Reading speed, xiii, *see also* Automaticity,
characteristics; Reading rate
Reading subskills, 7

Reading time, xiii
Response time, 90

S

Scanning difficulty, visual
and naming speed, 82–83
Semantic information
failure to make higher order connections
between word recognition and, 6–7
memory for, 31
Semantic memory retrieval and speed of
processing, 94–95
Sentences processing, 187, 191
Severe language impairment (SLI), and ERPs,
175–177
Shared limited capacity hypothesis, 38–39
Short-term memory (STM), 30–32, 52, 82,
see also Memory; Working memory
Simultaneous activation hypothesis (SAM),
76
Site-specific integration model, 198
Skill training, *see* Acceleration training; Brain
plasticity, training and
Speech, *see also* Auditory deficits; Auditory
modality; Prosody
vs. reading, information processing and
prosody in, 58–60
Speech perception, 147, *see also* Auditory-
phonological deficits
Speed of processing (SOP), xv, 8, 44, 90–91,
150, 170, *see also* Automaticity, characteristics; ERPs; Motor reaction time;
Visual reaction time
age-related changes in, 91–92
defined, 90
as domain-general skill, 92–97
as domain-specific skill, 97–99
dyslexia as caused by slow, 8, 239–240
among dyslexics, 99–104, 167–169,
192–194, 237
intelligence, G factor, and, 95–97
role within orchestration of reading,
236–240
visual system physiology and, 110–112
what influences, 91
within- vs. between-systems, 236

Stimulus onset asynchrony (SOA), 116–117, 121
Stress patterns of words and word identification, 57
Stroop effect, 37–40
Synchronization hypothesis, xvi, 211
Syntactic ambiguity, 54
Syntactic processing, 6, 26–27
Systems analysis approach, theoretical, 8

T

Temporal deficit hypothesis, see Auditory temporal deficit hypothesis
Transient deficit hypothesis, 101, 103, 119–124

V

Ventral auditory pathways, 132
Ventral pathways in cortex, 109–110
Verbal efficiency theory, 3, 35
Verbal proficiency model, 7
Vergeance control, 123
Vision, peripheral, 122–123
Visual cortex, 106–107
Visual deficits in dyslexia, evidence of, 117–119
    discovery and identification of a single stimulus, 113
    judgment of correlation between stimuli, 115
    judgment of temporal order of stimuli, 115–117
    separation between two stimuli, 113–115
Visual linguistic patterns, lower level, 118–119
Visual masking, 117–118

Visual-orthographic processing and dyslexia, 124–126
Visual persistence, 113
Visual processes, lower level
    and dyslexia, 112–119
Visual processing systems, two, 107–110
Visual reaction time, 157–163, see also Reaction time
Visual scanning difficulty and naming speed, 82–83
Visual-spatial attention, 121–122
Visual system, 106, 126
    physiology, 105–112
Vocabulary acquisition difficulty, naming speed and, 80–81
Vocalization, 33–34

W

Wernicke's aphasia, 220
Word and pseudoword processing, 10–13, 189–192, 231, see also Pseudowords
Word decoding, 5–6, 235, see also Automatic decoding; Decoding skills
Word decoding rate, 235–238
    determinants of, 236
    as indicator of dyslexia, 238
Word order in sentences, memory for, 30–31
Word reading fluency, improved through training, 225–226
Word reading skills, 7
Word recognition, 6–7, 154
    factors influencing, 44
    speed of, 43
    stages of, 2
Wording in sentences, memory for, 30–31
Words, meanings, and ideas
    failure to make higher order connections between, 6–7
Working memory (WM), 32, 154–155